GEORGE BOUSTRONIOS

A NARRATIVE OF THE CHRONICLE OF CYPRUS
1456-1489

CYPRUS RESEARCH CENTRE

TEXTS AND STUDIES IN THE HISTORY OF CYPRUS

- LI -

SOURCES FOR THE HISTORY OF CYPRUS
Edited by
Paul W. Wallace and Andreas G. Orphanides

VOLUME XIII

GEORGE BOUSTRONIOS
A NARRATIVE OF THE CHRONICLE OF CYPRUS
1456-1489

translated from the Greek by Nicholas Coureas
together with an anthology of Greek texts of the fourteenth
and fifteenth centuries relating to Cyprus
and translated by Hans Pohlsander

SHC

NICOSIA 2005

ISBN 9963-0-8092-8

CONTENTS

PREFACE

This is a new translation into English of the Chronicle by George Boustronios. It was written in Cypriot Greek early in the sixteenth century and records the events surrounding Cyprus' transition from Lusignan to Venetian rule. It was Professor Paul W. Wallace of the Greece and Cyprus Research Center at the University of Albany N.Y. who first suggested that a translation should be made based on Professor George Kehayoglou's recent edition of Boustronios's Greek text, and when he contacted Dr Nicos Orphanides, the then Acting Director of the Cyprus Research Centre, to enquire whether he knew of someone who could undertake this project I volunteered. My proposal received the support of Dr Orphanides, Professor Kehayoglou, Professor Wallace and Dr Petros Kareklas, at that time Permanent Secretary of the Ministry of Education and Culture of Cyprus.

In preparing the translation I would like to express gratitude to all of the above for endorsing my proposal. Furthermore, I thank Dr Rolandos Katsiaounis of the Cyprus Research Centre for supporting and encouraging the project up to its completion and Dr Chris Schabel, Assistant Professor at the University of Cyprus, for his invaluable suggestions on certain aspects of the translation. In addition, I wish to thank the outside scholar who read the draft of this work for his extremely constructive comments and observations, as well as my fellow worker and co-editor Professor Hans Pohlsander, whose translation of fourteenth and fifteenth century Greek texts at the end of this volume form an important complement to my own translation. I also express thanks to Anastasia Alexandrou and all the staff of Leivadiotes Printers who helped in producing this book. Last but not least I thank my wife Ersie and my children Eleni, Savvas and Constantina for their patience and forbearance with this work when it impinged on our domestic life.

List of Abbreviations

AOL	*Archives de l'Orient latin*
BEC	*Bulletin de l'Ecole des Chartres*
CICO	Pontificia commissio ad redigendum codicem iuris canonici orientalis: Fontes. Series III, 15 vols. Rome 1943-
DOP	*Dumbarton Oaks Papers*
EKEE	*Επετηρίδα Κέντρου Επιστημονικών Ερευνών*
ΚΣ	*Κυπριακαί Σπουδαί*
MY	*Μελέται και Υπομνήματα Ίδρυμα Αρχιεπισκόπου Μακαρίου Γ', Γραφείον Κυπριακής Ιστορίας*
ΠΠΚΣ	*Πρακτικά του Πρώτου Διεθνούς Κυπρολογικού Συνεδρίου*, 3 vols. Nicosia, 1971-1973
ΠΔΚΣ	*Πρακτικά του Δευτέρου Διεθνούς Κυπρολογικού Συνεδρίου*, 3 vols. Nicosia 1985-1987
RHC	*Recueil des historiens des croisades.* 16 vols. Paris, 1844-1864.
Lois	*Les assises de Jérusalem*, 2 vols. Paris, 1841-1843
REB	*Revue des Études Byzantines*

HISTORICAL INTRODUCTION

A Short History and Description of the Manuscripts of the Chronicle[1]

There are three extant manuscripts of the chronicle written by George Boustronios. All these manuscripts are undated, two of them, mss. A and B, contain solely the text of the chronicle itself, while the third, ms. M, also contains the text of the chronicle written by Leontios Makhairas as well as a shorter chronicle with some information on Cyprus. The first, the A manuscript, once belonged to Thomas Earl of Arundel (1592-1646), and is now to be found at the British Library in London under the classification Arundel (*codex Londoniensis, Arundelianus [graecus]*) ms. 518, ff. 1ʳ-143ᵛ.[2] The remaining two, the B and M manuscripts, are both located in Venice at the Biblioteca Marciana, with the B manuscript classified as *Marcianus graecus* VII.17 (1268), ff. 1ʳ-135ᵛ and the M manuscript as *Marcianus graecus* VII 16 (1080), where Boustronios's chronicle occupies ff.287ʳ-377ᵛ.

The A manuscript is made of paper of western manufacture and the sheets measure 21,8 x 15,7 cm without the binding, while with the binding they measure 22 x 19 cm. Today the manuscript consists of one blank protective folio at the beginning and a further 144 folios, of which the last is blank, while there is an additional blank protective folio at the end of the whole work. Hence without the initial and final protective folios, the manuscript consists of 18 full quires of 16 folios. The upper part of folio 1ʳ has been excised, and the main part of the manuscript has a double numeration. The initial numeration in yellowish ink consists of Greek numerals found at the top right hand corners of the each folio quire, hence ff. 9ʳ, 17ʳ, 25ʳ, 33ʳ, 41ʳ up until folio 137ʳ, although the numbering is faint in some of these folios or has been excised in the process of cropping the folio edges. The Greek numeral α for instance does not survive in folio 1ʳ, since its upper part has been excised, as stated above. A newer numbering system in Arabic numerals and in pencil is likewise found in the top right-hand corners of ff. 3ʳ-143ʳ, just beneath the older Greek numerals where these are present.

The more recent brown leather-backed binding that replaced the older covering was executed on 30 October 1963, according to a stamp found on the inside of the back cover. A paper stuck onto the spine of the manuscript bears the number 166 and the classification mark B.11 just below, possibly the previous classification of the manuscript. Under this is printed in gold foil: CYPRUS| CHRONICLE.| 1454-1474.|

---

[1] Unless otherwise stated, what follows in this section on the manuscripts derives from Τζώρτζης (Μ)πούστρους (Γεώργιος Βο(σ)τρ(υ)νός ἤ Βουστρώνιος) *Διήγησις Κρόνικας Κύπρου* (henceforth *Διήγησις*) ed. G. Kehayioglou (Nicosia, 1997), pp. 45*-60*.

[2] R.M. Dawkins, *The Chronicle of George Boustronios, 1456-1489* (Melbourne, 1964), p. 1 wrongly gives its classification as Arundel 308. See Kehayioglou, *Διήγησις, op. cit.*, p. 45* note 4.

BRIT.MUS.| ARUNDEL MS. 518. On both outer sides of the cover are found an emblem and the words: BIBLIOTHECA ARUNDELIANA while on the inside of the front cover the Arundel coat of arms is found with the motto NULLIUS IN VERBA. In the bottom left-hand corner of the cover, again on the inside, is the handwritten number 166.6, which must be an earlier classification, while on the recto of the initial protective folio is a stamp with the words ARUNDEL MS.518. At the bottom left-hand margin of folio 1^r is another stamp with the handwritten calligraphy Soc.Reg.Lond| ex dono HENR.HOWARD| Norfolciensis and a sequential list of the owners of the manuscript. The first known owner was Thomas the Earl of Arundel, a collector and patron of the arts who acquired it some time before his death in Padua in 1646, and the last was Henry Howard the duke of Norfolk, who must have donated the manuscript to the British Library in 1840 or shortly before that date.

Other than the partially excised folio 1^r the manuscript is in fairly good condition, with very few worm-eaten sections found on the top and bottom edges of certain folios. The whole manuscript, written by the same hand, has script in yellowish ink that frequently assumes darker shades and presents black blotches. This script, which appears stylistically to belong to the Cypriot 'notarial' style,[3] is highly legible, with the few additions, corrections or deletions in the text, the margins or the spaces between the lines having apparently been executed by the same hand using the same ink. The text is divided into paragraphs, with red ink having been used only for the almost completely extant large stylised 'T' projecting to the left of the first line of letters in the main text, which generally lacks headings, of folio 1^r. Such ink was not, however, used for the smaller capitals introducing new paragraphs, which likewise jut out to the left, as does the initial letter in the first line of every page (the capital of the first paragraph has been omitted by mistake only on folio 74^v, line 6). Each page contains 20 lines of text, with each full line containing around 30 characters. Folios 1^r-1^v are missing the initial four to five lines while folio 143^v where the text ends has only six lines, as do folios 93^v, 120^v, 131^v and 142^v.

In a later period, a different hand made notes on various pages of this manuscript in black ink. The most interesting of these are to be found in the blank space after the six lines of written text in folio 143^v, that is just after the end of the whole text. Among the notes are the words ο πϱοτο ο πϱοτονοταϱιως ϱ[ό]|δου, the hardly legible Greek letters αϕϰζ, or possibly αϕμζ, which denote the numbers 1527 or 1547 if indeed they were written with this intent, and, further down and in a different hand, the word μαϱι-γε (= Μαϱι[γ]έ<ττα>). It is not known whether owners of the manuscript made these notes, and those made by the first hand cannot greatly postdate the time the (now lost) parent manuscript had been written, possibly the beginning of the sixteenth century. The allusion to a Rhodian chief notary in conjunction with the number 1527 (or 1547) is interesting, especially if the number represents a date. This would suggest that the manuscript had either been sent to Rhodes at some point where it came into the possession of a Rhodian chief notary, or else had been acquired by a Rhodian chief

---

[3] On this style see G. Grivaud, 'Ο πνευματικός βίος και η γραμματολογία κατά την περίοδο της φραγκοκρατίας', in Ιστορία της Κύπρου, V, Μεσαιωνικόν Βασίλειον, Ενετοκρατία, ed. Th. Papadopoullos (Nicosia, 1996), 901-907.

notary who had come to Cyprus after the fall of Hospitaller Rhodes to the Ottoman Turks in 1522, something which I consider likelier. Numerous folios (ff. 4-5, 26-27, 35, 39, 46, 57-58, 62, 65, 67, 73, 84, 92, 98, 101 etc.) of this manuscript contain watermarks similar to watermarks common in Italy and particularly in Venice and the surrounding areas in the first half of the sixteenth century. The three discernible types consist of a 'cardinal's hat', a hat surmounted by a cross and a hat surmounted by a star with six or seven rays, indicating a type of paper attested for the period 1522-1535. In the light of the above, one can state conclusively that the A manuscript belongs to the early sixteenth century, although an exact date cannot be established, nor are the first owners known.

The B manuscript, located at the Bibliotheca Marciana in Venice, is made of western paper and measures 21,4 x 15,5 to 15,6 cm while the usual width of the written text in the manuscript is around 10cm. Today it consists of three initial folios (ff. I-III), 134 folios of text and a final folio bearing the number 136. Hence, other than the three initial folios and the single final folio, it is made up of 17 quires of 8 folios, all of which are complete with the exception of quire 16, from which the fourth and fifth folios have dropped out, although the more recent numeration of the manuscript is sequential, disregarding this lacuna. Furthermore, after quire 17 either a quire of eight folios has dropped out or, which is likelier, an isolated bound folio containing the end of the text, given that the final folio of this manuscript is now blank and bears on the recto side the number 136 according to its more recent numeration, whereas the penultimate folio is numbered 134. The main body of the manuscripts has a double numeration. The initial numeration, consisting of the Greek numerals β-ιζ (= 2-17) in yellowish ink, is found on the top right-hand corners of the recto folios 9^r, 17^r, 25^r, 33^r, 41^r, 49^r, 57^r, 65^r, 73^r, 81^r, 89^r, 97^r, 105^r, 113^r, 121^r and 127^r. The numbering of folio 1^r does not survive, while some of the Greek numerals are indistinct or have been excised in the process of cutting the folio edges. The newer numeration, consisting of Arabic numerals written in ink within a kind of semicircle, is likewise found on the top right-hand corners of the recto folios just below the initial numeration and continues up to the final black fol. 136^r located outside the body of the main text, thereby indicating the existence of the now lost fol. 135 but not of the two folios that had dropped out of quire 16.

The subsequent eighteenth century binding consists of a wooden board I cm thick with a dark brown leather cover, printed with geometrical designs. This secures the manuscript with a central clasp to which a small leather strap is joined. This binding is now covered by a dust jacket of thick green compressed paper. The top right-hand corner of folio 1^r, containing scribbles done in ink by an older hand (a sequence of eight multiplications written within hexagonal or parallelogram frames, as well as the addition of fifteen two-digit numbers), also has the later mark N 2. In the upper part of folio 1^v, written in ink and in very small letters, is the later annotation: Bekker Emmanuele pubblicò in *Abhandlungen der königl. Akademie der Wissenschaften der Berlin aus dem jahre 1841* il brano cart.1 lin. 1 bis 17-,[4] and further down an

---

[4] This is a reference to E. Bekker, 'Die ungedruckten byzantinischen historiker der St Markus Bibliothek', *Philologische und historische Abhandlungen der königlichen Akademie der Wissenschaften*, 1841 (Berlin, 1843), pp. 43-65.

annotation in ink written by a sixteenth or seventeenth century hand:

Cronica del regno di Cipro dall'anno 1456|fino al 1481. che venne in Italia la Regina| catherina cornara.-. On folio II recto an older hand has written in ink certain sums and scribbles, scarcely legible notes containing French and Italian words and a name: Havendo – bien passata – Il May (numbers follow) Zu_ (= Zuan) Zamb(er)lano|, as well as some prose extracts, possibly derived from Italian prose on the Trojan War. Folio II verso and the whole of folio III are blank, while on folio 136^v a more recent hand has written in pencil the older classification mark of the manuscript, XCI.6.| Class VII cod XXII. The round stamp of the Bibliotheca Marciana has been embossed in light blue ink in the right-hand margin of fol. 1^r.

The manuscript, apart from three lacunae, two in the middle and one on the last folio of the main text, survives in fairly good condition, with very few worm-eaten parts. The whole of the main section is written in yellowish ink, with some small blotches in certain places, by the same hand, similar but not identical to the hand of ms. A. This hand likewise belongs to the Cypriot notarial tradition. The writing is highly legible and most deletions, corrections and additions in the text, the area between the lines and the margins appear to have been done by the same hand using the same ink, which on occasion seems to have a more yellowish hue. There are more deletions and corrections than those in ms. A. Turning to the text itself, one observes that it begins with a decorative scroll drawn in red ink within a yellowish background. The title follows: Δ'ϊυγίσης κρονίκας. Κύπρου. αρχευγόντα. από την εχρονίαν. αυνςχ(ριστο)ύ, with the initial Δ likewise written in red ink. Red ink is used in only one other section of the manuscript: the stylised large capital T at the start of the third line of fol.1^r where the main text of the chronicle begins. The text is divided into paragraphs in which the initial capital letters as well as the initial letter of every first line in the pages of the manuscript jut out to the left (the capital of the initial paragraph is left out by mistake only on fol. 122^v line 7).

Each page of the manuscript contains around 20 lines, with 30-32 characters in each complete line, giving the manuscript much wider outer and bottom margins. Exceptions are the first page, beginning with the ornamental scroll and so containing 19 lines of text, and ff. 82^r and 97^v where the text continues down to the bottom right-hand corner of the twenty-first line so as to complete the paragraph. Subsequent notes executed by a different hand in a style of writing recall that of the Ms Paris, Bibliothèque Nationale de France, Grec 1390, the older of the two extant translations into Greek of the *Assises de la cour des bourgeois*, dated 1469. These are present in the margins of certain folios or in the spaces between the lines. Watermarks are discernible in fol. II as well as in several more folios of this manuscript (e.g. ff. 18, 23, 26, 31, 41 etc). That on fol. II resembles the type in the category 'letter A' that occurs in both the Veneto area and in southern France during the period 1331-1352, but these older initial folios of the manuscript must have been bound together with the main section of the manuscript in the sixteenth century, and the notes in Italian found on fol. II mentioned above date from this period. The watermarks present in the folios of the main text are representative of two distinct types, similar to those that are very common in Italy and especially in Venice, and found in Parma and the region around Venice during the first half of the sixteenth century: the hat surmounted by a cross and the anchor within a circle with a six-pointed star at the top. Both these types indicate a kind of paper attested for the period 1533-1538.

There is no information on the first owners of this manuscript, or even on the precise date at which it reached Italy. Nonetheless, the name Zuan Zamberlano appearing in fol. II of the manuscript suggests that a member of this family, prominent in Cyprus during the sixteenth century, when the island was under Venetian rule, had either owned or at least read the manuscript. This person was appointed chancellor of the district of Nicosia in 1526: in 1530 he and Antonello Bon made an unsuccessful attempt to buy the *casale* of Siria (now Kato Kivides) and after 1545 a salaried legal adviser of the *camera* on matters regarding taxation. One year later, in 1546, he was knighted by the doge himself and given the title 'magnifico', while in the general muster of troops held in April 1560 he is described as 'magnifico miser Zuan Zamberlan', although in 1557 he had declared himself relieved of all service. The title 'magnifico' attached to his name indicates that he was indubitably a nobleman, and as such he would easily be in a position to own the B manuscript, although this cannot be conclusively established.[5]

The M manuscript like ms. B is located in the Bibliotheca Marciana of Venice and as stated above includes other chronicles, notably the Cypriot chronicle of George Boustronios' predecessor, Leontios Makhairas. The following description shall first apply to the whole manuscript but later shall concentrate only to that part of the manuscript containing the chronicle attributed to George Boustronios.[6] The manuscript is made of western paper measuring 30.4 x 21.2 cm. At present it consists of three initial folios [I-III], 377 folios of text and two concluding folios. The main section of the manuscript was originally made up of 389 folios, twelve of which have dropped out, and consists of 40 quires. If the twelve lost folios are included, then the quires numbered 1, 3, 6, 8-13, 15-29, 31-35, and 37-40 formed set numbering ten folios, the quires numbered 5, 14, 17, 30-31 and 36 formed sets of eight folios and quire number 2 formed a set of twelve folios. The initial numeration by quires is faded to a degree making it almost illegible in most places, and other than this there are two additional numerations in Arabic numerals. The newer consecutive numeration of 1-377 done in pencil is present in larger numerals on the bottom right-hand corner of the recto folios, covering the whole main section of the manuscript and faithfully reflecting

[5] On Zuan Zamberlano see G. Grivaud and Aspasia Papadaki, 'L'institution de la *Mostra Generale* de la cavalerie féodale en Crète et en Chypre vénitiennes durant le XVIe siècle', *EKEE* XIII-XVI,1 (Nicosia, 1984-1987), pp. 528 and 536; B. Arbel, 'The Cypriot Nobility from the Fourteenth to the Sixteenth Century: A New Interpretation', in *Latins and Greeks in the Eastern Mediterranean after 1204*, ed. B. Arbel, B. Hamilton and D. Jacoby (London, 1989), pp. 179 and 187 and notes 21 and 80; *Ανέκδοτα έγγραφα της κυπριακής ιστορίας από το κρατικό αρχείο της Βενετίας*, 4 vols. ed. by Aikaterini Aristeidou (Nicosia, 1990-2003), IV, 53-55.

[6] The description of ms. **M** given here is based on Kehayioglou, *Διήγησις*, pp. 53*-58*. Another description, with understandable emphasis on that part of the manuscript containing the chronicle of Leontios Makhairas, is found in *Λεοντίου Μαχαιρά Χρονικό της Κύπρου: Παράλληλη διπλωματική έκδοση των χειρογράφων*, ed. M. Pieris and Angel Nicolaou-Konnari (Nicosia, 2003), pp. 27-32.

its present condition. The older consecutive numeration of 1-400, which does not record the total of the original number of folios in the main section with exactitude, covers the whole of this section other than the last folio (fol. 377 in the newer numeration), on which a later hand has erroneously written the number 401 in the top right-hand corner within a circle. Given that four folios dropped out after the folio numbered 400 in the older numeration, this number should read 405. The folios missing according to the older numeration are ff. 12, 42, 51, 306-307, 366-367, 392 and 401-404.

The binding consists of a bare wooden cover around 0.5 cm thick and only the spine of the book has been covered subsequently with a black leather binding. On the inside page and the three initial folios (ff. I-III) are stuck a small mark of the Bibliotheca Marciana bearing the classification number of the manuscript, the large logo of this library (BIBLIOTHECAE D.MARCI VENETIARUM) and a later annotation by the conservator Carlo Orlandini providing incomplete information on the lacunae of the manuscript following its conservation.[7] On fol. III[v], just off-centre, a hand possibly dateable to the seventeenth century has written in ink: Prioris huis Chronici auctor est *Leontius Machaeras*, ut patet| ex fol. 282. *verso.*| Sequioris autem *Georgius Bustronius*; sed tribus foliis caret.-,while at the top of the same page there is a subsequent annotation in ink and in very small letters resembling that found in ms. B, mentioned above: Bekker Emmanuele pubblicò in *Abhandlungen der königl. Akademie der Wissenschaften zu Berlin aus dem Jahre 1841* il primo| †brano† col. A. lin. 1 – bis col. B. lin. 8. A round stamp of the Bibliotheca Marciana in light blue ink has been affixed to the bottom of fol. 1[r].

From this point onwards various small and large annotations done in ink are discernible throughout various folios in the main text of the manuscript (the allusions to folio numbers that follow refer to the newer numeration unless otherwise stated). Given that ms. M, unlike mss. A and B discussed above, is a composite manuscript, it will be useful to break down the structure of the main text, which is divides into three sections:

1. Chronicle of Leontios Makhairas: ff. 1[r]-225[r], 226[v]-286[v] (=1[r]-239[r], 240[v]-305[v] in the older numeration)

2. Annalistic records, consisting of a note on the Venetian governance of Cyprus with dates and a short account on the arrival of the Ottoman Turks, stating by way of conclusion: 'αφής έμεινε η Κύπρο εις το χέριν τους ετραβένιασε τόσα κακά όπου να μηδέν τα δώση αφέντης ο θεός άλλου τόπου'. Also recorded are the advent of locusts, a plague, the advent of locusts in 1586, an earthquake in January 1577, and storms and flooding in Limassol in 1628. A different hand wrote a note wishing 'πολλά έτη' to Bishop Joachim of Limassol, and a hand different from the previous ones recorded a plague in 1589:[8] ff. 225[v]-226[r].

---

[7] Kehayioglou, Διήγησις, *op. cit.*, pp. 54*-55*.

[8] For these records see Leontios Makhairas, *Recital Concerning the Sweet Land of Cyprus entitled 'Chronicle'*, ed. R.M. Dawkins, 2 vols. (Oxford, 1932), II, 1 and note a; Kehayioglou, Διήγησις, *op. cit.*, p. 532; Pieris and Nicolaou-Konnari, Λεοντίου Μαχαιρά Χρονικόν της Κύπρου, *op. cit.*, pp. 48-50.

3. The chronicle attributed to George Boustronios: ff. 287^r-377^{v9} (=308^r-401^v [= 405^v]) according to the earlier numeration), which lacks a heading and has numerous lacunae, given that seven folios are missing from it. The annotations concerning that part of the manuscript containing the chronicle attributed to George Boustronios consist of sums, shapes and various letters. The most informative annotation chronologically is on fol. 376^r, which at the bottom has the following annotation, covering three lines: 'αχλδ (= the date 1634 [crossed out]) μαϱτηω-α-εφεϱανε τή Κϱωνιχανιαπε την Κυπϱων εμενα τον σαβα Κάπην.ι αχϰδ-μαϱτηω-α-. (= on March 1 1634 [year deleted] they brought the chronicle from Cyprus [to] me, Savvas Kappis, on March 1 1624). The surname Κάπης is also found in the left-hand margin of folio 66^v.

The ms. M survives in a fairly good condition, but nonetheless suffers some defects. These are the loss of the twelve folios already mentioned, the excision of part of the right side of fol. 377^r, part of the left side of fol. 377^v and of part of the lower section of fol. 357. One also mentions a minor excision of a section from the edge of fol. 309 and the major tear in ff. 339-346, which however were carefully restored during preservation and so retain their legibility. The manuscript has a few worm-eaten areas as well as a few traces of damp appearing more clearly at certain points, ff. 367-377 for example. The same hand wrote the main texts of sections 1 and 3 described above and it differs markedly from those that wrote mss. A and B. The manuscript, considerably bigger and bulkier than the other two, also exhibits several characteristics of the special care and the scriptural style usually encountered in contemporary ecclesiastical manuscripts. The ink used approaches black and occasional blotches appear. Section 2 and most of the annotations throughout the manuscript have been executed by various other hands, using a black type of ink differing from the ink of the other sections. The script in sections 1 and 3 is highly legible and careful, although the scribe, who must have been quite learned and was not particularly careful, and intervenes in the text on occasion. Short sections of the chronicle are frequently repeated, something that he is not always aware of, minor mistakes and deletions, additions and corrections to the main text, in the spaces between the lines or in the margins. These incidentally in section 3 occur far more frequently than is the case in mss. A and B, with most aiming at correcting the accentuation and spelling of an archetypal manuscript which in its inconsistencies regarding the accentuation cannot have differed markedly from mss. A and B. They also aim in places at making the text appear more erudite.

Sections 1 and 3 of ms. M are written in two columns per page, with an uneven number of lines per page and a variable width as regards the written text. There are usually 25-26 lines per column in the complete pages, while in the more densely

---

[9] Kehayioglou, Διήγησις, op. cit., pp. 56*-57* mistakenly gives the folio numbering as 287^r-337^v, but gives the correct numbering on p. 53* as well as on pp. 301 and 303, which show that the chronicle continues after fol. 376^v.

written ff. 66-68 the average is 36 lines. Another variation occurs on fol. 1^r, the columns of which contain only 15 lines because an ornate decorative scroll and the title of Leontios Makhairas' chronicle precede them. These are executed in red ink, also employed in the initial capitals of numerous paragraphs in sections 1 and 3. Such initial capitals are omitted by mistake, especially in the chronicle ascribed to Boustronios, while capitals larger and more stylised that the remainder are also found particularly in the same chronicle. Among them the letter K appears with notable frequency in ff. 300^r, 301^r, 302^v, 316^v and elsewhere. The whole text or a small section of text of certain paragraphs, once again especially in the text attributed to Boustronios, is written in red ink and with smaller letters. Examples of this can be found on ff. 307^r, 310^r, 314^r, 320^r, 326^v, 334^r and 370^r. The only watermark in the manuscript appearing in numerous folios throughout resembles the type in the 'anchor' category (an anchor within a circle surmounted by a six-pointed star) indicating a kind of paper attested for the period 1538-1561. There is no external information on the owners of this manuscript, although the date (1.3.1624) at which came into the possession of Savvas Kappis indicates that the manuscript reached Italy at or around this time.

The description of mss. A, B and M given above points to the conclusion that none of them is the archetype. Their palaeographic and scribal characteristics indicate a bifurcation in the manuscript tradition. The small self-contained mss. A and B belong to one branch and lack any apparent connection with the main centres of book production in Cyprus in the early sixteenth century or with any identifiable scribe active at that time. The second branch is represented solely by the large composite ms. M which perhaps aimed at constituting a concentrated edition of the chronicles on Cyprus written in the popular Greek dialect of the island, since it is a copy of the two most extensive Greek chronicles which are also chronologically sequential, despite their marked stylistic and structural differences, with the summary notes of section 2 later interposed. The Venetian provenance of the paper in conjunction with the watermarks of the main text in all three manuscripts, which present no great chronological divergences among themselves, were probably copied from an archetype before the middle of the sixteenth century.[10] Ms. A is probably the earliest, and may well have been copied in the second or third decade of the sixteenth century, that is to say not long after the time when the chronicle was created, with mss. B and M following in the chronological sequence. Ms. M may be dateable to a period with a *terminus ante quem* at the end of the 1560s, for this was the period when a greater interest was shown as regarded the concentration and utilisation of various Cypriot chronicles.

Although, surprisingly, there is no evidence for the existence of *scriptoria* in Cyprus in the numerous monasteries of the island, Latin or Greek, monks copied manuscripts on an individual basis, the best example being that of Abbot Ambrosios of the monastery of the Virgin Mary of Andriou in Nicosia, who copied at least eight religious manuscripts for various sponsors between the years 1530 to 1558. Various

---

[10] Grivaud, 'πνευματικός βίος', *op. cit.*, pp. 1089 and 1145 erroneously states that the three mss. date from the second half of the 16th century.

Greek religious manuscripts were copied between the years 1507-1512 for Orthodox religious communities in Sinai and Palestine, an indication that there was a demand for the copying of Greek manuscripts in Cyprus emanating from Orthodox religious in the eastern Mediterranean in general, not simply on the island, from the beginning of the sixteenth century. Furthermore, in around 1540 the Cypriot Hieronymos Tragoudistes, who was probably educated in Italy, returned to Cyprus and worked there as a musician and a copier of manuscripts, although he subsequently left the island for Italy.[11] In 1531 the Venetian doge Andrea Gritti expressed his wish for the two Greek manuscripts of the Assizes to be translated into Italian, a task completed in 1535, while at around the years 1556-1560 the young Leonardo Donà put together on his own initiative a collection of documents and translations the breadth of which presages the even more large scale project undertaken by Francesco Patrizi in the years 1561-1568. One notes that an Italian translation of the chronicle of George Boustronios is included among the translations compiled by Donà.[12] Hence the copying of the three extant Greek manuscripts of this chronicle in the early to mid-sixteenth century occurs within the wider context of the literary efflorescence that Venetian Cyprus experienced in this period.[13]

In concluding this discussion of the manuscripts, one notes that while all belong to the early or mid-sixteenth century it is impossible to date any of them with precision, or indeed to state with certitude whether they were copied in Cyprus or in Venice. It is, however, apparent from the notes to be found in each of them that prior to reaching Venice they were circulating in Cyprus and had Cypriot owners. The exception could be ms. A, the owner of which seems to have been a Rhodian chief notary who came to Cyprus, possibly following the fall of Hospitaller Rhodes to the Ottoman Turks in 1522. One can also say that these manuscripts, copied at a time of literary efflorescence in Cyprus and concerning a Greek chronicle that aroused enough interest to warrant an Italian translation, had a fairly broad circulation, as appears from the presence of marginalia written by different hands during various periods in the sixteenth century and beyond.

The Manuscripts of the Chronicle from their arrival in Venice until the Present Day[14]

Despite the fact that the three manuscripts of the chronicle reached Italy by the early seventeenth century and ultimately found their way into well known European

---

[11] D. Holton, 'Cyprus and the Cretan Renaissance: A preliminary study of some cultural connections', *EKEE* XIX (Nicosia, 1992), 519-520; Grivaud, 'πνευματικός βίος', *op. cit.*, pp. 900-901 and 1111.

[12] *Ibid.*, pp. 1112-1113, 1133-1139 and 1143-1146.

[13] Regarding which see Holton, 'Cyprus and the Cretan Renaissance', *op. cit.*, pp. 515-530; Grivaud, 'πνευματικός βίος', *op. cit.* pp. 1109-1204; D. Holton, 'A history of neglect: Cypriot writing in the period of Venetian rule', *Modern Greek Studies Yearbook*, vol. 14/15 (Minneapolis, 1998/1999), 81-96.

[14] Unless otherwise stated, this section derives from Kehayioglou, *Διήγησις, op. cit.* pp. 35*-43*.

libraries, the Bibliotheca Marciana in Venice and the British Library in London, they did not attract the interest of historians and palaeographers until well into the nineteenth century. First among them was J. Forshall, who in his preface to the first volume of the new series of the *Catalogue of Manuscripts in the British Museum*, which he wrote in 1834 but which was published in 1840 in London, alluded to a strange story of the affairs of Cyprus between the years 1456 and 1474, written as he said in barbarous Greek, possibly in the idiom of this island, when referring to the 35 Greek manuscripts of Thomas the earl of Arundel. The Latin description of the manuscript (ms. A) of the chronicle found in the same series attributes, albeit reservedly, the chronicle to George Boustronios, stating it to be an anonymous Cypriot chronicle, possibly of George Boustronios, in which the events taking place in Cyprus from the arrival of John, prince of Antioch, in the year 1456, up to the year 1474 are described, with the addition of a few things concerning Cyprus up to the year 1501, in which is mentioned the death of Morphou de Grenier, the count of Rochas. The description likewise states that the chronicle is written in barbarous Greek.

One year later, in 1841, the German philologist E. Bekker published a short commentary on this chronicle in an article on the unpublished Byzantine historians whose texts were at the Bibliotheca Marciana in Venice, including a few introductory lines from ms. B.[15] The French historian of Lusignan and Venetian Cyprus Louis de Mas Latrie also published two further extracts of the chronicle, taken from ms. A, along with a facing French translation in 1855, included in his three-volume work.[16] For the transcription of the published extracts and their translation into French he employed the services of two Greek literary men, I. Pitsipios and Sypsomos. The services of the latter in particular were utilized by a number of French classicists, and he worked as a copy editor for the publishing houses of Didot and Migne. The extracts published by Mas Latrie were reprinted in 1869 in the first edition of the three-volume work *Τα Κυπριακά*, compiled by Athanasios Sakellariou, and in 1873 the Greek publisher Constantine Sathas published for the first time a complete version of the chronicle in the second volume of his seven volume compilation of medieval Greek texts.[17] This publication was based on mss. B and M in the Bibliotheca Marciana, and Sathas used ms. A only to append the concluding passages referring to events in Cyprus following Queen Catherine Corner's departure for Venice in 1489. Sathas' friend D. Vikelas probably sent him these passages from London, although according to Dawkins he received them not from Vikelas but from Dr John Gennadios, a Greek diplomat in London.[18]

After Sathas' edition of 1873 no serious academic interest in the chronicle

---

[15] See note 4 above.

[16] L. de Mas Latrie, *Histoire de l'île de Chypre sous le règne des princes de la maison de Lusignan*, 3 vols. (Paris, 1852-1861), III, 82-85.

[17] 'Γεωργίου Βουστρωνίου Χρονικόν Κύπρου', in *Μεσαιωνική Βιβλιοθήκη* (= *Bibliotheca Graeca Medii Aevi*) ed. C. Sathas, 7 vols. (Venice, 1872-1894), II, 411-543.

[18] See Kehayioglou, *Διήγησις*, *op. cit.*p. 38*and note 11; Dawkins, *Boustronios*, *op. cit.*pp. 1 and 60.

occurred for over 40 years. During the First World War, however, the British scholar R.M. Dawkins, later Bywater and Sotheby Professor of Modern Greek at the University of Oxford, first read the chronicle while serving on board a Royal Navy warship in the Aegean. In the early 1920s, while on holiday in Italy, he had a transcription of ms. A made from photographs by the authorities of the British Library. He then prepared a preliminary draft of his translation of the chronicle into English while travelling in Tunisia in 1938, although he does not state which manuscripts this preliminary draft was based on. Not until December 1949 did he submit the final draft of his translation for publication in Australia, stating in his introduction that he used the Venetian mss. B and M as the basis of his translation but also incorporated some phrases from the London ms. A not found in the two Venetian manuscripts.[19] Professor James Stewart, a member of the Department of Archaeology of the University of Sidney, had encouraged Dawkins to have the chronicle translated in Australia, and his wife Eve prepared the excellent indices for this work. But when Dawkins died in 1955 this translation was still unpublished, and it was eventually brought out by the University of Melbourne in 1964, two years after James Stewart himself died at the age of 48.[20] Dawkins' translation subdivides the chronicle into numbered paragraphs and is prefaced by a brief introduction and summary of the narrative with numerous references to the third volume of George Hill's four-volume *History of Cyprus*.[21] This volume was published in 1948, only one year before Dawkins submitted his translation for publication. Other than the excellent indices on persons, places and subjects placed after the text, this edition also includes a map of Cyprus listing the places mentioned in the chronicle and various photographs, chiefly of coins but also including a portrait of Queen Catherine Corner attributed to the school of Bellini as well as a page from ms. A of the chronicle. Th. Papadopoullos, moreover, some time after 1952 expressed his intention to prepare a new edition of the chronicle with an accompanying English translation, notes and commentary. This was to be the second volume of the Belgian series titled *Biblioteca Graeca Aevi Posterioris*, but the projected edition never materialised.[22]

In 1978 a Bulgarian translation of the chronicle was published at the University of Sofia, reprinted in 1982. Professor Peter Tivčev, a member of the university's faculty of history, completed this translation, which like that of Dawkins is based on the text published by Sathas, although Tivčev also utilized Dawkins' translation of the chronicle into English.[23] The work in question consists of a brief introduction followed by the translated text, subdivided into five sections, these being the last years of King

---

[19] *Ibid.*, pp. vii and 1. On p. 1 he states that §§ 194 (final part), 256A, 266A, 279 and 283-284 of his translation have been taken from ms. A.

[20] Dawkins, *Boustronios, op. cit.*, p. ii; J.R. Stewart, *Lusignan Cyprus and its Coinage*, 2 vols. (Nicosia, 2002), pp. xxxi-xl (biographical note by C.E. Blunt).

[21] G. Hill, *A History of Cyprus*, 4 vols. (Cambridge, 1940-1952), volumes II and III of which are exclusively on Lusignan and Venetian Cyprus.

[22] Dawkins, *Boustronios, op. cit.*, p. ix: Kehayioglou, Διήγησις, *op. cit.*, p. 40*.

[23] P. Tivčev, 'Kipriska Khronika na Georgi Bustron', *Godishnik na Sofiiskiya Universit- Istoriteski Fakultet*, 72 (Sofia, 1978), pp. 121-184.

John II, the reign of Queen Charlotte, the civil war, the reign of King James II and, finally, that of Queen Catherine Corner.[24] More recently, in 1989, the Cypriot literary figure Andros Pavlides reprinted the text originally published by Sathas with the addition of Dawkins' subdivision of the text into paragraphs, although their number is somewhat reduced. His edition also includes a brief introduction, notes on the odd-numbered pages facing those of the text itself, a partial republication of the shorter chronicles and notes found on ff. 225^v-226^r of ms. M, a summary of the work, a conclusion describing the institutions of the kingdom of Cyprus, an index compiled by L.A. Louca, some photographs of coins, engraving and paintings and a map of Cyprus mentioning the places alluded to in the chronicle.[25]

Far more comprehensive and ambitious in scope is the complete edition of all three extant manuscripts of the chronicle, completed by Professor George Kehayioglou of the University of Thessaloniki and published in Nicosia by the Cyprus Research Centre in 1997.[26] Kehayioglou has transcribed mss A, B and M, published clockwise on facing pages so as to facilitate their comparison with one another, and has added his own composite text on the lower part of the even-numbered pages (text K). Text K is based on ms. A, which he considers to be the most authentic version of the chronicle, but includes extracts from mss. B and M not found in ms. A or which constitute better renditions than the corresponding sections present in ms. A. This makes Kehayioglou's edition completely independent of that published by Sathas over 120 years earlier. His edition consists of an extensive introduction with detailed discussions of the manuscripts, the language, the narrative, the author and the editorial principles underpinning this work. There follows a critical edition of the three manuscripts in the manner described above, clockwise on facing pages with a composite text on the lower section of the left-hand pages. The third section contains extensive notes on the texts, a glossary, and indices on the persons and places mentioned in the texts. In addition, three appendices are given. Appendices I and II publish the conclusion to the chronicle of Leontios Makhairas according to ms. M (the Venice manuscript) and three shorter fifteenth and sixteenth century chronicles, the first from fol. 225^v of ms. M, the second from the *Kleinchroniken* edited by Peter Schreiner and the third from the *Dated Greek Manuscripts from Cyprus to the Year 1570* edited by Constantine Constantinides together with Robert Browning.[27] Appendix III publishes a section of Florio Bustron's *Historia overo commentarii de*

---

[24] Kehayioglou, Διήγησις, *op. cit.*, pp. 40*-41* and 274*-275*.

[25] Γεωργίου Βουστρωνίου Διήγησις χρονίκας Κύπρου ... ed. A. Pavlides *et al.* (Nicosia, 1989); Kehayioglou, Διήγησις, *op. cit.*, p. 41* note 19 points out that Dawkins' text has 284 paragraphs, including five double ones (e.g. 266, 266A) whereas Pavlides' text has 270 paragraphs including one double one (267α and 267β). He also refutes Pavlides' claim to have used mss. B and M in the Bibliotheca Marciana in addition to Sathas' edition (see Διήγησις, p. 271* and notes 6-7).

[26] For a full reference see above, p. 13 and note 1.

[27] See P. Schreiner (ed.), *Die Byzantinischen Kleinchroniken*, 3 vols. (Vienna, 1975-1979), I, 212, no. 28.17; *Dated Greek Manuscripts from Cyprus to the Year 1570*, ed. C. Constantinides and R. Browning (Nicosia, 1993), p. 234, no.58.

Cipro, covering the years 1456-1489 and taken from René de Mas Latrie's edition of this chronicle.[28] The work ends with an English summary and three plates reproducing corresponding folios from mss. A, B and M of the chronicle.

It is important to note that Kehayioglou, following a detailed comparison on linguistic and structural grounds of the three extant manuscripts with each other and with the corresponding section in the chronicle of Florio Bustron, reaches the conclusion that ms. A offers an older and fuller version of events than mss. B and M in most cases where they differ, and closer for the most part as regards content and structure to Florio Bustron's account than the other two manuscripts. As regards ms. B, he considers it to be linguistically and in terms of palaeography closely akin to ms. A, although containing more corrections and additions. Ms. M he regards as the most recent and the one most subject to a subsequent reworking, given that it was commissioned to form part of a broader corpus of Cypriot chronicles and suffered from the carelessness of the scribe copying it, so that its main value is in completing certain lacunae of ms. B.

The origins and history of George Boustronios and the Bustron family

How little is known about George Boustronios, to whom the chronicle is attributed, appears from the fact that not even his origins are established with certitude. Jean Richard considered the Bustron (i.e. Boustronios) family to be bourgeois of Greek origin, Maurice Pinson considered George Boustronios' origin and his mother tongue to be Italian, like that of his kinsman Florio Bustron, and Peter Tivčev considered him to be 'a hellenized Cypriot Frank descended from the ancient Spanish family of Bustron.[29] None of these authors furnishes supporting evidence for his views, and Gilles Grivaud in a more recent work is correct in stating that his origins should be sought in Syria. The name Bustron or Boustron, Boustronios in its Hellenised form, has a clear affinity with the Syrian harbour town of al-Butrun, now in present-day Lebanon.[30] Given the extent of immigration from Syria to Cyprus throughout the Lusignan period and beyond, it is perfectly plausible to suggest that the Bustron family arrived in Cyprus from al-Butrun at some point in the Lusignan period.[31]

---

[28] See Florio Bustron, 'Chronique de l'île de Chypre', ed. R. de Mas Latrie in *Collection des documents inédits sur l'histoire de France: Mélanges historiques*, v (Paris, 1886), 373-459. Kehayioglou, *Διήγησις, op. cit.*, pp. 529 and 579 mistakenly attributes the edition to L. de Mas Latrie, but he names the editor correctly on p. 43*.

[29] 'Le compte de 1423', in *Documents chypriotes des archives du Vatican (XIVe et XVe siècles)*, ed. J. Richard (Paris, 1962), p. 30 note 9; M. Pinson, 'Observations sur la transcription des mots français et italiens dans le chronique de George Boustron', in *ΠΠΚΣ*, 3 vols. (Nicosia, 1971-1973), II, 213; P. Tivčev, 'George Bustron comme historien de l'île de Chypre au moyen age', *Etudes Balkaniques*, 4 (Sofia, 1982), 60.

[30] Grivaud, 'πνευματικός βίος', *op. cit.*, 1089 and note 98.

[31] J. Richard, 'Le peuplement latin et syrien en Chypre au XIIIe siècle', in *Croises missionnaires et voyageurs* VII (London, 1983); N. Coureas, 'The Place to be: Migrations to Lusignan and Venetian Cyprus', *ΚΣ* 66, 2002 (Nicosia, 2004), 125-145.

The family is first mentioned in Cypriot documents in the early fifteenth century. A statement of accounts prepared in the years 1422-1424 by an anonymous writer, possibly for a member of the Latin nobility, although neither the author nor the recipient are known, mentions a certain 'Quir Dimitri Boustron'.[32] The prefix 'Quir' is a corruption of the Greek κύριος, indicating that Demetrios Bustron was a member of the island's bourgeois, who at this time were mainly Greek or Syrian. The fifteenth century Cypriot chronicler Leontios Makhairas mentions a certain Thomassin Bustron as among the ordinary non-noble, people killed in 1426 at the battle of Khirokitia, in which the invading Mamluks defeated the army King Janus of Cyprus, capturing the king himself. He mentions that Thomassin, a tailor by profession, served in the royal army as an usher.[33] More important than either of the two Bustrons mentioned above was the cleric Paul Bustron. He was a canon at the Praemonstratensian monastery of Bellapais near Kerynia, and following the death of Abbot John some time before July 1445 the monks of the monastery had elected him abbot of the monastery. Savvas, however, the master chaplain of the church of Nicosia, contested his elections, having himself entered the monastery, assumed the regular habit customarily worn by the canons of the monastery, and been elected abbot during the time when the see of Nicosia was under the administration of Nicholas Bezas, a canon of Nicosia who had been appointed vicar general of the diocese, which was vacant at the time. Pope Eugenius IV appointed John, the cardinal priest of the church of St Lawrence in Lucina, to look into the matter, and the latter ruled in favour of Paul Bustron, whereupon the pope annulled Savvas' election, pronouncing Paul to be the lawful abbot and confirming his election.[34] Paul's election to the abbacy of the powerful Praemonstratensian monastery of Bellapais, other than being the first important office known to have been attained by a member of the Bustron family, also indicates that this family, or at any rate one part of it, were Roman Catholics and not members of the Greek church or of one of the eastern confessions (Jacobites, Maronites or Nestorians) to which Christians on Cyprus originating from Syria often belonged.[35]

Peter and Philip Bustron were two contemporaries of George Boustronios who both attained high office under King James II of Cyprus. Peter Bustron is mentioned as a royal *bailli* entrusted with the valuation of the *casale* of Porchades in a document dated October 1468, which mentions that his scribes assisted him in this task. He is also mentioned in February 1469 the *bailli* of a group of *casalia* collectively forming a territorial unit or *bailliage* that were joined to those of the royal estate on the king's

---

[32] Richard, 'Le compte de 1423', *op. cit.*, p. 30.

[33] Makhairas, *Recital, op. cit.*, I, § 685.

[34] W. Rudt de Collenberg, 'Etudes de prosopographie généalogique des Chypriotes mentionnés dans les registres du Vatican, 1378-1471', *MY* II (1984), 535 and 654-655; *Acta Eugenii IV*, ed. G. Fedalto, PCRCICO, xv (Rome, 1965), nos. 1313-1314, where Bustron is mistakenly rendered as 'Lutron'.

[35] N. Coureas, 'Non-Chalcedonian Christians on Latin Cyprus', in *Dei Gesta per Francos: Crusade Studies in Honour of Jean Richard*, ed. M. Balard, B.Z. Kedar and J. Riley-Smith (Aldershot, 2001), pp. 349-360.

orders. The *baillis* mentioned in the registers of 1468-1469 were entrusted with exploiting the royal estate, collecting its revenues and ensuring that the sums assigned from these to various persons were paid. In a second document of February 1469 Peter Bustron is mentioned as a *secrétain*, one of the officers of the financial office known as the *secrète*. This was the office entrusted with administering the royal estate and the kings' finances; brought over to Cyprus from the Latin kingdom of Jerusalem, where it existed at Tyre in the thirteenth century. On Cyprus Philip of Novara, writing in the second half of the thirteenth century, mentions the office, its *bailli* and its scribes. The *secrétains* formed a close-knit group whose number had no set limit, and many of its members appear from their names to have been of Greek or Syrian origin.[36] Philip Bustron like Peter was also a *secrétain*, and is mentioned in this capacity in no less than nine separate documents, in which he figures as a officer receiving payments from various nobles who gave the king money to secure a variety of offices, from serfs who paid sums to join the Greek priesthood or simply to be enfranchised. In these documents Philip Bustron is explicitly described as the officer of a new post created for forwarding payments to the men forming a troop or squadron under the command of Peter d'Avila, a Catalan who was one of King James II most prominent supporters, and who figures prominently in the chronicle of George Boustronios.[37] In several others he is simply mentioned as a *secrétain* of the *secrète*, while in one of the documents, dated 8 February 1469, a namesake of Philip Bustron is also mentioned. The latter is described as 'a squire of our chamber' and entrusted with the transportation to Famagusta of 100 bezants given by a certain Vassili Papa Georgi Lembiti from the *casale* of Letymbou in order to become a juror there.[38]

George Boustronios himself tells us very little about his own person, and most of the extant information on him derives from the chronicle attributed to him, where he always appears in the third person singular, hence the slight doubt over whether he is truly the author of the chronicle. From the chronicle one learns that at the time of the civil war that broke out between Queen Charlotte, the lawful heir to the throne of Cyprus following the death of King John II in 1458, and her half-brother James George Boustronios was himself a royal official. He was in the service of James, the future King James II, and an ardent supporter of his in the civil war, and he was also the *chevetain* at Salines, the administrative district deriving its name from the salt lake near the modern town of Larnaca, which was itself named Salines in the Lusignan period. The office of *chevetain* was relatively new in the Lusignan kingdom of Cyprus, coming into existence in the late fourteenth century and especially under King James I from 1388 onwards, when Cyprus was administratively divided into a dozen districts called *contrées* each of which was headed by a *chevetain*, who led a commission entrusted with assessing the districts for the payment of a new tax known as the royal tithe. Other than the *chevetain*, these commissions included a knight, a secretary and

---

[36] *Le livre des remembrances de la secrète du royaume de Chypre (1468-1469)*, ed. J. Richard with the collaboration of Th.Papadopoullos (Nicosia, 1983), pp. xi-xiv, xxi-xxiv and nos. 136, 220 and 230.

[37] *Ibid.*, nos. 78, 122, 124, 126, 152 and 176.

[38] *Ibid.* , nos. 125, 205 and 211-212.

a Genoese, and they were formed with the object of raising funds for the ransom of the king's son Janus, then a prisoner in Genoa. The *chevetains* were also entrusted with supervising the supplies due to their districts, or with the task of repurchasing them, and along with their deputies were empowered to arrest fugitive serfs. This empowerment indicates that they had judicial as well as fiscal authority, and since this authority to arrest fugitives was valid beyond the borders of the royal domain it had a public as opposed to a solely private nature.[39]

Mss. B and M of the chronicle, moreover, inform us that George Boustronios had a house in Larnaca, to which he sent the Catalan Jean Perez Fabrigues when the latter arrived at Salines on board a galliot.[40] This information is interesting because it was from the reign of King James II and especially during the Venetian period that Larnaca began to develop commercially and expand. Famagusta under Genoese occupation had been the only port for the entry of merchandise, in accordance with the treaty of 1383 concluded between Cyprus and Genoa, but on capturing the city in 1464 King James II abolished this monopoly, thereby creating the conditions for Larnaca to develop as a port. As late as 1467 the French traveller Nicolas le Huen found nothing but a church and a tavern there, but this relative obscurity was not to last. With the construction of houses and warehouses for the storage of merchandise at Larnaca people from Famagusta itself began to settle there, and Famagusta experienced decline. This decline is reflected in the reply the doge of Venice gave in 1491 to a petition sent to him by the citizens of Famagusta, rejecting their request to make it the only port of entry for merchandise, although he agreed to renew earlier prohibitions on the construction of new houses and warehouses at Salines, as Larnaca was then called. The repetition of such prohibitions bespeaks their ineffectiveness. By the end of the Venetian occupation Larnaca had become the main anchorage for Venetian ships in Cyprus, both on account of the salt loaded on board Venetian ships for dispatch to Venice, or for use as ballast in the course of the voyage there, and as the port of call for Venetian ships bound for Syria. The captain of Famagusta in 1509 reported that from an initial three houses Larnaca had become very populous. In 1543 600 persons lived there, according to the Venetian counsellor Dolfin and a document based on the census of 1563 records 1.000 people inhabiting the town, an increase of sixty six per cent within only twenty years.[41] Larnaca's importance as a port continued right through the Ottoman period, during which the European consuls and most European merchants were resident there.[42]

Members of the Bustron family, first appearing in Cypriot historical records of the early fifteenth century, continued to figure in the history of the island throughout

---

[39] Makhairas, *Recital, op. cit.*, I, §§ 618 and 621; Richard, *Livre des remembrances*, pp. xxi-xxii.

[40] See Boustronios (Coureas transl.), §82.

[41] Mas Latrie, *Histoire, op. cit.*, III, 489 no. 7; Hill, *op. cit.*, III, 812-813; B. Arbel, 'Cypriot Population under Venetian Rule: A Demographic Study', *MY* I (1984), 202-203.

[42] *Consulat de France à Larnaca – Documents inédits pour servir à l'histoire de Chypre*, ed. Anna Pouradier-Duteil Loizidou, 4 vols. (Nicosia, 1991-2002); Th.P. Ioannou, *Εμπορικές σχέσεις Κύπρου-Γαλλίας κατά τον 18ο αιώνα* (Nicosia, 2002).

the Venetian period and even beyond. Statistics on the population, livestock, produce, lands held by the clergy, and revenues of prominent families published by Mas Latrie, dateable to the early sixteenth century rather than to the late fifteenth as he suggests, mention a certain John Bustron as enjoying an annual income of 100 ducats, stating that the heirs of a certain 'Ser Zorzi Bustron' had the same income.[43] Peter Tivčev argues that the relatively modest income enjoyed by the heirs of George Boustronios indicates that he fell out of favour under the Venetians on account of having been a supporter of King James II, and so they sequestrated part of his estates, but this is a supposition without conclusive evidence to support it.[44] The 'Zorzi Bustron' of the statistics may simply have been a namesake of the chronicler, and quite a few persons named in these statistics had incomes of less than 100 ducats, sometimes as little as twenty. Furthermore, published documentation postdating Tivčev's article shows that the Bustron family included wealthy and even titled individuals in its ranks throughout the Venetian period.

On 21 August 1523 a certain Jason Bustron was granted permission by the Venetian Council of Ten to purchase the *casale* of Syrkati for 1.000 ducats. He had already given 400 ducats to purchase the *casale* of St Epiktetos near Kerynia, a transaction now annulled, and the Council of Ten stipulated that it required him to pay the outstanding balance of 600 ducats.[45] A letter of the Council of Ten dated 15 May 1525 also refers to a certain Bernardin Bustron, who was renting the *casale* of Peristerona near Morphou for the annual sum of 535 ducats, at the rate of ten bezants per ducat, 1.383 measures of wheat, 9.397 measures of barley and 179.75 *somme* of wine. On 7 July 1528 Bernardin Bustron sought the Council of Ten's permission to purchase the *casale* of Pano Koutraphas and Nikitari. The council's letter describes him as a Cypriot noble asking for this *casale* to be granted to him in perpetuity as a fief, stating that as another party was also interested in purchasing it, it would be sold to whoever offered the most advantageous terms.[46] On 22 March 1529 the Council of Ten approved the application a certain Zotin Bustron had submitted to buy the *casale* of Dikomo between Kerynia and Nicosia. Zotin had offered to pay 6.000 ducats for it within one month, at the rate of six *lire* and four *soldi* per ducat, and to pay the outstanding balance at the annual rate of 365 ducats. The council assented, but stipulated that the down payment of 6.000 ducats had to be made in fifteen days.[47]

A later Venetian document dated 9 April 1539 states that a certain Bernard Bustron, distinct from Bernardin mentioned above, was in the employment of the Venetian nobleman Sir Jeronimo together with Paleologo di Paleologi. Sir Jeronimo assigned them the task of having wheat, barley, pulses and biscuit loaded on board a ship belonging to the captain Manuel Emita, who had hired the ship to the nobleman

---

[43] Mas Latrie, *Histoire, op. cit.*, III, 493 and 500.

[44] Tivčev, 'Georges Bustron', *op. cit.*, p. 61.

[45] *Ανέκδοτα έγγραφα της κυπριακής ιστορίας από το κρατικό αρχείο της Βενετίας*, ed. Aikaterini Aristeidou, 4 vols (Nicosia, 1990-2003), III, 156-157.

[46] Aristeidou, *Έγγραφα, op. cit.*, III, 202-203 and 230-231.

[47] *Ibid.*, III, 263-264.

Andrea Marcello, a procurator of Sir Jeronimo. The cargo was to be dispatched to Venice or Corfu, both of which needed such supplies, at the discretion of the Venetian *proveditor* general of Cyprus and his officials, who had received instructions to this effect from the Venetian Council of Ten.[48] A letter dated 9 June 1540, moreover, states that the Venetian Council of Ten had examined a complaint of Jeronimo Bustron lodged against the nobleman Juan Marcello and his brothers, who were renting the *balliage* of Kouklia in Paphos and owed the public treasury rents worth 500 ducats from the previous September. The Venetian administrators on Cyprus had neglected to enforce payment of this sum, despite having received a letter from the previous Council of Ten. They were now reprimanded and ordered to compel Juan Marcello and his brothers to forward this sum to Jeronimo Bustron, who was clearly administering the *bailliage* and responsible for collecting its incomes for the public treasury.

Jeronimo Bustron reappears in this capacity in a subsequent letter of 14 July 1540, when the Council of Ten instructed the Venetian administrators of Cyprus to obtain from him the sum of 174 ducats and eight *gros* from the incomes of the *balliage* of Kouklia that he would deposit in the public treasury before the end of the coming September. They were to restore this money to the widow and heirs of Sir Alviso of Acre, who had been compelled to pay it to Alviso's creditor under a court decision that was subsequently overturned. One notes that Jeronimo Bustron was the viscount of Nicosia between the years 1549-1551 and once again between the years 1557-1559. His daughter Lucia, the wife of Scipio Podocataro, was captured during the fall of Nicosia to the Ottoman Turks in September 1570 and sent to Constantinople. Another member of the family, James Bustron, was kept imprisoned in Cyprus as a slave of Lala Mustapha Pasha, the commander in chief of the Ottoman army invading Cyprus.[49] The contribution of the Bustron family to the defence of Cyprus in the later Venetian period also appears in a list of feudatories and cavalrymen prepared on 28 April 1560 for Andrea Dandolo, the Venetian *provedittore* of Cyprus. It mentions Peter Bustron as furnished with one mount for the company of Count James de Nores, the liegeman Matthew Bustron as providing a mount armed with a corselet, while Philip and John Bustron were both furnished with mounts.[50]

The most famous Bustron of all, at least to posterity, is the chronicler Florio Bustron, a kinsman of George Bustronios who wrote a history of Cyprus in the later sixteenth century. His exact date of birth is unknown, but it was between the years 1500 and 1510. His studies, and whether he pursued them solely within Cyprus or in Italy too are also unknown, but his abilities as a jurist and as a linguist fluent in Greek,

---

[48] *Ibid.*, IV, 271.

[49] *Ibid.*, IV, 298-299 and 305-306; Chrysa Maltezou, 'Η περιπέτεια ενός ελληνόφωνου Βενετού της Κύπρου (1571)', in *ΠΔΚΣ*, 3 vols. (Nicosia, 1985-1987), II, 237-238; N. Coureas, G. Grivaud and C. Schabel, 'The Capital of the Sweet Land of Cyprus: Frankish and Venetian Nicosia', (publ. forthcoming), Appendix 1: The viscounts of Nicosia (by G. Grivaud).

[50] G. Grivaud and Aspasia Papadaki, 'L'institution de la *Mostra Generale* de la cavalerie féodale en Crète et en Chypre vénitiennes durant le XVIe siècle', *EKEE* XIII-XVI (Nicosia, 1988), 532 and 534.

French, Italian and Latin brought him to the notice of the Venetian authorities. In 1530 he appeared as a witness in an inquest against Thomas Ficardo, the former chancellor of King James II, and in 1531 he submitted a manuscript of the legal text known as the *Assises de la Cour des Bourgeois* to the three Venetian commissioners entrusted with gathering together the various manuscripts of this text to have it translated into Italian. The same commissioners assigned the task of preparing the translation to Florio himself, in his capacity as a notary. On completing the translation, published in Venice in 1535, he became a central figure in the administration of Venetian Cyprus, working from 1544 to 1566 as a notary or as a *secretain* in the fiscal department, translating feudal traditions, official acts of the Lusignan kings and lists drawn up by the tax commissions, as well as the *Livres des Remembrances*. He prepared a *pratico* or taxation register of the Marathassa district in 1549, completed the demarcation of the crown estates of Cyprus in 1566 and on his own initiative composed two treatises, one in 1552 on the rules of chivalry and another in 1554 on agricultural revenues. Various Venetian officers of state, including the *provedittore generalc* Bernardo Sagredo, praised his role in promoting good governance on Cyprus.[51]

His career in the Venetian administration does not appear to have brought him great wealth. His name does not appear in landed proprietors or those farming out public revenues in official documents, unlike certain other members of his family, and two notarial deeds of September 1562 and February 1563 mention a *Reverendus dominus presbyter Florius Bustronus Nicosiensis*, indicating that he had spiritual inclinations. The same deeds mention that Florio's brother John Bustron had adopted the habit of the Augustinians. Florio Bustron is last mentioned in 1568, when Stephen de Lusignan, who himself wrote two historical accounts on Cyprus after the Ottoman conquest of 1570, visited him in 1568 to consult a French manuscript of the *assises*. According to John Sozomeno, a certain Florio Bustron was killed on 9 September 1570 when the Ottoman troops took Nicosia by storm but his report is unconfirmed and may refer to a namesake.[52] His legal and administrative career in conjunction with the treatises he wrote would have been enough to make Florio Bustron a person of note, but what truly made him famous was his history of the island of Cyprus, surviving in five manuscripts and published in 1886 by René de Mas Latrie under the title *Chronique de l' île de Chypre*. René's title does not do justice to this work, the first attempt at historical synthesis undertaken by a Cypriot author writing according to the rules of Renaissance historiography with the express purpose of evoking the classical glories as well as the more recent Lusignan heritage of Cyprus so as to emphasize the importance of its civilisations, hence the dedication of his work *alli illustri signori conti ciprii*. This history, the culmination of his writings, was written between the years 1559 and 1566. Although lacking in originality it is nonetheless a masterly work of synthesis. The first part of his work on the historical geography, the

---

[51] Grivaud, 'πνευματικός βίος', *op. cit.*, pp. 1155-1156; *Idem.*, 'Florio Bustron, storico del rinascimento cipriota', in Florio Bustron, 'Chronique de l'île de Chypre', in *Collection des documents inédits sur l'histoire de France: Mélanges historiques*, V (Paris, 1886, repr. Nicosia, 1998), pp. vii-viii in the Nicosia reprint.

[52] Grivaud, 'πνευματικός βίος', *op. cit.*, pp. 1156-1157; *idem.*, 'Florio Bustron', *op. cit.*, p. viii.

classical monuments and famous persons of ancient Cyprus is inferior to the second and third parts dealing with the history of the Lusignan dynasty, given that his knowledge of Cyprus' geography and ancient history was limited. In the second and third parts of his history, however, his knowledge of events, his use of the major chroniclers writing in French, Latin and Greek and of documentary sources in Nicosia, as well as his generally detached and impartial approach, free of religiosity and scandal-mongering, make this one of the most important sources for the medieval history of Cyprus. His work greatly influenced Stephen de Lusignan in the composition of his own *Chorograffia* and *Description de toute l' isle de Chypre*, works lacking the clarity and readability of Florio's account but which nonetheless enjoyed a far greater diffusion.[53]

Several members of the Bustron family were seized and held in captivity by the Ottoman Turks. Not all of them were ransomed, as appears from contemporary documentation on the surviving members of the family. A letter of 1 July 1595 sent to King Philip II of Spain by the Spanish ambassador to Venice refers to the Cypriot noble Jason Bustron, who had become a Spanish secret agent in Ottoman Constantinople under an assumed name and for a yearly salary of 300 ducats. The letter states that Jason was descended from Spanish settlers in Lusignan Cyprus, a claim possibly advanced by Jason himself in order to facilitate his recruitment into Spanish service but which Tivčev believed to be true. It also states that Jason, a native of Cyprus, had been forced to flee to Venice with his mother and brothers following the Ottoman conquest, and had subsequently engaged in commerce in Constantinople and Anatolia, being fluent in Italian, Greek and Turkish. His recruitment as a Spanish secret agent was deemed especially valuable on account of his familial connections with the Ottoman sultan's household. Two daughters of his maternal aunt Lucia de Nores were married to Ottoman nobles, one to a Turkish prince and the second to a renegade *voevod* named Flangin. Jason was also related to none other than the first wife of Sultan Mehmet II, who was herself descended from the noble Cypriot family of Flatro. Subsequent correspondence of September 1600, the spring of 1601, June 1601 and February 1602 reveals that Jason was still serving the Spanish crown in Constantinople, had been instrumental in the recruitment of a second Spanish agent, Antonio Paronda, and had impressed the Spaniards with his capability enough so as to merit a rise in salary to 350 ducats annually This correspondence also reveals that Jason's brother John was also with him in Constantinople and assisting him in intelligence gathering. John, however, had become a Muslim following attractive proposals put to him by the sultan, which if rejected, however, could have led to his death, and had become the governor of a large territory surrounding the gulf of Naupaktos (Lepanto) in Greece.[54]

---

[53] Grivaud, 'πνευματικός βίος', *op. cit.*, pp. 1157-1168; *idem.*, 'Florio Bustron', *op. cit.*, pp. viii-xi.

[54] Tivčev, 'Georges Bustron', *op. cit.*, p. 60; Ισπανικά έγγραφα της κυπριακής ιστορίας (ις-ιζ αι), ed. I.K. Hasiotes (Nicosia, 1972, 2003²), nos. 19-21; Πηγές της κυπριακής ιστορίας από το ισπανικό αρχείο Simancas, ed. I.K. Hasiotes (Nicosia, 2000), no. 3.

John-Paul Bustron was another noble member of the family who entered Spanish service, but not before undergoing various tribulations, as appears in a letter of 28 February 1602 that he addressed to King Philip III of Spain. Losing his considerable estates after the Ottoman conquest, he was led into captivity along with his mother, one brother, three sisters and numerous other relatives. Some of them, and in particular his brother, continued to languish in captivity, but he himself had managed to escape after undergoing many troubles and expenses and make his way to Italy. There he had entered the Spanish army, serving in it for thirteen years and taking part in the military campaigns in the Netherlands and Picardy, where he had been wounded in action. On arriving in Italy after taking furlough he was informed that his brother had been located in Aleppo, Syria, where he was living in slavery. He betook himself there in order to ransom him, but failed to do so on account of the excessive sums demanded by the Turks, who humiliated and robbed him there. On his way to Syria he also stopped off in Cyprus on the instructions of Inigo de Mendoza, the Spanish ambassador to Venice, but the purpose of his mission there is not given. Returning to Italy, he was instructed to join the armada of Prince Doria, bound for the eastern Mediterranean, and he requested a salary from the king so as to meet his financial obligations towards his large family, especially the two sisters and nieces whom he had ransomed from infidel captivity.[55]

Two members from the branch of the Bustron family resident in Italy after the Ottoman capture of Cyprus entered the Roman Catholic priesthood in the seventeenth century. One was John-Matthew Bustron, who was born in Venice in 1581 and on entering the Greek college of Rome in 1592 studied theology and philosophy, obtaining a doctoral degree in both subjects. On his graduation in 1603 he held a number of offices at the college, and then moved to Padua, playing an active part there in the contemporary intellectual movements. By 1663 he was back in Venice, being described in 1666 as the librarian of the Bibliotheca Marciana, a post he had held since 1659, and as censor of Greek publications. He was distinguished chiefly as an epigrammatist and he died in Venice in October 1667. His contemporary George Bustron was likewise born in Venice in 1585, going to Rome and entering the Greek College in 1595. Completing his studies there fourteen years later, he entered the Order of the Jesuits in 1610, was ordained a priest, and taught theology and philosophy at the Jesuit College in Rome. He served for over 30 years as the archpriest of the Greeks at St Peter's church in Rome, where as the orator of the Greeks he transmitted the ideas of the counter-Reformation into Greek circles, translating the spiritual writings of the Spanish writer Juan d'Avila and of the Jesuit cardinal Roberto di Bellarmini in 1637 and supervising the edition of Neophytos Rodinos' Ἄσκησις Πνευ-ματική, published in 1641. He died in 1661 and was buried in the church belonging to the Jesuits in Rome.[56] No more is heard of the Bustron family from the second half of the seventeenth century.

---

[55] Hasiotes, Πηγές της κυπριακής ιστορίας, op. cit., no. 11.
[56] Paschalis M. Kitromilides, Κυπριακή Λογιοσύνη 1571-1878 (Nicosia, 2002), pp. 107-110.

The Chronicle as Literature

The chronicle of George Boustronios has traditionally been seen as a continuation of the larger and more renowned chronicle of Leontios Makhairas. Both chronicles are written in the contemporary Greek dialect then spoken on Cyprus, albeit in a more literary form than the colloquial Greek of the time. In chronological terms, George Boustronios' narration of the history of Cyprus commences in 1456, only 24 years after the end of the chronicle of Makhairas, which goes down to 1432, although the final section written by another hand takes the story down to 1458, the end of King John II's reign, in summary fashion.[57] One notes, however, that George Boustronios never refers to the chronicle of Makhairas, does not express any desire to continue it and does not furnish any information or inferences allowing one to conclude that he was familiar with the text of Makhairas' chronicle. As I will endeavour to prove below, the traditional interpretation is not valid in literary, chronological or even, to some extent, in historical terms.

Turning first to chronology, one observes that the true continuator of Leontios Makhairas in this respect was the anonymous author of a minor chronicle initially written in French and now surviving solely in an Italian translation in two manuscripts. The colophon of one of them states that the copyist Giovanni Tiepolo completed his copy on 28 October 1590. Consisting of six folios, the chronicle is, in precise terms, a reunion of three distinct texts, a chronological list of the Lusignan monarchs, a chronicle with 66 entries covering the reigns of Janus and John II and another four on events in the beginning of the fourteenth century, and finally four more detailed entries on the political events in the Latin kingdom of Jerusalem. These texts were not necessarily composed or copied by the same person. This chronicle fills the chronological gap of 24 years between the end of Makhairas' chronicle and the beginning of George Boustronios' narration.[58] It is unfortunate that there are manifest errors of chronology throughout the account, and the author appears to have based his narration on a list of the Lusignan kings of Cyprus and on various collections of annalistic historical notes. The information recounted for the years 1439-1459 allows one to conclude that he was a French speaker living in Nicosia and belonging to circles close to the royal court, who also had close contacts with the Greeks, hence he reported the election of Greek bishops and the union of the Latin and Greek churches at the council of Florence. The author also had a liaison with a Greek woman of his household, Perina Tiodorin (Theodorina) who bore him two children. The fact that the chronicle breaks off after the coronation of Louis the duke of Savoy in 1459 suggests that the chronicler died at this point or shortly after, although the possibility that he supported Queen Charlotte and went into exile cannot be discounted.[59] The chronicle, although written in French, clearly belongs in terms of content and structure to the

---

[57] Makhairas, *Recital, op. cit.*, I, 684-685 and II, 21.

[58] Grivaud, 'πνευματικός βίος', *op. cit.*, pp. 1084-1087; *idem.*, 'Une petite chronique chypriote du XVe siècle', in *Dei gesta per Francos: Crusade Studies in Honour of Jean Richard*, ed. M. Balard, B.Z. Kedar and J. Riley-Smith (Aldershot, 2001), pp. 317-339.

[59] Grivaud, 'πνευματικός βίος', *op. cit.*, p. 1085; *idem.*, 'Une petite chronique', *op. cit.*, p. 319.

literary genre of minor Greek chronicles copied in the margins of manuscripts, and
Jean Darrouzès has stressed their importance for the history of Cyprus. It is longer
than these Greek texts, however, and also differs in its final part, consisting of an
annalistic account of the Holy Land for the years 1257-1258 and 1263-1264. This part
of the text harks back directly to the Frankish thirteenth century tradition of
historiography.[60]

Turning to the literary character of the chronicle of George Boustronios and the
anonymous French chronicle directly preceding it chronologically, one discovers a
similar lack of sentiment in both accounts. The anonymous French chronicler is
completely dispassionate, except when mentioning the birth of his children.[61] George
Boustronios likewise writes in a manner that his kinsman Florio Bustron describes as
'senza alcune passione'.[62] In certain parts of his chronicle, however Boustronios
writes not dispassionately, but with strong though suppressed passion. Indeed, the
generally terse and dry style of his narrative make these rare outbursts of emotion all
the more dramatic, while the suppressed manner in which these emotions are
expressed does not lessen their force but paradoxically augments it. This comes
through with stark clarity when he recounts the career and doings of his *bête noir*,
James of Malta. He describes him as entering the service of King James 'barefoot and
dressed in a sackcloth, and chancing upon a crossbow he too went along with the
others to the forces assembled before Famagusta'. He goes on to describe how he
married the daughter of a former serf who had made much money, to accuse him of
malice and ingratitude towards his benefactor, the Catalan Peter d'Avila, and to
recount how he made friends with Carceran Chimi, a valet of King James II, only so
as to discover and denounce their conspiracy against the king's life. One of the
conspirators subsequently put to death was Demetrios [son] of Bustron. Although the
first name of Demetrios' father, a member of the Bustron family is not given,
Demetrios was almost certainly a kinsman of George Boustronios and possibly even
his own son, since the chronicler refers to himself simply as 'Bustron' elsewhere in the
text.[63] It is not hard therefore to understand his hatred and scarcely veiled contempt
for James of Malta.[64] His anger and frustration at not being able to harm him appear
with particular forcefulness when narrating their encounter at the depression of
Lefkomiatis, a village east of Nicosia. Queen Catherine Corner, the wife and successor
of King James II, had ordered James of Malta to betake himself to Famagusta
unarmed. Boustronios encountered him near Lefkomiatis while journeying in the
opposite direction, from Famagusta to Nicosia:

---

[60] Grivaud, 'πνευματικός βίος', *op. cit.*, pp. 1084-1085; *idem.*, 'Une petite chronique', *op. cit.*,
p. 320.

[61] *Ibid.* , p. 320.

[62] Florio Bustron, 'Chronique', *op. cit.*, p. 9 and note 3.

[63] Boustronios (Coureas transl.), §§ 93-95 and §194. I thank Prof. P. Edbury for the suggestion
that Demetrios might be the chronicler's son.

[64] Dawkins, *Boustronios, op. cit.*, p. 1 inexplicably states that the chronicler hated James of
Malta 'as an opponent of his favourite James II'.

Bustron, moreover, on seeing them, such as the one (i.e. James of Malta) who had caused the death of the young men whom the king had beheaded, and who had benefited on account of the evil visited upon others, while God, being just, had dispensed justice upon all who had been the cause of their demise, on beholding him without weapons Bustron did not move a muscle.[65]

This manifestation of strong emotions is all the more effective for being restrained and occasional in its expression. Nor does George Boustronios reserve emotion and employ vivid imagery solely for those hurting his relatives. A strong supporter of Queen Charlotte's brother James, whom he served in person, he graphically illustrates the admiration King John II had for his illegitimate son when recounting an ostensibly insignificant detail during the course of their meeting, after James' return from Rhodes:

In the morning the postulant mounted his horse and went to the king, coming into the king's presence …It was in addition extremely hot, and he took off his coat and remained in his shirt. And seeing him in his shirt, the king took great pleasure because he had a handsome body.[66]

The admiration shown by the king towards James parallels the chronicler's own admiration towards him, and the apparently insignificant aside about James staying in his shirt because of the heat provides a stark illustration of how by his mere physical presence James could evoke admiration. Later in the chronicle, when recounting the death on account of plague of the envoys Queen Charlotte had sent to the Mamluk sultan so as to obtain his support for her rule, he states sententiously that 'the emissaries whom they had sent from Cyprus died on account of the numerous transgressions they had committed in Cyprus. And on their death everything collapsed'.[67] In stating that the envoys had died on account of their sins, Boustronios resembles Makhairas, who also explains various calamities in terms of divine retribution visited on the sufferers on account of their evil ways. Hence Makhairas attributes the Genoese capture of Famagusta to the transgressions of the town's inhabitants, especially their predilection for sodomy and their cruelty towards slaves. Makhairas also attributes the Cypriot defeat at the battle of Khirokitia against the Mamluk invaders to the fact that put their trust in vain weapons, not in God.[68] Yet in explaining the calamities suffered by parties in terms of divine punishment for their transgressions, Boustronios is also harking back to a much older tradition. Writing in the sixth century after Christ, the Byzantine historian Procopius of Caesarea explained the destruction of Antioch by the Persians in the year 540 as having been brought about by divine judgement, although he expresses uncertainty as to the exact causes that prompted it.[69] This tradition of invoking divine intervention, running right

---

[65] Boustronios (Coureas transl.), § 194.

[66] *Ibid.*, § 20.

[67] *Ibid.*, § 41.

[68] Leontios Makhairas, *Recital, op. cit.*, I, §§ 482 and 670.

[69] Averil Cameron, *Procopius* (London, 1985), pp. 117 and 145.

through Byzantine and post-Byzantine historiography, is ultimately rooted in the Old Testament, which explains God's destruction of Sodom and Gomorrah as having occurred on account of the inhabitants' sinful way of living.[70]

The vivid imagery George Boustronios is capable of using also appears when he recounts how the abbot of the Benedictine monastery of the Holy Cross, seized by the Venetians in January 1474, had written to the pope stating of the kingdom of Cyprus 'it is in dire straits, and it now stands in the hands of the Venetians, which means that we have escaped the clutches of a dog and fallen into [those of] a swine'.[71] Although separated from him by nearly four centuries, the imagery Boustronios uses links him to another chronicler writing at the very beginning of Lusignan rule, Neophytos the Recluse. In explaining the failure of the Latins to expel the Muslims from Syria and Palestine, Neophytos stated of God that 'οὐδέ γαϱ ηὐδόκησεν η πϱόνοια κύνας εξε-ώσαι και λύκους αντεισάξαι (= for divine providence did not find it pleasing to drive out dogs and introduce wolves instead)'.[72] It is ironic for such similar imagery to be utilized by writers of historical events placed at opposite ends of the Lusignan period, the very beginning and the very end. Finally, in describing the final departure of Queen Catherine Corner for Venice, Boustronios likewise strikes a note of pathos and high drama when recounting her exit from Nicosia:

> And she went on horseback wearing a black silken cloak, with all the ladies and knights in her company, and six knights by her bridle and flanking her horse. Her eyes, moreover, did not cease to shed tears throughout the procession. The people likewise shed many tears. Besides, there were men drawn up, and all the soldiers had come to Nicosia. And as soon as she came out of the court, they let up the cry: 'Marco! Marco!'[73]

This dramatic yet restrained passage near the end of the chronicle provides a fitting and tragic climax to his story. Dawkins rightly remarks that 'In its position here at the end of the story we feel very much the hand of the artist'.[74]

Throughout the greater part of the chronicle, however, the style of writing, although terse and dispassionate apart from the exceptions discussed above, is nonetheless far from uniform. Brief paragraphs or even sentences alternate with prolix passages in which the events are recounted in great detail, suggesting that Boustronios' literary style is drawn partly from the calendrical accounts of the minor fifteenth century Greek chronicles and partly from the traditions of chronicle writing expressed by Leontios Makhairas in the same period.[75] Unlike Makhairas, however,

---

[70] Gen. 18-19.

[71] Boustronios (Coureas transl.), § 218.

[72] Neophytos the Recluse, 'Πεϱί των κατά την χώϱαν Κύπϱου σκαιών', *Μεσαιωνική Βιβλιο-θήκη (= Biblioteca Graeca Medii Aevi)*, ed. C. Sathas, 7 vols. (Venice, 1872-1894), II, 1.

[73] Boustronios (Coureas transl.), § 281.

[74] Dawkins, *Boustronios, op. cit.*, p. 7.

[75] Grivaud, 'πνευματικός βίος', *op. cit.*, pp. 1090 and 1092.

who was contemporary to only the later events recounted in his chronicle, Boustronios, whose chronicle covers a time-span of only 30 years, was a contemporary of and a participant in the events he narrates, covering the final period of Lusignan rule in Cyprus and the beginning of Venetian rule. His narration of events follows a strict chronological order, although there are some exceptions. Hence when introducing his account of Queen Charlotte's flight from Kerynia to Rhodes and her return to Kerynia via Paphos he begins with the words 'I forgot to write this previously'.[76] Similarly, after recounting the capture of Kerynia by King James' forces, he begins a new paragraph with the words 'In addition, on 29 August he took Famagusta, *as I stated above*' (my italics).[77] In fact the capture of Famagusta is not previously referred to in any of the three extant manuscripts. Either he forgot to mention it, or he confounded the capture of the Genoese vessels coming with provisions to relieve Famagusta in June 1461 with the capture of the town itself, or his previous allusion to its capture has been excised from the narrative. One notes that Florio Bustron dates the capture of Famagusta to January 1464,[78] not August, and that George Boustronios' chronicle is silent on events in Famagusta from November 1461 to July 1464, something strange for a contemporary chronicler.

This silence along with other lacunae lends credence to Grivaud's suggestion the three extant chronicles which all have gaps in the narrative derive from a dismembered original text.[79] The nine years of King James' reign from the capture of Famagusta in 1464 to his death in 1473 are dealt with in only ten chapters,[80] and three of them, considerably longer and more detailed than the others, deal solely with the plot against the king's life hatched by disgruntled nobles. In a similar manner, the chronicler devotes 24 lengthy and detailed chapters to the failed attempt of the 'Catalan party' to seize power by assassinating close relatives of Queen Catherine Corner and a single sentence to the thirteen years of her reign from her arrival in Nicosia in 1476 until her final departure in 1489.[81] It is possible that the events taking place during the reigns of King James II and Queen Catherine Corner, following the firm establishment of their rule, were deliberately excised in the Venetian period by an administration anxious to obliterate the memory of Cyprus' last monarchs and to habituate the Cypriots to the recently established Venetian governance. It is also possible, however, that the chronicler himself was uninterested in relating the more humdrum and everyday aspects of their reigns, concentrating instead on the intrigues, invasions, murders, warfare, confiscations and executions that marked the period from 1458 to 1474. Throughout his narrative he comes across very much as a 'dates and battles' historian of events.

This 'dates and battles' approach also manifests itself in the omissions in the

---

[76] Boustronios (Coureas transl.), § 85.

[77] *Ibid.*, § 88.

[78] Florio Bustron, 'Chronique', *op. cit.*, p. 411.

[79] Grivaud, 'πνευματικός βίος', *op. cit.*, pp. 1089-1090.

[80] Boustronios (Coureas transl) ,§§ 89-98.

[81] *Ibid.*, §§ 153-176 and 277.

chronicle of George Boustronios, especially when compared to that of the major Greek chronicle of Leontios Makhairas preceding his own. Makhairas chronicle has a didactic purpose, regarding the fate of Cyprus as determined by the providence of an almighty God and the history of the Latin kingdom established there as subject to both divine and diabolical interventions, reflecting the ongoing struggle between God, the protector of the Cypriots, and Satan, inspirer of the usurper Isaac Komnenos, the Genoese and the Saracens. It stresses Christian virtues and feudal values, regarding the Lusignan kings fighting the Muslims as on the side of God on account of their courage. It highlights the courtesy and knightly ethos of the Latins (Franks), condemns unchristian attributes such as envy, arrogance, and promiscuity, with particular strictures against blasphemy and sodomy, and espouses popular cultural traditions in showing devotion towards supernatural phenomena, belief in the miraculous powers of icons or sacred relics and observance of astrological manifestations.[82] None of these elements are present in George Boustronios' chronicle, which in general lacks both the religiosity and the sense of purpose running right through the chronicle of Leontios Makhairas. Peter Tivčev, discussing the chronicle from a Marxist perspective, concedes that 'the profound devoutness found so unashamedly in his predecessor (i.e. Leontios Makhairas) is not observable in Boustronios', although he also states that the chronicle 'resembling other medieval chronicles in this respect ... is permeated by religious perceptions and by the belief in divine providence appropriate to this period'.[83] This relative lack of religiosity should not be taken to mean that Boustronios is wholly impartial. He was an ardent supporter of both King James II and his wife and heir Catherine Corner, as will be discussed more fully in the historical section below. What characterizes his chronicle in general, however, is the lack of any didactic or edificatory purpose, no discussion of or even reference to the causes underlying specific events. The florid style, the wealth of expression, and the employment of a variety of narrative techniques used by Leontios Makhairas in his chronicle so as to attract the readers' attention are absent from that of Boustron, whose narrative lacks literary pretensions.[84]

George Boustronios' unpretentious style, impartiality and generally dispassionate way of recounting events are precisely those qualities which are valued today in historical writing, yet as David Holton points out he is paradoxically taken to task for them by none other that George Hill, whose two volume narrative history of Lusignan and Venetian Cyprus is still of great value notwithstanding the passage of time.[85] Hill, Dawkins, Tivčev and others have compared him unfavourably to Leontios Makhairas, viewing him as simpler, less original and less striking.[86] Since, however, the two chroniclers had markedly different approaches to their subject matter, as

---

[82] Grivaud, 'πνευματικός βίος', *op. cit.*, pp. 1073-1080.

[83] Tivčev, 'Georges Boustron', *op. cit.*, pp. 80-81.

[84] Grivaud, 'πνευματικός βίος', *op. cit.*, pp. 1090-1093.

[85] Holton, 'Cypriot writing', *op. cit.*, p. 85.

[86] Hill, *op. cit.*, III, 1107; Dawkins, *Boustronios, op. cit.*, p. 1; Tivtev, 'Georges Bustron', *op. cit.*, p. 83; Kehayioglou, *Διήγησις, op. cit.*, pp. 261-262*.

explained above, this comparison is not really relevant. More relevant is a comparison between the chronicle of George Boustronios and one written outside Cyprus sometime after 1573, namely the Χρονικόν περί των Τούρκων σουλτάνων (= Chronicle regarding the Turkish Sultans) written in the late sixteenth century and covering the period 1373-1513.[87] Boustronios' chronicle exhibits marked similarities with this later chronicle in chronology, linguistic features and style. The chronicle on the Turkish sultans concentrates on the rule of Sultan Mehmed II, 1451-1481, just as the chronicle of George Boustronios covers the period 1459-1489, while the alternation from direct to indirect speech found in both chronicles, the frequent inconsistencies in accentuation and the frequent use of direct speech are common to both chronicles.[88] Indeed, even Hill concedes that Boustronios' descriptions are 'almost as lively' as those given by Makhairas himself, while Tivčev considers his account to be more coherent and comprehensible than that of Makhairas, observing that 'his language is distinguished by its simplicity'.[89] His narrative is vivid and direct, and although his 'dates and battles' approach outlined above is not favoured by present-day historians stressing the value of analysis, discussion of underlying causes and the importance of social, cultural and economic factors in shaping historical events and processes one can hardly fault him for it, given that he was writing at the close of the middle ages and at the dawn of the Renaissance. Indeed, Boustronios' detailed recounting of intrigues, military operations, assassinations, conspiracies and personal quarrels give his narrative a journalistic flavour that is strangely but indubitably modern, and one could imagine him today as an excellent war or crime correspondent. In the light of the above one can state that in literary as well as in historical terms the chronicle of George Boustronios spans the transition from the medieval to the modern. Its 'watershed' quality both as a historical account and as a work of literature is precisely what makes it so distinctive and interesting.

The Language of the Chronicle and the Present Translation

David Holton in presenting and discussing a passage from Boustronios' chronicle has observed that the language is surprisingly modern, although remarking at the same time that the syntax preserves certain medieval features and elements of Cypriot phonology. He points out that 'we should not assume that it represents the unadulterated Cypriot vernacular of the time it was written', nonetheless concluding that 'the presence of idiomatic elements, particularly in the dialogues, and the natural flow of the narrative suggest that the language is not too far removed from the everyday speech of urban Cypriots of a certain educational level'.[90] In fact the chronicle makes the transition from the middle ages to the renaissance not only in literary and historical terms, as has been stated above and will be discussed in more

---

[87] E. Zachariadou, *Το Χρονικό των Τούρκων σουλτάνων (του Βαρβερινού ελλην. Κώδικα 111) και το ιταλικό του πρότυπο* (Thessaloniki, 1960).

[88] Kehayioglou, *Διήγησις, op. cit.*, pp. 237-238* and note 31.

[89] Hill, *op. cit.*, III, 1107; Tivčev, 'Georges Bustron', *op. cit.*, pp. 82-83.

[90] Holton, 'Cypriot writing', *op. cit.*, pp. 85-86.

detail below, but also linguistically. This is so because it illustrates, despite its use of Greek as a linguistic medium, the transition from French to Italian, from the Lusignans to the Venetians.

The Greek of the chronicle, like the Greek of contemporary or near contemporary texts, and here the Greek of the two extant translations of the *Assises de la Cour de Bourgeois* in particular springs to mind, is heavily impregnated by loan words from the Romance languages. It is not always clear, however, whether the original derivation is French or Italian. Words such as αρεστιάζω, ρικουμαντιάζω, κουφερτιάζω and μαντενιάζω could be derived from either, Ecclesiastical words such as τσανούνης and τσεντούρης originate from the Old French *chanoine* and *chanteor*, as do certain other words such as διυσπλαζίριν (Old Fr. *desplaisir*) or φούρμα (Old Fr. *Forme* = seat). Other words, for instance φορεστιέρικον (It. *Forestiero* = foreign), σπετσιέρης (It. speziere = spice seller) and λότζα (It. *loggia* = lodgings for merchants) are of clearly Italian derivation. The Greek of the chronicle is influenced by Romance expressions as well as loanwords. The expression έχει χρήσιν να κάμει (= he must do) clearly derives either from French *il a besoin de faire* or Italian *ha bisogno di fare*, and one cannot know with certitude which of the two it originates from. The Greek phrase να μεν δώσει φαστίδιον manifestly derives from the Italian *dare fastidio*, meaning to annoy or disturb. Loanwords from Catalan, Provençal, Arabic and Turkish are also found in the chronicle, but French and Italian are the predominant languages from which such words originate.

Both French and Italian had been present in Cyprus for centuries by the time Boustronios' chronicle was written. French was the official language of the Lusignan dynasty, spoken at the court, used in the drafting of legislation, in the courts of law, and in the documents drawn up in the royal chancery.[91] Yet by the time of King James II, the penultimate Lusignan king, the French of the chancery had become laced with Greek words, such as *frahte* (Greek φράκτης = enclosure), *climata* (Greek κλήματα = vines), *hrosomillie* (Cypriot Greek χρυσομηλιά = apricot tree), *protoquiporo* (Greek πρωτοκηπουρός = head gardener) and numerous others.[92] Queen Charlotte's relative ignorance of French and her fluency in Cypriot Greek were remarked on during her exile in Rome, and the French of Cyprus, cut off from regular contact with the French speaking lands of Western Europe had become archaic and anachronistic, infused with Italian, Greek and Spanish words.[93] This fact is reflected in the transcription of French and Italian words in Boustronios' chronicle. As Maurice Pinson has observed, the French utilized in Cyprus at the end of the Lusignan period, that is the mid-fifteenth century, had an artificial character, on account of being cut off from that of metropolitan France and because of the greatly reduced number of noble families able to speak correct French. Hence the transcription of French words into Greek is

---

[91] Grivaud, 'πνευματικός βίος', *op. cit.*, pp. 876-878.

[92] Richard, *Livre des Remembrances, op. cit.*, pp. 231-237.

[93] Mas Latrie, *Histoire, op. cit.*, III and note 1; Hill, *op. cit.*, III, 611; J. Richard, 'Culture franque et culture grecque: le royaume de Chypre au XVème siècle', in *idem., Croisades et etats latins d'Orient*, XVIII (Aldershot, 1992), 406-407.

incoherent and defective, reflecting the fact that Greek, despite ceasing to be the official language since the Byzantine era, had in practice become once again the chief spoken language.[94]

The situation regarding Italian was very different. Like French it had been present in Cyprus for centuries by Boustronios' time. Given the presence and activities in Cyprus of Venetian merchants from the late Byzantine period, since the twelfth century, and the increased migration of Italians and Italian speakers to Cyprus during the thirteenth and fourteenth centuries, especially from the mid-thirteenth century onwards, from both Italy and Latin Syria prior to the Muslim re-conquest, Italian was of prime importance in the commercial life of the island. Although not the official language of the Lusignan kingdom, unlike French, it possessed an important advantage in Cyprus over the latter. The French knights and nobility of the island had migrated there with Guy de Lusignan and in the course of the fifteenth century did not have their numbers regularly replenished by continual migration from overseas. With the passage of time their links with Europe were severed, their numbers were reduced by war and disease, and the use of French as a literary language ceased by the mid-fourteenth century. Italian, however, was constantly in use by the Venetian, Pisan, Genoese and Florentine merchants visiting Cyprus in the thirteenth and fourteenth centuries, of whom a certain number took up residence in the island. The Venetians and Genoese in particular maintained regular commercial ties with the island throughout the Lusignan period, and so an Italian language that was in regular and unbroken contact with metropolitan Italy was employed in Cyprus, especially in commerce.

Furthermore, from the mid-fourteenth century onwards many Cypriot students were studying law and theology at the Italian universities of Padua, Bologna, Rome and Naples, thereby creating an educated class fluent in this language.[95] Following the Venetian annexation of Cyprus in 1473 Italian also became the island's official language, supplanting both French and Greek in importance as an administrative and literary medium.[96] The unpublished Italian translation of Boustronios' own chronicle effected in the late sixteenth century, the Italian translations of the *Assises de la Cour des Bourgeois* executed in 1531, the Italian translation of Leontios Makhairas' chronicle known under the name of Diomede Strambali, the anonymous Italian chronicle known after its last owner, the Venetian nobleman Francesco Amadi, and the Italian chronicle of George Boustronios' relation Florio Bustron all illustrate its unchallenged literary and administrative dominance in Venetian Cyprus. Both languages are represented in George Boustronios' chronicle, but whereas the French present there was moribund, the Italian was very much the language of the future, at

---

[94] Pinson, 'Observations', *op. cit.*, pp. 213-220.

[95] A. Tselikas, 'Η διαθήκη του Petro de Caffrano και οι πράξεις εκλογής Κυπρίων φοιτητών για το Πανεπιστήμιο της Παδόβας (1393,1436-1569)', *EKEE* XVII (1987-1988), 261-292; Bianca Betto, 'Nuove recherché sulle studenti Ciprioti all' Università di Padova (1393-1489)', *Θησαυρίσματα*, 23 (1993), 40-79; Grivaud, 'Πνευματικός βίος', *op. cit.*, p. 880.

[96] *Ibid.*, pp. 880-881.

any rate until the Ottoman conquest of 1570.[97] In its language as in other areas, George Boustronios' chronicle represents a transition.

The present translation of the chronicle has been undertaken principally so as to make available an English translation based on the recent and extremely comprehensive edition of the Greek original prepared by George Kehayioglou. Other factors, however, also motivated this translation. One was the fact that Dawkins, using the older edition of Boustronios' chronicle as published by Constantine Sathas, based his own translation of ms. M, which as stated above appears to be the most recent of the extant manuscripts and the least complete. Taking advantage of the fact that Kehayioglou publishes all three extant manuscripts on facing pages I have effected a translation based on ms. A. In historical content it is the fullest of the three manuscripts, so that even Sathas in his edition of the chronicle added two final paragraphs from this manuscript to his edition of ms. M.[98] Dawkins in his translation, based on Sathas' edition, likewise added 'the few phrases from the London ms. which are not in the Venice ms.', commenting in comparing the two that 'the matter (in ms. A) is occasionally a little differently arranged and, particularly in the dialogues, made a little clearer and sharper'.[99]

In fact ms. A contains significant information not found in the other manuscripts. It mentions the year of the Mamluk invasion, omitted in the other manuscripts, and the fact that the admiral arrived 'along with numerous emirs, Saracens and foot soldiers' which the other manuscripts also omit. The word given for the Mamluk foot soldiers, χαλφούσιδες, derives from the Arabic *harâfish* meaning commoners or craftsmen, an indication of these soldiers' social background.[100] Mss. B and M wrongly render the name of James Salviati, a prominent Florentine nobleman and an avid partisan of King James, who richly rewarded his heir Jeronimo with several villages, as James Salah.[101] More serious is the wrong recording of King James' relationship with the Catalan Sor de Naves, who was instrumental in surrendering Kerynia to the king. Mss. B and M wrongly state that the king had him married to the illegitimate daughter of an uncle of his, whereas ms. A correctly states that he married him to one of his own illegitimate daughters, something confirmed in a letter of the Venetian Senate and also recorded in the chronicle of Florio Bustron.[102] Furthermore, ms. A is the only manuscript containing the important information that King James doubled the annual tribute the Mamluks received from Cyprus from 8.000 to 16.000 ducats, but once again reduced it to 8.000 shortly before his death.[103] Other important passages found only in ms. A are the incident in which a peasant from Paphos bewails

---

[97] Richard, 'Culture franque et culture grec', *op. cit.*, pp. 400 and 414-415.

[98] Sathas 'Βουστρωνίου Χρονικόν ', *op. cit.*, pp. cli (ρνα') and 543.

[99] Dawkins, *Boustronios, op. cit.*, p. 1. From ms. A Dawkins adds §§ 256A, 266A, 283-284 and the final part of 194 to his translation.

[100] Boustronios (Coureas transl.), § 43 and note.

[101] *Ibid.*, § 68 and note.

[102] *Ibid.*, § 87 and note.

[103] *Ibid.*, § 89 and note.

the lack of justice in Cyprus and the pardon Queen Catherine granted the brothers John and Charles Kallergis.[104] This is not to say that mss. B and M can be disregarded. They both contain words or phrases not found in ms. A, in particular the dramatic encounter between George Boustronios and James of Malta.[105] In this translation such words, placed in brackets < >, have been added throughout. Mss. B and M are also vital in providing details on the nobles' conspiracy against King James in 1470[106], on the plot against Venice engineered by Rizzo de Marinò and Tristan de Gibelet and on the details of Queen Catherine's final departure from Cyprus.[107] Where mss. B and M vary significantly from A this too has been recorded in the footnotes to the text.

A new translation of Boustronios' chronicle into English is needed, however, for another reason, the errors and shortcomings in Dawkins' own translation. As stated above, Dawkins prepared an initial draft in Tunisia in 1938 and a decade later revised his translation with reference to Sir George Hill's *History of Cyprus*, volumes II and III of which covered the Frankish and Venetian periods and were published in 1948. Dawkins, however, died in 1955, and J.R. Stewart himself died in 1962.[108] Hence both its translator and the person supporting its publication had died by the time it was finally published in 1964. Stewart himself admits that many difficulties arose impeding its prompt publication, and that in order to expedite matters he did not compile notes to accompany the translation.[109] Despite this disclaimer, the translated text does have some notes, as well as an excellent index compiled by Stewart's wife, Mrs. Eve Stewart. Other than the paucity of notes, the translation is marred by serious errors throughout, involving errors of dating, errors of identification of persons as well as misinterpretations of the text. Where such errors occur, they have been corrected and explanatory footnotes added.[110]

Certain procedures have been adopted in preparing this new translation of the chronicle from Greek into English. One concerns nomenclature. Dawkins simply transcribed all names from the Greek into Latin characters, retaining their Greek morphology even when the names were of French, Italian or Catalan provenance. Where possible I have restored names originating from the Romance languages to their original French, Italian or Catalan form, although first names have usually been anglicised, hence John instead of Jean or Juan, James instead of Jacques or Giacomo. Sometimes, however, it has seemed better to make an exception to this general rule, so I cannot claim complete consistency or uniformity. It should also be noted that although in translating the text my aim has been to render the Greek into clear modern English I have not in any way tried to embellish or polish the text in terms of

---

[104] *Ibid.*, §§ 194, 256 and 266.

[105] *Ibid.*, § 194.

[106] *Ibid.*, § 95 and notes.

[107] *Ibid.*, §§ 279-280.

[108] Dawkins, *Boustronios, op. cit.*, pp. vii-viii.

[109] *Ibid.*, p. v.

[110] See Boustronios (Coureas transl.), §§ 7, 9, 27, 50, 64-65, 68, 77, 89, 91, 95, 99, 113, 116, 162, 170, 205, 243, 252 and the relevant notes to these chapters.

vocabulary and style, since a translation should endeavour to convey as far as possible the author's style of writing as well as the meaning of the text itself. As regards Dawkins' division of the text into chapters, which is extremely sensible and facilitates referencing to the chronicle, this has been retained, but those chapters of his ending in B have been amalgamated with the preceding ones, hence 266 and 266B are now simply 266.

The Chronicle as History

Like other historical chronicles of Lusignan and Venetian Cyprus, the chronicle of George Boustronios is narrative rather than analytical. This can also be said for major Cypriot chronicles like those of Leontios Makhairas, Florio Bustron, Stephen de Lusignan, the anonymous chronicle named after its last owner, a sixteenth century Venetian nobleman called Francesco Amadi, for the minor Greek calendrical chronicles of the fifteenth century, and for the anonymous fifteenth century French chronicle surviving in Italian translation, discussed above. Where it differs from most major chronicles is in the period of time it covers. The chronicle of Leontios Makhairas begins with the fourth century Roman emperor Constantine and ends with the death of King Janus in 1432, although a sixth book which by general consent is seen as an addition written by another author takes the story down to the death of his successor, King John II, in 1458. The anonymous chronicle known as 'Amadi' begins with the conquest of Syria in the seventh century by the Caliph Umar and likewise concludes with the death of King Janus in 1432. The chronicle of Florio Bustron, George Boustronios' kinsman, commences with a description of Cyprus in antiquity, alludes to the visit of St Helena, mother of the Emperor Constantine, to Cyprus and takes the story down to 1489, when Queen Catherine Corner left the island, while the two chronicles of Stephen de Lusignan, the *Chorographia* and the somewhat fuller *Description*, begin with the names of Cyprus in antiquity and end with the seizure of the island in 1571 by the Ottoman Turks. Even the short anonymous fifteenth century French chronicle records kings and certain events in Cyprus from 1192 to 1459, while the chronicle on the Turkish sultans, written outside Cyprus and based on an Italian prototype, covers the years 1373-1513.

Unlike all the above chronicles, the chronicle of George Boustronios has a far more limited time span, covering the years 1456 to 1489, that is the closing years of King John II and the reigns of Queen Charlotte, her illegitimate brother King James II, his son, the short-lived King James III, and Queen Catherine Corner until her departure from Cyprus in 1489. In covering such a short period of time and with its heavy emphasis on the civil war between Queen Charlotte and her brother James the chronicle strangely resembles a Cypriot chronicle of the thirteenth century written by the famous jurist and nobleman Philip of Novara. He was a supporter of the powerful Cypriot noble family of Ibelin and he wrote a historical narrative on the war between the Ibelins and their followers, grouped around the young King Henry I of Cyprus, and the western Emperor Frederick II, at that time the suzerain of Cyprus.[111] This was a

---

[111] Filipo da Novara, *Guerra di Federico II in Oriente (1223-1242)*, ed. S. Melani (Naples, 1994), pp. 13-45.

civil war involving the Latin kingdom of Jerusalem as well as Cyprus, and the chronicle covers events from 1223 to 1242. Philip of Novara's chronicle has important points in common with that of George Boustronios. Both chronicles encompass a short period of time, several decades as opposed to centuries, both deal with civil strife as their main theme and in both cases the authors are not only eyewitnesses but also participants to the events, and highly partisan ones at that.[112] Philip of Novara, an avid supporter of the Ibelins, fought with them during the minority of King Henry I against the nobles in Cyprus and the kingdom of Jerusalem supporting the western Emperor Frederick II, while George Bustron likewise supported King James II against his sister Queen Charlotte, bringing forces up from Larnaca to support him.[113]

Both chroniclers cover periods of civil strife during which royal authority in Cyprus was destabilised, in the late 1220s and early 1230s on account of the minority of King Henry I and in the 1460s on account of the civil war between Queen Charlotte and her illegitimate half-brother James, who eventually prevailed and ruled as King James II, although his formal coronation did not occur until 1466.[114] In both cases outside powers were involved, among them suzerains of the kingdom of Cyprus. In the early thirteenth century the papacy supported the Ibelin nobles and their adherents against their opponents. They in turn drew support from the Western Emperor Frederick II who was the suzerain of Cyprus, for when the pope formally recognised Aimery in 1197 as king of Cyprus the Western Emperor had assumed suzerainty over the new Latin realm, an arrangement lasting until 1247.[115] Likewise in the later fifteenth century Queen Charlotte obtained the support of the Hospitallers of Rhodes, while her half-brother James solicited and eventually secured the support of another suzerain, the Mamluk sultan of Egypt.[116] Following the Mamluk invasion of 1426, the defeat and capture of King Janus at the battle of Khirokitia, and his eventual redemption from captivity in Cairo, the kingdom of Cyprus had been placed under the suzerainty of the Mamluk sultans.[117] This lasted from 1426 until 1517, when the Ottoman Turks defeated and conquered the Mamluks. Cyprus, under Venetian rule since 1473, now came under the suzerainty of the Ottoman sultans until they conquered it from Venice in 1571. Therefore in both civil wars taking place in Cyprus, that during the minority of King Henry I and that between Queen Charlotte and her half-brother James, the island was under the suzerainty of outside powers intervening in favour of one party.

---

[112] On Philip of Novara's partisanship see P. Edbury, *The Kingdom of Cyprus and the Crusades, 1191-1374* (Cambridge, 1991, 1994²), pp. 48-49 and 51-54.

[113] Boustronios (Coureas transl.), § 58.

[114] Hill, *op.cit.*, III, 631 and note 3, also 1159 (Addenda).

[115] Edbury, *Kingdom, op.cit.*, pp. 50-60 and 66; Melani, *Federico II, op.cit.*, pp. 21-36.

[116] Boustronios (Coureas transl.), §§ 37-43; Hill, III, 568-570; P. Edbury, 'Οι τελευταίοι Λουζινιανοί (1432-1489)', in Ιστορία της Κύπρου, IV, Μεσαιωνικόν Βασίλειον, Ενετοκρατία, ed. Th. Papadopoullos (Nicosia, 1995), 211 and 215-216.

[117] Hill, *op.cit.*, III, 489-490 and 492; R. Irwin, 'Οι εισβολές των Μαμελούκων στην Κύπρο', in Ιστορία της Κύπρου, IV, Μεσαιωνικόν Βασίλειον, Ενετοκρατία, ed. Th. Papadopoullos (Nicosia, 1995), 174-175.

Boustronios' chronicle resembles that of Philip of Novara stylistically as well as regarding subject matter. It has been pointed out above that Boustronios recounts isolated events in great detail while dealing very briefly with longer periods and even passing them over altogether. Hence Philip of Novara recounts the events of from the death of King Hugh I in 1218 to that of Rudolf the Latin patriarch of Jerusalem in 1224 in just over two pages and those from 1224 to the Emperor Frederick II's arrival in Limassol in 1229 in six pages, while devoting nearly sixty pages to an account of the civil war from the time of Frederick's arrival to the fall of Kerynia in 1233, following a long drawn out siege. The events from 1233 to 1239 are covered in little more than a single page, but those from the sailing of the crusade of 1239 under Count Thibaud of Champagne to the departure in 1242 of Richard Filangieri, the lieutenant of Frederick II, from the Holy Land for Apulia, following which the war between the Emperor and the nobles supporting the Ibelins was ended are recounted in over ten pages.[118] In this respect both narratives are somewhat disjointed, with heavy emphasis given on periods of civil strife and warfare, including sieges.

The interventions engineered by the Mamluks, the Hospitallers and finally, in every sense of that word, by the Venetians are recounted in full by George Boustronios. As a supporter of the victorious King James II he had access to written sources and refers throughout the chronicle to various letters as evidence for the events recounted.[119] He also gives a list of Queen Charlotte's supporters, a full account of the pillaging of their houses in Nicosia and what was found there, a brief account of the coins minted under James II, and he recounts in detail the confiscations and donations of incomes, movables and fiefs effected under both King James II and Queen Catherine.[120] All these features of the chronicle show that he knew how to use historical techniques to underpin his narration. Hill states that he 'records much just as he learned it from sources to which he had access without any idea of its proportional importance or its bearing on the general course of events'.[121] This criticism, which incidentally contains an indirect admission that he did have access to sources and learnt from them, overlooks the fact that as a chronicler heavily influenced by the short annalistic Greek chronicles of the fifteenth century he consciously chose not to discuss the importance or influence of what he recorded on events in general. It cannot be proven that he had no idea of the importance of the things he recorded, for in that case why did he trouble to record them in the first place? Indeed, as a contemporary and a participant in the events he was recording, he must have had some idea of their importance if only in order to decide what to record and what to leave out. And here it must be stressed that George Boustronios wrote, or at least finished, his chronicle at a time when Cyprus had passed under direct Venetian rule. Ardent supporters of King James II had been exiled from Cyprus or executed, as

---

[118] Novara, *Federico II*, *op.cit.*, pp. 66-243 (facing text and translation).

[119] There are allusions to letters in 44 chapters of the chronicle, for which see the index.

[120] See Boustronios (Coureas transl.) §§ 50, 63-68 and 73 for Queen Charlotte's supporters, the looting of their houses and for King James' coinage. For the incomes and fiefs awarded or confiscated consult the index.

[121] Hill, *op.cit.*, III, 1147.

he recounts quite clearly in his chronicle,[122] and so he may have chosen a generally dispassionate and annalistic manner of recording events to keep himself out of trouble. Nevertheless, his deliberately annalistic method of recounting events does result in an inadvertent obfuscation of the connections between events, in no discussion of cause and effect, and in a failure to place events within a wider context. In view of this, it will be helpful to give below a sequential account of the events recorded in the chronicle, to place them in a wider context and, most importantly, to recount important events omitted by the chronicler and the possible reasons for this. In historical terms, the chronicle is divisible into three main sections:

Section One: Events leading up of the civil war (§§ 1-37). This section commences with the marriage of Charlotte, legitimate daughter of King John II of Cyprus, to the Portuguese Prince John of Coimbra in 1456. Tensions in the court caused Prince John and Charlotte to move house to the residence of Count Peter of Tripoli, Charlotte's godfather. Following a murder committed allegedly by the Hospitallers and a fight outside the residence of Prince John, who was supposedly harbouring the murderers, the prince fell ill and died in summer 1457. Thomas the Chamberlain, a foster-brother of Queen Helena of Cyprus was accused of sending men to cause the fight outside Prince John's house and fled to Genoese Famagusta. Charlotte on returning to court complained to her illegitimate half-brother James that Thomas had caused her husband's death, and James had him murdered by two Sicilian brothers in his service. King John on hearing of this decided to deprive James, the postulant for the archbishopric of Nicosia, of the sees' revenues, and James betook himself to Rhodes, where he stayed for five months. He returned with his close friend William Goneme, an Augustinian canon also forced by court jealousies to flee to Rhodes, landing at Kerynia and coming to Nicosia in March 1458. In Nicosia James assassinated James Gurri, the viscount of Nicosia who was close to the late Thomas and Queen Helena, and sent Catalan supporters to loot the house of Thomas Gurri, his brother. King John II, who was extremely fond of his illegitimate son, had charges brought against him but these were not pursued, and he gave him back the revenues of the archbishopric. James also kept the spoils taken from the Gurri brothers.

James' enemies continued to intrigue against him, and he sent his servant George Bustron to a knight close to Queen Helena to refute rumours that he was planning to marry Charlotte to a nephew of the pope. Meanwhile King John had Charlotte betrothed to her first cousin Louis of Savoy, a union opposed by Queen Helena, who died, however, in April 1458. King John summoned James to the palace, and granted his request to have Hector de Chivides made viscount of Nicosia in the place of Francis Montolif. In June 1458 King John II died. James survived an attempt to poison him made by Carceran Suarez, the constable of Cyprus, who nonetheless continued to work against him together with his nephew Sir Bernard Rousset, admiral of Cyprus, Hector de Chivides, Francis Montolif and others, who had Charlotte crowned queen in October 1458. In December 1458 James and his supporters, who included his uncle Marcius, the Sicilians Rizzo de Marino and Nicholas de Morabit, made a failed attempt

---

[122] Boustronios (Coureas transl.) , §§ 176-177, 186, 226, 228, 255, 262, 274, 277-279.

to storm the court and kill nobles close to the queen, who other than those named above included Tristan de Gibelet and Garcia de Navarre, another Catalan constable, like Carceran Suarez. George Bustron learnt of this venture from one of Queen Charlotte's servants, who told him that she intended to bring charges against her brother before the *Haute Cour* but implored him to keep it secret. He nonetheless went and informed the postulant, who ordered him, the Greek bishop Nicholas, and other supporters to gather at his house, the archbishopric of Nicosia. Subsequently both sides disarmed on Queen Charlotte's orders, but following an inconclusive meeting with her James and his close supporters left Nicosia secretly and made their way to Egypt via Salines.

Section Two: The Civil War and the Reign of King James II (§§ 38-99). Following the arrival of James and his followers in Egypt Queen Charlotte sent her own envoys there, and each side solicited the support of the sultan. Eventually James, assisted by his supporters, especially the persuasive Augustinian William Goneme and Nassar Hous, prevailed, and in September 1460 a Mamluk invasion fleet alighted at Famagusta, where King Louis, the husband of Queen Charlotte, unsuccessfully tried to win the Mamluks over by presenting a gift of victuals to the Mamluk admiral. James' forces took Nicosia in late September and laid siege to Kerynia, where Queen Charlotte's supporters had gathered with their forces. While in Nicosia James proclaimed himself king, appointed William Goneme archbishop of Nicosia, had Rizzo knighted and made chamberlain of Cyprus and Nicholas de Morabit knighted and made viscount of Nicosia. He also recruited mercenaries there. During the siege of Kerynia Queen Charlotte's supporters, who had received Hospitaller reinforcements, once again unsuccessfully tried to win over the Mamluk commander Kun the Circassian through the offices of the Latin Bishop Nicholas of Limassol. When in late 1460 the Mamluks announced their intention of raising the siege in order to return to Egypt James personally implored them to leave some soldiers behind. Eventually a Mamluk emir called Janibek remained with 200 horse and 200 foot. In November 1460 William Goneme had George Bustron bring up 225 archers, consisting of serfs and emancipated peasants, from Salines to Nicosia. The Saracens in Kerynia and Nicosia meanwhile committed atrocities, beheading 27 persons and forcibly converting the sons of a priest to Islam. Goneme and Rizzo carried out raids against the Genoese in the Karpass peninsula. In December 1460 the king had various houses in Nicosia, presumably belonging to Queen Charlotte's supporters, systematically plundered, a measure probably applied to enrich his war chest.

Early in 1461 King James' forces secured Paphos in western Cyprus and then retuned to Nicosia via north west Cyprus, passing through Chrysochou, the monastery at Yialia, Pelendri, Marathassa, Yerakies and Pendayia, seizing money and valuables as they went, ostensibly to assist the king with money but in reality to enrich themselves. In February 1461 to supporters of Queen Charlotte, Carceran Chimi and Anthony Singritico, defected to James, a precedent that others were to follow. Hector of Chivides was killed in a surprise attack, and a galley setting forth from Kerynia to bring reinforcements from Rhodes ran aground at Pendayia. Meanwhile Sir Thomas Hariri and the nobleman Walter de Nores and his sons were apprehended and brought to Nicosia, where King James had to exert himself to stop Janibek from beheading them, and later from converting the youths to Islam. Hariri then swore fealty to King

James, but Walter de Nores refused to do so and so lost all his property, consisting of 36 villages. King James, however, admired his steadfastness, and later gave him an annual income of 365 bezants. He also secured the support of a Catalan pirate named James Zaplana, who had suffered shipwreck when sailing to the Karpass peninsula to practise piracy. Zaplana entered his service and later became constable of Cyprus.

In the spring of 1461 King James laid siege to Famagusta while continuing operations against Kerynia. He also defeated Genoese ships trying to re-supply Famagusta in a naval engagement, although he did not take the city until 1464. In Salines George Boustronios secured the continued support of the Catalan Jean Perez Fabrigues in late October 1461 while King James enlisted the support of the Sicilian knight Muzzio de Constanzo, who had sailed to Paphos with his galley, making him admiral of Cyprus granting him 'a wonderful income' from various villages and marrying him to the daughter of Sir Thomas de Verni, an old noble family. He also tried unsuccessfully to secure the support of a French galley captain who had sailed to Paphos at this time. Early in 1461, moreover, Queen Charlotte had sailed to Rhodes to solicit Hospitaller reinforcements. On her return she stopped off at Paphos, winning over the garrison to her cause, but King James had the town besieged by a force consisting of *turcoples*, that is light cavalry, and emancipated peasants, and it was eventually surrendered to King James, who granted a rich reward to Sir Peter de Naves, the garrison commander appointed by Queen Charlotte, for delivering Paphos.

When King James' forces took Kerynia in 1463 and Famagusta in 1464 James was effectively lord of Cyprus. James had Janibek and his Mamluk troops massacred, allegedly suspecting him wishing to seize Famagusta and kill him, overpowered an assassin sent to him by Janibek's sister and thwarted possible retribution on the part of the Mamluk sultan by judicious bribery. In 1469 a blight of the crops resulted in Cyprus being struck by famine and in 1470 a plague struck the island killing much of the population, although the king and those with him survived by betaking themselves to Akaki. The chronicler then describes at length a conspiracy against the king's life hatched by nobles angered and humiliated by his sequestrations and his sexual liaisons with their womenfolk, foiled by James of Malta, an impoverished adventurer whom the king had appointed *chevetain* at Pendayia and who had been helped by the Catalan Peter d'Avila. The chronicler reserves especial hatred towards him, for one of the nobles executed when he denounced the conspiracy after pretending to be party to it was his kinsman Demetrios [son of] Bustron. In 1471, a date the chronicler wrongly gives for 1461 King James sent Archbishop William Goneme to Rome, where he tried to secure papal recognition of his royal title and (he wrongly states, since it involved a separate mission taking place some years later) to arrange James' marriage to the daughter of the despot of the Morea. Neither plan came to fruition. In 1472 James, already married to her by proxy in 1468, formally married Catherine Corner, a member of the Venetian noble family that owned estates in Episkopi from the late fourteenth century onwards. She bore him a son, but James died of sickness only a year after the marriage, in March 1473. In his will, where the chronicler names the executors, one notes that five were Catalans or Aragonese, one was Cypriot and one Venetian. The king also disarmed the galleys he had maintained.

Section Three: The Imposition of Venetian Control through Queen Catherine (§§ 100-284)

Following the death of King James galleys were despatched to Venice and the Mamluk domains to announce this. Boustronios' account makes it clear, though it never states this explicitly, that various factions began preparing to take control over Cyprus, these being Queen Charlotte's supporters, foreign mercenaries of the late King James, the so-called Catalan party, and the Venetians, who ultimately prevailed. A young man named Valentine sent by Queen Charlotte in July 1473 to Cyprus was apprehended and executed as a spy, and officials of the king, notably his treasurer Phokas, were seized and interrogated. In August 1473 a Venetian fleet of 60 galleys arrived at Famagusta where Queen Catherine was residing, citing the impending birth of her son as a reason for not coming to Nicosia. The envoys Queen Charlotte sent to the admiral of this fleet to solicit his assistance in recovering her throne were rebuffed, and on the fleet's departure six galleys and an armed force remained in Famagusta. An emissary of King Ferdinand of Naples was expelled from Famagusta and sent to Paralimni just outside. Boustronios does not give the reason, but it was because he was trying to bring about the marriage between two illegitimate children of the late King James and King Ferdinand. A plot by Queen Charlotte's supporters to seize Kerynia was revealed following the seizure and interrogation of several friars, its perpetrators being seized and taken to Famagusta. Meanwhile the sultan received Queen Catherine's envoy to Cairo well, asking him to forward the tribute and indicating thereby that he recognised her. His detention of Queen Charlotte's envoys when they reached Cairo further indicated his recognition of Queen Catherine. In late August Queen Catherine gave birth to a baby boy, the short-lived James III. In September the Venetian *baiulo* left Nicosia for Famagusta and in October the Venetian fleet, about to leave Cyprus, returned to Famagusta after receiving instructions from two ships sent out to Cyprus 'from the West' presumably from Venice or one of its overseas possessions. In November 1473 Archbishop Louis de Fabrigues, the Catalan who had succeeded Goneme in 1471, returned to Cyprus with another envoy of King Ferdinand to arrange the projected marriage of King Ferdinand's illegitimate son to King James' illegitimate daughter.

It was at this point that matters came to a head. On 14 November Peter d'Avila, the Catalan who became constable of Cyprus after King James' death, rode out from Nicosia to Famagusta with an armed force and was told by someone he encountered that Sir Andrew Corner, Queen Catherine's uncle, her nephew Sir Marco Bembo, the Venetian doctor Gabriel Gentile and Sir Paul Chappe had all been murdered the previous night. During the night Sir Louis Alberic, a nephew of the Catalan Sir James Zaplana mentioned above, came to Nicosia from Famagusta. He stated that after Archbishop Louis had read a letter reportedly from the pope, berating the queen and the knights for allowing the four men about to be murdered to take over the kingdom, Rizzo de Marino, whom King James had appointed chamberlain of Cyprus, and his armed followers met up with them in the courtyard of the queen's palace in Famagusta and murdered them. On 15 November by some Sicilians arriving from Famagusta gave a more detailed version of these events. At this time Paolo Contarini, the Venetian captain of Kerynia, after some initial misgivings handed over the castle of Kerynia to

Sir Nicholas Morabit, the viscount of Nicosia, on receiving written instructions from Queen Catherine. Morabit surrendered it in turn to Sir Louis Alberic. On 17 November the faction behind the murders, called 'the Catalan nation' by the Venetians, sent an envoy to Venice, Sir Philip Podocatoro, and on 18 November the betrothal of King Ferdinand's illegitimate son to King James' illegitimate daughter was formally announced. It was also reported that King Ferdinand of Naples would send 20 galleys and 300 men to defend Cyprus on request, and at his own expense.

The galleys that came in the wake of the murders, however, were not Neapolitan but Venetian. In late November ten Venetian galleys under the command of the Venetian *provedittore* Sir Victor Soranzo arrived at Famagusta. Archbishop Louis went on board, clearly so as to negotiate, but came back downcast, an obvious sign that the negotiations had failed. The Venetians tried without success to secure the citadel of Famagusta by bribery, but now that they had forces available events began to move in their favour. In December Queen Catherine ordered Morabit to take possession of the citadel of Kerynia from Louis Alberic, having made him viscount of Nicosia for life, and gave him papers for the people of Nicosia, telling them that she would soon arrive there. Morabit duly took possession of the castle, accompanied by Rizzo. When the latter went to Nicosia and discovered from a servant that 300 armed men had landed from the Venetian galleys so as to seize him, he went with armed men to Famagusta to join his fellow conspirators. Meanwhile the people of Nicosia declared for Queen Catherine, and the role of the artisans under their leaders Stephen Koudouna, John the Black and others indicates a hitherto unprecedented participation in public events by the burgesses. The game was up for Rizzo, Archbishop Louis, James Zaplana and his nephew Louis Alberic, who fled Cyprus on 1 January 1474.

The rest of the chronicle essentially recounts how the Venetians consolidated their hold on Cyprus from January to May 1474 by bringing additional forces, taking over the castles and strong points, having their supporters rewarded and their opponents punished by death, confiscation of property, or exile. Of those who had fled Cyprus Tristan de Gibelet was captured in Rhodes, and he returned to Cyprus on board a Venetian galley. Two murderers of Queen Catherine's relatives, Mastichi and Nicolo Spezzieri, were hanged, and among those exiled were Farandetto, the castellan of Famagusta at the time the murders had been committed, foreign mercenaries of the late King James II, whom Boustronios calls 'Franks', a general term in Cyprus for all West Europeans, and members of the Kallergis family. Simon de Sant'Andrea, the Benedictine abbot of the Holy Cross, was taken to Famagusta and placed in custody when incriminating letters were found on him, and others placed in custody included Brother John de Riviolo, the archbishop's secretary, and the physician of the late King James, Estive Barthélemy, who was later released. Philip Podocataro who had gone to Venice on behalf of the party opposed to Venice was exiled. Certain elements in Nicosia took advantage of the unstable situation to loot a number of houses, and Viscount Nicholas Morabit had their leaders arrested and detained.

Throughout this period quarrels broke out among various parties, often over the appropriation of spoils, with accusations of disloyalty to the queen hurled at various persons. In March 1474 Queen Catherine deprived the Hospitaller Grand Commander of Cyprus, Sir Nicholas Zaplana, of the commandery, charging him with treason and requesting the Hospitaller Grand Master in Rhodes to appoint a new grand commander. The tumultuous events following the death of King James cannot have helped the administration of justice, for in May a villager from Paphos appeared before Sir Peter Bembo, a Venetian officer, complaining of the unjust detention of his son. But from May onwards the situation calmed and Queen Catherine came to Nicosia, where she stayed for the rest of her reign. Towards the end of the chronicle Boustronios recounts the dramatic but unsuccessful attempt of the two sworn enemies of Venice, Tristan de Gibelet and Rizzo de Marino in 1485 to engineer a marriage between Queen Catherine and the son of King Ferdinand of Naples, which ended with the Venetians capturing both of them. Tristan committed suicide, and Boustronios expressed ignorance of Rizzo's fate. In fact the Venetians had him imprisoned for some years and finally strangled. In 1487 the queen's mother came out to Cyprus and told her that the Venetian government wished her to abdicate, and in the following year her brother George Corner came to see her. Her abdication took place in February 1489, an incident that the chronicler narrates with consummate skill. The chronicle concludes with a raid on Cyprus in June 1489 carried out by Turkish pirate vessels and with the death of Morphou de Grenier, the count of Rochas, in 1501.

In the remainder of this historical introduction the omission of key events and the failure to place others in a proper context or to provide an adequate explanation for them will be discussed, since these weaknesses of the chronicle, already expounded above, concern precisely those things that are important for a present-day historian. At the beginning of the chronicle Boustronios recounts that Prince John of Coimbra and Charlotte left the royal court because of 'tensions' without explaining what these were and the causes behind them. These tensions were attributable to two factors. One was that the Portuguese John of Coimbra enjoyed the support of King Alfonso V of Aragon, a sworn enemy of the Genoese and the pro-Genoese Cypriot nobles such as James de Fleury, the titular count of Jaffa who according to an admittedly partial Genoese report took up residence in Genoese Famagusta on account of the opposition he encountered from Queen Helena, a granddaughter of the Byzantine emperor Manuel and the wife of King John II of Cyprus, and her pro-Aragonese supporters.[123] The second factor, given by later writers, was that despite having married Charlotte with the queen's support John turned against her policy of favouring Greeks. The queen was suspected of having an involvement in his sudden death, and given that Thomas the chamberlain of Cyprus was a favourite of hers, something that Boustronios does make clear, it is probable that Charlotte's accusations against him were true. James on hearing her complaints was only too glad to have Thomas assassinated, for thereby he would be rid of someone close to Queen Helena, who disliked him as the illegitimate son of Marietta of Patras, her husband's mistress.[124]

Boustronios likewise does not clarify, arguably on account of his partiality, why

---

[123] Hill, *op.cit.*, III, 531-533; Edbury, 'Λουζινιανοί', *op.cit.*, pp. 196-199.

[124] Boustronios (Coureas transl.), §§ 3-4; Hill, *op.cit.*, III, 532-535; Edbury, 'Λουζινιανοί', *op.cit.*, pp. 199-200.

Thomas Gurri and other knights supporting Charlotte accused James of trying to promote Charlotte's marriage to Sir Peter Louis, a nephew of Pope Callistus III, even though he explicitly states earlier that James friend, the Augustinian friar Salpous, had received papal instructions to bring this about.[125] Had James been instrumental in engineering such a marriage the pope would almost certainly nominate him to be the Latin archbishop of Nicosia, whereas at the time he was simply a postulant for this position, never having proceeded beyond minor orders. His father the king, moreover, had deprived him of the archbishopric's revenues following the murder of Thomas the Chamberlain.[126] Boustronios informs us that these revenues, which King John II eventually returned to James, amounted to 12.000 ducats per annum. This sum together with the booty of 6.000 ducats that James took from the houses of James and Thomas Gurri after having the former assassinated would have been vital in enabling James to pay his supporters and foreign mercenaries during the civil war that followed King John's death.[127]

Another cardinally important issue that the chronicler fails to clarify is why the Mamluk sultan Inal eventually supported James when he was on the point of recognizing Charlotte. Although it has been argued that he had been influenced by an embassy of the Ottoman sultan Mehmed II or by the fact that James' illegitimacy was no impediment in Mamluk eyes to his succeeding the throne, especially when the other candidate was female, the real reason is probably that James outbid Charlotte in increasing the annual tribute due to the sultan, the suzerain of Cyprus since 1426.[128] After recounting the massacre of the Mamluk commander Janibek and his followers, Boustronios states in the next chapter that:

> Furthermore, with Cyprus having been bound during the rule of King Janus to give 8.000 ducats annually [in tribute], King James promised another 8.000 and used to give (my underlining) 16.000, and once again, before he died, he had the sense to cut the [additional] 8.000.[129]

A superficial reading of the above passage, following as it does the massacre of Janibek and his troops, might lead the reader to conclude that the tribute was increased to placate the sultan after the destruction of his forces. The chronicler does state, however, that King James used to give (Greek ἐδίδεν) 16.000 ducats, making it clear that the sum was being given regularly. It is likelier that James promised to double the tribute while in Cairo, where he had to outbid his half-sister Charlotte, not after taking both Kerynia and Famagusta and thereby securing control over the entire island.

Boustronios narrates how from December 1460 onwards the king had his supporters break into and pillage the houses of various persons in Nicosia, while

---

[125] Boustronios (Coureas transl.), §§ 10 and 14-15.

[126] *Ibid.*, § 6; Hill, *op.cit.*, III, 538-539 and 542, esp. note 1; Edbury, 'Λουζινιανοί', *op.cit.*, p. 200.

[127] Boustronios (Coureas transl.), §§ 10 and 53.

[128] Hill, *op.cit.*, III, 557-559; Edbury, 'Λουζινιανοί', *op.cit.*, 207-208.

[129] Boustronios (Coureas transl.), § 89.

others on returning to Nicosia via north-west Cyprus after taking control of Paphos likewise engaged in rapine, seizing money and other valuable commodities, such as metals, textiles and sugar. Nowhere does he state explicitly that this was done, as in all probability it was, to raise funds for James' war chest, although the chronicler does state at one point that the his supporters discovering a hoard of coins at Pendayia arrogated much of the money amongst themselves, bringing the king only 15.000 *gros* coins.[130] Not does the chronicler give a satisfactory explanation of why the Mamluk commanders wished to leave Cyprus with their forces in late 1460, simply stating through the person of the Mamluk admiral that with the arrival of winter and rough seas the fleet had to set sail. In fact, as James himself stated in an address brought to the city of Florence by his envoys in October 1461, their reason for wishing to depart was because they had learnt that Sultan Inal was moribund and wished to be present at the inevitable jockeying for power that would take place after his death.[131]

Arguably Boustronios most significant, and possibly deliberate, omission concerns the massacre of the Mamluk emir Janibek and his troops ordered by James. He states that King James, king in fact as well as name following the capture of Kerynia and Famagusta, ordered the massacre because the emir Janibek wished to seize Famagusta, kill the king and retain Cyprus for himself.[132] The contemporary Mamluk historian Yusuf ibn Taghri Birdi, however, gives a different reason. According to him King James had Janibek and his soldiers massacred because they were kidnapping good-looking youths from their parents, and beat up the king's emissaries when they told them to cease. In a meeting that the king then arranged with Janibek the latter struck him, whereupon the king's followers killed Janibek and the 25 men escorting him. The Mamluk may have been kidnapping these youths so as to convert them to Islam and have them trained as Mamluks, as had happened in their own case.[133] It is not difficult to understand why Boustronios, who can hardly have been ignorant of the Mamluks' actions, did not mention these kidnappings. Queen Charlotte's supporters made much capital out of the fact that King James' forces included Muslim Mamluks who had been given permission to destroy churches, to introduce Islam and to kidnap children. Reports were circulating that King James had himself denied Christianity in the oath he had taken to the sultan. The text of the oath that James had allegedly taken, endorsed by Pope Pius II and circulated by the Hospitallers contains the fantastic charges that he had sworn, if failing in his obligations towards the sultan, to deny Christ, kill a camel over a baptismal font, and have sexual intercourse with a Jewess over an altar.[134] In Boustronios' defence, however, it should be stated that he does record Mamluk atrocities elsewhere in the chronicle and that if Janibek did indeed wish to become sultan he may have planned the seizure of Cyprus as a preliminary step.[135]

---

[130] *Ibid.*, §§ 63-68.

[131] Boustronios (Coureas transl.), § 56; Mas Latrie, *Histoire, op.cit.*, III 158; Edbury, 'Λουζι-νιανοί', *op.cit.*, p. 210 and note 105.

[132] Boustronios (Coureas transl.), § 88.

[133] Edbury, 'Λουζινιανοί', *op.cit.*, p. 219 and note 126.

[134] Hill, *op.cit.*, III, 557-558 and esp. 558 note 2; Edbury, 'Λουζινιανοί', *op.cit.*, p. 217.

[135] Boustronios (Coureas transl.), §§ 59 and 70.

The omission of a detailed account of the siege of Famagusta and the possibility that this was excised from the chronicle has been mentioned above. It is strange that §§79-85 deal with events taking place in October 1461 or shortly afterwards, §86 jumps to 1463 and §88 begins with the words '...on 29 August 1464 he (King James II) took Famagusta, *as I stated above* (my italics). Since none of the manuscripts refer to the town's previous capture, it is probable that Boustronios did recount it but that the section of the text dealing with it was excised under the Venetians, who perhaps wished to underplay the king's achievement in recapturing Famagusta following 90 years of Genoese occupation. It must be added here that the date of August 1464 that Boustronios gives for the city's surrender is wrong, and that he does not mention the terms under which it capitulated. These are given in detail in the sixteenth century account of his kinsman Florio Bustron, who dates the city's surrender to January 1464. It is likely that George Boustronios, who narrates the surrender of Kerynia immediately before that of Famagusta, gives the date of Kerynia's capitulation for the surrender of Famagusta, for Kerynia did indeed surrender in late August or shortly afterwards.[136] The terms of Famagusta's capitulation, completely omitted by Boustronios, are recorded by Florio Bustron and are referred to in King James' confirmation of duties payable on wine when he farmed them out in June 1468 to Catanio de Nigro and Louis Spataro. They are also referred to in the reply sent in August 1491 by the Venetian doge Augustino Barbaro to a request he had received from the city's inhabitants.[137]

One of the phenomena which Boustronios records but does not place in a wider context is King James' recruitment of foreign mercenaries. The chronicler himself was involved in this recruitment, urging the Catalan Jean Perez Fabrigues to stay in Cyprus because 'you shall have every favour from the king' as he told him. Indeed King James appointed him the commander of his galleys. He also records how the king 'gave a wonderful income to Sir Muzzio de Constanzo' a Sicilian knight captaining a galley that had reached Paphos, appointing him admiral and marrying him into one of the oldest Cypriot noble families, the de Verni. He tried without success to recruit another sea captain, described as a Frank, and even when the latter turned down his offer and eventually left Cyprus the king still gave him gifts worth 1.000 ducats on his departure, perhaps hoping that he would change his mind. Other foreign mercenaries he recruited included the Catalan pirate James Zaplana and, in all likelihood, the Savoyard soldiers taken prisoner at Sivouri, whom he had released in late 1460 and brought to Nicosia.[138] At this juncture it should be stressed that although the so-called 'Catalan party' opposing the Venetians after King James' death was largely made up of such mercenaries originating from Aragon, Catalonia or lands under Aragonese rule such as Sicily and the kingdom of Naples, not all 'Catalans' were opposed to the Venetians. The Sicilian Muzzio de Constanzo for instance remained loyal to Queen Catherine and

---

[136] Boustronios (Coureas transl.), §§87-88; Florio Bustron, 'Chronique', *op.cit.*, p. 411; Edbury, 'Λουζινιανοί', *op.cit.*, pp. 220-221 and note 131.

[137] Mas Latrie, *Histoire*, III, *op.cit.*, 485-492; Florio Bustron, 'Chronique', *op.cit.*, pp. 412-414; Richard, *Remembrances*, *op.cit.*, no. 29.

[138] Boustronios (Coureas transl.), §§ 57, 71 and 82-84.

Venice, and his descendants appear in the list of feudatories and cavalrymen drawn up in 1560 for the Venetian *provedittore* Andrea Dandolo. The same can be said for Nicholas Morabit, a Sicilian who like Rizzo de Marino was one of the king's initial supporters, becoming a knight, viscount of Nicosia and marshal of Cyprus. Unlike Rizzo, however, Morabit did not challenge Venetian control over Cyprus, serving Queen Catherine after the king's death without enduring exile or any other punishment.

King James was by no means the first Lusignan king to enlist foreign mercenaries. King Peter I began recruiting them on a large scale in the second half of the fourteenth century, much to the resentment of the Cypriot nobles, who were taxed heavily to pay for them and regarded them as a threat to their own power because they formed an alternative force under the king's command, other than the traditional feudal host made up of the native nobles in their capacity as royal vassals.[139] Boustronios himself along with other Cypriot knights and nobles may have felt the same way. Even though he himself, as stated above, help recruit Jean Perez Fabrigues to King James' cause, in time he may have come to resent their presence, and the rewards they had obtained. One notes that James of Malta, towards whom Boustronios felt particular hatred, was himself a foreign mercenary. His matter-of-fact mention of villages awarded by King James to various foreign mercenaries, something recorded even more thoroughly by Florio Bustron in his later chronicle, may mask feelings of envy and frustration, especially if he himself had not been rewarded similarly. When the Venetians exiled the 'Franks', as Boustronios called the West European mercenaries King James had recruited and then rewarded, he describes their sorrow at being separated from their families but does not express even a whisker of sympathy. The Franks in Famagusta were called traitors by Peter d'Avila's supporters who denounced them to the Venetian *provedittore* in Nicosia, and the chronicle stresses the anger felt by the people of Nicosia when Cypriot properties were given to Franks and when their leader John the Black and his men were ambushed by Franks lying in wait for them, who were subsequently exiled. He also highlights John's role in leading the protest made to the Venetian *provedittore* when the latter arrested Franks and Greeks in Famagusta for causing disturbances but released only the Franks.[140]

Another historical phenomenon that Boustronios fails to place in context is that of the emancipated peasants. He mentions them no less than five times throughout his narrative, relating how on one occasion he himself brought up 225 serfs and emancipated peasants armed with bows and crossbows to Nicosia on King James' orders, and how the king was pleased to see them, but does not explain how and why they obtained their freedom.[141] There were two classes of peasant in Lusignan and Venetian Cyprus: Firstly the *paroikoi* (Greek πάροικοι) who were serfs tied to the land owing their lords labour service on his domain and between a third and one half of their own produce and then the *francomati*, free peasants who had gained

---

[139] Edbury, *Kingdom, op.cit.*, pp. 176-177.

[140] Boustronios (Coureas transl.), §§ 187, 199, 255, 270, 274 and 276.

[141] *Ibid.*, §§ 35, 43, 58, 85 and 93.

emancipation on payment of a cash sum. This category were neither tied to the land nor bound by labour services, simply paying their lords one fourth to one third of their yearly income.[142] Following the sack of Alexandria in 1365, King Peter I of Cyprus had been forced to raise money for the war with Mamluk Egypt by allowing free peasants to purchase exemption from the poll tax, and after the ruinous war with Genoa in 1373-1374 a crown strapped for cash allowed serfs to purchase their way into the ranks of free peasants and both serfs and town dwellers to buy exemption from the poll tax. This process, continuing through the late fourteenth and fifteenth centuries, resulted in the free peasants outnumbering the serfs in early sixteenth century Venetian Cyprus.[143] The civil war between James and Charlotte, in which both sides needed money and fighting men, must have created opportunities for emancipation, and perhaps the serfs and free peasants whom Boustronios brought up from Larnaca hoped to buy their way out of serfdom or from having to pay the poll tax through service with King James' forces.

The most glaring lack of a proper context in Boustronios' account is at the point when he narrates King James' marriage to the Venetian Catherine Corner. He baldly states that James sent Sir Philip Mistachiel, who incidentally was a former partisan of Queen Charlotte now in his service, to Venice to arrange this marriage, which took place in 1472.[144] He does not state that Mistachiel went to Venice as early as 1467 and concluded the engagement in 1468, nor that Catherine Corner was a member of one of the oldest noble families in Venice with major financial interests in Cyprus on account of its large sugar plantations at Episkopi, acquired as far back as the 1360s.[145] He also leaves out related events in the wider European and Mediterranean political arena. Venice in October 1469 took Cyprus under her protection, and in return King James undertook to maintain two armed galleys at Venice's service for two to three months a year, denying harbour facilities or any other aid to powers at war with Venice. Venice's European enemies, the duchies of Milan and Florence, the Papacy and the kingdom of Naples were also supporters of Charlotte, while in the eastern Mediterranean both James and Venice were fearful of the growing Ottoman power, attempting to co-operate with the Ottomans' enemies, the Turcoman leader Uzun Hasan and the emirate of Karaman opposite Cyprus.[146]

When this co-operation failed to prevent Ottoman advances James seems to have

---

[142] Hill, *op.cit.*, II, 8-10; P. Edbury, 'The Franco-Cypriot Landowning Class and its Exploitation of the Agrarian Resources of the island of Cyprus', in *idem.*, *Kingdoms of the Crusades from Jerusalem to Cyprus*, XIX (Aldershot, 1999), 3.

[143] J. Richard, 'Le droit et institutions franques dans le royaume de Chypre', in *XVe Congrès International d'études Byzantines* (Athens, 1976), 6-7.

[144] Boustronios (Coureas transl.), § 97.

[145] F. Thiriet, *La Romanie Vénitienne au Moyen Age* (Paris, 1975), pp. 330 and 333; Edbury, 'Λουζινιανοί', *op.cit.*, p. 233; B. Arbel, 'A Royal Family in Republican Venice: The Cypriot Legacy of the Corner della Regina', *Studi Veneziani*, n.s. XV (1988), 131-152; *idem.*, 'The Reign of Caterina Corner (1473-1489) as a family affair', *Studi Veneziani*, n.s. XXVI (1993), 67-85.

[146] Mas Latrie, *Histoire*, *op.cit.*, III, 316-320; Hill, III, 611; Edbury, 'Λουζινιανοί', *op.cit.*, pp. 235-238.

tried to distance himself from Venice, thereby strengthening the hand of those adherents of his who wanted closer relations with the kingdom of Naples. Formerly Angevin, this kingdom was conquered in 1442 by King Alfonso V of Aragon and in 1458 his illegitimate son Ferdinand became king. Aragon, Sicily, Sardinia and southern Italy were now all under the control of Aragonese dynasties, with Aragonese ambitions extending to the Balkans and the eastern Mediterranean.[147] Although James finally did marry Catherine Corner late in 1472 an anti-Venetian reaction had meanwhile set in. As early as 1469 James and some of his Sicilian and Catalan supporters had begun entertaining the idea of a marriage alliance with the kingdom of Naples. This was not effective enough to stop James' marriage with Catherine, but in the spring of 1473 he refused to allow a Venetian galley bearing munitions to make port in Famagusta, perhaps fearful of Ottoman reprisals and of Venice's ability to protect Cyprus against them. Indeed the Ottomans inflicted a decisive defeat on Uzun Hasan at Bashkent in August 1473, shortly after King James' own death in July.[148]

Boustronios tells us nothing of all this, but he does mention the seven executors the king left in the will he had made before his death. All but two, the Venetian Andrew Corner and Morphou de Grenier, a former supporter of Queen Charlotte who originated from an old Cypriot noble family, were Catalans or Sicilians, mostly mercenaries he had hired in the war against Charlotte and subsequently rewarded.[149] Among this latter group Rizzo de Marino and John Tafur the titular count of Tripoli were to prove ardent supporters of King Ferdinand of Naples, and in the course of time Venice had the former exiled and the latter strangled.[150] Boustron also tells us that in his will King James ordered the release of the men obliged to do galley service. Although he presents the king as ordering this for humanitarian reasons, the dismantling of galleys assisting the Venetians and the appointment of predominantly Sicilian and Catalan executors indicate that towards the end of his reign James was distancing himself from Venice and placing trust in persons close to the kingdom of Naples.

These developments explain why the Venetians sent their fleet and troops to Cyprus in support of Queen Catherine, who for the first three years of her reign remained in Famagusta, within easy reach of these Venetian forces.[151] They also explain the arrival of King Ferdinand's envoy Severus to Cyprus in August 1473 to bring about the marriage of his master's illegitimate son Don Alonzo with Carla, King James' illegitimate daughter, although Boustronios does not mention these wedding plans in recounting his visit, only mentioning them when relating the return to Cyprus

---

[147] *Ibid.*, pp. 238-239; D. Abulafia, *The Western Mediterranean Kingdoms 1200-1500: The Struggle for Dominion* (London, 1997), pp. 204-210 and 223.

[148] Mas Latrie, *Histoire, op.cit.*, pp. 336-343; Edbury, 'Λουζινιανοί', *op.cit.*, pp. 234 and 238.

[149] Boustronios (Coureas transl.), §§ 50 and 98.

[150] *Ibid.*, § 228; Mas Latrie, *Histoire, op.cit.*, III, 431-435 and 441-442; Hill, *op.cit.*, 741 and note 4.

[151] Boustronios (Coureas transl.), §§ 113-114, 136, 143, 151, 163, 169, 215, 220, 227, 237, 272 and 275

of the Catalan Louis de Fabrigues, the archbishop of Nicosia, along with a second Neapolitan envoy.[152] Boustronios also fails to explain why King Ferdinand of Naples failed to support Rizzo di Marino, Archbishop Louis and their followers after the murder of Andrew Corner, Marco Bembo and Gabriel Gentile. Ferdinand's determination to concentrate on maintaining the peace in Italy and consolidating his power at home against Angevin attempts to unseat him and rebellious nobles within his kingdom provide a satisfactory explanation, as does his wish not to challenge Venice openly.[153]

Throughout Boustronios' account it is transparent that the people of Nicosia, burgesses, artisans and craftsmen, enthusiastically supported Catherine, but he does not give the reasons for this nor, on account of the very nature of his chronicle, does he place their actions in a broader context. Relations between Venice and Nicosia itself went back a very long way. The instructions given to a Venetian ambassador to Cyprus in 1302 allude to privileges that the Venetians had enjoyed in Nicosia from late Byzantine times. These included houses, a *loggia*, a church dedicated to St Nicholas, a separate quarter and a street. Medieval tombstones in the present-day Arab Ahmet mosque, built on the ruins of a medieval church, contain the names of prominent Venetians, such as Francesco Cornar (d. 1390), Antonio de Bergamo (d.1394) and Gaspar Mavroceni (d. 1402). P. Leventis has suggested that the Venetian quarter of Nicosia was located in the north and northwest part of the city, hence the Venetian names given to the four bastions Mula, Querini, Barbaro and Loredano located in this area when the new circuit of Venetian walls was constructed in 1567. The northern gate of this new circuit of walls, moreover, the present-day Kerynia Gate, was formerly named the *Porta Bemba* or the *Porta del Provedittore* after Lorenzo Bembo, the Venetian *provedittore* at the time.[154] The presence of a significant Venetian element in late medieval Nicosia would explain why the city came out so strongly in favour of Queen Catherine, who knew of this and in turn felt a strong affection for the city. On hearing in late November that the Venetian *provedittore* Victor Soranzo was en route to Cyprus with eight galleys, she sent messengers to Nicosia to have the city illuminated and the bells rung. Boustronios recounts how she granted an income in cash and kind to Stephen Koudouna, a prominent leader of the Nicosia populace, and how on leaving the capital for her final departure to Venice 'Her eyes ... did not cease to shed tears. The people likewise shed many tears'.[155]

Exile is a theme that occurs frequently in Boustronios' account, especially from 1474 onwards, following the flight of Archbishop Louis and his closest associates from Cyprus and the consolidation of Venetian power. Unfortunately Boustronios'

---

[152] *Ibid.*, §§ 115 and 152.

[153] Hill, *op.cit.*, III, 690-691; Abulafia, *Mediterranean Kingdoms, op.cit.*, pp. 223-235.

[154] Mas Latrie, 'Nouvelles preuves', *op.cit.*, pp. 54-55; Eutychia Papadopoulou, 'Οι πρώτες εγκαταστάσεις Βενετών στην Κύπρο', *Σύμμεικτα*, V (Athens, 1983), pp. 3134-315 and 329; P. Leventis, *Twelve Times in Nicosia, Nicosia, Cyprus, 1192-1570: Architecture, topography and urban experience in a diversified capital city* (Nicosia, 2005), pp. 123 and 327.

[155] Hill, *op.cit.*, III, 679 and note 4; Boustronios (Coureas transl.), §§ 188 and 281.

recording of the persons exiled is not always accurate. He omits the proclamation decreed and publicised on 8 January 1474, expelling all Catalans, Sicilians and Neapolitans from Cyprus, and does not mention the exile of Stephen Koudouna, a leader of the Nicosia populace, or of the knights Philip de Nores, John de Ras and John Attar, the last being a Cypriot knight who although allowed to return to Cyprus instead entered Venetian service and had a distinguished career, eventually dying in Venice. All of them were taken to Venice in December 1474 and were still being held in custody there in February 1475, when all other than Koudouna, who was detained until further notice, were released on condition that they remained in Venice unless the Council of Ten allowed them to leave.[156] He also fails to mention Simon de Sant'Andrea, the Benedictine abbot of the Holy Cross, exiled sometime after January 1474 and once again in 1475, and Garcia de Navarre, otherwise known as Anthony de Garcia, exiled in 1476.[157] Furthermore, he wrongly states that Marietta of Patras, the mother of the late King James, was exiled with the late king's illegitimate children Eugene and John in May 1474, although this did not take place until 1476.[158] He states that Morphou de Grenier, the count of Rochas, was exiled in May 1474 along with Peter d'Avila, the Spanish mercenary who had supported King James II and had become the constable of Cyprus shortly after the king's death in July 1473. In fact the count was not exiled until some months later, after the death of the infant King James III from malaria in August 1474, on account of his popularity among the people. He likewise fails to mention that the count was allowed to return to Cyprus in 1487, and so the last chapter of the chronicle recounting his death in 1501 and his burial at the cathedral of the Holy Wisdom seems confusing.[159]

Notwithstanding the above shortcomings, the chronicle of George Boustronios is an important source for Cypriot history and was recognised as such by the chroniclers of the Venetian period following him. The chronicler Florio Bustron, writing in the second half of the sixteenth century a work that essentially covers the history of the whole Lusignan dynasty from 1192 to 1489, states explicitly that for the reign of King James II, about whom many have written, some have deviated from the truth on account of hatred, others on account of invidiousness, and others on account of a bad narration. He praises George Boustronios, however, stating that he was a relative of his who had written much about this king in particular, and, as far as he could make out, had done so dispassionately, so that much of his account for the years 1458 to 1489 derives both from him and from his own father, who had himself witnessed certain events of this period.[160] A later chronicler, the Dominican brother Stephen de Lusignan, who was himself descended from the Lusignan royal family and wrote two historical accounts of Cyprus shortly after its capture by the Ottomans, the

---

[156] Mas Latrie, *Histoire, op.cit.*, III, 396-397 and 527; Hill, *op.cit.*, III, 695.

[157] Mas Latrie, 'Documents nouveaux', *op.cit.*, pp. 454-455 and 501-502;

[158] *Ibid.*, pp. 489-492; Hill, *op.cit.*, III, 726-727.

[159] Boustronios (Coureas transl.), §§ 277 and 284; Florio Bustron, 'Chronique', *op.cit.*, p. 454; Hill, *op.cit.*, III, 699-701.

[160] Florio Bustron, 'Chronique', *op.cit.*, pp. 8-9.

fourteenth century onwards was the *griparia*. Smaller than the *fuste*, it was a lateen-rigged type of galley, perhaps evolving from the Venetian *grippo* and in use as a merchantman and a naval transport by Latins, Greeks and Turks throughout the Mediterranean.[171] A development in the opposite direction led to the galleass, a larger version of the standard galley in which each oar was pulled by several oarsmen as opposed to one, allowing for larger oars and greater speeds. Another type of ship mentioned several times in the chronicle was the caravel, a small, light and fast ship that the Portuguese developed in the mid-fifteenth century for sailing against head winds and contrary currents.[172] The specific allusion to all these kinds of ship in Boustronios' chronicle forms vivid proof of how it spans the transition from the middle ages to the renaissance, nautically as well as chronologically.

---

[171] Boustronios (Coureas transl.), §§ 76, 82, 105, 209 and 283; Pryor, *Geography, op.cit.*, pp. 46, 66-69, 74, 169-170, 175, 180, 186 and 194-195; P. Earle, *Corsairs of Malta and Barbary* (London, 1970), p. 48 note; F. Braudel (transl. Siân Reynolds), *The Mediterranean and the Mediterranean World in the Age of Philip II*, 2 vols. (London, 1972-1973), I, 119, II, 868, 871 and 873-874.

[172] Boustronios (Coureas transl.), §§ 7, 9, 36, 71, 81, 209, 220, 237 and 241; Braudel, *Mediterranean, op.cit.*, I, 108; Pryor, *Geography, op.cit.*, pp. 43-47, 67-68, 72-73, 78-79, 83, 88-89, 162 and 180.

THE CHRONICLE OF
GEORGE BOUSTRONIOS

A Narrative of the Chronicle of Cyprus, Begun from the Year of Christ 1456

1. In the year of Christ 1456 the prince arrived from Portugal to marry Charlotte, the daughter of King John.[1] Her mother, moreover, was Lady Helena Palaiologina, the daughter of the despot of the Morea and the niece of the emperor of Constantinople. And so the said prince married Lady Charlotte. Indeed her mother Lady Helena was extremely sensible. Besides, she was always in ill health. Furthermore, the above prince married at the residence of the knight Sir Richard de la Baume[2], because ever since the royal court had been burnt King Janus, on his return from Syria, took possession of the residence of Sir Richard de la Baume and dwelt there, and it has remained the royal court down to this day.

2. Since, moreover, you know that jealousies are to be found in royal courts, it so happened that they spoke ill of the lord prince because he left the residence of his father in law and moved into the dwellings of the count of Tripoli, who was named Peter, opposite the citadel. This count was the uncle of the above-mentioned King John, and during his lifetime had christened the said Charlotte, granting her Lakatamia. And since the above prince also had his own means he took his spouse and departed from her father's house. Her father and mother were greatly displeased, for they had no other child.

3. Furthermore, after the passage of a few days, brothers set out from the hostel of the Hospitallers[3] and were going around one night when they set upon a young man named Sciarra, who himself was a good person, and killed him.[4] The young man

---

[1] Neither George Boustronios nor Florio Bustron give an exact date, but a recently published anonymous 15th century Italian chronicle dates John of Coimbra's arrival at Salines to 10 December 1456, and he reached Nicosia on 12 December. See G. Grivaud, 'Une petite chronique chypriote du XVe siècle', in *Dei gesta per Francos: Crusade Studies in Honour of John Richard*, ed. M. Balard, B.Z. Kedar and J. Riley-Smith (Aldershot, 2001), pp. 333 and 338.

[2] Florio Bustron, 'Chronique', *op.cit.*, p. 373 refers to the house as belonging to 'Ugo' that is Hugh, de la Baume. The la Baume (*alias* Balma) family was one of the oldest Latin noble families in the Eastern Mediterranean, appearing in Palestine in the early 12th century and in Cyprus after 1195. See J. Richard, *Chypre sous les Lusignans: Documents Chypriotes des Archives du Vatican (XIVe et XVe siècles)*, (Paris, 1982), p. 84; Hill, *op.cit.*, II 252, 255 note 2, 465 and 496 note 2, III, 534 and 549; P. Edbury, *Kingdom*, *op.cit.*, pp. 19 and note 26; *The Cartulary of the Cathedral of Holy Wisdom of Nicosia*, ed. N. Coureas and C. Schabel (Nicosia, 1997), nos. 43, 45 and 46.

[3] On the Hospitaller hostel in Nicosia, in existence before 1255 and mentioned in a document of King James II dated 3 March 1468. See Coureas and Schabel, *Cartulary*, *op.cit.*, no. 91; Richard, *Remembrances*, *op.cit.*, no. 146 and note 3.

[4] Disorderly conduct among Hospitallers on Cyprus impelled Ramon Zacosta, the Grand Master of the Order, in 1465 to order the seizure and deportation to Rhodes of insubordinate members who were wandering around the island, and in 1468 the murder of a layman by a Hospitaller was reported to King James II. See L. de Mas Latrie, *Histoire*, *op.cit.*, III, 91.

concerned had two brothers [who were] good men and had many friends besides. On seeing, moreover, that they had killed him on no pretext whatsoever, they laid the slain man on a stretcher, brought him to the court of the king and demanded judgement. And certain persons who happened to be there said to them: 'Know well that the friars who killed your brother are to be found in the home of the lord prince!' On hearing this they rushed off and went to the prince's house. The lord prince, moreover, was standing on the veranda, and on seeing the men who were hastening with great speed he gave the order for the doors to be locked. A great fracas then took place and they killed two servants of the prince, while one of them was also killed and many men were wounded. And the prince was greatly upset by this and fell mortally ill. Furthermore, certain persons came and told him that Thomas <the chamberlain>[5] had sent these people to come to his house. Indeed the prince was aggrieved over this, for the lady Queen Helena had brought Thomas over with her and he happened to be the son of her foster mother, while for the love of the queen the king had honoured him and had given him many revenues, making him, moreover, a knight and the chamberlain of the kingdom. And Thomas, on hearing that they had told the prince that he was the cause of the fracas, set forth and journeyed to Famagusta. The Genoese, moreover, accorded him great honour and kept him in good company.

4. Meanwhile the prince died after a few days.[6] Furthermore, he was buried in [the church of] St Francis, and there was much sorrow over his death, for he was a good looking and virtuous man. And Lady Charlotte remained a widow, while her father took her to his house straightaway with considerable grief. On the death of the prince the friends of the chamberlain at once made the news known throughout Famagusta, while he, without giving any thought to the matter came to Nicosia on hearing this and went to his house, which was the residence of a knight, Sir Rizzo Plan de Cardie, that happens to be right opposite the red bathhouse. Within it, moreover, the Lady Charlotte complained to her brother, the illegitimate son of her father, of how they caused her husband's death. That is to say [she complained] to James whom the king had appointed postulant, who was 17 years old, and to whom he had given the archbishopric with all its incomes and tithes, and who was high-spirited. Furthermore, hearing from the people of Nicosia and from many knights that the chamberlain was the cause, with them saying that 'the prince died on account of his provocation'. And they recounted many things for the postulant to listen to.

Two Sicilian brothers had arrived in Cyprus at that time, the one being [called] Linardus and the other Anthony, and Martinengo hired them as servants for the postulant. He, moreover, spoke to them over the affair of the chamberlain, and they

---

[5] The words in brackets < > are taken from mss. B and M. See Kehayioglou, *Διήγησις*, *op.cit.*, p. 4, ms. B line 17 and ms. M lines 17-18. Florio Bustron, 'Chronique', *op.cit.*, p. 374 and the anonymous 15th century Italian chronicle (Grivaud, 'Une petite chronique', *op.cit.*, p. 334) call him Thoma della Morea, indicating his Peloponnesian origins.

[6] Neither George Boustronios nor Florio Bustron give a precise date but the anonymous 15th century Italian chronicle dates it to 21 June 1457. See *ibid.*, pp. 334 and 338; *Les Lignages d'Outremer, introduction, notes et edition critique*, ed. M.A. Nielen in *Documents relatifs à l'histoire des Croisades* XVIII, Académie des Inscriptions et Belles-lettres (Paris, 2003), p. 170 ms. Vat. lat. 7806 A, fol. 251 dates it to '22 di zugno 1457'.

told the postulant that 'the chamberlain has a great summons at his house'. When the postulant heard this, and without anyone knowing anything, he got on his horse, taking Martinengo and the two Sicilians, and went to the chamberlain's house. Meanwhile the persons summoned had left, and he (i.e. the chamberlain) was alone. The chamberlain, having heard that the postulant had arrived, came down to the bottom of the stairs and welcomed him with great joy. Furthermore, he took him by the hand and they went upstairs. And in the course of the many things they talked about the postulant said to the chamberlain 'If it pleases you let these people go, so as to make room for us in order for me to talk to you!' So the chamberlain gave an order and his servants departed from there. And none remained other than the two Sicilians. The chamberlain then asked the postulant to order them outside, and the latter replied 'They don't know any Greek', The chamberlain, moreover, believed this, and once they were alone [the postulant] gave orders to the Sicilians and they killed him.[7] Furthermore, while the postulant was going down to get on his horse he narrowly escaped assassination by one of the chamberlain's servants, named Sergios. The postulant rode away and went to the house of the constable, Carceran Suarez,[8] and as soon as the commotion at the house of the chamberlain was heard everyone ran outside. The postulant told him (i.e. the constable) of how the incident came to pass. The constable, moreover, on hearing of it remained dumbfounded and did not allow him to dismount, and told him to go to the archbishopric. And he went forthwith and remained steadfast until the whole thing should blow over.

5. There was also a Cypriot knight called Sir James Gurri[9] involved in this affair, and

---

[7] Neither George Boustronios nor Florio Bustron, 'Chronique', *op.cit.*, pp. 374-375 date this murder, but the anonymous 15th century Italian chronicle (Grivaud, 'Une petite chronique', *op.cit.*, pp. 334 and 338) dates it to 13 July 1457.

[8] On this Spaniard, who in 1426 saved King Janus' life at the battle of Khirokotia, see 'Chronique d'Amadi', in *Chroniques d'Amadi et de Strambaldi*, ed. R. de Mas Latrie, 2 vols. (Paris, 1891-1893), I, 507 and note 1; Florio Bustron, 'Chronique', *op.cit.*, p. 386; Richard, *Documents, op.cit.*, pp. 130 note 4, 140 and 151; 'Pero Tafur and Cyprus', transl. C.I. Nepaulsingh, *Sources for the History of Cyprus*, ed. P.W. Wallace and A.G. Orphanides, IV (New York, 1997), 7, 12, 28 and 57-58.

[9] The Gurri, a family of 'White Genoese' originating from Syria, were among the 'White Venetians' or 'White Genoese' that is to say Oriental Christians who were subjects of Venice or Genoa, settled on Cyprus. They are mentioned in Makhairas, *Recital, op.cit.*, I, 354-355, § 375, II, 156, § 375. as well as in the Italian chronicles of 'Amadi' and Florio Bustron. See 'Amadi', *op.cit.*, p. 444; Florio Bustron, 'Chronique', *op.cit.*, p. 300. In Mas Latrie, *Histoire, op.cit.*, III, 17-18 note 5 it is stated that the Cypriot locality of Gourri to the west of the monastery of Makhairas acquired its name from this family. On Sir James Gurri and other members of the family see Richard, *Documents, op.cit.*, pp. 135 and 152-154; *idem., Remembrances, op.cit.*, nos. 30, 48 and 195.

[10] The viscount of Nicosia was the president of the Court of Burgesses. On this office and the Court of Burgesses see M. Grandclaude, *Etude critique sur les livres des Assises de Jérusalem* (Paris, 1923), pp. 13-15, 155-160; Edbury, *Kingdom, op.cit.*, pp. 187 and 193-194; J. Richard, 'Οι πολιτικοί και κοινωνικοί θεσμοί του μεσαιωνικού βασιλείου', and 'Το δίκαιο του μεσαιωνικού βασιλείου', in *Ιστορία της Κύπρου*, IV, *Μεσαιωνικόν Βασίλειον, Ενετοκρατία*, ed. Th. Papadopoullos (Nicosia, 1995), 345-346, 360-361 and 379-384; *The Assizes of the Lusignan Kingdom of Cyprus*, transl. N. Coureas (Nicosia, 2002), pp. 28-37.

he was a man of great sense who also happened to be the viscount of Nicosia,[10] and he was also in touch with Queen Helena. In addition, in order to satisfy Thomas' mother he maintained such close contact with the king as to cause displeasure to the postulant. The king, moreover, was resident in the houses of Lady Anne, near [the church of] St Catherine.[11]

6. Besides, King John was extremely angry over the killing of the chamberlain on hearing about it. Furthermore, they were afraid for the queen, Lady Helena. And so he (i.e. the king) gave the order and they commanded all men to congregate in the royal court.

So indeed it came to pass. The said King John was extremely fond of the postulant but on account of fearing the queen did not dare to show this openly, and so he ordered him to be deprived of the archbishopric. The postulant, moreover, was unable to stomach this, and he sought to recover the archbishopric by every means possible. Yet no remedy was at hand for him to have it. He was advised to go and converse with Sir James Gurri, and he would find a remedy. He did this, moreover, and conversed with him, and the latter sent him on his way, advising him to go out [of Nicosia] to [the monastery of] Mangana,[12] to the queen's confessor, while he would do everything possible with her ladyship the queen.

And he acted on the advice that he (i.e. Sir James Gurri) had given him. He got on his horse and rode straightaway to Mangana and conversed with her confessor, but no remedy was found enabling him to do anything. Therefore the postulant, on realising that there was no remedy enabling him to have the archbishopric, resolved to embark on the best possible course conducive to his life and his honour.

7. And so in the year of [Our Lord Jesus] Christ 1457[13] he took [with him] a priest of [the cathedral of] the Holy Wisdom named Sir Arnaud Moté as well as his valet, Martinique de Lieux, and ventured out one night from the Armenian quarter, out of the citadel adjoining the city walls. He had horses outside, and they rode off.

And he went to Salines and found Tafur's caravel.[14] Then they went on board and they set sail. In the course of their journey they encountered a Florentine galley[15] and

---

[11] This was a late 14th century Gothic church in Nicosia located to the north east of the Latin cathedral of the Holy Wisdom (St Sophia). For a description see C. Enlart, *Gothic Art and the Renaissance in Cyprus*, transl. D. Hunt (London, 1987), pp. 152-157.

[12] This was the largest and wealthiest Greek monastery in Cyprus. See J. Hackett, Ιστορία της Ορθοδόξου Εκκλησίας Κύπρου, transl. by Kh. Papaioannou, 3 vols. (Athens, 1923, Piraeus, 1927 and 1932), II, 154-155; Hill, *op.cit.*, III, 1072-1074; N. Coureas, 'Η Μονή Αγίου Γεωργίου των Μαγγάνων επί Φραγκοκρατίας', *Επιστημονική Επετηρίδα της Κυπριακής Εταιρείας Ιστορικών Σπουδών*, II (Nicosia, 1994), 275-286.

[13] All three mss. have 1456, as does Dawkins, *Boustronios, op.cit.*, § 7, but this must be mistaken as James left Nicosia for Rhodes after the death of John of Coimbra, which occurred in the summer of 1457. See Hill, II, 536 note 1; Edbury, 'Λουζινιανοί', *op.cit.*,, p. 200.

[14] A small, light and fast ship of the mid-15th century developed by the Portuguese for sailing against head winds and contrary currents. See Braudel, *Mediterranean, op.cit.*, I,108.

he (i.e. James) thought of going on board the galley for greater safety. So he motioned to the skipper, who took them on board and did them great honour, handing over the galley to him as though it had been his. They set sail at once, moreover, and came to Famagusta for tasks he had to fulfil.

Furthermore, on learning in Nicosia that the postulant was to be found in the galley in [the port of] Famagusta, they ordered a knight, Sir Bernard Rousset,[16] who was the admiral of Cyprus,[17] to go at once as a messenger to the skipper so as to have the postulant brought down from the galley. Indeed he exerted himself greatly, but found no way to bring him down, and the galley set sail and went to Rhodes. When, moreover, the Grand Master [of the Hospitallers] encountered him he was extremely pleased and did him great honour.[18] He sojourned in Rhodes for five months and the Grand Master covered his expenses. And he waited for news from Cyprus, to return for them to give him the archbishopric, but he never received any such news. Realising then that there were many knights and numerous persons hating him, he considered choosing the best course of action he could undertake.

8. At that time, moreover, there happened to be a monk in Cyprus, Brother William Goneme[19] of the Order of St Augustine,[20] and he was in great favour with the king.

---

[15] This was a larger version of the standard Mediterranean galley that the Florentines developed along with the Venetians and Genoese from the 13th century onwards. By the 15th century, the great Florentine galleys plied a regular route from Naples to Alexandria via Cyprus, returning via Beirut and Crete. See Pryor, *Geography, op.cit.*, pp. 43, 57 and 73.

[16] He was possibly descended from the prominent Genoese family of Rouss, established in Cyprus by the early 14th century. See *The Trial of the Templars on Cyprus: A Complete English Edition*, ed. Anne Gilmour-Bryson (Leiden, 1998), 69-70; N. Coureas, 'The role of the Templars and the Hospitallers in the movement of commodities involving Cyprus, 1291-1312', in *The Experience of Crusading*, ed. M. Bull, P. Edbury, N. Housley and J. Phillips, 2 vols. (Cambridge, 2003), II, 270-271.

[17] The office of admiral is attested from circa 1298-1299. See Mas Latrie, 'Nouvelles preuves', *op.cit.*, p. 52; *idem., Histoire., op.cit.*, II, 150, 162; 'Amadi', *op.cit.*, p. 400;

[18] The Grand Master was James de Milly (d. 17 Aug. 1461). On the Hospitallers in Cyprus and their conquest of Rhodes in circa 1308, see A. Luttrell, 'The Hospitallers in Cyprus after 1291', and 'The Hospitallers at Rhodes: 1306-1421', in *The Hospitallers in Cyprus, Rhodes, Greece and the West, 1291-1440*, I-II (Aldershot, 1979, repr. 1992,1997).

[19] On William Goneme see L. de Mas Latrie, 'Histoire des archevêques Latins de l'île de Chypre', *AOL*, II (1884), 293-297; Hill, III, 538 note 2 and 1092. On other members of this family see Richard, *Documents, op.cit.*, p. 149, note 2; *idem., Remembrances, op.cit.*, nos. 113, 124, 155, 157, 187-190, 195, 205-206, 208, 212, 214-215, 218,220, 222, 228 and 232-233; B. Arbel, 'The Cypriot Nobility from the Fourteenth to the Sixteenth Centuries: A New Interpretation', in *Latins and Greeks in the Eastern Mediterranean after 1204*, ed. B. Arbel, B. Hamilton and D. Jacoby (London, 1989), p. 181 and notes 34-37.

[20] The order of Augustinian canons was established on Cyprus early in the 13th century, and between 1206-1211 transferred to the Premonstratensian Order. By the mid 13th century the Augustinian (Austin) friars, who were mendicants as opposed to canons regular, were also established on the island. See N. Coureas, *The Latin Church in Cyprus, 1195-1312* (Aldershot, 1997), pp. 200-205 and 242-243. Hill, *op.cit.*, III, 1092 wrongly calls William Goneme an Austin friar, but Rudt de Collenberg, 'Le royaume et l'eglise latine de Chypre et la papauté de 1417 à 1471', *EKEE* XIII-XVI (1988), 172 describes him as 'O.S. Aug' (Ordo S.Augustini), hence he was a canon regular.

Furthermore, as you know, there are great jealousies to be found in all rulers' courts, and they knew well how to act in this fashion, and so they expelled the same Brother William from the king's court. He betook himself to Rhodes on account of his grievance, and there they held him in extremely high regard. The postulant conferred many honours upon him when he encountered him.

9. The postulant, perceiving that he was not going to receive any news from Cyprus decided to deliberate with the above-mentioned Brother William. And Brother William, listening to his complaints, said to him 'Do not be disheartened! I shall do everything that shall be to your honour and your pleasure'. Without anyone on Rhodes knowing anything, they armed two galleys, one belonging to John Balarca and the Florentine galley, as well as the caravel of John Perez[21] and the caravel belonging to John Tafur,[22] with the postulant and Brother William coming aboard, and came to Kerynia without anyone getting wind of anything. Furthermore, the postulant gave the order 'Let no one set foot on dry land!' And then, once it had become dark, they landed, he himself and all his men.

Then they came to Nicosia before daybreak, armed and on foot, on 1 March in the year [of Our Lord Jesus] Christ 1458.[23] They entered through the citadel adjoining the wall, through the Armenian quarter[24]. The Armenians, sensing their coming, began to create a disturbance. The postulant spoke to them forthwith and as soon as they recognised him they did not stir at all. The postulant, moreover, took those whom he wanted and went to the house of Sir James Gurri. They entered from the rear side of

---

[21] This was the Catalan John Perez Fabriges, the brother of Louis Perez Fabriges, the future Latin archbishop of Cyprus (1471-1475?), and a notorious pirate, who supported the postulant and was rewarded when the latter became King James II. Florio Bustron, 'Chronique', *op.cit.*, p. 418 states that after 1464 the king gave him as fiefs the *casalia* of Knodara, Koka, Moniatis, St Andronikos of Akaki, Mallia, Karpasso, Anglisidhes, Selino and other appurtenances. On Knodhara see also Richard, *Livre des Remembrances*, pp. 210-213 (doc. I). On his piratical activities see *Une enquête à Chypre au XVe siècle: Le sindicamentum de Napoleone Lomellini, capitaine Génois de Famagouste (1459)*, ed. Catherine Otten-Froux (Nicosia, 2000), pp. 60, 69, 74, 77, 143, 150 *et passim*.

[22] This supporter of the future King James II was likewise rewarded, becoming the titular count of Tripoli and captain of Famagusta. Florio Bustron, 'Chronique', *op.cit.*, p. 422 states that after 1464 the king granted him the *casalia* of Istinjo (Chio), Lassa, Askas, Tembria, Koutraphas, Plessia and Klavdhia. See also Mas Latrie, *Histoire*, *op.cit.*, III, 172, 355 note 1, 360, 402-403, 409, 412 and 512; *idem.*, 'Documents nouveaux', *op.cit.*, pp. 392-393, 423, 430, 433-440, 503-504 and 617.

[23] All mss. have 1 May 1457, but both the month and the year are wrong. James' return from Rhodes took place after the death of John of Coimbra in the summer of 1457 but before that of Queen Helena in April 1458, and so March should be read for May. Mss. **A** and **B** of the chronicle state below that Sir James Gurri, following his murder by James, was buried on 1 May 1458, and since once again March should be read for May, James and his supporters reached Nicosia arguably just before 1 March 1458. See Kehayioglou, Διήγησις, *op.cit.*, pp. 16-17, 20-21 and 348.

[24] Makhairas, *Recital*, *op.cit.*, I, 416-417, § 433 mentions the existence of an Armenian quarter in Nicosia. On relations between Cyprus and Cilician Armenia during the Lusignan Period see N. Coureas, 'Lusignan Cyprus and Lesser Armenia, 1195-1375', *EKEE* XXI (1995), 33-71.

the oven and came down and opened the door of the pathway, and then they all went up, and breaking down the doors they came into the bedroom where he lay asleep.

The said Sir James entertained a great fear over a Catalan valet of Dom Pedro, for a certain valet of the above-mentioned Sir James, called Gaves, had killed <a valet of Dom Pedro>[25], and on account of this he was in great fear. On hearing the commotion, moreover, he surmised that it was Dom Pedro and that he had come with his men to apprehend the murderer, and he did not realise that it was the postulant. And on finding poor Sir James in bed Tafur and Camus seized him and brought him outside to the loggia, where the postulant was standing. On beholding the postulant Sir James knelt in front of him and begged him forgiveness. Yet he was so cruel that he gave the order and they killed him,[26] and they pillaged his house.

10. The said postulant brought over from Rhodes a monk named Brother Salpous of the Order of St Augustine, who happened to be Cypriot, and he had come to King John from the pope so that he (i.e. the king) would take the pope's nephew, Master Peter [Louis], as a groom for his daughter Charlotte.[27] Furthermore, the postulant despatched the same Brother Salpous to the house of Sir Thomas Gurri, the brother of the above-mentioned Sir James. When the friar and Martinique along with numerous Catalans went to the house of the said Sir Thomas, they thoroughly looted it, and he ascended through a trap door and escaped, something in which Martinique assisted him.

The news reached the king at daybreak, of how 'the postulant came back to Cyprus and entered Nicosia, killing Sir James Gurri and his brother, and he wishes to kill all the knights'. The bell sounded the alarm, and all rushed together to the royal court. The postulant, moreover, took all the people and went to the archbishopric, staying there in force, for he was in low spirits and indifferent to death. On the way to the archbishopric they transported with them the things they had taken from the two brothers, Sir James and Sir Thomas, into the palace of the archbishopric, and whatever they had taken, silver, gold, *cartzias*[28] and merchandise, they made an estimate [coming to] 6,000 ducats. Furthermore, they brought poor Sir James to [the cathedral of] the Holy Wisdom[29] as though he had been a pauper and had him buried on 1 March [in the year] of Christ 1458. And they took his brother Sir Thomas to the royal court.

---

[25] The words in brackets < > are from mss. **B** and **M**. See Kehayioglou, Διήγησις, *op.cit.*, p. 17 line 18 (**M**) and p. 19, ms. **B** line 1 and ms. **M** line 1.

[26] The anonymous 15th century Italian chronicle (Grivaud, 'Une petite chronique', *op.cit.*, pp. 334 and 338) dates his assassination to April 1458 and Queen Helena's death to 17 March, but both George Boustronios and Florio Bustron, 'Chronique', *op.cit.*, pp. 379-380 place the queen's death after that of Sir James Gurri.

[27] This was the nephew of Pope Callistus III, on whom see Hill, III, 538-539, 539 note 1 on how various Cypriot chroniclers corrupted his name, and 542-543. For Pope Callistus III and his crusading interest in the eastern Mediterranean see K.M. Setton, *The Papacy and the Levant, 1204-1571*, 4 vols. (Philadelphia, 1976-1984), II, 161-195.

[28] A low value coin introduced under King James I of Cyprus (1382-1398). See D.M. Metcalf, *The Gros, Sixains and Cartzias of Cyprus 1382-1489* (Nicosia, 2000), pp. 133-147.

[29] This cathedral, often mistranslated as St Sophia, was the seat of the Latin archbishop of Cyprus. See Enlart, *Gothic Art, op.cit.*, pp. 82-130; Coureas and Schabel, *Cartulary, op.cit.*, pp. 21-54.

11. The king, moreover, seeing how the postulant had returned and entered Nicosia without authorisation, and had come and slain the viscount, gathered together all the knights and liegemen and held a session at the court. In addition he had charges brought against the postulant in the High Court,[30] maintaining that 'He has brought pirates, made an unauthorised entry into Nicosia, and has come in and slain the viscount of Nicosia. And I want to have justice from his person, after the manner the assize decrees'.

At once, moreover, all who simultaneously understood the king's desire, how in secret he loved the postulant, saw in each instance that it would be profitable to offer the best possible advice. And there were many knights wanting much harm to befall the postulant, having seen the manifold evils he had wrought. The king's court declared to him 'Know, our most high lord, from the charges you have brought against the postulant that it was no small crime that he committed. And on account of this it seems right to us for your lordship to send [men] for the capture of both him and his associates, and to have them brought before you'. It also appeared right to the other knights 'for the king to have him summoned to appear before him!' This, moreover, is what took place, and he ordered three knights, Sir Peter Pelestrine,[31] Sir William de Ras[32] and Sir Paul Croc to go and order him to appear before the king. The above-mentioned knights on arriving informed him according to their instructions, and the postulant answered them as follows:

12. 'Lords, know that I, the poor man, never set myself against my master, but have come for those who hate me and have tried to alienate me from my master! Furthermore, I greatly esteem my master's lordship, even if his wish is to my great detriment, and he orders me to appear before him. For this reason I want you to recommend me to his lordship and to tell him that I am prepared to die in his service, as I am obliged. But for reasons of good will, so that no harm befalls my own people, let his lordship offer me assurances and let him also give me that which he granted of his own free will! He made me a cleric and gave me the archbishopric with all its incomes and tithes, after the manner my uncle the cardinal[33] had possessed it.

Once my lord has done this, moreover, I am ready to live and to die serving him in every possible manner. Should his lordship not wish this on account of certain persons hating me, then let him take from me that which he gave me of his own

---

[30] On the establishment and workings of this court, which applied feudal law and to which all royal vassals, that is liege-men, had access, see Grandclaude, *Les livres des assises, op.cit.*, pp. 115, 117-118, 160-167; Edbury, *Kingdom, op.cit.*, pp. 113, 175-176 and 186-188; *idem.*, 'John of Jaffa and the Kingdom of Cyprus', *EKEE* XXIII (1997), 19 and 23-26; Richard, 'Το δίκαιο', *op.cit.*, pp. 375-379.

[31] See Richard, *Documents, op.cit.*, pp. 130, 140 and 151 regarding this knight.

[32] On this future viscount of Nicosia see Richard, *Remembrances, op.cit.*, nos. 155, 182 as well as Appendix 1.

[33] This was cardinal Hugh de Lusignan, *electus* to the Latin archbishopric of Cyprus sometime before March 1412 and appointed both archbishop and cardinal in 1426, while regent of Cyprus. See Mas Latrie, 'Histoire des archevêques', *op.cit.*, pp. 280-286; Hill, *op.cit.*, III, 1088-1089.

volition! Furthermore, once he has done this I am ready to appear before him. Otherwise, I consider it better for me to die, rather than for him to take from me that which he gave me'.

The knights turned back once they had heard the postulant's response and passed it on to the king and his counsel. And most of the knights and the remainder recognised the king's desire, for in secret he loved the postulant as his own child, but he was of a timid disposition, for he feared the queen greatly and did not dare to speak out, and it behoved all of them together to do, albeit unwillingly, what the postulant wanted. And so the king had a paper drawn up, stating that: 'the postulant should have the archbishopric with all its revenues and tithes!' just as his uncle the cardinal had possessed and held it, and he also secured [in his possession] his own men and the ships which he had brought with him. 'Let them not have any objections, and let them all go to the ships!' The king had this paper drawn up, moreover, in the presence of the Venetian *baiulo*,[34] Sir Peter Ramon, and of all his court, and he despatched it to the postulant.

13. And on beholding this paper the postulant set his household in order as he saw fit, and he himself got on his horse and went to the royal court. He found the people there armed, and on seeing them he burst out laughing. The king, moreover, secretly instructed those whom he knew and who loved the postulant to watch over him lest any should harm him. He (i.e. the postulant) went up to the chamber where the queen was lying down.

The king, on setting eyes on him, began to chide him and ostensibly made out that he was angry with him. In secret, however, he loved him greatly, and did that which he did to him for [the eyes of] the queen. Meanwhile he (i.e. the postulant) went about his business as he wanted to, and those hating him were desirous of his affection.

14. The postulant then found it convenient to implement his master's orders that 'The skippers should go with their men on board their ships and should not delay, on peril of their lives!', and a proclamation to his effect was made. Furthermore, the postulant sent word to the viscount, who was Sir Francis Montolif,[35] and on his orders carts were procured on which they loaded their weapons and clothes and the spoils they had pillaged from Sir James and his brother. The postulant, moreover, rode with them, with the *baiulo* keeping them company, and they rode as far as [the church of] St

---

[34] This officer first appears on Cyprus in notarial deeds of 1300, its first incumbent being Niccolo Zugno. See D. Jacoby, 'The Rise of a New Emporium in the Eastern Mediterranean: Famagusta in the Late Thirteenth Century', *MY*, II (1984), 169-171.

[35] The Montolifs were among the oldest Latin noble families in Cyprus. See Mas Latrie, 'Histoire des archevêques', *op.cit.*, pp. 286-287; Hill, *op.cit.*, II, 230, 244, 246-247, 261, 349, 377, 401, 410, 432, 440 note 1, 450 and note 1, 490, III, 502 note 3, 530, 542, 544 -545, 562, 598 and note 3, 600 and note 3 and 1091; Richard, *Remembrances, op.cit.*, nos. 87 note 1, 166 and note 20, 182, 195 and 225; Edbury, *Kingdom, op.cit.*, pp. 125-126, esp. notes 94 and 97, 139-142, 183, 188 and 192-193; Coureas and Schabel, *Cartulary, op.cit.*, nos. 65, 110-111 and 113.

Paraskevi.[36] Then they turned back, and the postulant went to the archbishopric with his men.

In this affair, besides, there were certain persons who planted a great many scandals among them, seeking ways to destroy him. This much they knew how to do, and they persuaded a valet of the postulant, Pierre de Hughet, who was a serf of Sir Simon Bernard and engineered a great betrayal against the postulant. For he used to sleep in the postulant's bedroom, and one night, while he (i.e. the postulant) was asleep in the tower of the archbishopric, he left the bedroom open and departed, [leaving behind him] six valets who were sleeping with the postulant. Furthermore, had these valets not sensed something, the postulant would have been assassinated. Despite this the postulant continued to like him, for he had brought him over from Rhodes and held him in high regard.

The postulant, moreover, received many entreaties and he forgave Sir Thomas Gurri, whom he employed to administer his court and the church, supposing him to have forgotten the death of his brother and the pillaging of his house, and he exhibited a great affection towards him. But Sir Thomas had not ceased to harbour bitterness over his brother and he was ever seeking an opportunity to wreak harm upon the postulant. For he knew how to do this much with the knights whom he knew and who hated him (i.e. the postulant), and he said to them, 'Do you know in truth that the postulant has an understanding with the pope's nephew, Sir Peter [Louis], for the latter to come and marry Lady Charlotte!' They said as much to the king, and they took him (i.e. the postulant) to the citadel, along with the queen and the king's daughter.

15. And the postulant, on discovering the treachery that had been engineered against him, desired to clarify everything forthwith. He sent his servant George Boustron to go to the knight Sir Thomas de Verni,[37] because his wife was one of the queen's damsels whom the queen held very dearly. George, moreover, set off and met up with Sir Thomas, to whom he said, 'Master, my master the postulant sends you many greetings, and conveys to your lordship the fact that certain conspirators imparted the news to the king and queen that he had come to an understanding with the pope's nephew, Sir Peter [Louis], for the latter to come and marry Lady Charlotte.

Furthermore, my lord the postulant has a great sadness and grievance towards his lord the king and his lady the queen, because they believe the words of those hating him. He knows, moreover, that her ladyship your wife, your lady, is on good terms with her ladyship the queen. And indeed, let her have a word with her ladyship the queen! Your lordship, moreover, must have a word with the lord king so that things become clarified in such a manner as to become manifest to their lordships. For the

---

[36] For this church see Makhairas, *Recital, op.cit.*, I, § 623 and notes 1-2, § 701, also § 594 note 1, stating that the Gate of St Paraskevi was in the area of the citadel, near the present Paphos Gate. G. Jeffery, *A Description of the Historic Monuments of Cyprus* (Nicosia, 1918), p. 92 alludes to a ruined church of St Paraskevi outside the present circuit of walls of Nicosia.

[37] This was an old Latin noble family in Cyprus. See Hill, II, 401, 410, 440 note 1, 479, III, 552 note 3, 555 and 563; Richard, *Remembrances, op.cit.*, nos. 145 and notes 3-4, 159 note 1 and 173; Coureas and Schabel, *Cartulary, op.cit.*, nos. 90, 110-112 and 130.

monk Brother Salpous used to be at the court of the postulant, and so let them give orders for his arrest, and they shall learn everything from his person and shall learn where the injustices spring from!'

The knight and his lady wife on hearing this went at once to the king and told him what they had heard, and to the queen likewise. And on the king's orders the viscount came and seized the friar in accordance with the postulant's wishes, and he also seized a canon of [the cathedral of] the Holy Wisdom, John Gradon, who had also come from Rome. They took both of them, moreover, to Kerynia, with their elbows bound behind their backs. Furthermore, had the postulant known that they were taking them to Kerynia he would not have allowed them to be taken, for he would have wished to interrogate them together with the viscount, given that they were clergymen. He thought, however, that they were taking them to the citadel (i.e. of Nicosia). They had sent them to Kerynia, moreover, so that matters would not be clarified in the king's presence. In addition, the viscount had them placed on the rack, with Sir John de Nores[38] also present, and had them subjected to numerous torments. But they confessed nothing to the effect that the postulant was responsible for Sir Peter [Louis], and their captors were greatly incensed. Besides, the queen was unwell, and they placed such great fear in her heart that she went and took up residence in the house of the Dominican friars, and she suffered apoplexy on account of her great grief.

16. Since Lady Charlotte had been widowed and had remained in this condition, her father betrothed her to the son of the duchess of Savoy, who was King John's nephew and first cousin to Charlotte. And her mother the queen did not wish to hear of such an evil taking place, and when she was about to die she had her daughter Charlotte summoned, placing her under a wish and a curse not to desire to take her first cousin as a husband.[39] Should he be married to him, moreover, she would be excommunicate,

---

[38] On John de Nores and other members of this old and prominent Latin noble family, attested in Cyprus from the early 13th century and surviving the Ottoman conquest of 1570, see *Lacrimae Nicossienses. Recueil des inscriptions funéraires la plupart françaises existant encore dans l' île de Chypre*, ed. T.J. Chamberlayne (Paris, 1894), pp. 123-129; Richard, *Documents*, *op.cit.*, pp. 127, 142, 150 and 154-155; Hill, *op.cit.*, II, 322, 329, 346, 473, 479, 486, III, 497, 509, 571, 621-622, 648-649, 674, 698 note 3, 807, 846 note 1, 979, 982 note 4 and 1031; W. Rudt de Collenberg, 'Les dispensations matrimoniales accordées à l'Orient Latin selon les registres du Vatican d'Honorius III à Clément VII (1223-1385)', *MEFRM* 89 (1977), pt. 1, 25, 37, 41-42, 74 nos. 90 and 98, 78 no. 117, 80 nos. 126 and 131, *idem.*, 'Recherches sur quelques familles chypriotes apparentées au pape Clément VIII Aldobrandini (1592-1605): Flatro, Davila, Sozomenoi, Lusignan, Bustron et Nores', *EKEE* XII (1983), 5-68; Richard, *Remembrances*, *op.cit.*, nos. 33 and note 2, 49 note 1, 60, 69, 73 and note 1, 87, 94, 95 and note 1, 130, 146-147, 151, 155, 174-176, 178-184, 198, [208]-212, 214, 216-221, 229 and 232-234; Coureas and Schabel, *Cartulary*, *op.cit.*, nos. 57, 62 and 136.

[39] Charlotte's mother Helena Paleologina belonged to the Orthodox confession of Christianity, which expressly prohibits marriage between first cousins. In the Roman Catholic Church the regulations of the Fourth Lateran Council of 1215 stated that dispensations for marriages up to and including the degree of first cousin were obtainable, although normally marriages up to the fourth degrees of consanguinity and affinity were forbidden. See C. Bouchard, 'Consanguinity and noble marriages in the Tenth and Eleventh Centuries', *Speculum*, LVI (1981), 268-287.

she would lose the kingdom and she would suffer her curse. She also had her husband King John summoned, placing him under oath not to wish to do such an evil ever, that two first cousins should come together. And within a short time Queen Helena died, on 11 April in [the year of] Christ 1458.[40]

17. Following the queen's death, moreover, the king gave orders for Sir John Montolif, the marshal of Cyprus[41], and Sir Odet Bussat[42] to go to Savoy as emissaries so as to bring King John's nephew Louis, the son of the duchess [of Savoy], to marry his cousin Lady Charlotte.

18.[43] On learning that the queen had died the postulant grieved greatly, and both he and his servants dressed in black. He also brought Sir Anthony Silouan,[44] who was a canon and the vicar of the [cathedral of] Holy Wisdom[45], and sent him to make his way to the king and to tell him that he had learnt of the death of the lady queen, to recommend him to his lordship and, should he perhaps decree this, to come before his presence. The latter, moreover, went and related this to the king. And on hearing this, certain knights who hated the postulant said to the king, 'The postulant should not go to the queen's funeral!' The vicar, besides, on perceiving this returned and told the postulant. When he heard it, he was upset greatly, and spent two days without leaving his home. The queen was buried, furthermore, in the house of the Dominican friars.[46]

---

[40] The anonymous 15th century Italian chronicle (Grivaud, 'Une petite chronique', *op.cit.*, pp. 334 and 338) dates her death to 17 March 1458.

[41] On the functions of this military office see Hill, *op.cit.*, II, 53; Edbury, *Kingdoms, op.cit.*, pp. 181-184; Richard, 'Οι θεσμοί', *op.cit.*, pp. 338-339 and 342.

[42] On this person and other members of his family see Richard, *Documents, op.cit.*, pp. 123-128, 131 and 153-157; *idem.*, *Remembrances, op.cit.*, nos. 94 and note 1, 195.

[43] In mss. **B** and **M** chapter 17 precedes chapter 18. See Kehayioglou, Διήγησις, *op.cit.*, pp. 34-37.

[44] The Silouan (*alias* Soulouan) family became prominent in the late 14th century and a church in Nicosia dedicated to St Nicholas was named after them. See Richard, *Remembrances, op.cit.*, nos. 167 and note 1, 195 and note 21, 196, 206, 208 and 219 note 3. Anthony Silouan may have been a nephew of King Janus, whose sister probably married James Silouan, his father. He enjoyed canonries in Nicosia and Paphos from 1430, a canonry in the Cathedral of Holy Wisdom in Nicosia from 1432, and in 1457 he was appointed archdeacon there. He is mentioned in 1468 as a beneficiary in the will of the late John Corner, receiving a clerical assize of 180 bezants, as well as one of 60 bezants from the lands of the Hospitaller Order. See *Ibid.*, nos. 195-196 and 195 note 21.

[45] The vicar or administrator administered the spiritualities of vacant archbishoprics and bishoprics. For other examples from Cyprus see Coureas, *Latin Church, op.cit.*, pp. 20, 64-66 and 74-75 The cathedral also had a dean, enjoying a double prebend and second to the archbishop in seniority. The papal legate Eudes of Châteauroux had recommended the appointment of a dean for the cathedral as early as 1249. See *ibid.*, p. 96 and note 154; *The Synodicum Nicosiense and other Documents of the Latin Church of Cyprus, 1196-1373*, transl. C. Schabel (Nicosia, 2001), pp. 166-167.

[46] See Coureas, *Latin Church, op.cit.*, pp. 211-215 for the establishment of the Dominican Order in Cyprus in the early 13th century. For 15th and 16th century descriptions of the Dominican house in Nicosia see Felix Faber, 'Evagatorium in Terrae Sanctae, Arabiae et Egypti Peregrinationem' (extracts), in *Excerpta Cypria, Materials for a History of Cyprus*, transl. C.D. Cobham (Cambridge, 1908, repr. Nicosia, 1969), pp. 43-44; Stephen de Lusignan, *Description de toute l'isle de Chypre* (Paris, 1580), fols. 31b-32b and 63b-64.

19. After the passage of a few days the king, [who] loved the postulant greatly, summoned him to appear at the palace. When the knights, moreover, discovered this, about how he had had the postulant summoned to appear at the palace, each of them sought to have his favour. And they brought him in accordance with the king's wishes, for the king had no one whom he loved more than the postulant. Besides, despite the wishes of every knight he had him sent for and brought to him, two hours into the night, along with the following: Sir Bernard Rousset, the admiral, Sir Hector de Chivides,[47] Sir Paul Croc and the *baiulo* of the Venetians, as well as numerous other valets. And keeping him company they brought him before the king. Furthermore, in the course of his entrance to the citadel they secured the doors opposite him and did not allow any of his servants to enter the citadel, but only him. Afterwards, moreover, the postulant learnt of this and he said 'Had I had knowledge of this, I would not have entered either'. On entering he approached the king, and the king took great pleasure in beholding him and showed him great affection. Besides, the knights on seeing him were all discomfited, and each one of them strove to have the postulant's goodwill. He remained, moreover, with his lord for three hours into the night, and then bade the king farewell. They kept him company and he came back to the archbishopric extremely pleased, and each one of them (i.e. the knights) sought to keep him company in view of the favour that the king had shown him. Furthermore, when the postulant entered the citadel and his servants did not enter, his mother learnt of it, and she sat on the step shedding many tears until she saw him coming out.

Once he had come home he went up to his bedchamber and made merry with his own people, telling them about the love that his lord had shown him. And at daybreak all the knights came to his residence and commended themselves to him, as the son of their lord. He, moreover, held them all in high regard, leaving aside whatever they had wished to do to him, and he mounted his horse and went to the king. As soon as the king set eyes on him he embraced and kissed him, placing all the affairs of the kingdom into his hands and having dinner with him. He (i.e. the postulant) bade him goodbye and came back to the archbishopric, and at midday he ascended the tower of the archbishopric together with his valets.

20. And while he was seated Hector de Chivides came and knocked on the door of the castle. They opened the door for him and on his entry he encountered the postulant playing backgammon with Silouan the vicar. One seeing Hector the postulant embraced and kissed him, seating him beside him, and Sir Hector took him by the hand and said to him: 'My lord, I wish to have a word with your lordship'. And he began to commend himself to him and among many other things he entreated him to remain in the king's favour so that he would appoint him viscount, and that on [the king's] so

---

[47] Chivides (*alias* Kividhes) is a village to the west of Lárnaca. Two persons bore this name during this period. The one mentioned above, 'the younger' was the lord of the *casale* of Thrinia, became viscount of Nicosia in 1458 at the request of the future King James II but later deserted him and was beheaded in 1461 during the siege of Kerynia. The king awarded his namesake the *casale* of Phiti in the Limassol district in 1469. See Richard, *Remembrances, op.cit.*, nos. 120 and note 1, 132, 149 and note 3; Aristeidou, Έγγραφα, *op.cit.*, III, 289; IV, 53-56, 63-64.

doing he would always be at his command. The postulant, moreover, said to him: 'don't worry Sir Hector, and I shall do everything with my lord's consent!'

Sir Hector on hearing this gave him as a present a nimble black horse that he owned, but the postulant did not wish to keep it. And thanking him Sir Hector bade him farewell and went away. In the morning the postulant mounted his horse and went to the king, coming into the king's presence. Furthermore, the king on seeing him showed a very good disposition towards him and great affection. It was in addition extremely hot, and he took off his coat and remained in his shirt. And seeing him in his shirt, the king took great pleasure because he had a handsome body. While they were conversing, moreover, he knelt before his lord and requested him the office of viscount for Hector de Chivides. The king on hearing him honoured his request, bestowed the office of viscount on Hector de Chivides and removed Montolif. The said Hector was at his home, like one not knowing anything, and they sent for and had him brought, giving him the office in line with the usual custom. Furthermore, he (i.e. the postulant) performed many favours for numerous other persons, and they did many bad things to him, yet the postulant overlooked as many things as they did to him and showed affection towards all of them.

21. One day, moreover, he organized a great summons at the archbishopric, with games and all forms of amusement. And these people attempted among themselves to create a disturbance, and summoning Marcius, the postulant's uncle, they said to him: 'Know that we have discovered that Sir Marco Corner has obtained the archbishopric of Cyprus for his brother, Sir Andrew!'[48] Marcius became angry on hearing this and came and found his sister, the postulant's mother,[49] saying to her: 'Do you know what news I have learnt from the lord who dined with the lord your son, and from Sir Thomas Gurri, which has displeased me greatly?' Sir Marco Corner has obtained the archbishopric for his brother, Sir Andrew'. His sister then said: 'Marcius, take note that those who told you this did not say it on account of the great love they have for him, my son, but those who hate him said it on account of being two faced, for my son to learn of it, to conceive a loathing for Sir Andrew, and for a great evil to transpire. For this reason show a little patience, so that we can verify it if perhaps it is true! And despite everything Sir Thomas Gurri [has said], the knights, on seeing that all the love of the king had fallen on the postulant, were, as regarded those hating him, preoccupied with how to do him harm'. And so Marcius held his peace, and the affair passed away.

---

[48] The Corner (*alias* Corner) family was the most prominent Venetian family in Cyprus in the 15th and 16th centuries, having established itself at Episkopi in the Limassol district, where it owned extensive sugar plantations, in the later 14th century. See F. Thiriet, *La Romanie vénitienne au Moyen Age* (Paris, 1975), pp. 330 and 333; Arbel, 'A Royal Family', *op.cit.*, pp. 134-152; *idem.*, 'Reign of Caterina Corner', *op.cit.*, pp. 67-85.

[49] This was Marietta of Patras, King John II's mistress. Hill, *op.cit.*, III, 528-529 relates Queen Helena's jealousy towards her and how she bit her nose off. On becoming king the postulant awarded her the *casalia* of Lyso, Pelathousa and Peristerona, lands at Polis and annual allowances of bread, wine, pork, olive oil, figs and onions for her household, for which see Florio Bustron, 'Chronique', *op.cit.*, p. 418; Richard, *Remembrances*, *op.cit.*, nos. 73 and 75; Aristeidou, Έγγραφα, *op.cit.*, I, 189-190 and 260-261.

22. Having eaten and entertained themselves, moreover, they went down to the courtyard and began shooting the crossbow. Afterwards all of them mounted their horses together with the postulant and went to the king, and found him ill. He died, moreover, within a few days in the monastery,[50] on 26 July [in the year] of Christ 1458.[51]

23. Furthermore, once the king was dead Sir Carceran Suarez, the constable of Cyprus, at once ordered a valet to remove the rings from his hand. And he had them sent to Lady Charlotte, and the postulant betook himself forthwith, before anyone else, and took an oath before the lady queen to live and die in line with her every command. All the knights and liegemen came after him and took an oath according to custom. Afterwards they brought down the king and had him buried within the same monastery. Once they had buried him, moreover, all the knights rode away and kept the postulant company, for him to go to the archbishopric.

And venturing forth from the castle the constable Sir Carceran Suarez, who exercised power within the citadel, would not let him pass, but had him dismount and had him conducted upstairs to the chamber where he slept, and gave orders for a splendid dinner to be readied, so that he could have dinner and sleep in his bed. Besides, he (i.e. the postulant) kept in his company those whom he considered suitable, his uncle Marcius, Sir John de Verni, Perrin d'Hughues, John Attar and George Boustron. The postulant, moreover, did not have any dinner on account of the great worry that came over him, and Perrin d'Hughes was on the point of killing him, had the postulant dined.

In addition his uncle had an evil premonition and told him to watch out. At daybreak, moreover, the constable gave orders for arrangements to be made for them to have lunch. And so indeed it came to pass. Furthermore, some of them ventured out and went to the postulant's mother, giving her to understand that the constable wished to poison her son. And his mother on hearing this gave orders for his food to be prepared in the archbishopric, and had it sent to the castle. The constable, moreover, on perceiving that the postulant did not wish to eat any of the food that he had had prepared, but only the food that his mother had readied for him, was greatly affronted and gave him extremely black looks. The postulant, moreover, on observing the black looks that he was giving him, immediately rode away and went to the archbishopric extremely discomfited. Indeed, it was from that day onwards that all evils between them began.

24. It is true that they comforted him from time to time, for Lady Charlotte had stated that she would hold him dearly just as her [late] lord had so held him, and would take care of the kingdom as she had no one more beloved than him. And at the break of day the postulant mounted his horse and went to the lady queen. Furthermore, on

---

[50] This was the Dominican house in Nicosia. See Mas Latrie, 'Documents nouveaux', *op.cit.*, p. 390.

[51] The anonymous 15th century Italian chronicle (Grivaud, 'Une petite chronique', *op.cit.*, pp. 335 and 338) and Bustron, 'Chronique', *op.cit.*, p. 384 give the same date.

seeing him she paid him considerable attention and said to him: 'We must arm our galley so as to send it to the lords of the West, to convey greetings to them and to inform them of the death of our good lord, and as regards this I have no-one closer than you in my affairs. I want you, moreover, to attend somewhat to the arming of the galley'.

The postulant, having listened to her instructions, intended to act in accordance with her wishes, and going to the archbishopric he had a bench set up [proclaiming]: 'Whoever so wishes can receive a wage to go to the galley!' And the people flocked to the archbishopric forthwith, in order to receive the wages. Besides, had they allowed him, he would have armed it within five or six days. But the constable, Hector of Chivides and Tristan de Gibelet,[52] who all hated the postulant, on seeing that the people of Nicosia loved him greatly had the bench taken away at once from the postulant's courtyard. The postulant, seeing this, did not wish to show any indication of knowing that those who hated him had once again begun causing trouble, and he pretended outwardly that he cared little about it. He used to go every morning, moreover, to [the cathedral of] the Holy Wisdom and listen to the service, and afterwards would mount his horse and go to the queen. Furthermore, the queen showed great affection towards him.

25. Besides, on seeing the good disposition that the queen showed him, they resolved to implement a plan with regard to the queen so as not to let him come to the court. And all of them, great and small, assembled in [the church of] St Dominic[53], Sir Carceran Suarez, Sir Bernard Rousset, the admiral who was [also] the constable's nephew, Sir Odet de l'Ingles, the chamberlain, Sir Hector de Chivides, Tristan de Gibelet, Sir Thomas Pardus who was the illegitimate son of a *marrano*,[54] Sir Francis Montolif and Master Peter Brion, the doctor, and Sir Thomas Gurri. These were the ones who stirred up the rest, whom I shall not name. They, moreover, came together and sat in council, and they decreed amongst themselves that 'They should no longer allow the postulant to come to the citadel with any man of his own, but only by himself!'

Furthermore, the postulant, not knowing this, got on his horse and went to the queen, and as soon as he had reached the door of the count of Jaffa Sir Thomas Pardus approached and gave him orders on behalf of the queen and of the lords who happened

---

[52] The Gibelets (*alias* Jubail) were a Latin noble family first attested in Cyprus in the early 13th century. See Hill, *op.cit.*, II, 48, 97, 111 note 5, 105, 112, 114, 123 and note 2, 124, 126, 241, 255 note 2, 262, 364, 366, 397, III, 549, 562, 598, 664, 688, 739-742, 746, 823, 1067, 1069 and 1070 note 4; Richard, *Remembrances, op.cit.*, nos. 10 note 1, 150 note 1, 121 note 1, 197 note 1 and 199-200; Edbury, *Kingdom, op.cit.*, pp. 18-19, 31, 51-52 and note 48, 55 and note 61, 64, 66-67 and note 100,105, 114 note 52, 173, 175, 189, 192, 205; Coureas, *Latin Church, op.cit.*, pp. 20, 38, 45, 58, 66, 68, 71, 73-76, 112-113, 116-117, 218, 236-237 and 239; Coureas and Schabel, *Cartulary, op.cit.*, nos. 41, 45-46, 53-55, 59-62, 109 and 130.

[53] For a description of this church, attached to the Dominican monastery and demolished in 1567 by the Venetians, see Stephen de Lusignan, *Description, op.cit.*, fol. 31v, 63v and 64.

[54] A *marrano* was a Jewish convert to Christianity originating from Spain.

to be in her confidence that no servant of his was to venture to enter the citadel, and to enter alone should he himself wish to enter. The postulant, on hearing this and not knowing anything, remained greatly distressed and returned to the archbishopric extremely dispirited, wishing moreover for the bell at the archbishopric to sound the alarm, so that the clergymen should congregate.

Had he indeed done so, a great commotion would have ensued. Being prudent, however, [and] to realize his aim in a better manner, he summoned Sir Anthony Silouan, the vicar, and sent him to the queen, so as to recommend him and to ask her whether the affront which the knights had administered to him today was perhaps on her orders. At his request, moreover, he went to the queen and spoke to her in the manner the postulant had instructed him. And the queen replied and said to him: 'Convey greetings to him on my behalf! Tell him in addition that the manifestation of my counsel is good, and so it seems to me too!' The vicar returned on hearing this and told it to the postulant. Furthermore, the postulant was greatly upset on hearing the queen's reply, and sought solace by himself in the fact that the message did not originate from the queen, reckoning that she would once again summon him to go to her. Yet his enemies knew how to do this much, insofar as they did not let her summon him to go to her.

26. Besides, after a few days had passed orders were given for the queen to be crowned. On decreeing the coronation they took her out of the citadel and brought her to the court where her father had ruled, to the royal court, the houses of which belonged to Richard de la Baume, and decreed 'Let the knights go to the citadel to keep the queen company, so that she may go to the court!' They did not, moreover, notify the postulant for him to go. Furthermore, with all of them assembled in the citadel, once it became dark they took the queen out and brought her to the court until the forty days following her father's [death] had passed. And on the passage of these forty days they gave orders for her to be crowned.

27. Besides, the postulant was greatly pleased on learning this, expecting, as head of the church, that they would summon him as well to go to her coronation. On Saturday, moreover, which was the eve of when she was about to be crowned, Sir Paul Chappe[55] arrived on behalf of the queen and said to the postulant: 'The lady queen sends you greetings and is coming tomorrow to [the cathedral of] the Holy Wisdom in order to be crowned. Her orders, moreover, are that "you are not to venture forth from your court, neither you nor your servants!" She also instructs you: "You are to summon the one who is in charge and are to order him to conduct the church [service] in the proper manner!" This, furthermore, is her behest'.

---

[55] An old Latin noble family first attested in Cyprus in the early 13th century. See Hill, II, 86 and note 4, III, 499, 524, 549, 671-672 and 674; Rudt de Collenberg, 'Les dispenses matrimoniales', *op.cit.*, pp 28, 34-35, 41-42, 50, 60 no. 19, 62 nos. 21-22, 64 nos. 32 and 41 and 68 nu. 61; Richard, *Remembrances, op.cit.*, nos. 149 note 2, 164 note 3, 170 and note 1, Coureas, *Latin Church, op.cit.*, pp. 44-45; Coureas and Schabel, *Cartulary, op.cit.*, no. 40.

[56] Dawkins, *Boustronios, op.cit.*, §27 has forty miles, but all the mss. have six. See Kehayioglou, *Διήγησις, op.cit.*, pp. 56-57.

And on hearing the order Sir Paul Chappes had given him, he said to him: 'I have heard the decree of our ladyship the queen, and commend me to her ladyship! Furthermore, tell her ladyship as regards the command that her ladyship has given me not to be present at her coronation, that I shall not depart from my home, neither I nor my servants! If, moreover, she so orders I shall go up to six miles[56] from the city!"

28. On Sunday morning, moreover, all the knights and all the common people conducted the queen to [the cathedral of] the Holy Wisdom. And she was crowned, and great rejoicing took place.[57] Besides, when the queen turned to go to the court her horse was frightened at the entrance of the doorway and the crown fell from her head, and all considered it to be a bad omen.

29. Let us now turn to the affairs of the postulant, whom those hating him worked against on a daily basis. He was, moreover, unable to tolerate this, and was concerned to do whatever he could. Furthermore, at the house of the postulant were Rizzo de Marino,[58] who was a Sicilian, Nicholas de Morabit[59] who was also a Sicilian, his uncle Marcius, Peter d' Hughet and many others. They, moreover, suggested to the postulant that they should go one night to the queen's court and kill the constable as well as the remainder who happened to be at the court. And so indeed it came to pass. He sent for and brought those who seemed suitable to him, revealed his plans and told them everything given by way of orders.

30. And on 15 December [in the year] of Christ 1458, in the fifth hour of the night, he took 85 men, all armed, and they set forth and entered [the church of] St Constantine,[60] next to [the house of] Sir Thomas de Verni. Furthermore, he gave Rizzo 25 men and told him to go from the far side of the royal court. In addition, he gave them an order to jump over from that side, while he too was to jump along with the remainder from the main entrance, so as to apprehend there those whom he had in mind.

---

[57] The coronation took place on 15 October. See Hill, *op.cit.*, III, 549 and note 3.

[58] On this prominent supporter of the postulant, later King James II, see Florio Bustron, 'Chronique', *op.cit.*, p. 418; Mas Latrie, *Histoire, op.cit.*, III, 391-392, 419-420, 431 and 433-435; Hill, *op.cit.*, III, 550 and note 2, 552 note 2, 559-560, 566, 591 note 3, 606-607, 652, 664, 666, 668, 672-673, 679, 684-685, 687-689, 711 and note 4, 739-742 and 823; Richard, *Remembrances, op.cit.*, nos. 148 and note 1, 149-151, 154-156, 166-169, 170 note 1, 181 note 1 and 185.

[59] On this supporter of the postulant see Mas Latrie, *Histoire, op.cit.*, III, 181, 251 and 272; Hill, *op.cit.*, III, 550, 552 and note 1, 559-560, 562 and note 1, 573 note 2, 591, 678-679 and 679 note 2; Richard, *Remembrances, op.cit.*, nos. 78 note 1, 146 and note 1, 147, 148, 155, 171, 173, 175, 177 and 184.

[60] This is probably the same as the Greek church of St Constantine mentioned in the will of Lord John of le Roi, viscount of Nicosia, which was drawn up on 13 February 1391. The will mentions houses adjoining the church that were to be maintained on a lifetime basis by the *turcopolier* John de Brie and his wife Philippa de Verni should her husband pre-decease her, and the de Verni family may have acquired these houses subsequently. See Coureas and Schabel, *Cartulary, op.cit.*, no. 112.

Indeed, had this plan been put into effect, a great evil would have ensued, for there was a great company in the court looking after the queen. There were Sir Carceran Suarez, Bernard Rousset, Sir Anton d'Eccles, Tristan de Gibelet, Hector de Chivides and another Catalan constable, Garcia de Navarre[61], as well as numerous others. And God thwarted it, for Peter d'Hughet remained in the archbishopric pretending to be ill, and on seeing that the postulant had taken his men and departed he straightaway leapt down from the archbishopric and went to the house of Master Pierre <Brion>[62], the doctor, telling him everything that the postulant had ordered. On hearing this, moreover, he (i.e. the doctor) sent word to the court at once and made it known.

Furthermore, as the postulant was venturing forth his mother stayed in the archbishopric together with Brother William, and they were sitting on the stairway. Besides, once Brother William observed that Peter was absent from his bedchamber, it crossed his mind that he had gone to make the affair known, and Brother William went at once, found the postulant and informed him of this. Furthermore, they heard a disturbance at the court and they secured the doors. And they (i.e. the postulant's followers) sensed that they had got wind of them, and the postulant returned at once with his followers to the archbishopric.

At daybreak, moreover, Phanes the queen's servant came to the house of George Bustron and said to him: 'Those were fine works which the postulant got up to last night! He wanted to enter the queen's court so as to kill her, and the queen has given orders for him to come down and give an explanation before the High Court'. Furthermore, he implored Bustron to keep it secret.

31. And on hearing it Bustron immediately went and told the postulant. On hearing this, moreover, he took Bustron and went to Nicholas, the Greek bishop,[63] and bringing him with him to the archbishopric detained him and all the clergymen with him. And he remained in the archbishopric to see how the affair would conclude.

32. Furthermore, on the 18 December the queen sent for Sir Peter Pelestrine, Sir Pago

---

[61] The mss. **B** and **M** both have 'Sir John de Navarre' but Garcia de Navarre is mentioned again towards the end of the chronicle. See Kehayioglou, Διήγησις, *op.cit.*, p. 59, line 10 of both mss. and pp. 242-243 line 3 of all mss.

[62] The words in brackets < > are from mss. **B** and **M**. See *Ibid.*, p. 59, ms. **B** line 14 and ms. **M** line 14.

[63] The 1223 agreement stated that the Greek bishops had to reside in the dioceses assigned to them, but the *Bulla Cypria* of 1260 allowed the Greek bishop of Solea within the Latin diocese of Nicosia to reside either in Solea or at the church of St Barnabas in Nicosia, although by the later 15th century Greek and other non-Latin bishops throughout Cyprus had usurped the powers of the Latin diocesans in Nicosia and the other cities, as Pope Sixtus IV observed in a letter of 1472. See Coureas and Schabel, *Cartulary, op.cit.*, nos. 78 and 94-95. For Bishop Nicholas see also Florio Bustron, 'Chronique', *op.cit.*, p. 388; Stephen de Lusignan, *Chorograffia, op.cit.*, § 374 pp. 87 and 206, § 426 pp. 97-98 and 216-217; *idem., Description, op.cit.*, folios 164b and 183.

Croc and Sir Nicholas Salah,[64] a chancellor, and they went to the postulant so as to seize him on the spot.

33. And on their way they told the postulant that which they had been ordered to do by the queen. He, moreover, replied: 'From that which you say to me, that I went to her ladyship's court to kill her, no-one shall ever prove that I sought to do such a thing and [commit] such treason'. And the knights on hearing this turned back and told the queen this, just as the postulant had told it to them. Once the queen and the knights had heard his reply, they immediately sat in council over what seemed right to them regarding the queen's summons for the postulant. And it seemed fit to them to send [word] for him to be arrested and brought before her ladyship. Besides, without making any deliberation both great and small took their weapons in order to go and arrest him, both him and his servants. On learning of this, moreover, the postulant gathered together all his ecclesiastical followers and stood fast. And they were all disposed to die for the postulant.

34. Furthermore, they (i.e. those close to the queen) considered George Bustron to be suspect because he was a servant of the postulant. The queen, moreover, gave orders and they wrote him a letter, stating: 'As one who is enfeoffed, he must come at once before the presence of her ladyship the queen! Otherwise he shall be deemed a traitor'. And on beholding the letter of the queen he took it and showed it to the postulant. The postulant, moreover, on seeing it said to him: 'Get ready to go! But simply consider how to respond! Besides, you know the cause of this'.

In addition, Bustron went off to his house and he summoned Sir Tristan de Gibelet and the admiral Sir Bernard Rousset, and they conducted Bustron amid great lamentations to the citadel and brought him into the presence of the queen. She, moreover, at once ordered the count, Sir James of Fleury[65] 'to take the abovementioned George and to ask him about the postulant's affairs, and what he is thinking of doing!' And he (i.e. George Bustron) told him: 'Lord, I inform your lordship [as follows]: His plan is that he has people assembled, other than his servants, because he has found out that they wish to go and arrest him, according to the orders of the lords and her ladyship the queen, and he is resolved to sound the alarm bell of the archbishopric and to die rather than to be arrested, and, should it be her command for him to appear before her with his retainers, he is prepared'. The queen then gave the order: 'Let everyone disarm!' by proclamation.

Furthermore, the postulant on learning of this likewise dismissed all his men. And then it seemed right to the queen and her counsel to summon the *baiulo* of the

---

[64] Like the Gurri, the Salah (*alias* Salah) were a prominent family of 'White Genoese' originating from Syria. See Makhairas, *Recital, op.cit.*, I, 354-355 § 375, II, 156 § 375; Florio Bustron, 'Chronique', *op.cit.*, p. 388; Richard, *Documents, op.cit.*, pp. 80, 128, 134-135, 141-142, 145, 147 and 150-153; Hill, *op.cit.*, III, 551, 648 and 650; Richard, *Remembrances, op.cit.*, nos. 1 note 4, 37 and note 2, 137, 195, 217-218 and 227.

[65] The titular count of Jaffa and a prominent supporter of Queen Charlotte, regarding whom see Richard, *Documents, op.cit.*, pp. 123-124, 126-131, 140-143, 146-147, 149-151 and 154-155; Hill, *op.cit.*, III, 533, 562, 580 and 589;

Venetians, Sir Peter Ramon, as well as Sir Peter Pelestrine and Sir Pago Croc, and they set off on behalf of the queen and said to him: 'Her ladyship the queen sends you greetings, and she has sent us to accompany your lordship, for you to come to the court'. He forthwith rode forth and appeared before the queen. In addition, they[66] sent Balian de Fresenges[67] to go in secret to the archbishopric with many men: 'And let them take from him whatever is there!' [he said].

On seeing this the valets who had remained in the house all departed. They (i.e. Fresenges' men), moreover, made away with whatever the postulant's house contained, because they had kept him at the court for a considerable length of time. Therefore they took whatever it held, but they did not remember to take his horses. On the postulant's entrance into the presence of the queen she spoke to him together with her counsel and then they dismissed him. He came by himself to the archbishopric and on dismounting went upstairs and discovered his house to have been plundered. He was, moreover, alone, because all the servants had left.

Furthermore, as soon as they had learnt that he had arrived, they all gathered together at once. And on seeing them he began to explain matters as they had come to pass. Listening to him all of them gave him comfort, and the queen gave him orders not to depart from his house until she should so command him. He acted, moreover, in line with her order and remained at home. And he made light of this and did not brood over it.

35. Besides, during those days there happened to be a lad named Kaloyeros,[68] who was a serf from Tremithoussa whom Sir Nicholas de la Tour[69] had emancipated. Furthermore, he remained as a servant of the postulant administering his cellar, and he had the whole household under his supervision. In secret, moreover, he schemed great acts of treason against the postulant and said many things to the knights regarding what he had in mind and what he was planning to do. And listening to the words of this lad the knights believed him and issued an order for persons to go to the archbishopric one night and to capture him (i.e. the postulant) dead or alive. Such, moreover, was their decision. Furthermore, on learning of this Balian de Fresenge went one night to the back of the archbishopric, and ascending it he informed the postulant.

---

[66] Ms. **A** has 'he' but mss. **B** and **M** both have 'they' which is correct in this context. See Kehayioglou, Διήγησις, op.cit., p. 65, ms. **B** line 13 and ms. **M** line 14.

[67] He is mentioned in Florio Bustron, 'Chronique', op.cit., pp. 389, 440 and 444 and was possibly related to James Fresenges, on whom see Richard, Documents, op.cit., p. 83 and note 11, 90-91 and 100; On Simon Fresenges, another possible relation to whom King James II awarded the casale of Cormia, see Florio Bustron, 'Chronique', op.cit., p. 420; Mas Latrie, Histoire, op.cit., II, 530; Stephen de Lusignan, Description, op.cit., p. 83 includes the Fresenges among the noble families of Cyprus.

[68] Florio Bustron, 'Chronique', op.cit., pp.389-390 likewise recounts Kaloyeros' nefarious schemes against the postulant.

[69] He is mentioned as a witness in a diploma of King John II of April 1441, in which the King promised James of Fleury that the casalia pertaining to his late wife would not revert to the royal domain, while Simon de la Tour, a possible relation, was buried in Nicosia where his tomb survives. See Richard, Documents, op.cit., pp. 148-150 and p. 150 note 1.

36. And the postulant on hearing this immediately placed one of his valets outside the door with a horse,[70] and he ordered him to go to [the church of] St George of Aglandja[71] so as to await him there. Besides, as soon as night fell the above mentioned Kaloyeros went to Carceran Suarez, the constable, and said to him: 'Now is the time if you wish to capture the postulant, and come at the fourth hour of the night!' Furthermore, the postulant at the second hour of the night took Brother William, his uncle Marcius, John de Verni, Nicholas Morabit, Rizzo de Marino and Nassar Hous[72], and dropping themselves down from the Armenian quarter they went to St George of Aglandja and found the valet. And the postulant rode out with John de Verni on horseback behind him, while the others went on foot[73]. And they went on to Salines, and on finding the caravel of Nicolo Galimberto[74] they went on board.

37. In line with the directions that the lad Kaloyeros had given them great and small sallied forth and went to the archbishopric to apprehend the postulant. And in the course of their venture they entered the chamber where he used to sleep and they cut the mosquito net <and the clothes, reckoning him to be asleep>[75] to pieces, and uncovering the bed they did not find him. Furthermore, they searched all the houses as well as inside the cistern, and they started a fire. The one who stated the fire, moreover, was James of Emesa[76]. Realizing that they were unable to find either him or his companions they returned greatly embittered.

Besides, at the break of day they left the gates of the city secured, reckoning him to be within the city. Furthermore, much later fishermen came from Salines and finding the gates secured asked: 'What is the reason?' And they were told: 'It is on account of the postulant'. And they said to them: 'We saw him in Salines and he went

---

[70] Mss **B** and **M** both have 'horses'. See Kehayioglou, Διήγησις, op.cit., p. 67 and line 19 of both mss.

[71] This locality near Nicosia was on the road to Salines (mod. Larnaca), the postulant's destination. The unidentified church of St George is perhaps St George of the Sataliotes or St George tou Colocasy. See 'Chronique de Strambaldi', in Chroniques d'Amadi et de Strambaldi, ed. R. de Mas Latrie, 2 vols. (Paris, 1891-1893), II, 254; Richard, Remembrances, op.cit., no. 195 and note 20.

[72] On this Mamluk and the possible etymologies of his name see Hill, op.cit., III, 552 note 1, 556 and 564.

[73] Mss **B** and **M** both state that all rode on horseback. See Kehayioglou, Διήγησις, op.cit., p. 69 line 8 of both mss. as well as p. 67 line 19 of both mss., which refers to horses in the plural. All of them must have completed the second leg of the journey, the 50 odd km from Aglanja to Salines, on horseback

[74] Hill, op.cit., III, 552 note 4 plausibly suggests that he is identical to the Venetian Galimberto mentioned below in §§ 190 and 244. Between 1464 and 1468 King James II granted him the casale of Polemidia in the Limassol district and the lands of St John, for which see Florio Bustron, 'Chronique', op.cit., p. 419.

[75] The words in brackets < > are from mss. **B** and **M**. See Kehayioglou, Διήγησις, op.cit., p. 69, ms. **B** line 13 and ms. **M** lines 12-13.

[76] Emesa (mod. Hims) is a town in Syria. Numerous Syrian Christians settled in Cyprus during the Lusignan and subsequent periods. See J. Richard, 'Le peuplement latin et syrien en Chypre au XIIIe siècle', in Croises, missionnaires et voyageurs, VII (London, 1983), 166-173.

on board the caravel of Galimberto'. On hearing this, moreover, they were extremely displeased. Besides, it did not cross their minds that he was going to Syria[77], but they thought instead that he was going to fall upon King Louis.

38. Furthermore, following the postulant's departure from Cyprus, a few days later a merchant ship arrived from Syria and stated that: 'The postulant went to Cairo and is negotiating the seizure of the kingdom of Cyprus, the sultan has been told that he is the king's son and many are of the opinion that he shall take it'.

39. And on learning this news in Cyprus,[78] they were agitated and began to man Kerynia and the remaining castles. Within a few days, moreover, another merchant ship arrived from Syria, which had come from Cairo. And they said that: 'they had seen the postulant in Cairo. Furthermore, he is preparing to take the kingdom of Cyprus and Flatro, an emir who happens to be Cypriot,[79] is placing obstacles in his path'. Besides, it seemed right to the queen and her counsel on hearing these tidings to send an emissary to Cairo, but part of her counsel said that they should wait in order to obtain a fuller picture. And they remained in a state of extreme anxiety.

40. In addition, in the year of Christ 1459 the emissaries from Savoy whom King John had summoned for the marriage of Charlotte arrived in Cyprus, and they brought King Louis[80], the lord of Aix,[81] Monsignor de Lornes and numerous Savoyards. On their arrival in Nicosia, moreover, they accorded them great honour and within a few days her ladyship the queen was married to the above-mentioned King Louis in [the cathedral of] the Holy Wisdom.[82]

---

[77] In medieval Cypriot usage 'Syria' referred to all the lands subject to the Mamluk sultans, including Palestine and Egypt.

[78] Mss. **B** and **M** both have 'and on learning the news in Nicosia (την χώραν)'. Sec Kehayioglou, *Διήγησις, op.cit.*, p. 71 line 11 of both mss.

[79] This emir may have been John Flatro, who had welcomed and served the Mamluk invaders entering Nicosia in 1426, or one of his descendants. See Hill, *op.cit.*, II, 484 and note 1. The Flatro were a French family first mentioned in Cyprus in 1350, rising to prominence in the 15th century, and surviving the Ottoman conquest of 1570. See Florio Bustron, 'Chronique', *op.cit.*, p. 419; Makhairas, *Recital, op.cit.*, I, § 693; W. Rudt de Collenberg, 'Les graces papales autres que les dispenses matrimoniales accordées à Chypre de 1305 à 1378', *EKEE*, VIII (1978), 229; *idem.*, 'Familles chypriotes', *op.cit.*, pp. 9-24; Richard, *Remembrances, op.cit.*, nos. 123 and note 4, 175 note 10 and 205. For the Greek monastery in Nicosia named after them see Stephen de Lusignan, *Description, op.cit.*, fol. 31b.

[80] Mss **B** and **M** *add.* 'his nephew'. See Kehayioglou, *Διήγησις, op.cit.*, p. 73, **B** line 2 and **M** line 3.

[81] He is called Ουντάν in all the mss. and Ουντάς further below in mss. **A** and **B**, for which see *ibid.*, pp. 72-73. This name is a corruption of the French 'le seigneur d'Aix', on which see M. Pinson, 'Observations sur la transcription des mots français et italiens dans la chronique de George Boustron', in *ΠΠΔΚΣ*, 3 vols. (Nicosia, 1971-1973), II, 216.

[82] George Boustronios and Florio Bustron, 'Chronique', p. 392 do not give exact dates for Louis of Savoy's arrival in Cyprus or his marriage to Queen Charlotte and do not mention his coronation as king-consort, but the anonymous 15th century Italian chronicle (Grivaud, 'Une petite chronique', *op.cit.*, pp. 334-335 and 338) dates his arrival to 1 October 1459, his marriage to 4 October, and his coronation to 7 October.

41. Besides, after several days they sat in council and gave an order for emissaries to be sent to the sultan. And they appointed the lord of Aix, Monsignor de Lornes and Sir Mounat. Furthermore, they went to Cairo taking many presents and on coming into the presence of the sultan they conveyed the news according to their instructions and returned to the place where they were resident. The sultan, moreover, showed himself well disposed towards them. Besides, a great plague raged in Cairo and the emissaries whom they had sent from Cyprus died on account of the numerous transgressions they had committed in Cyprus.[83] And on their death everything collapsed. Sir John de Verni also died, as well as a Rhodian youth from among the postulant's followers. Furthermore, on the news reaching Cyprus they were greatly displeased and after the passage of a few days they sat in council over whether to send another emissary, and they appointed Peter Podocataro.[84]

On going to Cairo, moreover, he presented himself before the sultan and also presented the gifts, conveying the message in accordance with his instructions, and once he had conveyed the message he went to the place where he was resident. And he approached the lords forthwith, bearing presents. Furthermore, all of them desired Lady Charlotte together with her husband to be the lords of Cyprus, as the rightful heirs of the kingdom. Besides, in line with custom they ordered the robe[85] so as to send it to the queen.

On learning of this, moreover, the postulant did not know what to do, and he called for Brother William and told him about it. And he (i.e. Brother William) told him: 'Place your hopes in God and do not be afraid, for there is no other king of Cyprus besides you! And sleep without worry and let me arrange things!' At night he

---

[83] Egypt and Syria suffered from recurring outbreaks of the bubonic plague throughout the second half of the 14th and the whole of the 15th centuries, on which see E. Ashtor, *A Social and Economic History of the Near East in the Middle Ages* (London, 1976), pp. 301-302. George Boustronios' attribution of the emissaries' death to their own transgressions vividly illustrates his partiality to the postulant, the future King James II of Cyprus.

[84] George Boustronios and Florio Bustron do not mention that John Dolfin, the Hospitaller commander of Nisyros, went with him, and that the Hospitaller Grand Master James de Milly sent him at the request of Queen Charlotte and her supporters, for which see Hill, *op.cit.*, III, 555-556 and 556 note 1. Peter Podocataro later supported James. See Florio Bustron, 'Chronique', *op.cit.*, pp. 392-393 and 420; Stephen de Lusignan, *Description, op.cit.*, p. 169; Richard, *Documents, op.cit.*, p. 78 note 10 and p. 79 note 11; *idem., Remembrances, op.cit.*, nos. 197, 199-200. The Podocataro were among the few Greek families ennobled under the Lusignans. See Mas Latrie, *Histoire*, III, 320 and 810; *idem.*, 'Histoire des archevêques', pp. 320-324; Makhairas, *Recital, op.cit.*, § 661 and 678; Hill, *op.cit.*, III, 469, 474, 489, 504 note 3, 518, 522, 524 note 4, 555-556, 559, 561, 564, 575, 577-578, 603, 676-678, 779 note 2, 841, 971 note 4, 984, 1004 note 4 and 1096; Also W. Rudt de Collenberg, 'Les premiers Podocataro: Recherches basées sur le testament de Hughes (1452)', Θησαυρίσματα XXIII (Venice, 1993), 130-182; Arbel, 'Cypriot Nobility ', *op.cit.*, pp. 187 and 189-190, and esp. note 95.

[85] The Mamluks conferred robes of honour as a mark of vassalage. See P.M. Holt, *The Age of the Crusades: The Islamic Near East from the Eleventh Century to 1517* (London, 1986), pp.142, 186 and 188-189; A.D. Stewart, *The Armenian Kingdom and the Mamluks: War and Diplomacy during the Reigns of Hetum II (1289-1317)* (Leiden, 2001), p. 72.

said goodbye to the postulant and took Nassar Hous with him, because he knew the language, and Brother William negotiated all night with the emirs in the course of his peregrinations and accomplished what he wanted. Furthermore, when dawn came he came to the postulant and said to him: 'Is this how you are sitting? Know that the queen's emissary is now on his way to the sultan, for them to give him his robe and the queen's robe, so as to go to Cyprus! For this reason you too must betake yourself to the sultan! And we shall see what will come to pass'.

42. And the postulant at once mounted his horse and went to the sultan. He also found the queen's emissary. Furthermore, orders were issued for him to be given the robe, with instructions that he should come to Cyprus. In addition, they brought the queen's robe and that of the emissary and as they took the robe in order to put it on the emissary suddenly the Mamluks all with one voice [shouted] 'Long live King James!' and snatching the robe put it on the postulant. Furthermore, they also placed the emissaries under his authority, as well as the robes of both the first and the subscquent emissaries, the emissary from Rhodes[86] and all the Savoyards. And the fleet was assembled forthwith and they conducted him to Cyprus. King Louis and the queen, moreover, went to Kerynia as soon as they learnt of this, and the capital was emptied, with some going to Famagusta and othcrs to the villages.[87]

43. Besides, on the 18 September [in the year] of Christ 1460 the fleet conducting the postulant appeared off Famagusta, disembarking <at Ayia Napa>[88] at Constantia, 80 ships great and small, the grand *dawadar*,[89] admiral of the fleet, along with numerous

---

[86] This was John Dolphin, the Hospitaller Commander of Nisyros, whom the Hospitaller Grand Master James de Milly had sent to Egypt at Queen Charlotte's request so as to support her claims, to effect an understanding between King Louis and the postulant if possiblc, and if not to ensure that Hospitaller goods, persons, animals and properties were not harmed in the conflict. He was still being detained in Egypt in June 1461. See Mas Latrie, *Histoire*, *op.cit.*, III, 86 and 96-99.

[87] The chronicler does not date these events, but they probably occurred before April 1460, when the duke of Savoy instructed his envoy Theobald de la Brigue to go to Genoa and seek Genoese assistance against James, who was planning to attack Cyprus with Mamluk aid and expel the Genoese from Famagusta, as indeed came to pass. The Venetian Senate wrote in April to Peter Ramon, the Venetian *baiulo* in Cyprus, instructing him not to interfere in the affairs of the kingdom of Cyprus, and in May to Louis of Savoy's ambassador, informing him that on account of Venice's good relations with the Mamluk sultan weapons could not be sent to Cyprus on board Venetian ships. See *Ibid.*, III, 99-104. In July 1460 Pope Pius II offered plenary indulgences for persons contributing for the defence of Cyprus against the Mamluks and a tithe raised in Savoy for the war against the Ottomans was re-directed to Cyprus. See Hill, *op.cit.*, III, 567 and note 1.

[88] The words in brackets < > are from mss. **B** and **M**. See Kehayioglou, *Διήγησις*, *op.cit.*, p. 77, ms. **B** line 12 and ms. **M** line 14. Constantia is north of Famagusta and Ayia Napa south of it, so it is impossible that they landed at both places. The Hospitaller Grand Master James de Milly stated in his letter of 6 November 1460 to the castellan of Amposta (Mas Latrie, *Histoire*, *op.cit.*, III, 111) that James landed 'near the coast of the town of Famagusta' and Constantia is far closer to Famagusta than Ayia Napa is.

[89] On the functions of this office see Holt, *Near East*, *op.cit.*, p. 222.

emirs, Saracens and foot soldiers.[90] And on the postulant's landing the people came forward and paid obeisance to him as for a king. In addition, he showed a good disposition towards them, and emancipated many of them. He straightaway gave orders to Rizzo and gave him eight Mamluks, so that he might go to Amasaria and to Salines to procure carts for transporting the artillery.

44. Furthermore, as soon as they declared him king <in Cairo>,[91] he had Sir Peter Podocataro bestow a knighthood upon Nicholas de Morabit,[92] and he also had him appointed the viscount of Nicosia, as well as having Rizzo de Marino knighted and made chamberlain of Cyprus. In addition, he awarded Morabit Nissou along with its dependencies, and [awarded] Rizzo Yenagra.[93] And Brother William was appointed archbishop of Nicosia.[94]

He also sent off his uncle Marcius along with many Mamluks, and they went to Sivouri.[95] In the castle, moreover, Sir Thomas Maches was the captain, while most of the constables happened to be outside the castle. Furthermore, had they been within they would not have captured it so quickly. The Saracens were circling it and the constables who happened to be within along with the other men surrendered to the king. There were also many Savoyards inside the castle. The captain surrendered as well, and he requested a safe conduct for his person, his wife and his possessions. As soon as he secured this, moreover, he immediately opened the gates of the castle. And they went in and once they had entered they asked for the Savoyards who were inside. Furthermore, they took them out, as well as the captain and the technicians.

---

[90] Ms. **A** gives the word χαλφούσιδες for the foot soldiers, while mss. **B** and **M** omit the words 'along with … foot soldiers'. Hill, 561 note 5 is unsure of this word's derivation, but rightly doubts Dawkins' suggestion (*Recital, op.cit.*, I, 332 and II, 672 note 3) that it derives from 'caliph', a high official. It probably derives from the Arabic *harāfish*, meaning commoners or craftsmen, as opposed to the aristocratic Mamluk cavalry. See Kehayioglou, Διήγησις, *op.cit.*, p. 497; *The Cambridge History of Egypt*, Vol. 1, *Islamic Egypt 640-1517*, ed. C.F. Petrie (Cambridge, 1998), 528.

[91] The words in brackets < > are from mss. **B** and **M**. See Kehayioglou, Διήγησις, *op.cit.*, p. 79, line 1 in both mss. No formal coronation, which could only take place in the cathedral of the Holy Wisdom in Nicosia, occurred, but some other form of inauguration. See Hill, *op.cit.*, III, 560, notes 2- 4.

[92] *Ibid.*, III, 559 observes that Sir Peter Podocataro was forced to dub Morabit and de Marino because Cypriot feudal custom required that only a baron of the kingdom in the king's presence could confer knighthoods.

[93] Morabit and Rizzo still held their *casalia* in 1468, for which see Richard, *Remembrances, op.cit.*, nos. 148 and 154. The first document states that Nissou was awarded to Morabit on 24 October 1460.

[94] See Mas Latrie, 'Histoire des archevêques', *op.cit.*, pp. 293-297 on his career as archbishop.

[95] On the construction of this fort, also called Castel Franc, under King James I see 'Amadi', *op.cit.*, p. 495; Florio Bustron, 'Chronique', *op.cit.*, pp. 24 (where he states that it had recently began to be ruined) and 352; Enlart, *Gothic Art, op.cit.*, pp. 475-477; Hill, *op.cit.*, III, 446 note 4 on its chronology; J-B de Vaivre, 'Sur les sites des châteaux disparus de Sigouri et de Gastria en Chypre', *Académie des Inscriptions et Belles-Lettres* (Paris, 1998), pp. 1007-1015.

And they left the garrison as they had been, appointing a Venetian captain, Philip de Pezzaro, because this Pezzaro had been a great friend of the postulant when the postulant had been in Cyprus, and after King James went to Syria the queen's advisers had the same Pezzaro incarcerated in Kerynia. He spent many days there, moreover, and they gave him freedom, and he went to Cairo, found King James and accompanied him. And he (i.e. King James) appointed him captain.

45. Besides, on 26 September [in the year] of Christ 1460 the king sent Brother William ahead with 50 Mamluks and foot soldiers to proceed to Nicosia so as to secure the people who had remained in the capital and, if he could, to capture the viscount Hector de Chivides as well. The Saracens, moreover, drew near, and the viscount always had good sentries, and a woman with some bread came from Lefkomiati[96] and said: 'While I was on my way I heard great shouts and blows, and I believe it to be the Saracens'. And the viscount did not believe her and he went down to the Gate[97] with five or six people, and the *muhtasib*.[98] Furthermore, the Saracens appeared shortly, and on beholding them he entered the capital, exited by the Upper Gate[99] and went to Kerynia. The Saracens, moreover, arrested the *muhtasib* along with his son George Hatit, and they wished to kill the *muhtasib*, reckoning him to be the viscount. And [eventually] they released him. In addition, the Saracens entered Nicosia and decreed that the *muhtasib* should retain his position, while also appointing Nicholas Morabit as viscount.

46. King James also entered Nicosia on 26 September [in the year] of Christ 1460, along with some of the Saracens. Besides, the admiral along with the fleet went and stationed themselves at some distance, at St Demetrios,[100] remaining there for three days.

---

[96] Once given by King James I to Hugh de la Baume, constable of Cyprus, later the Turkish Eski Sehir, this now lost village near Nicosia was directly east of it. See 'Amadi', *op.cit.*, p. 494; Florio Bustron, 'Chronique', *op.cit.*, p. 352; Richard, *Documents, op.cit.*, p. 146 and note 7, where he states that in 1385 John of Brie received it as a fief, but he gives no references; *idem.*, *Remembrances, op.cit.*, nos. 41, 79 and note 4, 124; G. Grivaud, *Villages désertés à Chypre (fin XIIe-fin XIXe siècle)*, *MY* III (Nicosia, 1998), pp. 180-181, 190, 197, 262 note 17, 380, 462 and 563(map).

[97] This was the Lower or Customs Gate on the east side of Nicosia, fronting the market. See Leventis, *Nicosia, op.cit.*, pp. 125,148 and 321.

[98] On this court officer (*alias* mathesep) commanding a company of 23 sergeants with police powers, see 'Abregé du livre des assises de la cour des bourgeois', ed. M. le Comte Beugnot, *RHC Lois*, II Paris, 1843), ch. 5-7, pp. 238-241; Edbury, *Kingdom, op.cit.*, p. 194; Holt, *Near East, op.cit.*, pp. 79-80. Under the Venetians this office became elective, for which see Arbel, 'Urban Assemblies', *op.cit.*, II, 212 and note 56.

[99] This was the Gate of St Paraskevi, near the church of that name mentioned above. For a discussion and various refs. See Leventis, *Nicosia, op.cit.*, pp. 145, 173-175 and 358.

[100] One locality of this name, now vanished, appears in 16th century Venetian taxation inventories for the region of Pendayia, and a second one in the Kerynia district, likewise unidentified, appears on a Venetian map of Cyprus of 1538. See Grivaud, *Villages désertées, op.cit.*, pp. 204, 468 and 475.

47. And on 29 September the Saracens and the king moved camp in order to go to Kerynia. The king, moreover, stayed behind so as to enrol those Christians whom he had recruited for a monthly wage. Furthermore, once the Saracens were on the march King Louis assigned men from Kerynia, and they came to Monadi[101] to dig up the roads, so that the Saracens would not be able to proceed, nor indeed their carts where they had the military equipment. And they narrowly missed being fallen upon. Had they (i.e. the Saracens) caught up with them none of them would have come back. For they had posted sentries and so they left. Furthermore, they found three men and killed them, and they assigned the foot soldiers to repair the roads. And the carts together with the fleet proceeded, and they went to Casa Epiphani.[102]

48. In addition, on the last day of September [in the year] of Christ 1460 the king arrived at Kerynia with the Saracens and the Christians, and he set up camp with the Saracens. Besides, three days afterwards the admiral of the fleet went away and set up camp on the side by Kamouza[103] along with the king and the prisoners whom he had brought over from Syria, Podocataro and Brother Christopher.

49. Furthermore, on the arrival of the sultan's fleet in Cyprus King Louis had sent Brother Christopher with presents to the admiral of the fleet, and he gave him the presents, oxen, slaughtered animals, chickens, loaves of bread, sugar and many other things. And as soon as he had presented them he (i.e. the admiral) gave them all to the foot soldiers, and he surrendered the abovementioned Brother Christopher into the power of King James. He, moreover, at once put him in irons and placed him along with the remainder,[104] together with the *luogotenente* de Bressan, Jaume de Geneve, Podocataro and other Savoyards. And he kept them good company.

50. Furthermore, the emir Kun the Circassian[105] set up camp in the royal *casale* and commissioned a cannon[106] that he had brought over from Sivouri, and they dragged it into the barbican. In addition, two emirs set up camp on the side of the Roman Catholic cathedral, and they set up two cannons that covered the side by Kamouza.

---

[101] This was the name of the pass through the Pentadaktylos Mountains. See Hill, *op.cit.*, III, 562.

[102] The present-day village of Kazaphani, located east of Kerynia and north of the Premonstratensian abbey of Bellapais. See Aristeidou, Έγγραφα, *op.cit.*, II, 83-84, 120-123; III, 171-173.

[103] A tower in Kerynia, on which see J.C. Goodwin, *An Historical Toponymy of Cyprus*, 2 vols. (Nicosia, 1976, 1984⁴), I, 461. Its name derives from the Arabic *dzamouz* meaning cow, not from Turkish as Goodwin suggests.

[104] The mss. **B** and **M** omit the rest of this sentence. See Kehayioglou, Διήγησις, *op.cit.*, p. 85, line 4 of both mss.

[105] The Circassians living beyond the eastern shores of the Black Sea were the dominant ethnic group among the Egyptian Mamluks by the late 14th century. See Holt, *Near East, op.cit.*, pp. 105-106, 127-129 and 178.

[106] Hill, *op.cit.*, II, 458 observes that artillery was first used in Cypriot warfare in 1404-1405, with both the Genoese and King Janus of Cyprus purchasing cannon from the Venetians. Holt, *Near East, op.cit.*, p. 193 states that the Mamluks used cannon only in siege warfare, not on the battlefield, and Kerynia provides a case in point.

Another emir, moreover, set up camp on the side of Sperouniou, placing two cannon there. Besides, the king placed a large piece of ordnance on the roof of a Greek church, causing great damage within Kerynia and killing 23 people. Furthermore, the king commissioned a large cannon and a Saracen fashioned it, and he had 500 olive trees[107] and many other trees cut down at Casa Epiphani for that cannon. And [nonetheless] it turned out to be defective.[108]

Subsequently scaling ladders and many siege engines were constructed. Kerynia, moreover, was strongly fortified and possessed considerable artillery, and it was difficult to take. In addition, there was a fine fleet in the harbour of Kerynia, a galley from Rhodes with a fine company of [Hospitaller] brothers, two well-armed galleys belonging to Sor de Naves,[109] Bonesme with his galleys and other ships that happened to be in the harbour. Furthermore, [present were] King Louis and the queen and the following lords: the count of Jaffa, Sir James de Fleury, Sir Morfou de Grenier, count of Rocha,[110] Sir John de Montolif, marshal of Cyprus and lord of Tyre, Sir Peter Pelestrine, Phoebus de Lusignan the lord of Arsuf,[111] Sir Walter de Nores,[112] Dom Pedro Palma,[113] a Portuguese, Sir Hector de Chivides, the admiral of Cyprus Sir Bernard Rousset, Dominic de Gibelet,[114] Sir Odet d'Inglés, Sir Thomas de Verni, the marshal of Jerusalem, Sir Francis de Montolif, Monsignor de Martirez, a knight from Savoy, Monsignor de Suna, Sir Guyot de Nores, Sir Harry Pezarte, Sir Peter Empalau,

---

[107] The mss. **B** and **M** have 'cultivated olive trees'. See Kehayioglou, Διήγησις, op.cit., p. 85, line 14 of both mss.

[108] Dawkins, Boustronios, op.cit., §50 wrongly stated that the cannon itself destroyed 500 olive trees and was then broken up. The trees in question were cut to fuel the furnaces in which the metal used for fashioning cannons was melted. On ordnance technology in Western Asia see K.N. Chaudhuri, Asia before Europe: Economy and Civilisation of the Indian Ocean from the Rise of Islam to 1750 (Cambridge, 1990, 2000⁴), pp. 101-103 and 326-330. On Mamluk difficulties in fashioning artillery see Holt, Near East, op.cit., p. 199; Ashtor, Economic History, op.cit., p. 331

[109] Sor de Naves, a Sicilian, later declared for James II. Florio Bustron, 'Chronique', op.cit., p. 418 states that after 1464 the king granted him the casalia of Lapithos, Vasilia, Kormakiti, Dikomo, Agridia, Koutraphades, Agyia, Lefkara, Stephani and Klepini, and Pissouri, as well as gardens at Kythrea and the impost known as the gabelle at Kerynia; See also Richard, Documents, op.cit., p. 132 note 1; idem., Remembrances, op.cit., nos. 46 and note 1, 151 note 2, 179 and note 4.

[110] He later declared for James and in 1468 was awarded as fiefs the casalia of Louroujina, Aplanda, Alexandretta, Pano Kividhes and Agridia. See Richard, Remembrances, op.cit., nos. 178-179. 'Rouchas' was another name for Edessa, a town in Northern Syria that became, the County of Edessa, one of the Latin states established in the wake of the successful First Crusade of 1099.

[111] He was the illegitimate son of Peter de Lusignan, the titular count of Tripoli. In 1468 King James II awarded Phoebus' son Hugh the villages of Meniko and Aglassica. See Florio Bustron, 'Chronique', op.cit., p. 422; Richard, Remembrances, op.cit., no. 150 and note 1.

[112] Florio Bustron, 'Chronique', op.cit., p. 397 adds Sassons and John de Nores after Walter.

[113] Ibid., p. 397 has Don Pietro de Dalmada.

[114] Ibid., p. 397 adds Tristan de Gibelet after Dominic.

Sir James Melin Croc, Sir Paul Croc, Sir William de Ras, Sir John de Ras,[115] Sir Simon Bragadin,[116] Sir John Bragadin, Sir Antoine de Bois and another knight, the Venetian Sir Andrea Corner, the auditor of Cyprus, all the above being knights. There were also many other burgesses and valets, whom I have not written down.

Besides, on seeing [matters], King Louis and the knights together with the whole company sat to deliberate what decision they should reach over the affair of Kerynia, which appeared to them in the manner that you are about to hear:

51. Firstly, they summoned Sor de Naves and appointed him captain over the men so that they would patrol the circuit of the walls of Kerynia. Secondly they appointed Brother Celli to supervise within the citadel, along with all the [Hospitaller] brothers whom he had in his company.[117] Thirdly they posted every knight and ordered the men to be ready when necessary. Fourthly they assigned the posts: 'Wherever they are needed the most, let every man be found at his post!'

52. Furthermore, when they had set everything in order, they sat in council in order to reach decisions, and it seemed right to all in unanimity to send an emissary outside, to the commander. And they sent Brother Nicholas, the Latin bishop.[118] As he ventured forth, moreover, from the gate of Kerynia, he was taken to the tent of the admiral of the fleet. And he was sitting on a mat with King James beside him. Furthermore, as the bishop entered the tent he fell forward and prostrated himself before the chief emir. Next he greeted the king, saying to him: 'My lord and her ladyship the queen send greetings to your lordship'. And the king thanked them. The bishop, moreover, had received instructions to convey the message to the admiral and to present the gifts as well. And while presenting them he said to him: 'Lord emir and great *dawadar*, my lord commends himself to your lordship and says: "As regards your arrival, you have

---

[115] Both Sir William and his son Sir John de Ras later served under King James II, and are identical with Glimin (Guillaume) and Gioan d'Arras whom Florio Bustron ('Chronique', *op.cit.*, pp. 420 and 422) lists among those receiving fiefs from the king after 1464. He also had both of them made members of the High Court (Mas Latrie, *Histoire, op.cit.*, III, 245-246 and 272).

[116] Florio Bustron, 'Chronique', *op.cit.*, p. 397 omits Sir John de Ras and Sir Simon Bragadin.

[117] Although James had previously spent five months in Rhodes, once he secured Mamluk support the Hospitallers were implacably opposed to him, seeing his victory as strengthening the Mamluks' hold over Cyprus. See A. Luttrell, 'Τα Στρατιωτικά Τάγματα', in Ιστορία της Κύπρου, IV, Μεσαιωνικόν Βασίλειον, Ενετοκρατία, ed. Th. Papadopoullos (Nicosia, 1995), 752 and note 68.

[118] This was Nicolas de Courio, the Dominican Latin bishop of Imbros, or, less likely, titular Latin bishop of Hebron. He became a bishop sometime before 13 September 1458, when the royal court granted him the garden of Faquelatos in Nicosia (J. Richard mistakenly states that 'the king' granted it, but King John II died on 26 July 1458) and died sometime before October 1468 when his will, in which he left 25 gold ducats to the secretary Thomas Petropoulos and various articles to the Dominican house in Nicosia. He is not to be confused with Nicholas the Greek bishop of Nicosia. See Hill, *op.cit.*, III, 616-618; Richard, *Remembrances, op.cit.*, no. 24 and note 1, no. 104 and note 2 and no. 175 and notes 3 and 4.

arrived, and welcome! And as regards the outgoings that our master the sultan expended to have the postulant crowned king and to send him hither, he is welcome!" Should you decree it, I shall convey my message, as I have been instructed'.

And the commander said to him: 'Said that which you are about to say and I shall listen to you!' He said to him: 'O lord, know that Cyprus is a domain of the lord sultan, and we are all his slaves![119] For this reason, if lordship saw fit to listen to things that were improper, and his lordship heard them and spent money fitting out his fleet and sending it to Cyprus so as to take it from those to whom it belongs and who were never at fault with him, and who despite everything are the rightful heirs, and yet on account of words he was given to hear he placed it into the hands of others, [know that] should the sultan perhaps so wish my lord King Louis is prepared to dispatch to your lord every outlay he expended on his armada and everything else'. When he had heard this, he replied to him: 'I have heard everything that you said to me, and it appears to me that you have spoken well. Nonethcless I wish to tell you this. The sultan sent him here to be the overlord. What is to become of him?'

53. The emissary, moreover, responded and said to him: 'In connection with what your lordship says, what shall become ot him, I inform your lordship that while living the lord king his father had him join the church and awarded him the archbishopric, which has an annual revenue of 12,000 ducats. Furthermore, should he perhaps desire it, it will always be his. Besides, should he not wish to be a clergyman let them make him a prince so that he can have a large income from whatever they arrange for him, and let the two brothers remain loving one another. On this being done, moreover, my lord sultan shall be pleased'. The commander having heard this told the emissary to return to his lord and to tell him on his behalf that: 'I have listened to everything and I shall do everything according to what is best'.

And the emissary on hearing the emir's reply bade him farewell and on his return to Kerynia said everything that the emir had told him. On hearing it the knights and as many others were in Kerynia held a session to deliberate what to do over the affairs of the lords, and it seemed right to all of them to take far greater care than what they had hitherto taken. In addition they had no fear other that Kerynia might be taken from the landward side. Many, moreover, were of the opinion that it could be taken only with difficulty: 'For it is all made of rock'. They remained nonetheless in a state of great concern.

54. Furthermore, after eight days had passed since the emissary had come out, they observed that they (i.e. the Mamluks) had taken up their tents and had set a fire, burning all their siege engines and departing like defeated men. Besides, they left behind all the victuals that they had, for a message had come from the admiral of the fleet to the commander of the land forces that: 'Winter has arrived, and a galley along

---

[119] Following the Mamluk invasion of 1426 and the defeat and capture of King Janus at the battle of Khirokitia Cyprus was placed under Mamluk suzerainty. See 'Amadi', *op.cit.*, p. 514; Hill, *op.cit.*, II, 490 and 492; Irwin, 'Οι εισβολές , *op.cit.*, pp. 174-175.

with many landing craft has been shipwrecked, so it is necessary for the fleet to set sail'.[120]

Once the commander of the land forces heard this, he took the fleet away from Kerynia. Once those who were within Kerynia observed that the camp had been lifted and that they had set fire to it, it seemed extremely strange to them, and they reflected: 'Did they perhaps do it to deceive us, and have they set up some ambush?' They remained confined, moreover, in a state of great unease, and none dared to come out of Kerynia. Furthermore, two Muslims who happened to be the children of Christians from Lesbos, who had been captured and made Muslims, deserted from the camp, and entering Kerynia they told them the reason why the host had departed. On ascertaining the truth, moreover, they ventured out and finding many victuals brought them into Kerynia. And they did not dare to venture forth.

55. In addition, once the host had departed from Kerynia, it came to Nicosia and made camp at St Demetrios, remained there until the day after the morrow and then lifted camp so as to leave and cross over (i.e. to Syria).

56. The king on seeing them began to weep, to fall at the Saracens' feet and to implore their commander not to abandon him, to go without securing the kingdom in line with the order he had from the sultan. There was, moreover, no solution, and he (i.e. the commander) said to him: 'As to what you tell me, and as to the fact that the sultan sent us to secure you as king, you speak the truth. But winter is upon us and you have heard that the commander (i.e. of the fleet) has summoned us, and I must follow his order'. The king burst into tears on hearing this, falling at his feet and at those of all the emirs. They, moreover, all rode off together and made their way towards Famagusta so as to cross over. Furthermore, the king remained in Nicosia and was greatly upset with his followers and at a loss regarding what was to come about. And he took counsel with those few whom he had, telling them that: 'I came with the help of God and the sultan to be king of Cyprus, and the commander had taken away the host and I do not know what to do'.

Brother William, moreover, said to him: 'Do not be downhearted! Even though we see that we are all doomed, nonetheless it is necessary for us to save our persons, our honour and our property. Our advice is that you should ride now and go to the fleet, meet up with the commanders and fall at their feet with great entreaties for them to take pity on you and to leave you a commander with 200 Mamluks and the same number of foot soldiers. Besides, if they take pity on you and you do this, we reckon before God that you shall remain master of Cyprus'. Furthermore, he did just as Brother William had told him. And he went away and found the admiral of the fleet and falling at his feet and wept a great deal.[121] The admiral and the whole fleet,

---

[120] King James II maintained in an address of 3 October 1461 brought to Florence by his emissaries that the Mamluk emirs were anxious to depart because they had learnt that Sultan Inal was moribund, and desired to be present at his death in the hope of succeeding him. See Mas Latrie, *Histoire*, op.cit., III, 158.

[121] Florio Bustron, 'Chronique', op.cit., p. 399 states that King James told the admiral that if he did not leave him 200 foot and 200 horse then he too would return to Cairo. Under Sultan Khushkadam (1461-1467) Mamluk reinforcements were apparently sent twice in late 1461, but they went reluctantly and returned quickly. See M. Ziada, 'The Mamluk Conquest of Cyprus in the Fifteenth Century', Pt. II, *Bulletin of the Faculty of Arts*, vol. 2, Pt. 1 (Cairo, 1934), 59-60.

moreover, were extremely sorry for him on seeing him. Besides, the admiral at once called an emir named Janibek, appointing him commander and giving him 200 Mamluks and 200 infantrymen. And the fleet set sail straightaway and departed.

57. Meanwhile King James, bringing the Saracens and the infantrymen with him, came to Nicosia. On his way past Sivouri, moreover, he gave orders and they released all the prisoners whom he had sent there while he had been encamped before Kerynia, Sir Peter Podocataro, Brother Christopher, James de Geneve and many Savoyards, bringing them to Nicosia.

Furthermore, on 7 November [in the year] of Christ 1460 he spent the night with the Saracens at Kalamoulli.[122] At once, moreover, they sounded the alarm bell at [the cathedral of] the Holy Wisdom, so that the soldiers in the king's pay would come forth and appear before him. And on hearing the proclamation and the alarm bell they took up arms immediately and appeared before him.

58. In addition, the king on his way to Famagusta[123] said to Brother William: 'George Bustron is the *chevetain* at Salines. Tell him to bring the serfs and the emancipated peasants, both mounted and on foot, to Nicosia!' Brother William, moreover, acted in accordance with his orders. He sent for and brought all the serfs and the emancipated peasants, 225 of them, with crossbows and bows. Furthermore, they entered Nicosia and going to the archbishopric they found Brother William, and they remained until the morning, and in the morning they went before the king. The king, moreover, appeared well disposed on seeing them. In addition, the king on entering Nicosia kept the Saracens in his company and settled their commander in the citadel, sending the other emir to [the house] of the count of Tripoli, others to the houses of Sir Hugh Soudan,[124] others to the houses of Giovanni Ridolfo, others to the houses of Benedetto Pallavicini, and others to various houses.[125] He himself, moreover, went to the royal court.

59. And on 9 November [in the year] of Christ 1460 the carts with prisoners in them arrived from Sivouri, and they were taking them to the citadel. Furthermore, the king on learning of this at once mounted his horse and turned them back, brought them to the court and had them taken upstairs into a chamber.

Besides, on the same day during the evening the king took the Mamluks and the

---

[122] A place in the diocese of Limassol, renowned because the cross of Tokhni had been thrown there following its theft in 1318. See Makhairas, *Recital, op.cit.*, I, § 67-69. In 1367 it belonged to John le Bufle, and after 1464 James II gave it as a fief to Philip Ceba, the *bailli* of the *secrète*, together with Axilou and Salamiou. See Florio Bustron, 'Chronique', *op.cit.*, p. 421; Richard, *Documents, op.cit.*, p. 84 and note 9.

[123] Mss. **B** and **M** have 'the king having gone to bring the Saracens'. See Kehayioglou, Διήγη-σις, *op.cit.*, p. 99 line 14 of both mss.

[124] A counsellor of King Janus in 1427, he was chamberlain of Cyprus in 1433, an office he was still holding in 1438 and 1442. See Mas Latrie, *Histoire, op.cit.*, III, 18; Richard, *Documents, op.cit.*, pp. 129 note 2, 142 and note 2 and 151.

[125] Ms **M** omits 'and …various houses'. See Kehayioglou, Διήγησις, *op.cit.*, p.101, **M** line 5.

Christians in order to go to Kerynia. And he arrived two hours into the night at Casa Epiphani, remaining there until daybreak. In addition, as soon as he arrived Rizzo took a Mamluk <named Ali>[126] and climbed up into an almond tree, and they kept a look out as to whether people would come out from Kerynia. Furthermore, they relaxed their vigil and began to come out. Besides, Rizzo was watching them and made their departure known, and the Saracens fell upon the hapless villagers and killed them. In addition, in Kamouza they apprehended a good man who was going to grind corn in Lapithos and who bore a sword and a buckler, and they brought him into the presence of the king. He, moreover, knelt down and kissed his knee, saying to him: 'Lord, as regards why I ventured out, I did so that your lordship might apprehend me'. But whatever he had to say, he (i.e. King James) had no mercy, and he gave orders to a black man and had him beheaded.

In addition, on the same day the Saracens apprehended the wife of the priest Phantes from Lapithos along with her two children, the young men, and they put them on camels and brought them to Nicosia, making the children learn Saracen (i.e. Arabic) letters, and in the space of a few days they converted them to Islam. Furthermore, on that day they seized 27 persons <exiting from Kerynia>[127], and after beheading them they brought the heads in sacks to Nicosia. The king, moreover, was not there, [and none were there] other than 100 Saracens. And 600 people subsequently exited from Kerynia and came as far as the royal estate, and their spirits did not sustain them for venturing any further.

60. Besides, on the 20 November [in the year] of Christ Brother William went to the Karpass peninsula and met up with the *bailli* of the Karpass, Sir Alessandro Tarantin,[128] and performing an ambush they killed some Genoese, 35 persons, and Famagustans from [the town of] Famagusta who had ventured out to practise piracy. And Brother William returned to Nicosia.

61. In addition, on 25 November [in the year] of Christ 1460 the above-mentioned Brother William went once again to the Karpass and went to Famagusta. Furthermore, he encountered the Famagustans and killed 40 Famagustans. He had with him, moreover, 100 Saracens, and bringing the Saracens with him he came to Nicosia.

62. Besides, on 6 December Rizzo sallied forth and went to the Karpass, because the *bailli* had sent word to him <by letter>[129] that: 'A Genoese galley has set sail from

---

[126] The words in brackets < > have been added from mss. **B** and **M**. See *ibid.*, p. 101, line 14 in both mss.

[127] The words in brackets < > missing from ms. **A** are taken from mss. **B** and **M**. See *ibid.*, p. 103, line 10 of mss. **B** and **M**.

[128] The *baillis* of the kingdom referred to here were those entrusted with the exploitation of the royal domain. They had scribes to assist them and in the mid-15th century they were found at Morphou, Akhelia, Limassol, Karpass, Lefkara, Pelendri, Lemba and Emba. But their powers, unlike those of the *chevetains*, did not extend beyond the limits of the royal domain and so did not have a public character. See Richard, *Remembrances, op.cit.*, pp. xxii-xxiii.

[129] The words in brackets < > are from mss. **B** and **M**. See Kehayioglou, Διήγησις, *op.cit.*, p. 105 line 6 in both mss.

Famagusta and has gone to raid this area, and on board it has a Genoese skipper whom the king had hired and had in his service, and who left and went to Famagusta'. Going there, moreover, Rizzo apprehended him and despatched him to the king, also sending him the things that he had seized, 25 hundredweight of soap, an abundance of grain and many other things. And as soon as they fetched this skipper to him the king had him sent down to the bridge, and they hanged him by the feet.[130]

In addition, on the 12 December they brought John, the chamberlain's lad, and him too they hanged by his feet.

63. And on 15 December the king sent [for persons] and destroyed the house of Niccolo de Candia, and he took the things stated below, which Stephen Koudouna[131] had in his possession: 250 iron pieces, 80 other broad strips (of iron), 180 other strips,[132] five beds and a large chest, along with the furnishings of the house.

64. Besides, on the same day they broke open the house of Demetrianos, the father of <Sir Peter of >[133] Petra, taking from him five tables with worked tufts of animal hair, 125 unrefined camlets,[134] 20 sacks of Marrakech hair, one sack of refined hair, one sack of spun hair and movables: Those they took from him [were] 500 valued ducats, one sack of cochineal, silks and linens worth an additional 500 ducats.[135]

On the same day they broke open the house of Nicholas Halab[136] and took the following, placing them in trust in the possession of Sir André Denes: one sack of

---

[130] Florio Bustron, 'Chronique', *op.cit.*, pp. 400-401 also narrates the developments in the Karpass, and states that the hanging took place 'al ponte della piazza'. Cypriot chroniclers mention this bridge, known variously as the bridge of the pillory, of the *Berlina*, of the prisons or of the cotton market, more than any other bridge in Nicosia. For references see Leventis, *Nicosia, op.cit.*, pp. 384-385.

[131] On his role as a popular leader in Nicosia under Queen Catherine, see below.

[132] The large quantity of metal mentioned suggests that Nicolo di Candia possessed a warehouse. On the storage of metals in such depots, called *fondacos* in the later Middle Ages, see Olivia Remie Constable, *Housing the Stranger in the Mediterranean World: Lodging, Trade and Travel in Late Antiquity and the Middle Ages* (Cambridge, 2003), pp. 206, 211-212 and 334-337.

[133] The words in brackets < > are from mss. **B** and **M**. See Kehayioglou, Διήγησις, *op.cit.*, lines 1-2 of both mss. On 9 July 1468 King James II granted a manor house at Petra, now part of the royal estate, to Sir Anthony de Lorsa, who had been entrusted with the upkeep of a lighthouse in the area. See Richard, *Remembrances, op.cit.*, no. 38.

[134] On the history and importance of camlet production in medieval Cyprus see D. Jacoby, 'Το εμπόριο και η οικονομία της Κύπρου', in Ιστορία της Κύπρου, IV, Μεσαιωνικόν Βασίλειον, Ενετοκρατία, ed. Th. Papadopoullos (Nicosia, 1995), 420-421.

[135] Dawkins, *Boustronios, op.cit.*, § 63-65 and note 33 states that he was uncertain as to the meaning of the goods appearing in this and the following two paragraphs, and so he gives only a summary translation.

[136] His surname indicates that he originated from Aleppo in Syria.

Marrakech hair, two sacks of refined hair [and] one sack of hair from the covered market,[137] which were all worth 500 ducats.

65. On the same day they broke open the house of Savvas the joiner,[138] taking the following from him: 250 pieces of steel, 60 other strips and other things. The things they took were worth 1500 ducats.[139]

66. And on 29 December they broke open the house of Sir Anthony Hadid and took the following: twelve wagons[140] and many other things. They did not, moreover, find the coins (*cartzia*) because he had hidden them under the earth. Furthermore, they said that he had ten thousand ducats.

67. They also went to [the house] of Simon Bragadin and found 150 broad and narrow iron strips inside a well, and another 60 strips, while in his other house [they found] 200 pieces.

On 4 June[141] they broke open the house of William Metaxas taking 20 litres (= 48 kilograms) of silk[142] cocoons, eight litres of other muslins and other quantities worth 500 ducats.

68. In addition, following the king's arrival in Cyprus he despatched James Salviati,[143] Niccolo d'Inglés and Nasar Hous together with a Mamluk, and they went to Paphos, to all the localities and to the citadel of Paphos. Furthermore, they conferred with the garrison commander, Sir James Mahes,[144] informing him of the coming of the fleet that

---

[137] Boustronios has 'το σουκ'. Such covered markets or *souks*, formerly called *funduks* or *fondacos*, existed throughout the Mediterranean (Constable, *Housing the Stranger, op.cit.*, pp. 201-233 and 266-354.) but only Boustronios mentions one for woollens in Nicosia. For markets in Nicosia see Leventis, *Nicosia, op.cit.*, pp. 385-387; Coureas, Schabel and Grivaud, 'The Capital', *op.cit.*, pp. 35-38.

[138] Mss. **B** and **M** have 'Savvas the Venetian'. See Kehayioglou, *Διήγησις, op.cit.*, p. 107, line 8 of both mss.

[139] Ms. **M** has 150 ducats. See *ibid.*, p. 107 line 10 of **M**.

[140] Ms. **M** has 'loaded wagons'. See *ibid.*, p. 107 line 12 of **M**.

[141] Mss. **A**, **B** and **M** all have June, but this is probably a scribal error for January, since the preceding passages refer to events taking place in November and December, while subsequent passages deal with events in February. See *ibid.*, p. 108, **K** line 2.

[142] Mss. **B** and **M** have 'dyed silk'. See *ibid.*, p. 109, line 2 of **B** and **M**.

[143] Mss. **B** and **M** both have 'Salah', as does Dawkins, *Boustronios, op.cit.*, p. 26 § 68, but Florio Bustron ('Chronique', *op.cit.*, p. 401) and Stephen de Lusignan (*Chorograffia, op.cit.*, p. 90 § 391) have Gianuto or Jacomo Salviati, which is correct. Salviati, a Florentine noble and an ardent partisan of James, had accompanied him to Cairo and received from him Sir James Gurri's house in Nicosia, where he died. Florio Bustron states that his heir Jeronimo Salviati received from King James II as fiefs the *casalia* of Omodos, Axilou, Simou, Salamiou, Paliometokho, Thrinia, Platanisto, Kallepia, Stavrokomi and Anarita, but a document of 1512 lists the last five as villages of the royal domain once belonging to Gianuto Salviati, indicating that King James had given them to him as opposed to his heir Jeronimo. See Florio Bustron, 'Chronique', *op.cit.*, pp. 401-402 and 422; Mas Latrie, *Histoire, op.cit.*, III, 97 and note 4, 512; Richard, *Remembrances, op.cit.*, no. 145 and note 2; Aristeidou, *Έγγραφα, op.cit.*, III, 101-102 and 290.

[144] He has the same surname as the commander of Sivouri, the above-mentioned Sir Thomas Mahes.

had brought King James, and told him on the king's behalf to hand over the castle. And he said to them: 'Guarantee me my person, my property and my comrades who happen to be in the citadel, and I shall do everything for the lord king!' And he offered him a guarantee. They opened the gates immediately, moreover, and surrendered. Besides, they (i.e. King James' emissaries) entered and they left the above garrison commander in the citadel, as he had been previously. Furthermore, he swore an oath to be loyal to the king and had the men of the citadel swear likewise. Besides, they left things there and proceeded to the region of Chrysochou, to the monastery of Yialia,[145] doing many bad things to a monk there.

And from there they went to Pelendri and arrested Santini, torturing him so that he would confess the whereabouts of his valuables. He took them, moreover, to a storeroom, and they discovered a pitcher full of *gros* coins[146] able to hold three sack-loads of wine. Furthermore, they arrogated them among themselves, and from them they did not bring the king anything other than 15,000 [*gros*]. In addition, from there they proceeded to Marathasa, belonging to the Count de Rochas, to Yerakies, and seizing the head priest they tormented him, took his valuables and brought him to Nicosia as well, inflicting many sufferings upon him. Besides, from there they ventured to Pendayia and took the valuables of the *chevetain*,[147] John de Milan,[148] taking 2,000 ducats from him.

And then they went to Hariri's vineyard at St Dometios, taking 16 cases of sugar and many other things from him.[149] Then they went to Khrysida belonging to Sir William d'Acre[150] and took his valuables, silver and gold worth 2,000 ducats. <His secretary, moreover, was the cause of this, because he took three pieces of jewellery and they betrayed him. Furthermore, James [of Chios?] (i.e. the secretary) was responsible for many evils befalling the Christians, and he died as soon as he returned home.>[151]

---

[145] One of the three Georgian monasteries founded in north west Cyprus prior to the Latin conquest of 1191, along with Lacrona and St Savvas. See Catia Galatariotou, *The Making of a Saint: The Life, Times and Sanctification of Neophytos the Recluse* (Cambridge, 1991), p. 62 and note 100.

[146] For the *gros* coinage of the first half of the 15th century see Metcalf, *Corpus, op.cit.*, III, 43-99.

[147] A royal officer entrusted with the collection of taxes and royal revenues when local government was reorganized in the late 14th century and the island divided into twelve districts under these officers. See Richard, *Remembrances, op.cit.*, pp. xxi-xxiii; Edbury, *Kingdom, op.cit.*, pp. 194-195.

[148] Possibly identical with the man mentioned in 1468 in connection with the purchase of a vineyard at Pera. See Richard, *Remembrances, op.cit.*, nos. 212-213.

[149] Hariri mentioned here is perhaps the same person as Luke Hariri described below as a valet of Morphou de Grenier, the count of Rochas.

[150] Khrysida is a locality near the village of Kythrea. The William d'Acre mentioned here may be the same as the one undertaking to settle three Syrians from Episkopi and their families in the *casale* of Potimata. See Richard, *Remembrances, op.cit.*, no. 228 and note 1.

[151] The section in brackets < > is not found in mss. **B** and **M**. See Kehayioglou, *Διήγησις, op.cit.*, p. 111 lines 11-13.

69. In addition, in February of the same year, 1460[152] Carceran Chimi and Anthony Synglitico[153] left Kerynia, and coming to the king they recommended themselves. And the king was well disposed towards them, asking them about matters in Kerynia, how they were faring within it. He also asked him about Hector de Chivides and about the remainder, whether they were in the habit of coming out of Kerynia. They, moreover, told him: 'Lord, King Louis has developed a longing to eat veal, and Sir Hector [de Chivides], hearing this has promised him to bring it. Besides, he is coming out on Wednesday in order to go towards the area of Lapithos to discover some for him'. The king, moreover, on hearing this came out of Nicosia and taking company with him he spent the night at Monadi. And as soon as dawn broke, in accordance with his information, he mounted his horse and fell on him, and he killed him, severed his head and brought it back to Nicosia, hanging it on the bridge of the lower central street (Kato Mese).[154]

70. Furthermore, during those days the galley of Brother Boussole ventured out <from Kerynia>[155] to journey to Rhodes, and it was shipwrecked on its arrival at Pendayia. In addition, they apprehended Sir Walter de Nores, Sir Thomas Hareri, Sir Walter's two children and numerous other Cypriots, and they brought them to Nicosia. And on their final arrival in St Dometios,[156] the commander Janibek rode out, and he went to St Dometios, discovering that they were bringing them in irons and with chains around their necks, and the emir was going to behead them. But Brother William implored him a great deal and he did not behead them. Besides, the emir was attracted to the youths, and he wished to convert them to Islam, but the king arrived and he saved them with many entreaties.

Furthermore, he brought them into Nicosia, all on foot, and <the Saracens>[157] took them down to the central (i.e. Mese) street[158] and showed them the viscount's

---

[152] The year in medieval Cyprus began in March, so this is really February 1461. See Dawkins, *Boustronios*, *op.cit.*, p. 26 note 43.

[153] Florio Bustron, 'Chronique', *op.cit.*, pp. 419 and 424 includes John Chimi as well as Philip and John Synglitiko, possible relations of the above two men, among those granted fiefs after 1464 by King James II. On the importance of this family under the Venetians see B. Arbel, 'Greek Magnates in Venetian Cyprus: the Case of the Synglitiko Family', *DOP*, no. 49 (1995), 325-337; Aristeidou, Έγγραφα, *op.cit.*, I, 352-353, II, 26-28, 79-80, 250-252, III, 196-198, 200-204, 248-250, IV, 159-162, 166-168, 176-178, 240-243.

[154] Florio Bustron, 'Chronique', *op.cit.*, p. 402 also describes this incident, describing the bridge in question as that 'of the *Berlina* in the square of Nicosia'. See Leventis, *Nicosia*, *op.cit.*, pp. 384-385 for references to this bridge by Cypriot chroniclers. For the daily stipend of a bezant a day the king awarded him see also Richard, *Remembrances*, *op.cit.*, no. 33, stating that it was drawn from the toll known as the *gabelle*, levied at the Customs Gate in the east of Nicosia. Later, however, he presided over the royal *secrete* or treasury, for which see *ibid.*, nos. 217-218.

[155] The words in brackets < > are from mss. **B** and **M**. See Kehayioglou, Διήγησις, *op.cit.*, p. 113, ms. **B** lines 9-10 and ms. **M** line 9.

[156] A village south west of Nicosia which King James II awarded as a fief to his Sicilian admiral Muzio de Constanzo. See below §84 and Florio Bustron, 'Chronique', *op.cit.*, p. 418.

[157] The words in brackets < > are from mss. **B** and **M**. See Kehayioglou, Διήγησις, *op.cit.*, p. 113, ms. **B** lines 19-20, ms. **M** line18.

[158] i.e. the famous 'Mese' street where the bridge of the pillory mentioned above was located.

head, and they said to them: 'Behold your viscount!' On seeing it, moreover, they were saddened greatly. And they conducted them to the court of the king and put them on the ground floor, while they placed Sir Walter and Hariri upstairs in a chamber. Besides, they spent many days there, and they brought them out to swear fealty to the king. In addition, the king asked Sir Walter give him the oath, but he did not wish to swear fealty to him as king, stating: 'I had but one oath of fealty, and I have given it'. And the king took away his villages, 36 of them. Subsequently he awarded him for his livelihood a stipend of one bezant a day throughout his life.[159] <And Hariri swore fealty to him (i.e. the king). >[160]

71. In the same year,[161] moreover, a galleass set sail from Famagusta and went to the region of the Karpass to engage in piracy. And the *bailli* Alessandro Tarantin went out there with his companions and captured all of them, as well as the skipper. Furthermore, he beheaded him, while he brought the remainder to Nicosia.

At the same time Sir James Zaplana[162] came to the area of the Karpass to engage in piracy, and it was his good fortune that the ship was wrecked. In addition, the *bailli* of the Karpass captured him, him and all his company, and they took them all away on foot. The king, moreover, was encamped near Famagusta and they brought them into his presence. Besides, he did to each one of them that which seemed right to him, and he sent Sir James to his tent, into the hands of Stephen the Chiot.[163] The king also sent him a crimson undergarment made of velvet, took off his irons and had him brought before him, and held him extremely dearly.

72. Furthermore, on 22 March 1461 the king ventured forth to go to Famagusta and he took scaling ladders and many siege engines in order to be able to take it. He

---

[159] Florio Bustron, 'Chronique', *op.cit.*, p. 403 also recounts this incident, pointing out that 'the fealty of Sir Walter' became a legendary expression for obduracy. He enumerates Vasilia, Kormakiti, Myrtou, Karpasia, Kambyli and Margi among the villages taken from him. This notwithstanding, in time he gained royal favour and is mentioned in early 1469 as the lieutenant of the royal administrators and *bailli* of the *secrete*. See Richard, *Remembrances*, *op.cit.*, nos. 33 and note 2 and nos. 217-219.

[160] The words in brackets < > are from mss. **B** and **M**. See Kehayioglou, Διήγησις, *op.cit.*, p. 115, line 8 of both mss. Thomas Hariri subsequently became *bailli* of the *secrète* and was granted the village of Stromato as well as the mills of Petonakhi by King James II sometime after 1464. See Florio Bustron, 'Chronique', *op.cit.*, pp. 415 and 419.

[161] See note 152 above.

[162] *Ibid.*, pp. 403-404 states clearly that the besieged Genoese sent the Catalan corsair James Zaplana to the Karpass to secure supplies for them prior to his capture. This notwithstanding, King James II took him into his service, granting him the *casalia* of Agrinou, Tokhni, Vouda, Maroni and Ardana. He also became a bailiff of the kingdom and governor of the royal treasury by December 1471. See *ibid.*, p. 418; Mas Latrie, 'Documents nouveaux', *op.cit.*, pp. 410-411, 415 note 3, 423, 430, 432, 435, 437, 439 and 446; Richard, *Remembrances*, *op.cit.*, nos. 69, 159-165, 168-169, 171, 191, [193-194], 207, 226 and Appendix I, doc. 2.

[163] Sometime after 1464 King James II granted him a flourmill at Kythraea. See Florio Bustron, 'Chronique', *op.cit.*, p. 422; Richard, *Remembrances*, *op.cit.*, no. 97 records an increase in the incomes granted to a certain Constantine of Chios, a possible relation.

appointed Peter de Naves the commander on the side towards Trapeza,[164] with scaling ladders, 50 Christian men and 30 Saracens. The king, moreover, was with the remainder, who were all on foot, he alone being mounted. And on the final arrival of all the commanders with the scaling ladders on the side of the arsenal, where the tower was, they discovered a hole and began to widen it with picks. Besides, the scaling ladders were found to be short, and they joined them together. Furthermore, they were not able to accomplish anything, and they turned back, inflicting much damage on the vineyards and also burning many settlements.

73. In addition, know this also, that when the king came he had nothing for his expenses! And he minted copper specie, *cartzias* and *sixains*, with six *cartzias* to every *sixain*. Furthermore, he extracted all the copper piping of the baths, and this was the pretext for destroying the baths. He also took many items of copper from the households. This currency, moreover, was in use for three years, until he mastered the kingdom. And then he abrogated it and had silver *gros* minted showing him on horseback, and he had *cartzias* minted too.[165]

74. Besides, on 15 April 1461 the king went to Kerynia to organize an ambush. As he was going, moreover, Nicholas Morabit was with him, and he galloped from the Roman Catholic Church to the ditch of the barbican. And King Louis had an ambush organized in there, and as he was galloping Diego de Cacciorla seized him by the reins [of his horse], while James the son of Sir Martin dragged Morabit down so as to kill him. He safeguarded himself, however, cut the reins of the horse, got away and appeared before the king. In addition, as soon as he arrived in Nicosia he granted him three *presteries*,[166] Vyzakia, Kafkallos and Athasin, as well as two large vineyards, and also appointed him marshal of Cyprus, marrying him to the daughter of Sir Louis de Nores. Furthermore, his wife died in the space of a few days.[167]

75. In addition, on the 15 May 1461 Sir Sor de Naves arrived at Salines with two galleys so as to remain constant in the service of the king, as the latter had instructed him. And on his arrival at Salines King James and the emir came down from Nicosia

---

[164] This *casale*, 8 km to the west of Famagusta, had been sacked in 1426 by the Mamluks and given as a security in 1445 to Genoese creditor of King John II. In 1469 King James II ordered the revenues from the *gabelle* tax levied in Nicosia to be allocated to Philip Syngritico, the commander of the fortress of Sivouri, so as to finance its reconstruction. See *ibid.*, no. 133 and note 3.

[165] On the coinage of King James II see Metcalf, *Gros, Sixains and Cartzias, op.cit.*, pp. 99-111, 121, 123-124, 128-132, 134-136, 149 and 157; J.R. Stewart, *Lusignan Cyprus and its Coinage*, 2 vols. (Nicosia, 2002), I, 76-78. The *gros* coins showing him on horseback follow Renaissance models.

[166] The *presteries* (Gk. προαστιό) were hamlets, smaller than the *casalia* and often dependent on them. See J. Richard, 'Agriculture in the Crusader States', in *A History of the Crusades*, ed. K.M. Setton, 6 vols. (Philadelphia/Madison, 1955-1989, V, 269-270; For *presteries* in the Venetian period see Aristeidou, Έγγραφα, *op.cit.*, I, 347-349, III, 123-125, IV, 65-66, 69-71.

[167] Two persons had this name, one being the marshal of Cyprus whose widow was still alive in 1468 and the other being the one mentioned here, described as 'the auditor's son' in two royal charters of King John II. See Richard, *Documents, op. cit.*, pp. 142 and note 1, also 150 and note 3.

and conferred with him, giving him all necessary victuals and papers for him to go to Tripoli and bring Saracens and other things that he had ordered. The king, moreover, returned to Nicosia so as to take his land forces and go to Famagusta. Furthermore, he went there and set up camp on the side of St Nicholas, while the emir [did the same] opposite the Limassol Gate along with all the Saracens.

76. Besides, the galleys from Genoa arrived on 2 June 1461 with great quantities of victuals for Famagusta, which belonged to Leonardo de Grimaldi, and they also brought a captain to Famagusta, Babilano[168] Gentile Palavicino. In addition, Sir Doria d'Imperiale arrived with a small galley (*fuste*) of 22 oarsmen[169] in the company of this ship, [and] with a Cretan *griparia*[170] loaded with provisions.

As soon as the king learnt of this, moreover, he went at once and caught up with the ship in the waters off Salines, and having no time (i.e. to summon reinforcements) he straightaway aligned the ships that he had, and they fought and captured the ship and those accompanying it, along with a large amount of supplies on their way to Famagusta.

77. Furthermore, on 6[171] June [in the year] of Christ 1461 Sir Sor de Naves, whom he had sent to Tripoli, returned. And he committed a great treason against the king, for he brought 60[172] Mamluks, 50 infantrymen, 20,000 bows and arrows, a barrel of gunpowder, a small galley and two cannons, with the galley in question belonging to Benedict Cartagena,[173] and he entered the harbour of Famagusta, granting the cannon to the Genoese and taking the remainder and going to Kerynia.

78. King James, moreover, observing the treason of Sor de Naves took his land forces away from Famagusta. Furthermore, the Famagustans and the Genoese sat in council so as to send persons to bring victuals for Famagusta, and they sent Sir Luke Amelin[174]

---

[168] The Genoese captains of Famagusta were elected for one year. Babilano Palavicino succeeded Giovani di Parma and preceded Raphael de Andoria. See Otten-Froux, *Une enquête, op. cit.*, p. 16.

[169] The *fuste*, the same size as a frigate, was an extremely fast type of light galley often favoured by corsairs. See Pryor, *Geography, op. cit.*, pp. 74, 175, 180 and 186; Earle, *Corsairs, op. cit.*, p. 48 note; Aristeidou, Ἐγγραφα, *op.cit.*, II, 366-369.

[170] The *griparia* was a lateen-rigged type of galley even smaller than the *fuste* used by Venetian and Ottoman seamen as a merchantman or naval transport. See Pryor, *Geography*, pp. *op. cit.*, 46 and 180.

[171] Dawkins, *Boustronios*, ch. 77 has 6 June, but all the mss. have 7 June. See Kehayioglou, Διή-γησις, *op. cit.*, pp. 120-121.

[172] Florio Bustron, 'Chronique', *op. cit.*, p. 406 has 60. Mss. **A**, **B** and **M** of the text all have six, but this must be wrong. See also Hill, *op. cit.*, III, 574 and note 1.

[173] Benedict Cartagena later declared for King James II. Florio Bustron, 'Chronique', *op. cit.*, p. 422 states that after 1464 the king granted him Curdaca (Akourdalia?), Anaphotia and 150 measures of wine.

[174] Amelin is perhaps a corruption of Lomellini. Napoleone Lomellini was captain of Famagusta ín 1456 and his son Luke was sub-castellan of Famagusta from 26 December 1457 onwards. On Luke Lomellini see Otten-Froux, *Une enquête, op. cit.*, pp. 20, 30-31, 33, 40, 44 *et passim*.

as a negotiator to bring supplies. Besides, twenty-five armed men ventured out of Famagusta on 28 September and went to Stylloi, procuring slaughtered cattle and piglets to the number of nearly 1,000.

79. In addition, on 2 October 1461 twenty-five men came out of Famagusta carrying weapons, and proceeding to Akrotiri they captured three men whom they took to Famagusta.[175] The captain, moreover, had them tortured, and they confessed that they had killed many people from Famagusta since the war had begun. And <on Saturday>[176] they hanged them.

80. Besides, on 9 October Sir Imperiale's galley set sail to journey to Corycos from Famagusta so as to fetch wheat. Furthermore, Anthony Lombardo, a burgess of Famagusta, was appointed the skipper, and on 5 December it returned to Famagusta loaded with supplies of all kinds.

81. And on 30 October the captain of Famagusta sent the caravel of Franceschetto d'Alma on a voyage to Ancona tò bring wheat. The Genoese also appointed as their emissary to Genoa an envoy [who was] a burgess of Famagusta, Lazarus Chalco,[177] along with John d'Andrea. In addition, during the voyage of the above emissaries to Genoa John d'Andrea turned back to Ancona and found the caravel loaded with wheat. They came, moreover, to Famagusta with 3,000 *modii*.

82. During these days a Catalan vessel arrived at Salines, belonging to Borja Johniel, as well as a galliot[178] belonging to Michel de Martin. Besides, John Perez [Fabriges] was on board the galliot. And on disembarking he set eyes on George Bustron who was a *chevetain*. In addition, he (i.e. George Bustron) sent him to his house <in Larnaca>.[179]

---

[175] The Genoese foray to Akrotiri refers to the place name Akrotiri on the south coast of the Karpass peninsula, 3km west of Cape Elea (Goodwin, *Toponymy, op. cit.*, I, 132) not the Akrotiri peninsula west of Limassol.

[176] The words in brackets have been added from mss. **B** and **M**. See Kehayioglou, Διήγησις, *op. cit.*, p. 123, line 10 of **B** and **M**.

[177] Florio Bustron, 'Chronique', *op. cit.*, p. 407 gives his surname as Laico. Is he identical to Lazaro Lercari(o), mentioned as a burgess of Famagusta in the proceedings of 1459 against Napoleone Lomellini, a former captain of Famagusta? On Lercari see Otten-Froux, *Une enquête, op. cit.*, pp. 38, 44, 48, 50, 61, 81, 85 *et passim*.

[178] A galliot was a small galley of 17-23 benches and 2-3 men to an oar, favoured by corsairs until the 17th century. See Pryor, *Geography, op. cit.*, pp. 67-69, 169-170, 180 and 194-195; Earle, *Corsairs, op. cit.*, p. 48 note.

[179] The words in brackets < > have been added from mss. **B** and **M**. See Kehayioglou, Διήγησις, *op. cit.*, p. 125, line 5 of mss. **B** and **M**. On the development of Larnaca from the time of King James II onwards see Hill, *op. cit.*, III, 812-813; Arbel, 'Cypriot Population', *op. cit.*, pp. 202-203. The mention of 'Larnaca' in the later **B** and **M** manuscripts indicates that the name was gaining ground in the 16th century, and it never appears in the *Livre des Remembrances* of the *secrete* for the years 1468-1469.

Furthermore, he had supper and slept there, and he asked him to write a letter to the king so as to recommend him, and, should he so wish, to give him a cargo ship[180] for him to export 1,000 *modii* of wheat and take them to Rhodes. The *chevetain*, moreover, wrote a letter and sent him on to the king. And the king on examining the letter did not show any favour towards him. Besides, John Perez, seeing that he had not shown any favour to him returned to Salines so as to embark on the galliot. In addition, the *chevetain* detained him, telling him to have patience: 'And you shall have every favour from the king'. And so he remained in Cyprus.

83. On the same day two galleys came to Paphos, the one belonging to a Sicilian knight, Muzzio de Constanzo,[181] while the other requested a safe-conduct so as to enter the harbour of Paphos. Furthermore, Sir John Mistachiel[182] was the captain in Paphos, and he had a safe conduct drawn up for him, sending a letter to the king. In addition, the king on hearing of this immediately mounted his horse and went to Paphos, cancelling the safe-conduct that Mistachiel had had drawn up. Besides, he impounded the galleys and had Sir John Mistachiel appointed skipper to guard them until he should return to Nicosia to appoint a skipper.[183] He came, moreover, bringing with him the two skippers of the galleys, and he [eventually] appointed John Perez skipper of these galleys.

84. In addition, within the space of some days he gave a wonderful income to Sir Muzzo de Constanzo, Vavla, Kornokipos, Lympia, Kakotrygeti, the Arsos of Mesaria and other villages. Besides, he appointed him admiral and married him to the daughter of Sir Thomas de Verni, while also granting him the houses of Benedetto Pallavicini. Furthermore, he held the other skipper, the Frank, in high esteem, and he wished to have him married and to give him incomes. He, however, was married and did not wish to remain, and he requested permission to depart. The king, moreover, listening to him granted him many presents, to the value of 1,000 ducats in ducats and objects, and allowed him to leave.[184]

85. I forgot to write this previously. With the host of the Saracens having departed from Kerynia and having gone to cross over (i.e. to Syria), the Mamluks and the foot soldiers remained with the king. And the lords who were within Kerynia sat in council with King Louis, and it appeared fitting to them that: 'Lady Charlotte should go to the

---

[180] This may have been the carrack, a 15th and 16th century merchant ship evolving from the cog, which had been introduced into the Mediterranean from northern Europe in the 14th century and displaced the traditional round ship as a cargo vessel. See Pryor, *Geography*, *op. cit.*, pp. 39-43.

[181] Muzio de Constanzo declared for James, becoming admiral of Cyprus and regent following King James' death. See Richard, *Remembrances*, *op. cit.*, nos. 159-165, 182 and pp. 214-215 (doc. II).

[182] He may be identical to the John Mistachiel knighted in 1473, and made viscount of Nicosia in 1489. See *ibid.*, no. 6 note 1.

[183] Florio Bustron, 'Chronique', p. 423 states that after 1464 King James granted John Mistachiel the *casalia* of Stroumbi and Polemi. On his family background and the possibility that he became knighted and the viscount of Nicosia by 1489, during the reign of Queen Catherine, see Richard, *Remembrances*, *op. cit.*, no. 6 note 1.

[184] This episode is also recounted in Florio Bustron, 'Chronique', *op. cit.*, pp. 407-408.

[Hospitaller] grand master in Rhodes together with her husband so as to bring forces and seize the kingdom!' Furthermore, she took the galley from Rhodes and that belonging to Sor de Naves and went to Rhodes, and the grand master together with all the lord entertained them greatly and kept them good company.

In addition, within the space of a few days she returned to Cyprus once again and disembarked at Paphos, making port by the castles. Sir John Mistachiel was the garrison commander, moreover, and at the sight of them he forthwith turned the castles over to the power of the queen. And the queen immediately appointed Sir Peter Palol garrison commander, and took Sir James Mahes to Kerynia, while the queen herself returned to Kerynia. They organized, moreover, great celebrations in Kerynia. Besides, after the passage of a few days Sor de Naves set sail from Kerynia together with his galleys, and taking Peter de Naves with him he went to Paphos so as to relieve Peter Palol and place Peter de Naves in the castles.

Furthermore, while going past Pendayia, Sor de Naves ventured to practise piracy. And Demetrios de Coron[185] happened to be the *chevetain* in Pendayia, and on seeing the galleys he rode out at once with those few men who happened to be there, and going to the coast they engaged in a fine battle. Besides, six persons from the galley were killed in the fray, and three from the other side, while many were wounded from both the one side and the other.[186]

In addition, the [men in the] galleys, seeing that they had no advantage, went to Paphos and relieved Palol, installing Peter de Naves. He (i.e. Peter Palol), moreover, returned to Kerynia. Furthermore, when King James learnt that Sor de Naves had gone to Paphos, appointing Peter de Naves garrison commander, he went to Pendayia, relieved Demetrios de Coron and sent him to Paphos as the garrison commander. And on his way there he issued a command, and all the *turcoples*[187] and the emancipated peasants came into his presence. Besides, he had the castles[188] surrounded and caused them great anxiety.

---

[185] James II later granted this person, probably originating from Coron in the southern Peloponnese, Episkopio as a fief, and then Kapouti and Strovolos in exchange for it. A representation of him and his wife survives in the frescoes of the church of Panayia tes Podithou, founded in 1502 at Galata. See Florio Bustron, 'Chronique', *op. cit.*, p. 422; Richard, *Remembrances, op. cit.*, nos. 51 and note 5, 60 and 105; S. Frigerio-Zeniou, *L'Art "Italo-Byzantin" à Chypre au XVIe siècle* (Venice, 1998), pp. 13-15 and 17-19; A. Aristeidou, Άγνωστα στοιχεία σχετικά με τους κτίτορες της εκκλησίας της Παναγίας Ελεούσας (Ποδύθου), *EKEE* XXX (2004), 171-190.

[186] For this incident see also Florio Bustron, 'Chronique', *op. cit.*, pp. 409-410.

[187] On this type of light cavalry see J. Richard, 'Les Turcoples au service des royaumes de Jérusalem et de Chypre: Musulmans convertis ou Chrétiens orientaux?', in *Croisades et etats latins de l'Orient*, X (Aldershot, 1992), 259-270.

[188] Throughout this chapter the fortifications of Paphos are called castles (Gk. καστελλία) in the plural in all three mss., but the Frankish and Cypriot forces are described as in *the castle* (sing.). Dawkins, *Boustronios, op. cit.*, §85 invariably employs the singular form in his translation, but perhaps the Greek mss. have the plural form because Paphos had one functioning castle by the harbour and another known as Saranta Kolones, a 13th century Hospitaller foundation abandoned after the earthquake of 1222, on which see P. Megaw, 'A castle in Paphos attributable to the Hospital?', in *The Military Orders:Fighting for the Faith and Caring for the Sick*, ed. M. Barber (Aldershot, 1994), pp. 42-51; J. Rosser, 'Archaeological and Literary Evidence for the Destruction of "Saranta Kolones" in 1222', *EKEE* XXX (2004), 39-50.

Peter de Naves, moreover, had Franks and Cypriots within the castle who used to sally forth from the castle and fight with [the forces of] Demetrios of Coron. Sir John Mistachiel also happened to be in Paphos, and coming to the king he obtained his permission to go and speak with Peter de Naves, if he wished.[189] In addition, he gave him leave and had a letter drawn up for him addressed to Demetrios de Coron, for the latter to allow him to negotiate with Peter de Naves. And going to Paphos Mistachiel asked Peter de Naves, should it please him, to grant him a safe conduct so that he could speak with him, since he had permission from King James. He, moreover, granted him a safe conduct at once.

Furthermore, Mistachiel went to the castles, Peter de Naves came out and they conferred, and each bade farewell to the other and went away. And in the morning they came together, and following many promises that Mistachiel gave Peter de Naves the latter returned the castles to King James. He also wrote a letter to King James, and sent it with Balian Salah.[190] King James was greatly pleased on seeing this letter. Besides, King James immediately gave orders and they wrote a charter, giving it to Balian Salah, and he granted Salah the villages of Sir Alexander Cappadoca,[191] Koka and Moniatis, because he had brought the news. But after a few days he took them and gave them to Benedetto from the Morea.

They came, moreover, to Nicosia from Paphos, and all the Mamluks along with many Christians went and brought Sir Peter [de Naves] into Nicosia with great honour, bringing him before the king. In addition, they settled him in the houses of Pallavicino, and he (i.e. the King) granted him a considerable income.

86. Besides, in the year of Christ 1463 they sent Fleury the count of Jaffa from Kerynia as an emissary to Constantinople. His wife's sister, moreover, was married to a pasha, both being Kantakouzenes. Furthermore, the pasha came to an agreement with the count that he should bring his wife to Constantinople so that her sister might see her, or his children. And the count summoned her, but his wife did not wish to go under any circumstances, nor send her children.[192] In addition, neither his wife nor his children having gone, the pasha had the count placed in custody, and a few days later they severed him down the middle and burnt him,

---

[189] Florio Bustron, 'Chronique', *op. cit.*, p. 410 states that he requested a safe-conduct from the king, who then granted him leave to speak to Peter de Naves.

[190] Probably identical with the Balian Salah to whom King James II in July 1468 granted an annual stipend. See Richard, *Remembrances, op. cit.*, no. 37.

[191] He belonged to an old Greek family prominent in the royal *secrète*. See John Richard, 'Le casal de Psimolofo et la vie rurale en Chypre au XIVe siècle', in *Les Relations entre l'Orient et l'Occident au Moyen Age*, IV (Aldershot, 1992, repr. 1996,1999), 127; *idem., Documents, op. cit.*, pp. 12, 14, 79 and 81; *idem., Remembrances, op. cit.*, no. 20 and note 1.

[192] His wife was the Greek noblewoman Zoe Kantakouzene, who bore James de Fleury three sons, Manuel, Hercules and Jason. Regarding Zoe and possible reasons why James de Fleury was put to death in Constantinople see Hill, *op. cit.*, III, 589 and note 4; E. Brayer, P. Lemerle and V. Laurent, 'Le Vaticanus Latinus 4789', *REB* 9 (1951), pp. 47-105 and esp. 64-77; Richard, *Documents, op. cit.*, pp. 124, 129-131 and 151.

87. By 1463, moreover, King James had placed Kerynia in such dire straits that [those within] could no longer live. Besides, they were eating dogs and cats, while an egg was worth a *marcello*.[193] Furthermore, the commander within was Sor de Naves, and following negotiations King James married him to his illegitimate daughter.[194] And it was on account of him that he took Kerynia.[195]

88. In addition, on 29 August 1464 he took Famagusta, as I stated above.[196] On capturing it, he appointed Conella [Nicholas Morabit][197] garrison commander within, and said to him: 'Should they come, even at night perhaps, to tell you to open the castle, do not open upon your life!' Furthermore, Janibek the commander of the Saracens wished to capture Famagusta so as to be powerful, to retain Cyprus and to kill the king. And he went at night and told Conella to open [the gates] for him, that he might enter with the Saracens. He, however, did not open [the gates] for him, and he said to him: 'I have orders from the king not to open for him even if he comes at night in person'.

In the morning, moreover, Janibek complained about this to the king, and he sent him away with fine words, but Janibek remained angry. In addition, the king secretly

---

[193] This Venetian coin was worth one third of a ducat. See Kehayioglou, Διήγησις, *op. cit.*, p. 474.

[194] Florio Bustron, 'Chronique', *op. cit.*, p. 411 also states that King James II had Sor de Naves wedded to an illegitimate daughter of his. Mss. **B** and **M** (Kehayioglou, Διήγησις, *op. cit.*, p. 135 line 9 of both mss.) and Dawkins, *Boustronios, op. cit.*, p. 30 § 87 state that Sor de Naves married an illegitimate daughter of King James' uncle, but Kehayioglou (Διήγησις, *op. cit.*, pp. 392-393) observes that the word 'uncle' was added in ms. **B** by a different hand, and that ms. **M** copied this from a lost ms. incorporating this addition. The Venetian Senate's letter of 18 May 1469 to King James II, moreover, alludes to the death of his natural daughter who had been promised as a wife to Sor de Naves. See Mas Latrie, *Histoire, op. cit.*, III, 308-309.

[195] Sir William de Ras left Kerynia in around this time, and obtained a safe conduct from Peter Ramon Zacosta, the Hospitaller Grand Master, to visit Cyprus in Queen Charlotte's service in September 1463. He subsequently declared for King James II, as stated in a note to §50.

[196] George Boustronios is wrong about the date, although Kerynia may have capitulated in August, for which see Edbury 'Λουζινιανοί', *op. cit.*, pp. 220-221 and note 131. Florio Bustron, 'Chronique', *op. cit.*, p. 411 states that Famagusta capitulated in January 1464, and on p. 415 mentions John de Ras as one of the witnesses to its surrender, clear evidence that by now he and his father William de Ras were serving King James II. Other witnesses he mentions are Archbishop William Goneme, Michael de Castellatio and Anthony d'Euchanta, who were the bishops of Paphos and Famagusta, Morphou de Grenier the count of Rochas, John Tafur, Rizzo de Marino and Jeronimo Salviati. George Boustronios does not refer previously to the capture of Famagusta in any of the chronicle's extant manuscripts. This implies that part of his narrative has been lost, or that he confused the capture of Genoese ships bringing supplies to relieve Famagusta in June 1461 with the capture of the town itself. The chronicle is silent on events in Famagusta from November 1461 to July 1464, and perhaps these were later excised, on which see Grivaud, 'Πνευματικός βίος', *op. cit.*, pp. 1089-1090. For the terms of Famagusta's capitulation see Florio Bustron, 'Chronique', *op. cit.*, pp. 411-416; Mas Latrie, *Histoire, op. cit.*, III, 485-492.

[197] Florio Bustron, 'Chronique', *op. cit.*, p. 416 has Conella Morabito, the first name being a variant of Nicholas. See also Hill, *op. cit.*, III, 1187.

sent word to Nicosia that: 'All the Franks and the soldiers must be present in Famagusta at midnight!'[198] Furthermore, he ordered the Saracens: 'They must go and remain at Mesaoria!' Besides, he kept two Saracens in his company, Curcuma and James who had been christened, for he himself had christened him, while Curcuma was a valiant man, and he loved him.[199] In addition, the Franks and the soldiers arrived at midnight, and he despatched them. The <Saracens> moreover, were sleeping, and they killed all of them.[200]

89. And the commander Janibek had a sister, a great lady in Cairo. Furthermore, once the news that they had killed her brother arrived she went to the sultan at once and asked him to administer punishment for her: 'Because you sent my brother to Cyprus, and he exerted himself to make a swine king, and yet he killed him, him and your fleet'. Besides, as soon as he had killed him the king sent an emissary to the sultan forthwith, with great presents and with complaints that he (i.e. Janibek) had wished to kill him in order to seize the kingdom. The sultan and the emirs, moreover, were fond of him. Furthermore, with Cyprus having been bound during the rule of King Janus to give 8,000 ducats annually [in tribute], King James promised another 8,000 and used to give 16,000,[201] and once again, before he died, he had the sense to cut the [additional] 8,000.[202] And the sultan never wished to give a hearing to the sister of Janibek <for King James had many people in Syria who were fond of him, and he gave them rich

---

[198] Mss. **B** and **M** have 'All the soldiers, Franks and Greeks, must be present well armed in Famagusta at midnight!'. See Kehayioglou, Διήγησις, op. cit., p. 137.

[199] Florio Bustron, 'Chronique', op. cit., p. 416 states that King James retained three Saracens, the third one being Janibek's chamberlain. On p. 419 he states that King James II granted Curcuma the casale of Mamonia in Paphos as the fief sometime between 1464 and 1468.

[200] The words in brackets < >, not found in ms. **A**, have been added from mss. **B** and **M**. See Kehayioglou, Διήγησις, op. cit., p. 137, lines 7-8 of mss. **B** and **M**. One notes that the contemporary Mamluk historian Yusuf ibn Taghri Birdi states that King James II had Janibek and his men killed because they had begun kidnapping good-looking youths from their parents, possibly so as to convert them to Islam and send them to Egypt to train and serve as Mamluks. When the king's emissaries told them to desist, they were beaten up. In the ensuing meeting between the king and Janibek the latter hit King James, whereupon the Cypriots present killed him and the 25 Mamluks accompanying him. See P. Edbury, 'Λουζινιανοί', op. cit., p. 219.

[201] George Boustronios does not state exactly when King James II doubled the tribute to the Mamluks. He must have done so either to placate the sultan after massacring Janibek and his troops, or when arriving in Egypt to enlist Mamluk support for seizing the throne. The prospect of a double tribute would certainly have given them good reason to support him in preference to Queen Charlotte, the lawful heir. The Venetian claim to the Mamluk sultan in 1474 that Rizzo de Marino had instigated the massacre (Mas Latrie, Histoire, op. cit., III, 391-392) is not very credible, for they were then urging the Mamluks to arrest Rizzo if he entered Mamluk territory, and so their accusation had ulterior motives. Perhaps the sultan did not avenge Janibek's murder because he saw him as a threat to his rule and so was glad to be rid of him. On how Mamluk emirs considered a threat by the incumbent sultans were sent on military campaigns far from Cairo see Stewart, Armenian Kingdom, op. cit., pp. 107-108 and note 181.

[202] Dawkins, Boustronios, op. cit., § 89 inexplicably has 'before Janus died mad he cut off the eight thousand', and has clearly misinterpreted this passage, found only in ms. **A**. For the relevant passage see Kehayioglou, Διήγησις, op. cit., p. 136. ms. **A** line 20.

presents as well>.[203] Besides, the sultan forwarded numerous complaints to King James.

90. Furthermore, Janibek's sister, seeing that the sultan was not going to begin a vendetta for her, sent a Saracen overseas. He came, moreover, to Famagusta in the guise of a merchant, found the king on the beach, approached him and dealt the king a stab on the neck. And the king turned around, giving him a light blow, and he fell on the beach immediately. In addition, they fell upon him from behind and killed him.[204]

91. Besides, in 1469 there was widespread famine in Cyprus because of a great blight[205] of the crops, and wheat came to cost ten (ducats?) per *modius*, while many died of famine. Furthermore, the king made considerable provision to help the island, and he sent for and brought wheat and assisted the island until the [next] crop arrived and the island was succoured.

92. In addition, a great plague struck in 1470 and lasted for two and a half years. Besides, three parts of the island died, and the island remained devastated.[206] The king, moreover, < took those who seemed suitable to him and >[207] went to Akaki, and was looked after and none of them died.

93. Furthermore, I inform you that among the foreigners who entered the service of the king there was a certain James of Malta. And when he came to Cyprus he was barefoot and dressed in a sackcloth, and chancing upon a crossbow he too went along with the others to the forces assembled before Famagusta and fashioned some weapons, and they gave him a monthly wage together with the others. After a short time, Nicholas de Palermo, who had been a serf of the count of Tripoli, and who on being enfranchised became a tavern-keeper[208] and made a lot of money appeared, and he took the above-mentioned James as a husband for his daughter. The above-mentioned James, moreover, became a *cittadino* (i.e. a burgess). Furthermore, the king appointed him *chevetain* in Pendayia.

Besides, Peter d'Avila was the cause of his good fortune. And yet in secret he

---

[203] The words in brackets < > have been taken from ms. **M**. See *ibid.*, p. 137, ms. **M**, lines 16-18. It was at this time that King James sent William Goneme, the Latin archbishop, to Cairo with 1.000 pieces of camlet and merchandise worth 20-25.000 ducats. See Edbury, 'Λουζινιανοί', *op. cit.*, p. 220 and note 128.

[204] Florio Bustron, 'Chronique', *op. cit.*, p. 417 recounts this incident in greater detail.

[205] Dawkins, *Boustronios, op. cit.*, § 91 does not give a translation of the word μύρτος. For its meaning of blight see Kehayioglou, Διήγησις, *op. cit.*, p. 477, and for other outbreaks of blight, droughts and famine in Cyprus see Grivaud, *Villages désertés, op. cit.*, pp. 435-436. The fact that the chronicle does not mention the placing of Cyprus under Venetian protection on 4 October 1469 (see Mas Latrie, *Histoire, op. cit.*, III, 316-320), an event of momentous importance, vindicates Dawkins' assertions regarding its parochial character.

[206] On the recurrence of plagues in Cyprus see Grivaud, *Villages désertés, op. cit.*, pp. 439-440.

[207] The words in brackets < > have been taken from mss. **B** and **M**. See Kehayioglou, Διήγησις, *op. cit.*, p. 139, lines 12-13 of mss. **B** and **M**.

[208] On taverns in Nicosia see Coureas, Grivaud and Schabel, 'Frankish and Venetian Nicosia', *op. cit.*, p. 37.

always used to say bad things about Peter d'Avila. At the time of the plague, moreover, Peter d'Avila went to Morphou, as did James himself along with Carceran Chimi and many others on account of the plague. The said Carceran was a valet of the king, while Sir John Mistachiel happened to be his father in law, and he had found the men at arms that Peter d'Avila had hired, and he was there in order to organize the squadron.

The above-mentioned James was also there, and he struck a great friendship with Carceran Chimi, and in the course of their great friendship each revealed himself to the other, with Chimi telling him everything his heart contained, and they became like brothers. In addition, since it was manifest that King James was inflicting numerous wrongdoings and great humiliations upon the Cypriots, and that they were extremely discontented, while Carceran Chimi was likewise greatly dissatisfied. As soon as they had returned with James, Carceran said to him: 'Would your heart have the strength to do that which I would do?' And James said to him: 'Sir Carceran, would that your heart had as much strength as mine has! Tell me what it is that you wish to do, and you shall acknowledge me, as though you yourself had done it!' Furthermore, Chimi replied and said to him: 'Should the king perhaps have done something shameful to you, what would you do to him?' James responded and said to him: 'I would kill him'. They said many other things besides, and then fell silent.

94. After the plague had passed, moreover, they all returned to Nicosia. In addition, one day Carceran Chimi with many people who were expressing complaints as regarded the matter of the king. One complained because he had taken his villages from him, another complained that he had taken what was his, yet another complained that he had committed a shameful act in his home, another about his kinswoman, and they were complaining to each other and saying: 'It would be better for us to be dead than to endure the shame that we have suffered from our lord'.[209]

And Chimi, listening to their complaints, did not display any outward sign. In September, moreover, by his misfortune,[210] Carceran happened to be with the above-mentioned James, and he said to him: 'Let us get together tomorrow morning to converse!' He replied to him: 'With pleasure!' And they said goodbye to each other. Furthermore, as soon as it was daybreak James made his way to the house of Carceran Chimi. They rode off, moreover, and going to [the church of] St John[211] they heard

---

[209] Florio Bustron, 'Chronique', *op. cit.*, pp. 425-432, closely followed by Hill, *op. cit.*, III, 648-650, gives a far more detailed account of this conspiracy, mentioning things omitted in this chronicle, such as the failed attempt to ambush the king on his return to Nicosia from Famagusta, Peter d'Avila's denunciation of the plotters during the muster of the troops, the trial before the High Court and the king's delayed and hypocritical decision to 'pardon' the conspirators because he considered that the executioner had already despatched them.

[210] Ms. **A** has 'their misfortune' but I have adopted the singular as found in mss. **B** and **M**, since the following pages make it clear that this is correct. See Kehayioglou, Διήγησις, *op. cit.*, p. 143, ms. **B** line 16 and ms. **M** line 15.

[211] This was almost certainly the Cistercian abbey of Beau Lieu outside Nicosia, ceded sometime after 1469 to the Observant Franciscans, who renamed it St John de Montfort after the saint buried there. See Richard, *Remembrances*, *op. cit.*, no. 219 and note 2; *idem.*, 'The Cistercians in Cyprus', in *The Second Crusade and the Cistercians*, ed. M. Gervers (New York, 1992), pp. 203-204.

mass. And Chimi said to James: 'What do you think about the indignities that the king inflicts on us, and the way he humiliates us daily. Besides, we must find a solution'. James replied, moreover, saying to him: 'Does it seem to you that I have any greater pleasure other than this?' And then Chimi revealed to him whatever was in his heart, as well as about all the young nobles who were in the habit of talking to Chimi. In addition, he said to him: 'I am ready and first'. Besides, on coming out of the church Chimi said to James: 'I beseech you brother, as a faithful friend, that the words we spoke be between us, since nothing can be done. For discontent brings about many things, and one says whatever comes immediately to mind. For this reason I implore you, keep it secret!' And James said to him: 'Carceran, don't you know me. It's not the first time that we have expressed complaints to each other'. Then they took their leave of each other.

95. Furthermore, James went to the court, to the king, and told him everything he knew, both truths and falsehoods. The king, moreover, ordered him upon his life that no one should learn that he had come to him.[212]

In addition, he gave orders for a general muster[213] [of troops] to take place <at the back>[214] by the customs house[215] on Sunday, and there were found to be 700 cavalry.

Furthermore, after two days he sent for and seized all three children of Chimi, as well as Nicholas [the son] of Constantine, Demetrios [the son] of Bustron, John Sabah, James Salaha, Balian de Nores and Marcello. And they brought them before him one by one, and he said to them: 'is this what I deserve, for having established you?' In addition, Nicholas [the son] of Constantine had a grievance because <the king> had established a fencing joust,[216] <so that the champions might contest in court. And he had directed the above-mentioned Nicholas to judge, because he himself was a

---

[212] King James II rewarded James of Malta, who was clearly an *agent provocateur*, by granting him the *casale* of St Andronikos 'de Curicho' and the fruit market of Nicosia (Florio Bustron, 'Chronique' *op. cit.*, p. 424). See also Richard, *Remembrances, op. cit.*, nos. 8 and note 2, 78 and 122 on James of Malta's appointment as *chevetain* of Pendayia.

[213] These musters of troops were characteristic of the Venetian period. See G. Grivaud – A. Papadaki, 'L'institution de la *mostra generale* de la chevalerie féodale en Crète et en Chypre vénitiennes durant la XVIe siècle', *Studi veneziani*, n.s. XII (1986), 165-199.

[214] The words in brackets < > are from mss. **B** and **M**. See Kehayioglou, Διήγησις, *op. cit.*, p. 145, line 16 of both mss.

[215] Dawkins, *Boustronios*, translates τουχιάναν as market, but I consider it to derive from the Italian *dogana* (French *douane*) meaning customs house. It must have been near the Market or Customs Gate in eastern Nicosia, on which see Leventis, *Nicosia, op. cit.*, pp. 145 and 357.

[216] Dawkins, *Boustronios, op. cit.*, § 95 and Hill, *op. cit.*, III, 648 misinterpret this event, Dawkins thinking that Nicholas was to judge a music contest and Hill that he was to give a solo performance (see also Kehayioglou, Διήγησις, *op. cit.*, pp. 273*-274*). The Greek τζόγια της σκλίμας means a fencing joust (τζόγια from Old French *joste* = joust: σκλίμα from Old French *escremie* = swordplay. See A. Hindley, F.W. Langley and B.J. Levy, *Old French-English Dictionary* (Cambridge, 2000), pp. 288 and 379.

champion and a valiant man>.[217] Nicholas, moreover, judged the champions who were competing, but at the judgement it appeared to the king that he had judged them badly, and so on his orders Nicholas was beaten, and he had a grievance that he had injured him in front of the whole of Nicosia, he being a good man and valiant as a person. Besides, the king was holding a dagger <in front of him. Furthermore, the king observed that his eyes were upon his dagger, and the king straightaway put it behind him. Indeed, Nicholas was thinking of snatching it, so as to kill the king>.[218] And while he was talking to him, had he not put the dagger behind him Nicholas would have killed the king. <And he (i.e. the king) said to him: 'Huh, is this why I honoured you?'

In addition, he had them all put in gaol and in irons, and had them guarded well>.[219] A great evil and lamentation took place, moreover, among their wives and kinsmen and kinswomen, while the king's mother, <the barons>[220] and the knights made appeals. Indeed, there was no way <for the king to climb down>.[221] He arrived at the decision to have all of them beheaded, and he gave orders for carts to take them away, and they took Nicholas, Marcello and Demetrios and beheaded them. Besides, the carts returned to take the others as well. The king, moreover, entered his chamber and locked himself in, <so that they would not cause him to have scruples>.[222]

In addition, his mother arrived, as well as all the people with the women and their children and relatives, battered, ragged <and barefoot>[223], and his mother knocked and they forced open the doors, and all of them, great and small, fell at his feet in tears. Furthermore, he granted them (i.e. those remaining) a reprieve from the awful death and he had them placed in solitary confinement, and they remained in isolation until the king died.[224] Besides, on coming out of the chamber he asked: 'Did they behead Nicholas [the son] of Constantine?' And they said to him: 'They beheaded him'. He, moreover, said: 'May God bless him!' For the king was extremely fond of Nicholas. Furthermore, on his (i.e. the king's) death they allowed them (i.e. the surviving conspirators) to be released.

96. In addition, in the year 1471 he despatched the archbishop to Rome, sending him there on numerous errands; firstly to persuade the pope to have him crowned king of

---

[217] The words in brackets < > have been taken from mss. **B** and **M**. See Kehayioglou, *Διήγησις, op. cit.*, p. 147, lines 4-6 of mss. **B** and **M**.

[218] The words in brackets < > have been taken from mss. **B** and **M**. See *ibid.*, p. 147, lines 8-11 of mss. **B** and **M**.

[219] The words in brackets < > have been taken from mss. **B** and **M**. See *ibid.*, p. 147, lines 11-13 of ms. **B** and lines 11-12 of ms. **M**.

[220] The words in brackets < > have been taken from mss. **B** and **M**. See *ibid.*, p. 147, line 14 of mss. **B** and **M**.

[221] The words in brackets < > have been taken from mss. **B** and **M**. See *ibid.*, p. 147, line 15 of mss. **B** and **M**.

[222] The words in brackets < > have been taken from mss. **B** and **M**. See *ibid.*, p. 147, lines 18-19 of ms. **B** and line 19 of ms. **M**.

[223] The words in brackets < > have been taken from ms. **B**. See *ibid.*, p. 148, line 2 of ms. **B**.

[224] Florio Bustron, 'Chronique', *op. cit.*, p. 432 states that they were gaoled in Kerynia and released after the king's death, whereupon they went to Rhodes.

Cyprus and secondly to negotiate his marriage with the daughter of the Despot of the Morea, who happened to be in Rome under the guardianship of Cardinal Nicaeas.[225] And on journeying to Rome he presented himself before the pope and conveyed the message. The pope, moreover, <despite everything that he ventured>,[226] did not wish to have him (i.e. King James) crowned because the rightful heir was still alive. Besides, regarding the marriage with the despot's daughter he (i.e. the archbishop) took every measure along with the cardinal and the others. And on coming to Cyprus the archbishop brought a bishop along with him so that the wedding would take place. Furthermore, since the pope did not wish to have him crowned, the king for his part did not wish to proceed with the marriage.

97. And he sent Sir Philip Mistachiel[227] to Venice to bring about the marriage with the [present] queen, Catherine. He brought her, moreover, in the year of Christ 1472 and he married her in Famagusta. Besides, great celebrations were organized. <And the king lived on for one year from when he had married>.[228] In addition, he lived in the kingdom, from the time when he returned to Cyprus, for twelve years and eight months, dying at the age of 33.[229]

98. His will: <And he took to his bed on 27 March 1473>. Furthermore, sensing that he was sick in body, he wished to make a will, and the notary was Sir Thomas Ficardo, his chancellor.[230] Besides, he had appointed as executors of the will in the kingdom

---

[225] George Boustronios does not name the archbishop or the pope. Florio Bustron ('Chronique', *op. cit.*, p. 432) and Stephen de Lusignan (*Chorograffia, op. cit.*, pp. 96 and 215, §§ 417-419) both give Pius II as pope and Louis Fabregues as archbishop, although Pius died in August 1464 and Louis did not become archbishop until 1471. I suggest that 1471 is a misreading of 1461, when Pope Pius II unsuccessfully tried to persuade King James to marry his niece, and angered by his rebuff refused to recognize him as king. Boustronios mistakenly conflated this episode with the later marriage proposal of Pope Paul II, Pius II's Venetian successor, who in 1466-1467 suggested that James should marry Zoe Palaiologina, the daughter of the late Thomas, despot of the Morea. James turned this down also, although Pope Paul granted him his coronation. Cardinal 'Nicaeas' is in fact Cardinal Bessarion, who was Zoe's guardian. See Hill, *op. cit.*, III, 557-558, 628-629, 631 and note 3 and Addenda 1159.

[226] The words in brackets < > have been taken from mss. **B** and **M**. See Kehayioglou, Διήγησις, *op. cit.*, p. 149, line 14 of ms. **B** and lines 14-15 of ms. **M**.

[227] Florio Bustron, 'Chronique', *op. cit.*, pp. 432-433 mistakenly has Philip Podocataro. On Sir Philip Mistachiel, mentioned as the captain of Paphos under King John II in 1452 and a former supporter of Queen Charlotte who later accepted King James II, see Mas Latrie, *Histoire, op. cit.*, III, 48, 53, 126, 178 and 316; *idem.*, 'Documents nouveaux', *op. cit.*, p. 423; J. Darrouzès, 'Notes pour servir à l'histoire de Chypre', ΚΣ XXIII (1959), 45; Richard, *Remembrances, op. cit.*, no. 6 note 1, and on other members of the family no. 37 note 1 and no. 220.

[228] The words in brackets < > have been taken from mss. **B** and **M**. See Kehayioglou, Διήγησις, *op. cit.*, p. 151, line 4 of mss. **B** and **M**.

[229] For descriptions of King James II's reign, see Hill, *op. cit.*, III, 621-656; Edbury, 'Λουζινιανοί', *op. cit.*, pp. 223-239.

[230] Thomas Ficardo also served Queen Catherine as her emissary to the Mamluk sultan following the death of King James, and appears in a list of Cypriot feudatories in the early 16th century. See Mas Latrie, *Histoire, op. cit.*, III, 405-406 and note 6, 419-420 and 420 note 1, 499; *idem.*, 'Documents Nouveaux', *op. cit.*, pp. 518-521 and 521 note 2, where 1480 should read 1489 (Hill, *op. cit.*, III, 742 note 4); Hill, *op. cit.*, III, 696, 725, 731, 735, 741 note 4, 742 and note 4; Ανέκδοτα έγγραφα της κυπριακής ιστορίας από το κρατικό αρχείο της Βενετίας, ed. Aik. Aristeidou, 4 vols. (Nicosia, 1990-2003), I, nos. 11 and 17. The village of Phikardou in the Troodos Mountains derives its name from his family, who held it as a fief.

John Tafur, the count of Tripoli, who was also the captain of Famagusta, Sir John Perez [Fabrigues], the count of Jaffa and of the Karpass,[231] as well as captain of the galleys, the count de Rochas, Morphou de Grenier, Sir Andrea Corner, the auditor of Cyprus who was the queen's uncle, Sir John Rognon, Sir Rizzo Marino, the chamberlain and Peter d'Avila, the constable.[232]

He appointed the men in question as executors, and he said: 'Should God perhaps do His will regarding my person, I leave my wife, who happens to be pregnant, lady and queen of Cyprus. In addition, should she give birth to an heir, let my son have the kingdom! Should he die, moreover, let the illegitimate Eugenius have the kingdom. And should Eugenius die, let John have it. Furthermore, should none of them perhaps live, let my illegitimate daughter have it![233] Should she too happen to die, then let the closest heir from among the Lusignans have it. This indeed is my will. I also bequeath a considerable treasure that I built up by numerous means. As for the galleys that I maintained in armed readiness, let them disarm all of them, for I kept the crews in a state of extreme oppression!'

99. The king in question died on 5 July [in the year] of Christ 1473.[234] As there was no wax in Cyprus they took him and buried him crudely, until some wax should arrive so that they could bury him properly.[235] They buried him, moreover, in Famagusta, in [the cathedral of] St Nicholas, <and cut him open>,[236] extracted his entrails and anointed him with balsam. They also released the men serving in the galleys and let out the nobles who were in solitary confinement.[237]

---

[231] The county of the Karpass was created in 1472, and among the witnesses were John Tafur the count of Tripoli, Sir James Zaplana, Sir John de Ras and Sir Rizzo de Marino. See Mas Latrie, 'Documents nouveaux', *op. cit.*, pp. 421-423.

[232] Hill, *op. cit.*, III, 674, note 1 correctly observes that Peter d'Avila was not constable at that time, but acquired this office subsequently.

[233] Her name was Carla. On King James' illegitimate children see Mas Latrie, 'Documents Nouveaux', *op. cit.*, pp. 564-568; Hill, *op. cit.*, III, 654-656; Aristeidou, Ἔγγραφα, *op.cit.*, I, 187-189.

[234] George Boustronios and Florio Bustron ('Chronique', *op. cit.*, p. 433) wrongly date his death to 5 June 1473, which Dawkins (*Boustronios, op. cit.*, § 99) misreads as 11 June. Hill, III, 651 note 2 rightly points out that since his surviving epitaph reads 6 July the chroniclers are wrong about June, and that George Boustronios' statement that he was bedridden from 27 May is a calculation backwards from the mistaken date given in June. Kehayioglou (Διήγησις, *op. cit.*, pp. 152-153 all mss. and 405-406) dates his death to 5 and not 6 July. This is the most convincing date, as it explains the chronicle's statement below that the news of his death reached Nicosia on 6 July. He probably died on the night of 5-6 July, hence the date 6 July found on his epitaph.

[235] After death the cadavers of kings and nobles, in Cyprus and in Europe, were washed and anointed with odoriferous plants, eviscerated and embalmed, and wax must have been used in these processes. See B. Imhaus, 'La mort dans la société franque à Chypre', *EKEE* XXIV (1998), 45-47.

[236] The words in brackets < > have been taken from mss. **B** and **M**. See Kehayioglou, Διήγησις, *op. cit.*, p. 153, ms. **B** line 7 and ms. **M** line 7.

[237] James II's release of the galley crews and his nomination of testamentary executors who were all, other than the Venetian Andrea Corner and Cypriot Morphou de Grenier, Sicilians or Catalans strongly suggest that he wished to distance the kingdom from Venice, for which see Edbury, 'Λουζινιανοί', *op. cit.*, pp. 238-239.

100. In addition, on 19 July 1473 the queen had 1,000 *modii* of wheat sent to Nicosia, <because it> was still expensive, <and it was sold>[238] at two and a half[239] per *modius*.

101. Besides, as soon as the king died they sent Andrea Casoli, a burgess of Famagusta,[240] as a messenger to Syria so as to inform the sultan of the king's death. Furthermore, the Venetians also sent a galley to Venice from the fleet, to announce the king's death and for them (i.e. the Venetian government) to tell them what to do.

102. And on 6 July [in the year] of Christ 1473 the news that: 'the king has died' reached Nicosia. According to custom, moreover, all the constables[241], the Venetian *baiulo*, Sir Muzzo de Constanzo, the admiral of Cyprus who was also regent in Nicosia, Sir Paul Chappes, whom King James had appointed seneschal, Sir William de Ras who was the viscount of Nicosia, the Greek bishop Nicholas, Anthony Silouan, the vicar of the great church (i.e. the cathedral of the Holy Wisdom in Nicosia) and Sir John de Ras, who had come from Famagusta and had proclaimed the queen in Nicosia and throughout all the castles, assembled.

They also took the oath [of fealty] to Niccolo de Morabit, who was the garrison commander in Paphos, and the queen summoned him to come. They sent for Cortese[242] and Sir John Attar as well, and every liegeman gave an oath to the queen. **103.** In addition, Morphou de Grenier, the count of Rochas, came to Nicosia from Famagusta on 29 July [in the year] of Christ 1473. Besides, he assembled the populace of Nicosia[243] and told them that: 'The Queen has been detained from her arrival in Nicosia because she is about to give birth this month. And I came on her behalf to tell you this, and she holds you very dearly. Furthermore, I wish to make everything known to you'. Meanwhile, he comforted them with many other tidings, and the people were pleased on hearing them and said to him: 'Lord, recommend us to her ladyship and tell her ladyship that we are her subjects, at her command, ready to live and to die in her name!' The count, moreover, remained in Nicosia on her behalf. In addition, the admiral and Peter d'Avila went to Famagusta, and he (i.e. the admiral)

---

[238] The words in brackets < > have been taken from mss. **B** and **M**. See Kehayioglou, *Διήγησις, op. cit.*, p. 153, line 12 of ms. **B** and line 11 of ms. **M**.

[239] None of the three mss. specify a unit of currency. Dawkins, *Boustronios, op. cit.*, §100 adds '*gros*' before per *modius*.

[240] Probably identical with the Andrea Cazulli mentioned in the context of charges brought against Napoleone Lomellini, the Genoese Captain of Famagusta, in 1459. See Otten, *Une enquête, op. cit.*, pp. 142 and 235 (note 156).

[241] The words 'ούλοι οι κοντόσταβλοι (= all constables)' are present in all three mss. but this is probably an error on Boustronios' part for 'ούλοι οι κουβερνούρηδες', that is all governors or royal councilors.

[242] Florio Bustron, 'Chronique', *op. cit.*, p. 433 has count Cortese.

[243] The people of Nicosia showed an unwavering loyalty towards Queen Catherine, and wept during her final departure from Cyprus, on which see below. For the development of urban assemblies in Nicosia into permanent institutions by the close of the 15th century see Arbel, 'Urban Assemblies', *op. cit.*, pp. 206-210.

returned to Nicosia after a few days, and they appointed him to the office of chamberlain, just as he had enjoyed it while the king was alive. Peter d'Avila, moreover, remained in Famagusta, while he sent for and took his wife there as well. And he had Benedict Cartagena appointed in his place.

104. Besides, on 30 July the queen sent [word] from Famagusta to Nicosia so as to take the porphyry sarcophagus from [the cathedral of] Holy Wisdom and have the king placed within it. Furthermore, the churchmen on hearing this sat in council and decided [as follows]: 'It must not come out of [the cathedral of] the Holy Wisdom! And let anyone who wishes to take it be excommunicate!' Besides, they sent word of this to the queen. The queen, moreover, gave orders for word to be sent to the pope,[244] so that he would issue a decree.

105. In addition, on the last day of July a brigantine[245] arrived from Rhodes to ascertain the death of the king, which had been sent by Queen Charlotte, and setting anchor in the area of Chrysochou it dropped off Valentine, a youth[246] in the service of Sir John de Montolif, so as to find out everything that was taking place and to return forthwith. And following his disembarkation he came to Pendayia. As soon as they recognised him, moreover, they seized him and took him to the *chevetain* of Pendayia, and they interrogated him regarding the reason he had come. And he said to them: 'I came on a brigantine to find out about the death of the king. The brigantine in question has a knight on board who is Sir John de Gibelet, as well as Odet Boussat, a valet of the queen, and many others, and they have numerous letters on them'.

The *chevetain*, moreover, had this Valentine sent straightaway to Famagusta on account of the brigantine. In addition, they armed a ship at once and John Perez went on board as captain, going off in search of the brigantine. Furthermore, on 3 August John Perez returned, not having been able to discover anything. And on 11 August the above-mentioned Valentine was beheaded and quartered.

106. Besides, on the 12 August they arrested Phokas, who was [serving] in the king's chamber, and whom the king had regarded very dearly. Furthermore, they arrested him because he was cognisant of the king's affairs, so that they might find out something from him.

107. On 16 August 1473, moreover, the count of Tripoli, Sir John Tafur, Peter d'Avila and the chancellor set out and entered the citadel of Famagusta so as to interrogate the above-mentioned Phokas. They put him on the rack many times, and they did so on account of the king's money, but he confessed nothing. And they said: 'Sixty thousand ducats have been lost'.

---

[244] Pope Sixtus IV (1471-1484) on whose involvement with the eastern Mediterranean see Setton, *Papacy and Levant, op. cit.*, II, 314-381.

[245] This was a small oared vessel fitted with sails that had 6-16 benches with one man to each oar, making it smaller than a galliot but slightly larger than a frigate. See Braudel, *Mediterranean, op. cit.*, pp. 119, 868, 871 and 873-874; Earle, *Corsairs, op. cit.*, p. 48 note.

[246] Florio Bustron, 'Chronique', *op. cit.*, pp. 435-436 when recounting this incident describes Valentine as 'un giovene', which Hill, *op. cit.*, III, 598, wrongly translates as 'son'.

108. Furthermore, on 19 August[247] a letter from Famagusta arrived in Nicosia, sent on the queen's behalf to the viscount, Sir William de Ras, ordering him to find Marin de Bonaventura, that they might show him the queen's letter and tell him on her behalf that they [had orders] to arrest the person [whose name] was written down. And in accordance with her command they seized him, [a person] who happened to be in the service of Sir Rizzo [de Marino], immediately, and they took him to Famagusta. Besides, they had him tortured, but he confessed nothing and they released him.

109. The viscount went to the house of Marietta Bragadin on the same day, ordering Luke her brother on behalf of the queen, to go to Famagusta immediately, and should he not wish to they would send him against his will. Luke, moreover, on hearing this rode off at that instant, and he went to Famagusta, and he also took the privileges of Marietta and of Claire, his sister, as well as his own, and going to Famagusta he paid homage to the queen on his own account and for all the others together.

110. Furthermore, Sir John Arognon[248] died on the 20 August.[249] And he was poor when he arrived in Cyprus, but he was a Catalan from a good family and the king conferred many benefits upon him and married him to Lady Margaret, the daughter of Franceschin de Bandes,[250] giving him a fine income. He died, moreover, in Famagusta and he was buried in [the church of] St Francis,[251] a monk.

111. On the same day they sent Andrea de l'Orsa as an emissary to the sultan, on the part of the queen.

112. <And on the same day they sent Constantine de Chio[252] to Syria to bring back Andrea Casoli>.[253]

---

[247] Mss. **B** and **M** both have 17 August. See Kehayioglou, Διήγησις, op. cit., p. 159 line 13 of both mss.

[248] Florio Bustron, 'Chronique', op. cit., p. 421 states that between 1464-1468 King James II granted him the fief of Kalavassos in the Larnaca district and 200 measures of wine. See also Mas Latrie, Histoire, op. cit., III, 181 and note 3, 493; idem., 'Documents nouveaux', op. cit., pp. 409-410; 'Richard, Remembrances, op. cit., nos. 158 and note 3 and 185.

[249] Mss. **B** and **M** both have 18 August. See Kehayioglou, Διήγησις, op. cit., p. 161 line 13 of both mss.

[250] Dawkins, Boustronios, op. cit., § 110 names him de Santes, following ms. **M**, but mss. **A** and **B** both have de Bandes (Kehayioglou, Διήγησις, op. cit., pp. 160-161). The de Bandes were a prominent family of burgesses of Famagusta and Florio Bustron ('Chronique', pp. 422 and 448) also has this form. On this family see P. Edbury, 'Famagusta in 1300', in Cyprus and the Crusades, ed. N. Coureas and J. Riley-Smith (Nicosia, 1995), p. 315 and note 70; Gilmour Bryson, Templars, op. cit., pp. 429-430. Florio Bustron, 'Chronique', op. cit., p. 422 recounts how between 1464 and 1468 King James II gave Lady Margaret, the daughter of Franceschin de Bandes, the casalia of Katokopia and Syriati as fiefs.

[251] This was the church attached to the Franciscan convent in Famagusta, for a description of which see Enlart, Gothic Art, op. cit., pp. 262-267.

[252] He was a soldier of King James II, who in December 1468 increased his annual stipend by 100 bezants, to be taken from the revenues of the tax on livestock known as the maréchaussée. See Richard, Remembrances, op. cit., no. 97.

[253] The words in brackets < > are taken from mss. **B** and **M**. See Kehayioglou, Διήγησις, op. cit., p. 163, lines 2-3 of mss. **B** and **M**.

113. On the same day the Venetian fleet arrived in Famagusta, sixty galleys. And they came victorious[254], seizing the castle at Makri.[255] In addition, they captured numerous Turks and hanged them, and they also took much wheat. Furthermore, they executed 26 people from the ships, those ships that they had captured off Rhodes.

Besides, Queen Charlotte on learning the news sent two friars, [who were] French knights, as emissaries to the admiral of the Venetian fleet, stating that: 'King James, who held the kingdom unjustly, has died. Why should others take it while the heir is living? For this reason, so long as the rightful heir of the kingdom is living his lordship should be prepared to offer her every means of assistance so that she may have her kingdom! For all that is fair requires this, since the preceding kings always regarded you very dearly, as well as your affairs and the revenues that you had in Cyprus, and you are bound by justice to assist her'.

And the admiral replied: 'As regards what you say, that the bastard was holding the kingdom unjustly and that now the queen wants it as the heir, I reply to you: he held the kingdom as king, just as the sultan appointed him. In addition, I am obliged to work for my ladyship (i.e. Queen Catherine) rather than for her ladyship Queen Charlotte. And this is my answer'.[256] The emissaries went back and the fleet came to Cyprus, to Famagusta. Besides, the queen at once sent out all her knights, and they went to the littoral. Furthermore, the admiral of the fleet together with many gentlemen disembarked, and they arrived at the palace where the queen was, while the admiral greeted her and listened to her very attentively. The queen, moreover, thanked him, and they returned to the ships.

114. In addition, the fleet set sail on the same day[257] and went to Corycos.[258] Six

---

[254] Dawkins, *Boustronios, op. cit.*, §113, misread κερδεμένα as meaning 'gained' as opposed to 'victorious' and so thought that the Venetian fleet, made up of 60 galleys, had in fact had captured 60 galleys from the Turks. See Kehayioglou, *Διήγησις, op. cit.*, pp. 162-163, where a careful reading of all three mss. makes it clear that the galleys in question were the Venetian fleet itself, not captured Turkish galleys. It is stated below that 26 prisoners from Turkish ships captured off Rhodes were executed. Had the captured ships numbered 60 one imagines that the number of persons executed would have been far greater.

[255] This is a town located on the southern Turkish coast, now called Fethiye. See A. Luttrell, 'The Hospitallers on Rhodes confront the Turks, 1306-1421', in *The Hospitallers of Rhodes and their Mediterranean World*, II (Aldershot, 1992), 104.

[256] Florio Bustron, 'Chronique', *op. cit.*, pp. 434-435, has the Venetian commander cite additional justifications: might and not laws determined the right to kingdoms, the Genoese as well as Charlotte had lost the kingdom, and Catherine, a daughter of Venice, had been appointed heir along with the son she had had by James, which meant that Venice was obliged to uphold her.

[257] Mss. **B** and **M** both have 19 August. See Kehayioglou, *Διήγησις, op. cit.*, p. 165 line 8 of both mss.

[258] King Peter I of Cyprus had acquired Corycos (*alias* Gorhigos) early in 1360 (Makhairas, *Recital, op. cit.*, §§112-116) and it remained a Cypriot possession until 1448, when the emir of Karaman seized it (Florio Bustron, 'Chronique', *op. cit.*, p. 384; Mas Latrie, *Histoire, op. cit.*, III, 48-56 and 59).

galleys remained behind in Famagusta along with 50 soldiers and two Greek commanders, the one named Rhalles and the other Demetrios.[259]

115. Besides, on the same day the emissary of King Ferdinand (of Naples), named Severus, made his entrance, and in his discussion with the governors he spoke very bluntly, with arrogance.[260] Having heard him they expelled him and exiled him in Paralimni, outside Famagusta.

116. Furthermore, on 20 August <1473>[261] they apprehended Matthew, the chief cantor[262], together with his company and Friar Desiderius, as well as a canon, a friar and George Leotario, placing them on the rack. Matthew, Desiderius and Friar Anthony confessed, moreover, and said that: 'A veneration takes place on 15 August at Apsinthi[otissa] and Akheiropoiete, and the whole of Kerynia goes to the above-mentioned venerations', and that they had wanted to hold the castle for [Queen] Charlotte. The bishop of Limassol,[263] moreover, had them brought into his presence, and he divested all three of them of every right to confer the sacraments. And then they were beheaded and quartered.

117. <And on the same day> they also hanged the youth who had come over from Rhodes in order to spy.[264]

118. Furthermore, on the same day the count de Rochas sent John de Navarre to Kerynia with 15 men, along with their horses, and another 25 from Famagusta so as to bring others who were said to be conspirators in Kerynia. And on the presentation of

---

[259] This action signalled the beginning of the Venetian military presence on Cyprus.

[260] Severus had come to further the negotiations for the marriage of King James II's illegitimate daughter Carla with Don Alonzo, the illegitimate son of King Ferdinand of Naples, an issue which George Boustronios only mentions below and which Archbishop Louis Perez Fabrigues had promoted (Florio Bustron, 'Chronique', *op. cit.*, p. 436). King Ferdinand (1458-1494), the natural son of King Alfonso of Aragon and Naples (1416-1458) succeeded his father to the throne of Naples with the support of Pope Pius II (1458-1464), the famous literary figure, on whom see Setton, *Papacy and Levant, op. cit.*, II, 196-270.

[261] The number in brackets < > is from mss. **B** and **M**. See Kehayioglou, Διήγησις, *op. cit.*, p. 165, ms. **B** line 16 and ms. **M** line 15.

[262] Dawkins, *Boustronios, op. cit.*, §116 translates the Greek τσεντούρην as 'officer', Kehayioglou, Διήγησις, *op. cit.*, p. 494 suggests 'centurion', and Florio Bustron, 'Chronique', *op. cit.*, p. 437 has Centurione as Matthew's surname. I have translated τσεντούρης as cantor, since his companions belonged to the clergy and Bishop Antonio di Zuco of Limassol divested all of them of every form of sacring (τσεντούρης = French *chanteor* = cantor: see Hindley *et al.* Old French-English Dictionary, *op. cit.*, p. 112).

[263] This was a certain Anthony di Zucco, who may have succeeded Peter de Manatiis in around 1456-1460 and himself died in March 1479. See Giuseppe della Santa, 'Alcuni documenti per la storia della chiesa di Limisso in Cipro durante la seconda metà del sec. XV', *Nuovo archivio Veneto*, XVI (1898), 153-158, 161, 169-170 and 186 (doc. IV).

[264] The words in brackets < > are from mss. **B** and **M**. See Kehayioglou, Διήγησις, *op. cit.*, p. 167, ms. **B** line 6 and ms. **M** line 5. This incident recalls Valentine's secret arrival in Cyprus on behalf of Sir John de Montolif and Queen Charlotte, but it cannot be the same youth, for as seen above Valentine was beheaded and quartered.

the queen's charter the captain [at Kerynia] had them all arrested, Demetrios Psichistes, his son, his son in law and a further five foreigners. They conducted them to Famagusta, and one of them got away, while the others were taken to Famagusta and placed on the rack. They did not, moreover, confess, and they released them.

119. Furthermore, a letter from Famagusta arrived on the same day: 'A Frenchman who was at [the church of] St Nicholas of Silouan[265] must be apprehended! Also King Louis' shoemaker! And let them be despatched to Famagusta!' And they were found guiltless and were released.

120. Besides, on the same day the messenger Andrea Casoli arrived from Cairo. The sultan showed himself well disposed towards him, having him clothed in cloth of gold. He ordered the tribute to be sent to him.

121. Furthermore, on this day the queen had Sir Paolo Contarini appointed captain in Kerynia, and Sir Peter de Vales the castellan there.

122. Besides, Queen Charlotte also sent an envoy from Rhodes to the sultan, [Bernard de] Rivesaltes, as well as Nicolin di Miglias. And the sultan did not receive him, and had them both detained at Cairo.[266]

123. In addition, a Venetian galley arrived from Rhodes on the same day, and inside there was a youth named Nicholas who had brought a young lady from Rhodes with him, and he was the brother of Valentine, whom they had beheaded and quartered. And they seized him as soon as he disembarked and took him to the palace, and had him interrogated over how he had come from Rhodes, bringing the young lady as well. And he told them: 'My lords, I fell in love with her and eloped with her from Rhodes'. They had them both placed in custody so as to ascertain clearly the reason for their arrival.

124. Furthermore, on the 21 August they brought two persons from Famagusta to Nicosia, the Frenchman, whom they beheaded, and the other, whom they dispatched to Kerynia and likewise beheaded.[267]

---

[265] On 31 March 1468 King James II conferred this church and its revenues on a lifetime basis to his chaplain, Brother Paul, who would enter into possession of it on the death of the present incumbent, Prior Peter Omode. Opposite the church were the houses belonging to Nicolin Sedit and Andos Lakhanas, whose names indicate a Syrian origin. See Richard, *Remembrances, op. cit.*, nos. 167 and 206 and no. 206 note 2.

[266] Florio Bustron, 'Chronique', *op. cit.*, p. 434 omits Bernard de Rivesaltes. Both he and George Boustronios below state that the sultan had the envoys handed over to Queen Catherine's ambassador, for him to despatch them to her so that she might do as she pleased with them. The ambassador in question was probably Andrew (*alias* Anthony) de Lorsa, who returned to Cyprus on 26 October, as mentioned below. Queen Catherine seems to have allowed them to return to Rhodes, for on 1 July 1474 they both received a safe-conduct from the Hospitaller Grand Master Gianbattista di Orsini at Queen Charlotte's request (Mas Latrie, *Histoire, op. cit.*, III, 127 note 3).

[267] This refers clearly to the Frenchman and King Louis' shoemaker, mentioned above (§119) as having been arrested, sent to Famagusta and then released. Clearly the authorities had in the meantime apprehended them once more.

125. On the 22 [August], moreover, an emissary from the pope arrived bringing much news from Italy.

126. And on the 23 August the emissary from Syria arrived, and as soon as he touched dry land he went off, because he learnt that they wished to seize him.[268]

127. And on the same day they released Nicholas and the young lady who had arrived from Rhodes.

128. Furthermore, on 24 August Sir Paolo Contarini was appointed captain at Kerynia.[269]

129. In addition, on 27 [August] the queen went into labour and on the 28 she gave birth to a strapping baby boy. And he was proclaimed King James [III], and after living for one year he died.

130. On the 29 [August], moreover, the news that she had given birth reached Nicosia, and there were celebrations for three nights running, while all the prisoners were set free.[270]

131. And on 3 September a ship from Rhodes reached Famagusta, and Sir Louis Alberic, Zaplana's nephew, arrived. Furthermore, the king (James II) had honoured him greatly on his [previous] arrival in Cyprus on account of his regard for Sir James [Zaplana] <his uncle>, granting him an income of 1000 ducats <a year>[271]. Sir Louis, moreover, on perceiving that the affairs of King James were unsettled, returned every income that he had given him and went straight back to Rhodes. Indeed it was Sir James Zaplana, once he had learnt about it, the death of the king, who had sent him to

---

[268] Hill, *op. cit.*, III, 660 states that this reference to an unnamed envoy from Syria is incomprehensible. One notes, however that Venice in this period had poor relations with the Mamluks of Egypt, who were suspicious of her dealings with Uzun Hasan, the Turcoman ruler controlling the lands east of Syria. In 1473 the Mamluks seized a Venetian envoy sent from Cyprus to contact Uzun Hasan, and by the middle of this year relations were so bad that Venetian merchants bound for Alexandria and Beirut were forbidden to go ashore. See E. Ashtor, *Levant Trade in the Later Middle Ages* (Princeton, 1983), pp. 454-456. Perhaps the envoy from Syria was a Mamluk fearing arrest by the Venetians in retaliation for the seizure of the Venetian envoy, hence his flight.

[269] Paolo Contarinii was a cousin and a devoted supporter of Queen Catherine.It was at this time, on 24 August 1473, that the Venetian Senate wrote to the captain-general Peter Mocenigo instructing him to go to Cyprus with the fleet to protect the island and Queen Catherine, to join forces with the admiral of King Ferdinand of Naples in operations against the Ottoman Turks, but to hasten back to Cyprus forthwith with his fleet if the said admiral resolved to go there without him. See Mas Latrie, *Histoire, op. cit.*, III, 348-350.

[270] On 2 September the Venetian Senate wrote to Queen Catherine assuring her of Venetian protection, and informing her that it had given Mocenigo instructions to keep at least five galleys permanently stationed in the harbour of Famagusta. See Mas Latrie, *Histoire, op. cit.*, III, 348, note 2.

[271] The words in brackets < > in this sentence have been added from mss. **B** and **M**. See Kehayioglou, *Διήγησις, op. cit.*, p. 171, ms. **B** lines 15-16 and ms. **M** lines 12-13.

Cyprus, for Sir James happened to be in Rhodes over an issue that he had with his eldest brother, and he sent him over to find out how things were going.

132. Besides, on 6 September[272] a ship from Syria arrived bringing a written message that the envoy of Queen Catherine: 'had been received by the sultan, who also placed into his hands Charlotte's envoy and Nicholas di Miglias'. Furthermore, he had them brought back to Cyprus and also sent a Mamluk envoy.

133. And on 10 September the Count de Rochas went to Famagusta, <the queen having summoned him.>[273] And he left the admiral in his place.

134. On the same day, moreover, Nicholas Morabit was appointed viscount and William de Ras was divested [of this office].[274]

135. In addition, on the 12 September the Venetian *baiulo* ventured forth from Nicosia and went to Famagusta by coach.[275]

136. Besides, on the same day two galleys of the fleet arrived on the part of the captain, [stating] that: 'The ships that happened to be in Cyprus should sail before him', and the trumpet sounded forthwith, with everyone entering the ships at once, 'and all the soldiers must take their mounts and present themselves to the captain!' And they went straightaway, and there were 18 ships.

137. Furthermore, on 14 September a ship from the [Mamluk] sultan arrived, bringing the queen a message that she should immediately despatch the king's treasure chest and all the valuables pertaining to him, because they were his. For the sultan did not know that the queen had given birth and had an heir.[276]

138. On this day, moreover, Brother William [Goneme] died and they buried him in

---

[272] Ms. **A** wrongly has 'December' and I have followed mss. **B** and **M**. See *ibid.*, p. 173, line 2 of both mss.

[273] The words in brackets < > are taken from mss. **B** and **M**. See *ibid.*, p. 173, line 7 of both mss.

[274] In exchange for relinquishing his office Queen Catherine granted William de Ras an annual stipend of 100 ducats. Sometime before August 1477, when his son John submitted a claim to the Venetian Senate on his behalf, it was revoked by the Venetian *provedittore* and councillors on Cyprus along with estates and distinct localities that King James had given him in exchange for his ancestral properties, despite a royal privilege stating that he was to enjoy them, and the yearly income of 200 ducats they yielded, without this being contested. In March 1479, however, the Venetian Senate restored to him the annual income of 100 ducats. See Mas Latrie, 'Documents nouveaux', *op. cit.*, pp. 494-495.

[275] Mss. **B** and **M** both have 'on the same day', that is 10 September. See Kehayioglou, Διήγη-σις, *op. cit.*, p. 173 lines 11-12 of both mss. Clearly the Venetian *baiulo* would have felt safer in Famagusta, where the Venetian galleys were stationed.

[276] Florio Bustron, 'Chronique', *op. cit.*, p. 434 states that on learning that the queen had given birth to a son the sultan withdrew this demand, and that the Venetian Senate wrote to the captain-general in Crete (i.e.Mocenigo) asking him to grant every favour and assistance to the queen, a probable reference to their letter of 24 August mentioned above.

[the monastery of] St Augustine.[277] This person had done many good things for the monastery, had bequeathed it a village and had also had the hostel built. And as his executors he assigned the *baiulo* of the Venetians, the dean of the great church and the vicar of the great church.[278]

139. And on the 22 September Sir John Mistachiel was knighted in Famagusta and was appointed the emissary to Venice on the part of the queen.

140. Furthermore, on the same day the commander of the fleet landed the Venetians, with many gentlemen among them, at Famagusta.

141. In addition, this fleet sailed away from Famagusta on 2 October. As it was leaving, moreover, two ships from the West arrived and conferred with the commander, and the fleet returned forthwith to Famagusta.

Besides, on the same day a ship belonging to Marufus arrived in Famagusta loaded with corn. Furthermore, there also came one belonging to the pope loaded with corn, and they took it. Yet another ship arrived loaded with corn, and they took it. On board this ship, moreover, was the patriarch who possesses Psimolophou.[279] And when King James came, he took the villages from everyone and took this village as well, and as soon as the patriarch learnt of this he sent an emissary to the king to regain it, but was unable to do so, and the king rented it from the patriarch for 200 ducats a year. And they impounded the above ships on this pretext. The queen sent Sir James to Salines on learning of this, and he found the ships and the patriarch. In addition, he gave him 400 ducats and had the galley brought back to Famagusta along with all its victuals.

142. On the same day, moreover, John Perez was brought from Famagusta at the point of death and taken to the archbishopric, for his brother was the archbishop.[280]And Luke of Jerusalem, the *bailli* of the royal court, died on this day.[281]

---

[277] William Goneme had relinquished the office of archbishop sometime before 3 June 1469, when the Venetian Senate instructed the College to write to its ambassador at Rome informing the Venetian pope Paul II of the unsuitability of a Catalan nominee for this post on account of the intrigues of King Ferdinand of Naples in Cyprus. He died an Augustinian canon. See Mas Latrie, *Histoire, op. cit.*, III, 310 and note 1, *idem.*, 'Histoire des archevêques', *op. cit.*, p. 297

[278] The 'Great Church' refers to the Latin cathedral of the Holy Wisdom in Nicosia.

[279] This was the titular Latin patriarch of Jerusalem. On his possession of the *casale* of Psimolophou see Richard, 'Le casal de Psimolopho ', *op. cit.*, pp. 121-153.

[280] His brother Louis Perez had been archbishop from 1471, as stated above, and certainly before 27 December 1472, the date of a signed letter of King James II accrediting him as his envoy to the Holy See, for which see Mas Latrie, 'Documents nouveaux', *op. cit.*, pp. 417-418. One notes that Queen Catherine herself later described Count John Perez Fabrigues as a traitor in a letter of 20 March 1474 to Doge Nicholas Marcello of Venice (*Ibid.*, p. 449) in which she proposed granting the titular county of Jaffa, which he had held, to her cousin George Contarinii.

[281] This information is not found in mss. **B** and **M**. See Kehayioglou, Διήγησις, *op. cit.*, pp. 176-177. Luke of Jerusalem is mentioned as a good friend of King James II and as the *bailli* of Phinikas, a locality in the Paphos district forming part of the Little Commandery of the Hospitallers on Cyprus (Richard, *Remembrances, op. cit.*, no. 147). A certain Manuel of Jerusalem is mentioned in a document of May 1413 regarding the division of water rights at the *casale* of Kythraea (Mas Latrie, *Histoire, op. cit.*, II, 504), while Tristan and Jerome of Jerusalem appear in a list of fief-holders for the years 1510-1521 (*Ibid.*, III, 500).

143. Furthermore, on the same day a written message was brought to the viscount, and it stated: 'We make it known to you that the government of Venice has sent us an envoy [stating] that we must hold back 15 galleys from the fleet for the defence of the island, and, should it be necessary, we must send word to the commander to hold back the whole fleet. And so organize major festivities throughout Cyprus!'

144. Besides, on 2 October[282] the person who had been placed in custody on account of the king's money was released, as were George the lute player and Philip the maker of bridles, who were not guilty as regarded Kerynia.

145. Furthermore, on 2 October Peter d'Avila was knighted in Famagusta. A great disturbance took place and many were killed. And had Peter d'Avila not secured the Porta Maris[283] in time, a great calamity would have ensued.

146. In addition, Viscount Morabit issued a proclamation on 21 October, that: 'All the prostitutes must go to the camel yard and the coach station,[284] and let none be found in the vicinity, and whoever might be found shall be banished from Nicosia!'

147. And on 24 October John Perez the count of Jaffa died, and he was buried in [the cathedral of] the Holy Wisdom.

148. On 26 October, moreover, a written message from Famagusta came into the hands of the admiral and the viscount that: 'They must go to the count of Jaffa's house and register his possessions and houses both within and outside Nicosia, as well as the villages of the church!' And they did so, also taking his written records. Furthermore, his wife on discovering this mounted her horse at once and went to Famagusta. And the queen after seeing her left her in [the enjoyment of] her possessions.

149. And on the same day Anthony de l'Orsa arrived from Cairo, where he had gone as an envoy, and he brought news that: 'the Sultan is well disposed towards Cyprus and he should be sent 24,000 ducats [in tribute] for three outstanding payments, and a good present because the queen has entered into her kingdom!'[285]

150. In this month the queen appointed Sasson de Nores constable of Jerusalem.[286]

---

[282] Mss. **B** and **M** both have 12 October. See Kehayioglou, Διήγησις, op. cit., p. 177 line 13 of both mss. The unnamed person released was possibly Phokas, on whom see §§106-107 above.

[283] The Greek πόρτα του γιαλού must refer to the Porta Maris (alias Porta Comerhii) on the eastern seaward side of the walls. For references see Otten, Une enquête, op. cit., pp. 56, 61, 162, 191, 194-195, 209, 225, 232, 234, 237, 239, 241 and 262.

[284] The coach station is also mentioned in Makhairas, Recital, op. cit., §§434 and 443.

[285] Ms. **M** states: 'because the **child** has taken possession of the kingdom'. See Kehayioglou, Διήγησις, op. cit., p. 179, line 18.

[286] Mss. **B** and **M** both have 'on the same day'. See ibid., line 1 of both mss. Sassons de Nores, despite having been a supporter of Queen Charlotte and with her at the castle of Kerynia, later became one of King James II's most prominent officers. He was present with him at the surrender of Famagusta in 1464, received the casalia of Pyla and one half of Arediou between 1464 and 1468, and on 14 September 1468 he appointed him chief bailiff of the kingdom and supervisor of the secrete in the place of James Zaplana, who was to be assigned other duties. His mother probably originated from the old Latin family of Sassons (alias Soissons), established in Cyprus since 1197. See Florio Bustron, 'Chronique', op. cit., pp. 397, 415 and 423; Chamberlain, Lacrimae, op. cit., pp. 151-153; Richard, Remembrances, op. cit., nos. 69, 87, 130, 146-147, 155, 174-176, 178-184, 198, [208]-212, 214, 216-221, 229 and 232-234; Coureas and Schabel, Cartulary, op. cit., no. 46.

151. And on 30 October the queen despatched three letters sealed with [the emblem of] St Mark, sent by the government of Venice, to Nicosia, and they were read out in [the cathedral of] the Holy Wisdom. And they stated: 'We learnt of the king's death and were greatly saddened. Secondly, we have learnt that the whole island is at peace and that all the lords desire you to be queen, and we have derived great pleasure from this. Take care as far as possible to be mindful of your life and that of your child, and do not concern yourself over the other matters! For we too wish to offer you assistance in whatsoever matters you require it. We have, moreover, written to the commander of the fleet, [instructing him] to send you five galleys to be at your service. Furthermore, notify us should you have any additional requirement!'

152. And Brother Louis the archbishop arrived on 5 November 1473, whom King James had sent as an envoy to King Ferdinand to betroth his illegitimate daughter to King Ferdinand's illegitimate son. He also brought an envoy along with him.[287]

153. In addition, on 14 November Peter d'Avila together with Franks and Greeks, as many as were salaried, rode out with their weapons and went to Famagusta, with Peter d'Avila as their captain, so as to receive orders on what to do. On their way they encountered a certain person named Ringo. And Peter d'Avila asked him: 'What is the news from Famagusta?' And he said to him: 'Know that the queen's uncle Sir Andrew Corner was assassinated on Saturday, before 3 a.m., and her nephew Sir Marco Bembo, as well as Sir Paul Chappe and Master Gabriel Gentile, the doctor'. And he (i.e. Peter d'Avila) asked him: 'How did this come about?' And he told him: 'I don't know anything to tell you other than what you have heard', and saying goodbye to him he departed.

And in the first hour of the night Sir Louis Alberic, Zaplana's nephew, arrived from Famagusta, and conveyed the news to Morabit, to Sir Muzzio di Constanzo and to Sir John de Ras, narrating the event to them as it had come to pass, and said to them:

154. 'My lords! Know that the pope had sent a letter through the archbishop to the queen and to all the knights.[288] "Know that you have been shamed before the whole

---

[287] Hill, *op. cit.*, III, 670 and notes 2-3 states that Archbishop Louis arrived on 15 November, immediately after the murder of Andrew Corner, Marco Bembo, Gabriel Gentile and Paul Chappe by members of the Catalan party, that the name of the envoy was Simonetto di Belprato, and that the betrothal of the two natural children was successfully concluded. For how this and related ventures eventually came to nothing see *ibid.*, III, 677-678. See *ibid.*, III, 758 on how 5 November may be correct after all, since it would have given Archbishop Louis time to have the pope's letter read to his supporters in Nicosia and to arrange the murders of Corner, Bembo, Chappes and Gentile in Famagusta.

[288] Florio Bustron, 'Chronique', *op. cit.*, pp. 437-438 refers to two letters, one to the queen and the other to the knights; Lusignan, *Chorograffia, op. cit.*, p. 98 § 430 and p. 217 § 430 refers to a letter sent to the governors and commissioners, in which the pope accused Corner and Bembo of killing King James II by poison with their acquiescence, while in *Description, op. cit.*, fol. 184b, he states that the pope's letter was addressed to all the princes of the kingdom of Cyprus and that he named in writing those he accused of having poisoned the king. No such letter from the pope in question, Sixtus IV (1471-1484), survives in the papal registers, but sometime before August 1472 he wrote a long letter denouncing the usurpation of the powers of Latin diocesans in Cyprus by Greek and other non-Latin prelates, as well as abuses such as simony, marriage within the prohibited degrees of consanguinity and affinity, divorces and the ordination of morally unsuitable persons, See Coureas and Schabel, *Cartulary, op. cit.*, no. 94.

world! For we have learnt of the death of the king, [and] how you let Sir Andrew Corner, Sir Marco Bembo, Sir Paul Chappe and Gentile the doctor take over the kingdom".

155. Besides, as soon as the Cypriot lords received the letters, he sent word to them to do that which they did. They did not, moreover, reckon any further than this, and on reading the letters they all gathered together at Zaplana's house. And he imparted a diabolical notion in their minds, saying to them: "Know that I have learnt for certain that Sir Andrew has appointed a captain, the Italian James Visconti and his company, to be at the ready to hear the alarm bell [and] all together to jump into the houses of the constable and the count de Rochas, as well as into the house of the count of Tripoli and the house of Rizzo, and to kill them!"

And they (i.e. the Cypriot lords) also said this to the people of Famagusta:[289] "All together must be prepared and at the sound of the bell must all come armed to the palace!" And this is what happened, and on the Saturday of 15 November,[290] before 3 a.m. the bell sounded the alarm. Furthermore, the knights and all the people hastened to the palace, as he had given them to understand, having first gone to the queen's courtyard. Sir Paul Chappe,[291] moreover, was coming on horseback, and riding behind him was Sir Peter Gurri, and they encountered Rizzo and his men as soon as they entered the courtyard. And as soon as Rizzo set eyes on Chappe, he struck him with a lance and it went right through him, from one end to the other. Gurri fled.[292] In addition, they seized Chappe by the legs and threw him into a pit, while the doctor Gentile[293] went into the queen's chamber so as to escape. And the archbishop came and encountered him near her as he stood there armed, and he did not recognise him and said to him: "Stand here in company with the queen!" Rizzo, moreover, came in behind him and found him, and on seeing him said to him: "Is this where you are, you

---

[289] This allusion to the people of Famagusta as a whole is an example of their importance in public affairs in the 15th century. For other examples see Florio Bustron, 'Chronique', *op. cit.*, pp. 411-416; Arbel, 'Urban Assemblies', *op. cit.*, pp. 206 and 210-211.

[290] This date is given in all mss. (Kehayioglou, Διήγησις, *op. cit.*, pp. 184-185). The murders took place, however, on 13 November 1473, not 15, which was a Monday, and this is clear from the allusion in §153 above to Peter d'Avila and his men riding out to Famagusta on 14 November and learning from Ringo of the murders that had taken place at 03.00 on Saturday. See also Hill, *op. cit.*, III, 757.

[291] Sir Paul Chappe, the seneschal of the kingdom, had served the Lusignan royal house from the time of King John II. See Florio Bustron, 'Chronique', *op. cit.*, pp. 387, 423 and 438; Mas Latrie, *Histoire*, *op. cit.*, II, 520 note 2, 525, III, 66 note 1,126, 241 note 1(p. 242), 354 note 4; Hill, *op. cit.*, III, 524 and note 2.

[292] Peter Gurri fled to Rhodes and was given a letter of safe conduct by the Hospitaller Grand Master on 1 July 1474,at Queen Charlotte's request. See Mas Latrie, *Histoire*, *op. cit.*, III, 126 and note 9, 127 and note 3, 397 and note 3.

[293] A supporter of King James II, who had granted him as fiefs the *casalia* of St Theodoros, Patriki, Paliometokho, Klavdhia, Dora and Chito. See Florio Bustron, 'Chronique', *op. cit.*, p. 421; Mas Latrie, *Histoire*, *op. cit.*, III, 240 note 5, 261 note 8, 353-354, 354 note 5, 361 note 1; Richard, *Remembrances*, *op. cit.*, no. 181.

traitor?" The queen on hearing him exclaimed: "Sir Rizzo, leave him here!" And he did not heed her command, but seized him by the chest and dealt him two blows, and discovered him to be armed. He next seized him by the hair, and dragging him outside drew his sword out of its scabbard. He, however, eluded them and entered the cookhouse building, and they entered this building and killed him.

Furthermore, Sir Andrew departed and went off to seek refuge in the citadel. And they caught up [with them] and killed both him and Sir Marco Bembo. The matter then came to an end. In addition, with the cessation of the disturbance they sent me to journey to Kerynia, at the queen's behest, so that they would surrender Kerynia to me in the queen's name'.

Sir Louis then said goodbye to them and went to Kerynia. The knights, moreover, were standing by in Nicosia with vigilance.

156. And on 15 November[294] the admiral and the viscount rode out, and made a proclamation on the part of the queen: 'Let all persons remain at home and occupy themselves with their own affairs! Besides, in five or six days the queen is coming to Nicosia and shall attend to every business. And let none, great or small, dare to carry weapons, on pain of being hanged!' On the same day, moreover, 30 Sicilian men arrived from Famagusta and we learnt the news more fully.[295] And they said:

157. 'Lords, know that regarding the constable and the remainder of his company, the count of Tripoli, Sir John Tafur and Rizzo, the devil entered their hearts, they hatched a conspiracy and a great treason took place! For the constable and the remainder of his company decreed that: "the bell must sound the alarm before 3 a.m.!" Furthermore, in line with their decree, as soon as the bell had sounded and the knights and all the people of Famagusta had heard it, they were to arrange for all to congregate at the queen's palace.

On hearing the bell, moreover, Sir Peter Gurri armed himself and went to Sir Paul Chappe's house, found him in bed and said to him: "My lord, don't you hear the bell sounding the alarm? Get up and mount your horse, for us to go to the courtyard and see what the matter is, as we are committed [to do]!" And so he got up and mounted a horse, with John Cappadoca[296] following them on foot, and they went to the courtyard. Furthermore, Louis Alberic came upon them and said to Chappe: "Come in so that I can talk to you!" In addition, on entering he found Cortese and said to him:

---

[294] Dawkins, *Boustronios, op. cit.,* §156 following ms. **B** (Kehayioglou, *Διήγησις, op. cit.,* p. 187 line 11) has December, but this is far too late, especially as all the other actions of the conspirators were immediately after 15 November.

[295] The Sicilians had been under the command of Captain John Visconti, their Italian commander, who was imprisoned by the murderers to cover their actions, but they and many others arriving in Nicosia revealed everything that had transpired. See Florio Bustron, 'Chronique', *op. cit.,* p. 440.

[296] One wonders whether he is identical with the John Cappadoca mentioned as having accompanied Queen Charlotte in 1467 into exile. See W. Rudt de Collenberg, 'Les Lusignan de Chypre', *EKEE* X (1980), 195, no. 688.

"Grasp my hand so that I can dismount!" And Cortese[297] said to him: "There is no need to dismount". Peter Gurri, moreover, dismounted behind him, and Rizzo and his men killed him, who took him away and threw him into the pit.

Besides, Gentile the doctor on hearing the bell armed himself, went to the courtyard and entered the queen's chamber, reckoning on helping her, for he did not know that the bell was for him. And Rizzo straightaway entered the queen's chamber and seized him by the hair, against the queen's wishes, and five or six men fell upon him. And he said to Rizzo: 'What blameworthy thing did I do and you wish to kill me?" Furthermore, they were unable to kill him, other than Rizzo who raised his apron of chain mail and giving him a lunge in the stomach slew him. Sir Andrew, moreover, happened to be at home with a goldsmith named Tomasso, and on hearing the bell at around midnight said to his people: "Look out of the window! What's the matter?"

And looking down they saw people entering and coming down. Furthermore, Sir Andrew on hearing this got up, while Sir Marco Bembo likewise got up, and they went to the *baiulo's* house so as to ascertain what was happening. In addition, as they were going the count of Tripoli came upon them while they were armed and said to Sir Andrew: "off to your house!" And Sir Andrew did not pay any heed, but instead pressed on to the *baiulo's* house, and the *baiulo* said to him: 'Know that they sent word to me not to venture out from my house!" Sir Andrew, moreover, on hearing this was displeased and pressured [him] greatly to go to the citadel, and the *baiulo* did not wish to go.[298] And Sir Andrew mounted his horse, while Marco Bembo was on foot, and they all went to the castle walls so as to enter the citadel, reckoning that they would open the citadel for them.

In addition, he cried out to the castellan, telling him to open up for them. He, however, said to them: "My lords, we have an order from the governors that should our ladyship the queen come herself, in person, we must not open for her". Sir Andrew on hearing this did not know what to do, and he went and climbed up onto the

---

[297] This was John Cortese (*alias* Cortez), sent by the royal councillors to Paphos with John Attar after the death of King James II to receive the vassals' oath to Queen Catherine, and later imprisoned for his part in the murders. See also Florio Bustron, 'Chronique', *op. cit.*, p. 433. Mas Latrie, *Histoire*, *op. cit.*, III, 396 and 408-410 has decrees of the Venetian Council of Ten of 16 November 1474 and of 30 October 1476, ordering the incarceration and possible torture of Cortese and the despatch to Venice of the family of Michael Cortese. The latter, possibly related of John Cortese, is mentioned in a document of February 1469, in which King James II ordered the transfer of the annual stipend of 500 bezants and of incomes in kind enjoyed by him to Michael Sabourguada. See Richard, *Remembrances*, *op. cit.*, no. 131.

[298] Sir Andrew Corner also asked Josaphat Barbaro, the Venetian envoy to Cyprus and her ambassador to Uzun Hasan, to accompany him, but he likewise declined. Barbaro sent a detailed report to the Venetian Senate, dated 15 November, describing the murders, the actions of the kingdom's governors after them, especially as regarded obtaining control of Kerynia, and Queen Catherine's meeting with the Neapolitan embassy over the marriage of King James II's illegitimate daughter Carla with Alonzo, the natural son of King Ferdinand of Naples. In this letter Barbaro accuses the deceased Andrew Corner of vacillation and indecisiveness, especially in supplying and reinforcing the garrison of Famagusta. See Mas Latrie, *Histoire*, *op. cit.*, III, 353-361 and esp. 357-358.

abutment of the citadel. Furthermore, the count and Rizzo came and cried out to the castellan, asking him if anyone had entered the citadel. And he said to them: "No one came other than Sir Andrew". Sir Andrew, hearing them from there where he was standing, said to them: "What do you want?" And they said to him: "Come, the queen is summoning you!" He, moreover, came out from where he had been standing and appeared before them. Casoli, who was a burgess of Famagusta [and] was the viscount of Famagusta, also happened to be there, together with a burgess, and on seeing Sir Andrew on foot he too dismounted and brought him his horse for him to mount it.

In addition, Rizzo on seeing that he had given him his horse insulted him greatly. Furthermore, they brought along his packhorse and Sir Andrew mounted it. And the count of Tripoli said to him, to Sir Andrew: "I'm going, and you come along with Sir Rizzo!" And he responded to the count: "I'm coming with you". Rizzo on hearing Sir Andrew dealt a knife blow to his head and falling upon him killed him and threw him into the moat of the citadel. Besides, a convert to Christianity[299] called Mastiches killed Sir Marco Bembo, throwing him too into the moat. Furthermore, upon his killing them all disturbances ceased. In the morning, moreover, they seized John Visconti, the captain of the Italians, and they placed him in custody so as to tidy up their treasonable acts'.

158. And on 15 November 1473 Sir Louis Alberic sent a written message from Kerynia that Sir Paolo Contarini did not wish to surrender Kerynia to him: 'Besides, he says that he does not wish to give Kerynia to a foreigner who has neither a wife nor children nor a fief on Cyprus, but should it be her (i.e. the queen's) command, let her send Nicholas Morabit, so that he might surrender it to him!' And they sent this message to Famagusta, to the queen. Furthermore, the queen instructed the captain of Kerynia in writing to surrender the castle to Morabit as soon as he set eyes on the order. She also gave written instructions to Sir Nicholas Morabit to appoint a viscount in his place, while he himself should go and take possession of Kerynia. He, moreover, appointed his father in law, Sir Balian Fresenge, in his place, and went to Kerynia.

In addition, on his arrival the captain and everyone said to him: 'Welcome, my lord!' Furthermore, during his entrance he also admitted Sir Louis Alberic and Sir Tuzio[300] de Constanzo, and secured Kerynia. In addition, they approached the inner castle, and Sir Paolo Contarini said to Morabit: 'Guarantee my life for me and I shall give you the citadel!' He, moreover, guaranteed him, and he (i.e. Contarini) opened it up for him. And immediately all those in Kerynia said to him with one voice: 'We place the castle into your hands and not in anyone else's'. Furthermore, on receiving

---

[299] Hill, *op. cit.*, III, 673 and Dawkins, *Boustronios, op. cit.*, p. 40 and note 69 translate μαρράνος as a converted Muslim, but this word of Spanish origin also refers to converted Jews, some of whom may have been on Cyprus among the Catalans there, so I have taken it to mean a convert to Christianity.

[300] Ms. **M** has Τζουάν, which Dawkins, *Boustronios, op. cit.*, §158 translates as John, but mss. **A** and **B** have Τούτσου and Τουτσίου respectively, Tuzio was the son of Muzio de Costanzo, and in 1570 his own son Bruto Muzio held the Hospitaller Commandery of Templos. See Luttrell, 'Τα στρατιωτικά τάγματα', p. 755 and note 77. The reference to 'John' in ms. **M** is completely isolated and must be mistaken. For the variants see Kehayioglou, Διήγησις, *op. cit.*, pp. 194-195.

it he kept it for himself and said to them: 'My lords, know that our lady the queen has told me in writing to take the citadel into my hands and not to give it to anyone else!' He also told Sir Louis: 'You must have patience, for me to write to the queen [to discover] what she commands me to do'.

159. Besides, he wrote a letter to the queen. On 17 November, moreover, the constable Sir John Zaplana arrived in Kerynia, and he went there with great anger because Morabit had not surrendered Kerynia to his nephew. In addition, on coming to Kerynia he found it secured. And word reached Morabit that: 'The constable has come and is standing outside, and should it be your wish then open the citadel for him to enter!' Morabit on hearing this stood there wondering whether to open for him for a long time, and eventually had [the gates] opened for him. And he (i.e. the constable) entered, and he had the citadel opened for him as well. Furthermore, he entered uttering many threats against Morabit because he had not surrendered the castle to his nephew, and angry words were exchanged.

Morabit, moreover, on seeing Zaplana so enraged said to him: 'My lord constable, I marvel greatly at your person. Besides, it seems to you that you are setting eyes on people not aware of their honour, and you are extremely angry. I had no intention of doing anything else, other than in accordance with the command that I had from our lady the queen. Your lordship, moreover, can take this any way he likes, because the queen sent word to me to take Kerynia into my hands and not to give it to anyone else!' And the constable on seeing this made his farewells and came to Nicosia, while Morabit stayed in Kerynia with Louis Alberic, remaining until the 18 November. He then surrendered the castle into the hands of Sir Louis Alberic, he himself coming to Nicosia. In addition, on the 19 November Morabit journeyed from Nicosia to Famagusta, as well as Sir John de Ras.

160. Furthermore, on the same day Sir William de Ras came from Famagusta and said that: 'They were scrubbing the queen's palace and they even took the queen outside, and everyone came and swore an oath to her, while they set up a table and paid every person to whom they owed money'.

Furthermore, they appointed an envoy to go to Venice, Sir Philip Podocataro, to whom they granted the village that had belonged to Sir Gentile, Dora and Chito, and they also gave him his (i.e. Gentile's) houses. Besides, they appointed him vice-chancellor and gave him 300 ducats. And he went on board a Venetian ship with a subject of King Ferdinand for company, and disembarked on 17 November [in the year] of Christ 1473.[301]

---

[301] Cf. Florio Bustron, 'Chronique', *op. cit.*, p. 451 describes this episode more fully, stating that Philip Podocataro was sent to Venice to make excuses for the misdeeds committed, and that those behind them forced the queen to write letters to the Venetian Senate justifying the murders. The Senate, however, which had found out the truth by another means, ordered the galley to return forthwith to Cyprus and Podocataro to depart from any Venetian territory within six hours on pain of facing the judgement of the Venetian government. He was also temporarily deprived of the *casalia* given to him, although in time they were restored on the Venetians ascertaining that he was blameless regarding the murders and taking him into favour again. See also Hill, *op. cit.*, III, 677-678.

161. In addition, on 18 November[302] the news reached Nicosia that: 'King James' illegitimate daughter had been betrothed to King Ferdinand's illegitimate son, and King Ferdinand had promised on all occasions the kingdom might need them to send 20 armed galleys with 300 foot soldiers for guarding the place, with King Ferdinand shouldering the expenses'.[303]

162. Furthermore, on 23 November Morabit went to Famagusta. The queen, moreover, sent word to him and he left Sir Simon Fresenge[304] as viscount in his place. And as soon as he arrived the archbishop, the governors and as many persons as happened to be in Famagusta came out before him and let him in, and they put him up in Rizzo's living quarters.

163. In addition, on the same day ten galleys from the fleet arrived along with the *provedittore* Sir Victor Soranzo,[305] and the government of Venice had sent them for guarding Cyprus. They found out, moreover, about that which had taken place in Famagusta, and having found out about it none wished to disembark. Furthermore, they did not let them enter the harbour and they remained outside, at St Catherine's. And they forthwith set one galley apart and sent it to Venice, in order to convey the news of how things had transpired and to send them word on what to do.

On learning of this, moreover, the governors of the kingdom went down to the seashore to deliberate so as to go to the ships and confer with the *provedittore*. It seemed right to them to send the archbishop to go on board the ships and speak to the *provedittore*, and they sent for and obtained a safe-conduct. Furthermore, the archbishop went on board the galley and many words were exchanged, and among the many things said they requested possession of Famagusta or Kerynia. And hearing this, the archbishop said to them: 'My lords, you ask for something that you cannot have, because the late king made a will and left governors in the realm, and things cannot be done other than in accordance with the decree that he gave. I shall return now and speak to them, and I shall tell them what you request. You shall, moreover, receive an answer'. And the archbishop made his farewells and came back extremely

---

302 Mss. **B** and **M** both have 19 November. See Kehayioglou, Διήγησις, *op. cit.*, p. 210, line 1 of both mss.

303 Simonetto di Belprato, the Neapolitan envoy, had conveyed King Ferdinand's offer of men and ships to Queen Catherine in Famagusta, on the evening of the 15 November. See Mas Latrie, *Histoire, op. cit.*, III, 361-362.

304 Dawkins, *Boustronios, op. cit.*, §162 mistakenly gives his surname as Francis, but see Florio Bustron, 'Chronique' *op. cit.*, p. 420 where he figures among the feudatories of King James II, who awarded him the *casale* of Cormia in the Paphos district, a locality abandoned sometime before 1550 (Grivaud, *Villages désertés, op. cit.*, p. 240). Strambaldi, 'Chronique', *op. cit.*, II, 266 alludes to another Simon Fresenge in the early 15th century.

305 Florio Bustron, 'Chronique', *op. cit.*, pp. 441-442 states that previous to this a Venetian galley commanded by Coriolano Cippico arrived at Famagusta announcing Soranzo's impending arrival with eight galleys for the kingdom's defence, and adding that if necessary the whole Venetian fleet commanded by the captain-general would arrive. Queen Catherine was so pleased that she had Nicosia illuminated and the bells rung there. When Soranzo arrived Florio Bustron like Boustronios states that he had ten galleys (p. 442).

discomfited, telling the governors just as they had told him. Besides, the ships remained offshore by St Catherine's and none were allowed to disembark.

164. And on 24 November Anthony de l'Orsa happened to be in Famagusta, and he had a Portuguese named Janico Cuzzo in his service. The abovementioned Anthony, moreover, briefed the abovementioned Janico to go to the citadel, to speak to the castellan, the castellan being Farandetto, and to promise him 1,000 ducats[306] on the part of the government [of Venice], for which he would surrender the citadel of Famagusta. And he spoke to him. Furthermore, the castellan consented and [thereby] deceived him. And in the morning the castellan went and reported it to the governors, and they sent men at once and seized him (i.e. Janico), placing him in custody in order to learn about the matter clearly. In addition, Anthony del'Orsa fled and went on board the Venetian galley.

165. Besides, on 25 November Nicholas Morabit went to the citadel, to the queen, and he greeted her. She showed him a favourable disposition, and he said to her: 'My lady, your ladyship sent word for me to come and I have come according to your behest'. The queen, moreover, hearing this gave the archbishop orders to send him away, and she said to him: 'As regards your arrival, you did well to come! But go home and rest until our ladyship decrees [otherwise]! Furthermore, she considers you a highly regarded, trustworthy and meritorious servant of hers'. And he took his leave.

166. In addition, on 1 December [14]73 the queen sent word to Morabit to be present at her court. He, moreover, went there, entered the palace and greeted her, while she gave him orders to go to Kerynia as captain because she could not entrust Kerynia in other hands: 'Because the king considered you to be an extremely valuable and trustworthy servant, on account of this I want you to go immediately and take possession of the citadel from Louis Alberic'.

167. And hearing this Morabit said to her: 'My lady, do you wish me to go according to your command?' And she said to him: 'Such is my wish'. He, moreover, kissed her hand and paid homage to her son [King] James [III]. Besides, she conferred the office of viscount upon him for his whole life, as well as the right to put a person of his choosing in his place. And he took his leave of her and went away. In addition, the queen gave Rizzo orders to go to Kerynia together with Morabit in order to take the castle from Louis Alberic and give it to Morabit in accordance with her command.

168. Furthermore, she also gave them signed papers. They, moreover, came to Nicosia, circulated around Nicosia and gave comfort to the people, telling them that: 'Her ladyship the queen is coming soon to Nicosia'.

---

[306] Mss. **B** and **M** have 2.000 ducats. See Kehayioglou, Διήγησις, *op. cit.*, p. 203, line 18 in both mss. Florio Bustron, 'Chronique', *op. cit.*, p. 443 likewise has 2,000 ducats.

[307] Victor Soranzo records Louis Alberic's reluctance to surrender the castle of Kerynia to Nicholas Morabit in a letter of 9 December, stating that Louis had been forewarned of the queen's intentions and had declared that he had no intention of leaving Kerynia. It remained to be seen what effect the arrival of Morabit and Rizzo di Marino would have on him, for if he disobeyed much scandal and discord would ensue. See Mas Latrie, 'Documents Nouveaux', *op. cit.*, p. 430.

And on 7 December they ventured forth from Nicosia and went to Kerynia, and he (Nicholas Morabit) left his father in law Balian Fresenge as viscount in Nicosia. Furthermore, as soon as Sir Louis caught sight of them from Kerynia he secured the citadel. He spoke to them, moreover, and they did not display the queen's command. In addition, on seeing it he immediately opened the inner castle for them, admitted Rizzo and spoke to him, and they both slept inside the citadel while Morabit remained outside, in the castle.[307] And on the day after the morrow they opened the inner castle, admitted Morabit and surrendered the citadel to him. Furthermore, Sir Louis opened the barbican gate and departed from Kerynia without encountering Morabit, and he came to Nicosia. Rizzo, moreover, remained for three days with Morabit and [then] came to Nicosia.[308]

169. Besides, at night one of Rizzo's servants arrived from Famagusta, bringing him a written message that 300 armed men had disembarked from the galleys in order to seize him. And on hearing this Rizzo brought together 50 men to guard him throughout the night, while in the morning he began riding, with good horses, and went to Famagusta.

170. In addition, four days had not gone by when the men from Dalmatia[309] killed a good man[310] [in the service] of the count of Tripoli, outside Famagusta. And the pretext was that the count of Tripoli, who also happened to be the captain of Famagusta, ventured forth and opened the Sea Gate, went out and conferred with the *provedittore*, and returned to Famagusta. Furthermore, as soon as the day broke Zaplana learnt about it and was extremely upset over it, saying: 'He should not have gone out to confer alone, without our counsel'. On account of this, moreover, Zaplana was angered, and on learning of it the queen and her counsel issued a command to Zaplana, emanating from the queen and the governors: 'Let him not venture forth from his house, upon his life and all his goods!'[311] And he acted thus, in accordance with her command. Furthermore, following the passage of two days he sent her requests to allow him to appear before her, so that she would give him orders to come to Nicosia. And she gave him the orders. He, moreover, brought 25 men with their horses along with him, and on his arrival in Nicosia the people of Nicosia did not let him enter, telling him to go back and bring the queen.

---

[308] Florio Bustron, 'Chronique', *op. cit.*, p. 443, states that Alberic went to the archbishopric in Nicosia, and that Rizzo di Marino departed from Kerynia one day after him.

[309] Dalmatia was the coastal area to the south-east of Venice, now part of Croatia, and many men from Dalmatia served as mercenaries in the Venetian forces. *Ibid.*, p. 443 likewise states that the Venetians disembarked 300 armed men on Cyprus, and the men from Dalmatia must have been among them.

[310] Dawkins, *Boustronios, op. cit.*, §170 has 'a good many', but I assume 'man**y**' is a misprint for 'man'.

[311] In his letter to the doge of Venice dated 17 December 1473, the *provedittore* Victor Soranzo states that Zaplana was so angry over this with the count of Tripoli that he had ridden out of the city with around 40 horsemen and that the count of Tripoli was about to follow him, but the archbishop, acting on the queen's orders, prevented him from doing so, and personally exited from Famagusta and told Zaplana that he was under orders to return. See Mas Latrie, 'Documents nouveaux', *op. cit.*, pp. 439-440.

A certain Dominic Lachanas who had an illegitimate child was involved in these intrigues. <And he said to him (to his child)>:[312] 'And give me a pen and some paper for me to settle accounts with the market.[313] I wish to go quickly, moreover, for Rizzo is hiding in our home and I believe that he wishes to send a written message to Famagusta!' And the lad was making his way to Sir Leo's place, and he went there and said it to him. Sir Leo, moreover, happened to be with Stephen Koudouna and told him about it, and he also said to Koudouna: 'Rizzo <has come to Nicosia and he is hiding in Dominic Lachanas' house. What is more, I believe that he>[314] came for no reason other than to hang you, both you and many others'. Koudouna on hearing this went off and gathered many young men. He also went to Dominic's place in search of Rizzo, and he did not find him.[315] In addition, they all determined a course of action in Nicosia in order that the queen should come, otherwise they would not let anyone enter Nicosia, neither from Famagusta nor from anywhere else. And so it came to pass.

171. Besides, they sounded the alarm bell immediately and they all assembled at Koudouna's house. Furthermore, they held counsel and appointed leaders from amongst themselves, Stephen, John the Black, John of Emesa[316] and numerous others,[317] hoisted the queen's banner and proceeded to the royal court. On their entry, moreover, they found the admiral and placed him under confinement on the part of the queen, so that he would not venture forth from his house. And so it came to pass. Besides, they said to him: 'We want our lady the queen to come to Nicosia'. And the admiral said to them: 'Do what you like!'

In addition, he wrote to her ladyship the queen at once, so that she would find a way to come to Nicosia. Furthermore, as soon as the admiral had sent the letter,[318] Sir John de Ras came in order to enter Nicosia. They, moreover, did not let him, until he had given them an oath that he would live and die alongside them, and then they let him in. Benedict Cartagena arrived in his wake, and they did not let him in until he too had given an oath.

---

[312] The words in brackets < > are taken from mss. **B** and **M**. See Kehayioglou, Διήγησις, *op. cit.*, p. 211, **B** line 1 and **M** line 1.

[313] Dawkins, *Boustronios, op. cit.*, §170 translates φούντικας as factory, but I consider market to be more appropriate, especially as the chronicler mentions τον φούντικαν των πωρικών i.e. the fruit market in §189, also mentioned in Florio Bustron, 'Chronique', *op. cit.*, p. 449 as the *fontego delle frutte*.

[314] The words in brackets < > are taken from mss. **B** and **M**. See Kehayioglou, Διήγησις, *op. cit.*, p. 211, lines 6-8 of both mss.

[315] Florio Bustron, 'Chronique', *op. cit.*, p. 444 does not mention that Rizzo di Marino was still in Nicosia, now in hiding. This can be dismissed as an unfounded rumour, for both Boustronios and Florio Bustron (*Ibid.*, pp. 443-444) state that he left the capital with an armed escort for Famagusta on learning that the Venetians had landed 300 men in Cyprus.

[316] He was a supporter of King James II, who granted him the *casale* of St John of Malounda (San Gioan de Malondos) between the years 1464-1468. See *ibid.*, p. 419.

[317] *Ibid.*, p. 444 states that among them were *alcun altri mastri di scrimia*, that is persons with exceptional perception and acumen.

[318] *Ibid.*, p. 444 states that Balian Fresenge and Peter Bussat sent this letter.

172. Besides, on 29 December the count of Tripoli came to Nicosia, as well as Peter d'Avila, in order to confer with the people of Nicosia. And on hearing of this the people all gathered together, on horseback and on foot, and coming to the Taxation Gate they secured it and appointed Sir John de Ras as captain. The abovementioned lords, moreover, stood outside, and all the people came out of Nicosia. And on the fourth hour of the day the count of Tripoli and Peter d'Avila sent forth Philip Singritico, who was the captain of Sivouri,[319] and he parleyed with the people of Nicosia, with Sir John de Ras and with the leaders, saying to them:

'My lords, know that her ladyship the queen has given orders to the count of Tripoli and to Peter d'Avila, and they are coming to confer with you so that you can tell them what you are asking for!' And they all exclaimed with one voice: 'We want our ladyship the queen to come to Nicosia, and to live and die in her name and that of our lord!' The captain of Sivouri, moreover, on hearing this said to them: 'Do you want me to go and fetch them, for you to speak to them so that they might see your enthusiasm?' And they said to him:[320] 'Let them come!' And the captain went, as well as Benedict Cartagena, Sir Philip de Nores, Stephen Koudouna, John of Emesa, Master Nicholas de Pis, Anthony the basket maker and Pierre the Savoyard, who were constables, in order to speak to the lords who had come from Famagusta. In addition, the captain went and told them that he had spoken to the people 'in accordance with your orders, and they said that they want their lady and their lord to come to Nicosia, and they said that your lordship should go'.

Furthermore, the lords approached Nicosia, and the abovementioned artisans and the whole of Nicosia appeared before them. The lords, moreover, on setting eyes on the populace dismounted and conversed with them, saying to them: 'Our ladyship the queen, having heard of the love that you have for her, has derived great pleasure and holds you in high regard. And she has ordered us to come and see what you are asking for'.

173. On hearing this, the artisans and the people said to them: 'My lords, you are welcome as regards your arrival! We wish to know whether you are good and loyal subjects of our ladyship the queen and we want you to take an oath for us upon the Holy Gospels that you will live and die justly and loyally with us, under the banner of our lady the queen and of our lord, without deceiving us with words. In addition, upon your doing this we shall hold you as our beloved lords and we shall open the gates for you to enter Nicosia. This, moreover, is our wish'.

174. And the lords replied: 'As regards what you say, that we should take an oath for

---

[319] Philip Syngritico was appointed captain of Sivouri under King James II in place of Philip de Pezzaro, whom the king had appointed to replace Thomas Mahes, as stated in §44. He also granted him the *casale* of Terra, lands at Androlikou, exemption from the tax known as the *rate* and an income from the revenues obtained from the *gabelle* levied at the entrance to Nicosia. See *ibid.*, p. 419; Richard, *Remembrances, op. cit.*, nos. 115, 133 and 156.

[320] Ms. **A** has 'them' instead of 'him', but I have adopted 'him' found in mss. **B** and **M**, as the preceding sentence makes it clear that Syngritico alone spoke to them. See Kehayioglou, *Διή-γησις, op. cit.*, pp. 214-215, ms. **A** line 4, ms. **B** line 3 and ms. **M** line 3.

you, we are ready to do so'. And the leaders sent for and brought the master chaplain, <Sir Simon of Antioch>[321] along with the Holy Gospels. Furthermore, the count of Tripoli and Peter d'Avila dismounted and took the oath.

On their taking of the oath, moreover, they opened the gates for them. And they went in, and they immediately brought Sir John de Ras and other knights. Besides, they appointed Sir John de Ras as captain and kept good watch throughout the night, issuing orders on what had to be done. In addition, they mounted their horses and went to Famagusta.

175. And as soon as they had mounted Luke Hariri, a valet of the count de Rochas, came up and said to them: 'My lords, know that just as you departed from Famagusta, Sir James Zaplana happened to be hidden outside Famagusta! Furthermore, as soon as you arrived, he immediately sent word to the archbishop and to Rizzo to come outside Famagusta, to speak to him and, if they could, to bring the count de Rochas out along with them. On hearing this, moreover, they mounted their horses and went out from Famagusta. And after a short time the count de Rochas also ventured forth. And John de Naves, who happened to be at the Famagusta Gate to guard the place, did not allow him to exit, but instead turned him right back and sealed the gates straightaway. Besides, the archbishop, Rizzo and Zaplana departed. And I do not know anything else to tell you, because as soon as these events transpired they sent me to bring you the news'.[322]

And on hearing this, they went as of necessity to Famagusta, leaving John de Ras as the lieutenant in Nicosia and also Benedict Cartagena, in the name of the queen. And they (Ras and Cartagena) came to [the cathedral of] the Holy Wisdom together with everyone, both mounted men and those on foot, and he (Ras) said to them:[323] 'All of you assemble together this evening, in the plain of Trachonas.[324] Furthermore, they appointed Anthony de Bois with 25 horses, Benedict Cartagena with 25 horses and Sir John de Ras with the remainder, and issued an order: 'Let them patrol around Nicosia throughout the night, with every captain attending his watch!'

176. And <on Saturday> on 1 January [14] 74[325] [in the year] of Christ news arrived from Famagusta that: 'the archbishop, Sir James and Rizzo have boarded a foreign

---

[321] The words in brackets < > are taken from mss. **B** and **M**. See *ibid.*, p. 217, ms. **B** lines 5-6 and ms. **M** lines 2-3.

[322] The Venetian *provedittore* Sir Victor Soranzo had 700 men landed in Famagusta on 31 December (Hill, *op. cit.*, III, 685 and note 3). With Nicosia and Kerynia already under the control of Queen Catherine's supporters and Famagusta as well now, the Catalan party had no option other than to flee.

[323] Ms. **A** has 'him' instead of 'them' as found in mss. **B** and **M**, and I have adopted 'them' as being manifestly correct. See Kehayioglou, Διήγησις, *op. cit.*, ms. **A**, p. 218 line 8, ms. **B**, p. 219 line 7 and ms. **M**, p. 219 line 6.

[324] A *casale* situated northwest of Nicosia. Florio Bustron, 'Chronique', *op. cit.*, p. 418 states that King James II had given it as a fief in 1464-1468 to a certain Pero Zerbas, along with various other *casalia* and 100 measures of wine in the Marathassa district.

[325] Ms. **A** has 1473 given that the New Year began on 1 March. See Kehayioglou, Διήγησις, *op. cit.*, p. 218 ms. **A** line 13.

galley belonging to King Ferdinand, and have gone away.[326] On learning of this in Famagusta, moreover, they brought out two Venetian galleys and sent them on their trail in order to seize them. Furthermore, as soon as they learnt about this in Nicosia, they issued an order: 'Let them seize their servants, wherever they might find them, and bring them to Sir John de Ras!' And on the same day the archbishop's nephew arrived with letters in which the queen sent word that: 'Let no one create difficulties for the servants of the archbishop, John (sic) Alberic and Rizzo until her ladyship should give orders!' <Over which matter Sir John the Ras asked whether the Venetian galleys had indeed gone after them. And they told him: 'They had ordered them [to do so] and then they let things be'>.[327]

177. In addition, on the morning of 2 January Alfonso, the illegitimate son of Carceran Suarez, arrived, who was together with Zaplana, and he told them about it, saying to them: 'My lords, I do not know anything to tell you, other than what I saw. I saw the archbishop coming out of Famagusta, and Rizzo as well, in order to speak with Zaplana. As soon as they came out, moreover, they secured the gates. And straightaway they went to the coast, dismounted, placed the bridles in the saddle and let the horses go. Zaplana, moreover, said to me: "Will you come with me?" And I said to him: "No!" And he said to me: "Take off my cuirass and my helmet for me!" Furthermore, he took them and threw them into the boat, as well as some silver coins that I was holding for him, and I bid him farewell. And he said to me: "Go to my house and tell my wife not to worry!" And I do not know anything else to tell you'.

178. Besides, on the same day a message from Famagusta arrived, that: 'As soon as the count of Tripoli and Peter d'Avila reached Famagusta, they found the gates secured. This news, moreover, reached the queen straightaway. And the count de Rochas and all the others rode out together with their weapons, and they opened the gates and brought them inside'.

179. In addition, they arrested the archbishop's secretary on the same day, in order to torture him and learn everything. This person showed them numerous papers that they had drawn up and he also disclosed many persons who were with them. Furthermore, <they> confiscated their moveable effects and horses and also deprived them of their fiefs. <They also condemned them as traitors>.[328]

180. And on the same day a message from the queen arrived to Sir John de Ras that he should forthwith send [people] to confiscate the villages of the archbishopric, of Zaplana and of Louis Alberic. <And this is what he did>.[329]

---

[326] Florio Bustron, 'Chronique', *op. cit.*, p. 446 includes Louis Alberic among those fleeing, and Boustronios' references to the sequestration of his fixed property below does indeed verify this. Hill, *op. cit.*, III, 687 states that the fugitives took 60.000 ducats' worth of gems and money with them.

[327] The words in brackets < > are taken from mss. **B** and **M**. See Kehayioglou, Διήγησις, *op. cit.*, p. 221, lines 6-8 of both mss.

[328] The words in brackets < > are taken from mss. **B** and **M**. See *ibid.*, p. 223, ms. **B** lines 8-10 and ms. **M** lines 9-11.

[329] The words in brackets < > are taken from mss. **B** and **M**. See *ibid.*, p. 223, ms. **B** line 13 and ms. **M** line 14.

181. On 3 January, moreover, the *proveditorre* of the Venetians sent two written messages to Nicosia, one to Sir John de Ras and the other to the populace of Nicosia, and he also sent them a New Year's Day gift of 40 ducats.[330]

182. Besides, on the same day Sir John de Ras received a message from the queen, and it wrote: 'For many and various tasks and fealties that he has performed in the kingdom, we have appointed our dear count de Rochas as regent and have also given him his fief, Marathassa, Alexandra, Letymbou and Diorimi. Furthermore, we have appointed Peter d'Avila constable of Cyprus and have given him Rizzo's villages, Yenagra and Stremmata and the two country estates of Pelendri, and we have also given him his (Rizzo's) houses in Famagusta and have given him Zaplana's houses in Nicosia as well, that used to belong to the count of Tripoli and are right opposite the citadel. In addition, we have given him the Armenian vineyard[331] in St Dometios.[332]

183. And on the same day there came a written message from <Famagusta> that: '<The Queen>[333] has granted an amnesty to each person regarding whatever [wrongdoings] he had committed. Let none cause them any trouble!' Furthermore, the proclamation took place, excluding those who had fled (i.e. from the kingdom).

184. On the same day, moreover, a written message came from the queen, and the people from Famagusta went to Zaplana's house and took whatever was found, as happened with [the house] of Louis Alberic. And they apportioned them among themselves.

185. In addition, on the same day Benedict Cartagena sent [persons] to Zaplana's

---

[330] The loyalty that the inhabitants of Nicosia had steadfastly expressed to Catherine must have pleased the Venetians especially. Not only did it emanate from the island's capital, but also from the one major inland city not within direct range of their fleet. The Venetian Senate's determination to retain Cyprus appears in its letter of 20 December to Peter Mocenigo, the captain-general of the Venetian fleet (Mas Latrie, *Histoire, op. cit.*, III, 362-364), stating that even if something might have happened to Queen Catherine or her heir, the young King James III, the kingdom could not fall into alien hands, and had to be recovered if it had. The captain-general was empowered to obtain ships and reinforcements from Crete, and if this was not feasible to summon galleys from the regular lines of Beirut and Alexandria to his aid. He could purchase abundant grain from Syria. Above all, he was to bring order to the kingdom by any means necessary and to have the fortresses of Famagusta, Kerynia and elsewhere placed under castellans and men loyal to Venice.

[331] 'Armenian vineyards' at St Dometios are mentioned in a document of 8 October 1468 as forming the inheritance of Johnne David, the widow of Nicholas Minas, and her son John. They were also found in the village of St Sergios near Famagusta in the area of Kythraea north east of Nicosia and in Kalamoulli in the Larnaca district. See Mas Latrie, 'Nouvelles preuves', *op. cit.*, p. 123; Makhairas, *Recital, op. cit.*, § 637; Richard, *Remembrances, op. cit.*, nos. 210 and 214-215.

[332] These properties were not the only reward he obtained. On 5 January 1474 the Venetian Senate ordered the captain-general Sir Peter Mocenigo to promise Peter d'Avila even more that the annual stipend of 1.000 ducats he was already receiving, and to do everything to attach him to Queen Catherine's cause.

[333] The words in brackets are taken from mss. **B** and **M**. See Kehayioglou, Διήγησις, *op. cit.*, p. 225 ms. **B** lines 11-13 and ms. **M** lines 10-12.

house and took his falcons, as well as Alberic's.[334] Furthermore, they conducted a search <in Nicosia>[335] on the part of Peter d'Avila.

186. Besides, they said on the same day: 'The Venetian fleet has arrived at Salines, 40 galleys'. And it was lies. A galley arrived at Famagusta, moreover, and said that: 'the fleet is coming soon'.[336] It also said that it had come across King Ferdinand's galley, which had Zaplana, the archbishop and Rizzo on board. And it said that: 'It is heading for Naples'.

187. Furthermore, on the same day a written message arrived from Famagusta, from the constable, to the viscount that: 'Let this brother[337] take the houses and estates of Gabriel Ferrier[338] as well as the houses and estates of Bonaistre!' And on hearing this, the people of Nicosia were agitated. Saying, moreover: 'It does not seem right to us that they should take the estates of Cypriots and give them to Franks' they left the message sealed, in order to convey it to the queen.[339]

188. And on 19 January the queen granted Stephen Koudouna 1,000 bezants a year from [the revenues of] the Taxation Gate, as well as 100 *modii* of wheat and 100 measures of wine.[340]

189. In addition, on 20 January[341] the queen appointed Gonsalvo Perez[342] captain of

---

[334] Cyprus in the Lusignan and Venetian periods was famous for its falcons and falconers. See Novara, *Federico II*, *op. cit.*, pp. 142-143, lines 177-179; Aik. Aristeidou, 'Το κυνήγι με γεράκια στην Κύπρο από την αρχαιότητα μέχρι την τουρκοκρατία', *EKEE* XX (1994), 146-157; B. Arbel, 'Venetian Cyprus and the Muslim Levant, 1473-1570', in *Η Κύπρος και οι Σταυροφορίες/Cyprus and the Crusades*, ed. N. Coureas and J. Riley Smith (Nicosia, 1995), pp. 167-168.

[335] The words in brackets < > are from ms. **M**. See Kehayioglou, *Διήγησις*, *op. cit.*, p. 225 line 18.

[336] The Venetian fleet under the command of the captain-general Peter Mocenigo arrived in Famagusta on 3 February 1474 and visited the queen, promising her every assistance. A tribunal operating under his direction put on trial and punished numerous persons, noble or commoner, who were considered to have acted against Venice. See Florio Bustron, 'Chronique', *op. cit.*, pp. 447-448; Stephen de Lusignan, *Chorograffia*, *op. cit.*, pp. 122-123 and 240-241 §606; Hill, *op. cit.*, III, 695-705.

[337] This is possibly Brother Gomez, concerning whom see below.

[338] He is mentioned twice in Florio Bustron, 'Chronique', *op. cit.*, pp. 395 and 448.

[339] These confiscations, if they took place, must be seen as part of a wider set of punitive measures. Hill, III, 695 states that on 8 January a proclamation was publicised expelling all Catalans, Sicilians and Neapolitans from Cyprus, while those more directly implicated in the murders were hanged.

[340] In mss. **B** and **M** the order of § 188-189 is reversed. See Kehayioglou, *Διήγησις*, *op. cit.*, p. 229, ms. **B** lines 9-11 and ms. **M** lines 9-10. Koudouna later fell under suspicion was exiled to Venice along with other notables in May 1474. George Boustronios and Florio Bustron, 'Chronique', p. 453 do not mention him by name among those exiled, but see Mas Latrie, *Histoire*, *op. cit.*, III, 397 and note 5.

[341] Mss. **B** and **M** both give 19 January for the events narrated in this paragraph. See Kehayioglou, *Διήγησις*, *op. cit.*, p. 227, ms. **B** line 15 and ms. **M** line 14.

[342] He was a supporter of King James II, who between 1464 and 1468 granted him the *casalia* of Paliometokho and Kataliondas, as well as 100 measures of wine and a yearly income of 800 bezants. Kataliondas was taken from the surgeon Bartélemy Estive, who received other *casalia* in exchange, and awarded to Gonsalvo. See Florio Bustron, 'Chronique', *op. cit.*, p. 423; Richard, *Remembrances*, *op. cit.*, no. 86 and note 2.

Famagusta, relieving the count of Tripoli. She also knighted Philip de Nores and gave him Agrinou. Besides, she knighted John Attar and granted him the other part of Apalaistra. Furthermore, she exempted him from the property rentals customarily paid to the admiral. The king, moreover, had honoured Master Anthony Garcia[343] the tailor, who had been a companion of Peter d'Avila when he had departed from Kerynia, just as he had honoured the others, granting him Epikho and betrothing him to a widowed noblewoman who had been married to Sir William Strambali.[344] The queen[345] knighted him as well and granted him the fruit market of Nicosia, as well as two estates that James of Malta had possessed in Kythraea, which she had confiscated from him because he was a traitor.

190. In addition, on 21 January they relieved the castellan of Famagusta and appointed Galimberto, a Venetian.[346]

191. Furthermore, on the same day they appointed John de Navarre[347] seneschal of Jerusalem and gave him the estates of Brother Gomez.

192. And on 22 January 1474[348] they sent off Sir John de Aragon[349] and Bernardin

---

[343] All the mss. have 'Garcia', but Florio Bustron, 'Chronique', *op. cit.*, p. 449 has Anthony Perez.

[344] On the king's right to remarry widowed noblewomen and the legal procedure followed see Makhairas, *Recital, op. cit.*, I, §277. The Strambali were an important family under King James II, for John Strambali was the royal treasurer and a secretary of the *secrète* and Simon was a royal administrator. They remained important under the Venetians, and after the Ottoman conquest of Cyprus migrated to Cephalonia, where they continued in importance throughout the 17th century. See Richard, *Remembrances, op. cit.*, nos. 1, 22, 35-36, 93, 187-191, 193-194, 196 and note 8, 203, 205-212, 216-222, 224-226, 229 and 232-234; G.N. Moschopoulos, 'Η κυπριακή οικογένεια Στράμπαλι στην Κεφαλονία (16ος-17ος αι.)', in *ΠΔΔΚΣ*, 3 vols. (Nicosia, 1985-1987), II, 249-258.

[345] Ms. **A** has 'the king' but mss. **B** and **M** both have 'the queen' (see Kehayioglou, *Διήγησις, op. cit.*, pp. 228-229) as does Florio Bustron, *Chronique, op. cit.*, p. 449, and I regard the latter as preferable chronologically.

[346] This was the implementation of the Venetian Senate's instructions to Peter Mocenigo on 20 December 1473, mentioned above. *Ibid.*, p. 449 adds that as well as Galimberto in Famagusta, the Venetians placed Paul Contarinii as castellan at Kerynia, Giovanni Penal at Paphos and Andrew the Provençal at Chrysochou. Cypriot soldiers were dismissed from the entrance to the palace, and Italians replaced them, Cretans were posted at the city gates, and Nicolo Benedetti replaced John François as the commander of the arsenal. George Boustronios narrates some of these events below.

[347] John de Navarre, as seen above (§118), had helped secure Kerynia against Queen Charlotte's supporters in August 1473 and was among those of King James II's supporters granted unspecified amounts of grain, vines and estates between 1464 and 1468. See Florio Bustron, 'Chronique', *op. cit.*, p. 422.

[348] Ms. **A** has 1473 because the New Year formerly began on 1 March. See Kehayioglou, 'Διήγησις', *op. cit.*,p. 228 line 16.

[349] A knight named John de Aragon, possibly identical to him, is mentioned as owing 600 ducats to the treasury of Cyprus, and on 8 March 1490 the Venetian Council of Ten decided to extend his period of repayment to twelve years. He is also mentioned as a witness in a document of October 1496 regarding the payment of tithes owed to the Latin archbishopric of Nicosia. See Aristeidou, Έγγραφα, *op. cit.*, I, 214-215 no. 20; Coureas and Schabel, *Cartulary, op. cit.*, no. 137

Salah,[350] and these two went to the villages of Zaplana and Louis Alberic, to take possession of them in the queen's name and to conduct a search regarding whatever they had. They went, moreover, to Kolossi and to the castles and found Brother Francis the lieutenant there along with the other brothers.[351] In addition, they showed them the queen's command that 'they must reveal to them whatever effects of Zaplana happened to be within the castle and the village of Kolossi! Furthermore, they would be considered traitors if they did not reveal them'.

And on hearing the abovementioned command, the lieutenant said to them that: 'Nothing shall be found, and Zaplana has nothing belonging to him in Kolossi'. Sir John de Aragon on hearing this, moreover, said to the lieutenant and his company: 'A religious service must take place and you must swear to us that there are no possessions or effects of Zaplana are to be found here'. And on agreeing to the oath, they had to tell the truth and to reveal everything that Zaplana possessed. Besides, they opened one chest and found a gold-threaded crimson cloth, a gold-threaded blue cloth, many velvet stuffs, a great quantity of silver and much <powdered>[352] sugar, which they estimated at 4,000 ducats [in value].

193. Furthermore, on 23 January the queen sent a letter to Sir John de Ras that: 'He should appoint William de Ras in his place[353] and he himself should go to Famagusta, and should also give orders to the people of the archbishop, of Zaplana and of Rizzo to go unarmed to Famagusta, on pain of the gallows!'

194. She also wrote a letter to [John] Cortese: 'Upon his life, let him too be present unarmed in Famagusta!' This person on account of his humiliation went forth two hours before daybreak, and took his wife along with him, hoping that the queen would take pity on her and him. In addition, she wrote to Sir William: 'He too (Cortese) must

---

[350] He was supporter of King James II, who granted him the *casale* of St Photios between 1464 and 1468. One village with this name is found in the Karpass peninsula, and the other in the Paphos district. See Florio Bustron, 'Chronique', *op. cit.*, p. 423; Grivaud, *Villages désertés, op. cit.*, pp. 125, 242-243 and 446.

[351] The Grand Commandery at Kolossi had been conceded on 26 February 1471 to Brother Nicholas Zaplana, then the commander of Baules in the Hospitaller priory of Catalonia (Mas Latrie, *Histoire, op. cit.*, III, 93). Nicholas was related to James Zaplana, hence the suspicions, ultimately proven, that James Zaplana had had valuables spirited away there for safekeeping. As a result of this, Nicholas Zaplana was then deprived of this commandery, and the Hospitallers were asked to appoint a successor. This was the Venetian Mark Crispo, an uncle of Queen Catherine's, appointed in 1474 as the administrator but not the Grand Commander. Marco Malipiero, also a Venetian, succeeded him, and the Hospitaller Grand Commandery was gradually but permanently attached to the Corner family. See Hill, *op. cit.*, III, 698; Luttrell, 'Τα στρατιωτικά τάγματα', *op. cit.*, p. 753.

[352] The word in brackets < > is taken from mss. **B** and **M**. See Kehayioglou, *Διήγησις, op. cit.*, p. 231, **B** line 12 and **M** line 11.

[353] In his place as the captain of Nicosia, the office the people of Nicosia had conferred on John de Ras in November 1473, when they allowed him to enter Nicosia once he had sworn fealty to the queen, for which see above.

turn up in Famagusta, unarmed!' as well as to Louis Alberic,[354] Peter d'Avila, James of Malta and Matthew's brothers. James of Malta, moreover, on hearing of this command said: 'I'm going upon my own head! But they are threatening to kill me wherever they find me, and now they are ordering me to go to Famagusta without weapons. Furthermore, should they come across me on the way, they shall kill me'. And on hearing him Sir John de Ras said to him: 'I shall guarantee you your life so that no evil may befall you presently, and get ready to go in accordance with the queen's command!'

All three of them, moreover, straightaway mounted their horses and rode to Famagusta. <And George Bustron came across them at the depression of Lefkomiatis while he was coming from Famagusta. Bustron, moreover on seeing them, such as the one who had caused the death of the young men whom the king had beheaded, and who had benefited on account of the evil visited upon others, while God, being just, had dispensed justice upon all who had been the cause of their demise, on beholding him without weapons Bustron did not move a muscle>.[355]

195. In addition, on 24 January [in the year] of Christ [14] 73[356] a piece of news reached Nicosia that: 'The count de Rochas, governor of the kingdom, gave a horse to a youth, Therianos, which had belonged to John d'Augustine. Furthermore, following the lords' departure he too (John d'Augustine) was found to be a traitor and he was exiled as well. He had, moreover, sold the horse to Barberotto, a man from Famagusta. Besides, he (Barberotto) went and issued a court summons against the count regarding why he had taken it and given it to Therianos before Gonsalvo Perez, who was the captain of Famagusta. And the captain went to the court, found the count de Rochas and began speaking to him with tremendous arrogance, telling him that: "I am the captain of Famagusta and I have authority to dispense justice to everyone. Your lordship took the horse and gave it there where you wanted".

Furthermore, the count on seeing that he was speaking to him so crudely, got up from the bench and stood. And Gonsalvo drew his dagger while Sir John de Ras dealt him a kick, and he fell down. The count, moreover, remained extremely resentful, and the people of Famagusta on hearing about this all rushed to the count de Rochas' house in order to kill the Franks. Besides, the count, in order for the affair to blow over, went to the galley and had a conversation with the *provedittore* until the matter had settled, and he then came back. In addition, Gonsalvo went away to enter the queen's chamber, so as to speak to her, but they did not let him, and after a short time the *provedittore* sent 25 men from Dalmatia and they conducted Gonsalvo to the galley'.

---

[354] One finds it hard to believe that the queen wrote a summons to Louis Alberic, since he had departed from Cyprus with Rizzo de Marino, Archbishop Louis Perez Fabrigues and James Zaplana on 1 January 1474.

[355] The words in brackets < > are taken from mss. **B** and **M**. See Kehayioglou, Διήγησις, *op. cit.*, p. 233, **B** lines 11-17 and **M** lines 10-16. George Boustronios is clearly referring to James of Malta when speaking of 'the one who had caused the death of the young men whom the king had beheaded' for James was the one who had secretly given them away.

[356] Ms **A** wrongly has 1473 for 1474. See *ibid.*, p. 232 ms. **A** line 18.

196. Furthermore, on 25 January two Venetian galleys came from Venice to Famagusta bringing Tristan de Gibelet[357] with them, in irons. They had, moreover, found him on board the galley of King Ferdinand, on which the lords had taken flight. And he said to them: 'The aim of Zaplana and of Rizzo was to go to the sultan, but <their crime and> the weather drove them to Rhodes and they disembarked', <while Tristan de Gibelet also disembarked>[358]. They seized him and had him brought to Cyprus, to Famagusta.

197. And he[359] said that: 'The Venetian fleet is to be found at Rhodes, 46 galleys'.[360] In addition, the archbishop wrote a letter to her ladyship the queen, stating: "the reason why I left was none other than that no evil should come to pass".[361] <And> he recommended the countess.

In the same month they hanged Mastichi[362] as a traitor, as well as Nicolo Spezzieri, because they admitted that they had killed Sir Andrew Corner and Sir Marco Bembo, and that they had other things in mind but God revealed them.

---

[357] He was the only conspirator captured, but he was subsequently released or escaped to resume plotting against Venice with Rizzo di Marino, for which see Hill, *op. cit.*, III, 688 note 4 and §278 below.

[358] The words in brackets < > in this and the preceding line are taken from mss. **B** and **M**. See Kehayioglou, Διήγησις, *op. cit.*, p. 237, **B** lines 7 and 11-2, **M** lines 7-8.

[359] Mss. **B** and **M** have 'they'. See *ibid.*, p. 237, ms. **B** line 8 and ms. **M** line 9.

[360] It had arrived there to seize the Neapolitan galley transporting Archbishop Louis, Rizzo, Zaplana and Louis Alberic, and on 25 January the Venetian captain-general Peter Mocenigo arrived and demanded the fugitives from the Hospitaller grand master. Grand Master Orsini, however, refused to let him seize this galley, which was in Rhodes harbour, or to arrest the fugitives. Mocenigo departed and set sail for Cyprus, but Orsini, fearing that the Venetians might attack Rhodes, compelled the fugitives to leave the island in February. See Hill, *op. cit.*, III, 688.

[361] The archbishop nonetheless continued to draw revenues from the see of Nicosia through his agent and supporter on Cyprus Anthony di Zucco, the Latin bishop of Limassol, who had them regularly despatched to Rome in his capacity as administrator of the property of the archbishopric of Nicosia. Queen Catherine tried to remove him by having him sent on an embassy to Venice in late 1473, and following his return to Cyprus sometime after March 1474 she wished to expel him again, but could not do so due to the favour he had curried with the *provedittore* Francesco Giustiniani and her councillor Peter Diedo. On arriving back in Cyprus Bishop Anthony di Zucco complained to Pope Sixtus IV of having been robbed of 200 ducats of revenue over several years by the royal officials. Sixtus promulgated a bull threatening spiritual penalties on those acting thus at the expense of Anthony or his successors. In November 1475 Queen Catherine sent a letter to Doge Peter Mocenigo of Venice reporting the bishop's activities in favour of the exiled Archbishop Louis and urging his expulsion. After the translation of Archbishop Louis to Capaccio in March 1476, Bishop Anthony tried unsuccessfully to succeed him, but the pope appointed the Venetian candidate, Victor Marcello. See Mas Latrie, 'Documents nouveaux', *op. cit.*, pp. 454-455, 488 and 492; *idem.*, *Histoire, op. cit.*, III, 456 note 1; *idem.*, 'Histoire des archevêques', *op. cit.*, p. 301; Hill, *op. cit.*, III, 724-725 and 725 note 1.

[362] Demetrios of Patras, also called Mastachi, who was incarcerated in Venice in November 1474 on the orders of the Venetian Senate (Mas Latrie, *op. cit., Histoire*, III, 396) is unlikely to have been a relative, for above Mastichi is described as a *marrano*, a Jewish or Muslim convert to Christianity.

198. And on the 26 [January] a command came to Sir William de Ras that: 'He must send Father John de Riviolo[363] to Famagusta, under close guard!'

199. Besides, on the same day certain men of the citadel who had been with Peter d'Avila arrived from Famagusta, because they had been expelled from Famagusta. And they went to the *provedittore* and to the count de Rochas and said to them: 'My lords, we are not secure because the Franks remain in Famagusta and we should not trust them because we have discovered them to be traitors once already. We declare, moreover, to your lordship that they should disappear from Famagusta! And if they do not, give us orders for us to go!' Furthermore, the lords, on seeing this, [realised] they had to expel them from Famagusta and have them brought to Nicosia. In addition, on their arrival in Nicosia they did not allow them to enter the city and sent them away. And they went to Lefkomiatis and remained there in great fear. They also wrote a letter and sent it to Famagusta, to the queen and the governors. <And the queen and the governors wrote a letter>[364] and they were admitted into Nicosia.

200. In addition, on 27 January they appointed Sir George Contarini count of Jaffa,[365] in Famagusta, and they gave him as incomes [the revenues of] Vavatsinia with its appurtenances, as well as Dhali, Platanistasa and Kalopsida.

201. Besides, on 28 January Sir Paul Contarin went to Kerynia as the captain there, and Nicholas Morabit departed.[366]

202. On the same day, moreover, the queen sent written orders to Muzio de Constanzo, the admiral, to go to Famagusta. And she also sent word to the people in the city: 'Let none cause him any discomfort! Furthermore, let his house be well guarded, <because I want him for my own matters!'>[367]

203. And on the same day the *provedittore* sent [men] and had Camus[368] taken to Famagusta, and he placed him on boards the galley along with the rest.

204. On the same day, moreover, the queen sent word that Farandetto, who had previously been the castellan at the citadel of Famagusta, when they had killed Sir Andrew, should be sent to Famagusta, so that they could ascertain in truth the reason why they had not opened for Sir Andrew so that he could enter the citadel. And as soon as he arrived, the queen gave orders for him to be interrogated. In addition, he told them in the course of his interrogation that: 'My lords, you are doing me a great

---

363 He was Archbishop Louis' secretary and administrator, on which see below.

364 The words in brackets < > are taken from mss. **B** and **M**. See Kehayioglou, *Διήγησις*, *op. cit.*, p. 239, **B** lines 11-12 and **M** lines 10-11.

365 He was appointed in place of John Perez Fabrigues, the brother of Archbishop Louis who had died on 24 October 1473, as mentioned above.

366 On this appointment see also Mas Latrie, 'Documents nouveaux', *op. cit.*, pp. 441-442.

367 The words in brackets < > are taken from mss. **B** and **M**. See Kehayioglou, *Διήγησις*, *op. cit.*, p. 241, lines 3-4 of both mss.

368 Franceschin Camus was a supporter of King James II, who between 1464 and 1468 had granted him the *casalia* of Sia, Margo and Cormia, purchased from John Imperator, and Peristerona in the region of Mesaoria. See Florio Bustron, 'Chronique', *op. cit.*, p. 423.

injustice. You know that during that night, when they killed Sir Andrew, the count of Tripoli who happened to be the captain of Famagusta came, and he ordered me three times, upon my life, not to open the citadel to admit Sir Andrew, and should I open it I would be a traitor! For this reason I, not knowing about the matter, had to do just as he ordered me to'. Furthermore, they took him and presented him to the *provedittore*, and the *provedittore* had him sent to the galley until they were to interrogate him. He was exiled, moreover, along with the rest.

205. Besides, on 31 January a great scandal was about to take place regarding Garcia de Navarre[369] and [John of] Emesa. Garcia was in the company of Peter d'Avila and happened to be a tailor, and on his arrival in Cyprus the king honoured him and also gave him incomes. In addition, on the king's death Peter d'Avila had him knighted and he was given an additional income of 300 ducats, <and these things were not sufficient for him>[370] and he was not content. Besides, he had a hostel outside Nicosia,[371] [formerly] belonging to [the late] Sir William Strambali, and because the king had wedded him to his wife he acquired the hostel as well.[372] He did not have the authority, moreover, to conduct slaughters outside, but Garcia wished to do so without any right whatsoever.[373] In addition, [John of] Emesa was the tenant and he sought to forbid this on the part of the queen: 'He had better not dare to do something that is not customary!' And they exchanged sharp words. Furthermore, he drew out a dagger in order to stab [John of] Emesa, and had other people been absent a great calamity would have ensued. And John went straightaway to Sir John de Ras, who was the queen's deputy and told him of the incident. Having listened to him, moreover, he sent word of it to Nicholas Morabit, and he rode over and came to Sir William de Ras, and he too

---

[369] He is also called Master Anthony Garcia in this chronicle, for which see §189, where it is also mentioned that King James II had granted him the *casale* of Epikho, and that Queen Catherine had granted him the fruit market of Nicosia as well as two estates that James of Malta had possessed in Kythraea, subsequently taken from James because he was a traitor. Garcia was exiled to Venice in 1476, and in a letter of 15 March 1480 he asked permission to return to Cyprus, or to bring his wife to Venice if this were not granted. See Mas Latrie, 'Documents nouveaux', *op. cit.*, pp. 501-502.

[370] The words in brackets < > are taken from mss. **B** and **M**. See Kehayioglou, Διήγησις, *op. cit.*, p. 243, **B** lines 7-8 and **M** line 8.

[371] By 1474 five such hostels, called *canutes* (Gr. χανούτιν: a word of Armenian origin) and serving bread, meat and wine, were located outside the city walls of Nicosia, and by 1531 their number had increased to twelve, a development that hastened the decline of hostels located within Nicosia. On such hostels see Coureas, *Assizes*, *op. cit.*, Codex One, articles 101 and 103-104, Codex Two, articles 101-103; Coureas, Grivaud and Schabel, 'Frankish and Venetian Nicosia', *op. cit.*, p. 37.

[372] Dawkins, (*Boustronios*, *op. cit.*, §205) following mss. **B** and **M** which have 'ἔξω τῆς πόρτας' misinterprets this passage, regarding the hostel as being located outside the door of Sir William Strambali. Ms. A correctly has 'ἔξω τῆς χώρας', meaning outside the city. See Kehayioglou, Διήγησις, *op. cit.*, pp. 242-243, ms. **B** line 8, ms. **M** line 9 and ms. **A** lines 8-9.

[373] The viscount of Nicosia strictly controlled the existing slaughterhouses of Nicosia and a law of 1305 prohibited the raising of meat prices from Christmas Eve until the second week after the New Year. See 'Banns et Ordonances des rois de Chypre', *RHC Lois*, II, ed. M. le Compte Beugnot (Paris, 1843), p. 367, no. XXII. It appears that Garcia was seeking to evade these controls by slaughtering animals at the hostel outside Nicosia.

mounted his horse and they [both] went to the Taxation Gate to conduct an inquest. And on seeing that the matter was about to turn ugly, they found a way and reconciled them.

206. In addition, on the same day they brought the abbot of [the monastery of] the Holy Cross, Brother Simon de Sant'Andrea, to Famagusta, and they placed him in the citadel. And they said that: 'They apprehended a letter that he was sending to his brother the pope, which wrote: "My dear brother, I make it known to you that by God's power the tyrannical bastard who ruled the kingdom with great tyranny has died! The kingdom, moreover, has been left with great grievances. Furthermore, he left the queen pregnant, and she gave birth to a strapping lad. And King Ferdinand [of Naples] is secretly seeking to acquire the kingdom, while on the other hand Charlotte is also seeking it. Besides, it is in dire straits, and it now stands in the hands of the Venetians, which means that we have escaped from the clutches of a dog and fallen into [those of] a swine".[374] He wrote numerous other things, moreover, and they discovered other letters in the archbishop's hands, and he was writing many and varied things that they sent for and had brought'. Furthermore, they confiscated whatever the Holy Cross possessed, including <the village>.[375]

207. And on 1 February they released Gonsalvo from the galley.

208. Besides, on the 2 February Stephen of Chios the *chevetain* of Chrysochou arrested Gabriel Ferrier, and they discovered 105 ducats on him and had them sent to the queen, as well as the abovementioned Gabriel. And they placed him on board the galley straightaway.

209. Furthermore, on 3 February Sir Peter Mocenigo, the captain of the fleet, came to Famagusta, with twelve galleys and four galleasses,[376] and there were twelve horses on each galley.[377]

---

[374] Florio Bustron, 'Chronique', *op. cit.*, pp. 447-448 who also recounts this incident has the abbot state that the kingdom has fallen 'nelle onge de lione' i.e. to a lion cub. Dawkins, *Boustronios, op. cit.*, §206 likewise has 'a lion's whelp', an interpretation that Hill, III, 697 note 5, regards as more appropriate to Venice, whose emblem was the lion of St Mark. The word κουκούτιν, however, undoubtedly means pig (Makhairas, *Recital, op. cit.*, II, 234, § 713 note 1). Given the abbot's hostility to Venice, is it not hard to credit him with this characterization.

[375] The words in brackets are taken from mss. **B** and **M**. See Kehayioglou, Διήγησις, *op. cit.*, p. 245, **B** line 14 and **M** line 14. The travellers Nicolo de Martoni and Felix Faber, who visited Cyprus in 1394 and 1483 respectively, both mention this village. See Cobham, *Excerpta Cypria, op. cit.*, pp. 27 and 38. Confiscations apart, the abbot, who supported Queen Charlotte, was banished from Cyprus, but was able to return there and even visit his monastery on account of the favour shown to him by the Venetian *provedittore* Francesco Giustiniani. He was banished once more by Queen Catherine and her councillors, and in November 1475 she recounted these things in a letter to Doge Peter Mocenigo of Venice, expressing bitterness at the audacity with which such persons could come back to Cyprus on account of someone's favour and because her power to react was greatly circumscribed. See Mas Latrie, 'Documents nouveaux', *op. cit.*, p. 455.

[376] A galleass was a large galley. See Pryor, *Geography, op. cit.*, pp. 43-57, 67-68, 72-73, 78-79, 83, 88-89, 162 and 180.

[377] Hill, *op. cit.*, III, 695-696 observes that following his arrival and landing of troops, which astonished the people of Famagusta on account of its occurrence in mid-winter, the prosecution of persons seen as inimical to Venice intensified. Mocenigo headed a tribunal including the *provedittore* Victor Soranzo, Count George Contarinii of Jaffa, the Count de Rochas, Constable Peter d'Avila and Chancellor Thomas Ficardo.

210. On the same day, moreover, the *turcoples* of Paphos brought Perico de Villafranca and Peter of Armenia[378]. And they placed them in irons in the galley.

211. Besides, on 5 February they brought the archbishop's secretary[379] and placed him in the citadel of Famagusta.

212. And on the same day John the Black arrived in Nicosia with three men, without having taken orders from the queen, and he told the populace and the artisans to go to Famagusta to greet the commander of the fleet. They, moreover, went and greeted him, and they came back.

213. In addition, a proclamation was made on 6 February[380] on the part of the queen: 'Let none carry weapons, neither great nor small!'

214. And on the same day the captain of the fleet made a proclamation: 'let none from the fleet dare to spend the night in Famagusta, but only in the galleys!'

215. Furthermore, on 7 February [14] 73[381] [in the year] of Christ Marco Venier the queen's nephew came, who was the captain in Crete. And as soon as he had learnt about [the murder of] Sir Andrew he came, bringing 70 men and 36 horses.[382]

216. In addition, on the same day they took Master [Estive] Barthélemy,[383] the

---

[378] Florio Bustron, 'Chronique', *op. cit.*, pp. 447-448 mentions both as being implicated in the murder of Sir Andrew Corner. It also states that Peter of Armenia among others was detained in connection with the flight of Archbishop Louis, then released, but eventually summoned to appear for transportation to Venice. Perico de Villafranca may have been related to James de Villafranca, mentioned in two documents of 5 November 1468 as purchasing together with John de Milan vineyards at Pera and Naya from Peter Goul for 300 bezants, and undertaking to grant eight bezants a year to a Greek nunnery in the vicinity, the identity of which cannot be conclusively established. See Richard, *Remembrances, op. cit.*, nos. 212-213 and 212 note 5.

[379] Brother John de Riviolo, already mentioned in §198.

[380] Ms. **A** has 3 February, but 6 February as found in mss. **B** and **M** makes more sense given that this event follows those of 5 February recounted in §211-212. See Kehayioglou, Διήγησις, *op. cit.*, p. 247 line 13 in both mss.

[381] Ms. **A** mistakenly gives 1473 for 1474, and dates Venier's arrival to 5 February. See *ibid.*, p. 246, ms. **A** lie 17; p. 247, line 17 of mss. **B** and **M**.

[382] The Venetian writer Navagero states that he arrived with 50 crossbowmen whom he brought at his own expense in the hope of receiving a fief from Queen Catherine, but she simply knighted him and then sent him away, so that he had to sell an estate on Crete to pay for his men. Determined to exact revenge, he arrived back in Cyprus in 1478 and was placed in command of the Famagusta garrison, but his plot to assassinate Queen Catherine on 8 April 1479 and then seize the kingdom for Queen Charlotte was betrayed beforehand. Venier was arrested, confessed everything, and was hanged with the other conspirators on the same day. See Hill, *op. cit.*, III, 604 and note 6 and 730-731.

[383] This doctor is described as a surgeon in a document of November 1468 in King James II exempted him from payment of the annual sum of 200 bezants on the *casale* of Kataliondas, which the doctor clearly possessed, as well as from paying the tax known as the *rate*, an annual payment of 25 bezants payable half in cash and half in wheat. See Richard, *Remembrances, op. cit.*, no. 86. A Venetian report of 1510-1521 mentions the *casalia* of this doctor as having been reincorporated in the royal estate, although Kataliondas is not named among them. See Mas Latrie, *Histoire, op. cit.*, III, 512.

doctor, to Famagusta, and placed him in the citadel. The chief groom of the count de Rochas took his mule, moreover, and sent it to the count's house. And on learning about it in the court they send persons and commandeered it. Furthermore, he spent some time in the citadel, and taking him out they put him on board the galley and interrogated him, and he was clean.

217. And on 8 February the commander of the fleet appeared before the queen along with the *provedittore*, and greeting her they said to her: 'Give us orders, if you have some order, on what to do with the traitors who happen to be in your land, regarding whom we have some in our power, some in the citadel and some in the galleys! And tell us what to do!' Besides, with the queen and the lords standing near her, Sir George Contarini, the count of Jaffa, the count de Rochas and Sir Peter Bembo, all listening, Sir George spoke and said to them: 'My lords, regarding what you told our lady, her ladyship has heard you, and shall send word to your lordships when the time is ripe'. And the captain and *provedittore* on hearing this said goodbye and went to the galley with a large escort.

218. Besides, in the third hour of the night the queen sent for and brought the chancellor, together with her counsellors. Furthermore, they wrote that which she wanted and she gave it to the chancellor, while he took it to the commander of the fleet and to the *provedittore*. In addition, the count de Rochas, Sir George Contarini, Peter d'Avila, Sir John de Ras and Sir Thomas Ficardo, the chancellor, ventured forth in the morning, and they went to the galley where the commander and the *provedittore* were, told them the things that they had to say, returned, brought the response to the queen, bade her farewell and left.

In addition, as soon as they had eaten they rode off, went to the seashore, entered the galley and conversed with the commander and the *provedittore*. They, moreover, called the captain of the galley so as to release the persons mentioned below and have them placed in the citadel: the knight Sir John Cortese,[384] the knight Sir Camus, Brother Simon de Sant'Andrea, the abbot of the Holy Cross, the valet Peter de Lignana,[385] the canon Father John de Riviolo, Master Bernard, the king's tailor,[386] Franciscetto Lombardo and Peter de Marino, [all] in irons, < as well as Perrico de Villa[franca] and Francesco, [who were] in irons, and Farandetto>.[387]

---

[384] A possible relation of Michael Cortese mentioned above.

[385] He was a soldier from Piedmont and a supporter of King James II, who between the years 1464-1468 granted him the *casalia* of Sarama, Aplanda and Kryo Nero, while in a document of 27 October 1468 he is mentioned as the captain of Kerynia Castle. He was clearly released or else made his escape following his arrest and detention, for he died in 1476 as a mercenary soldier of Duke Charles the Bold of Burgundy. See Florio Bustron, 'Chronique', *op. cit.*, p. 420; Richard, *Remembrances, op. cit.*, no. 76 and note 3.

[386] The tailor of King James II, he is mentioned in a document of 8 September 1468 as receiving 25 measures of corn, and in a later document of 13 October 1468 as the beneficiary of an annual subvention consisting of 36 measures of wheat, 36 measures of wine and 90 measures of pulses. See *ibid.*, nos. 58 and 138.

[387] The words in brackets < > are taken from mss. **B** and **M**. See Kehayioglou, Διήγησις, *op. cit.*, p. 251, **B** lines 11-12 and **M** lines 11-12.

Besides, once they had taken them to the citadel, the commander, the *provedittore*, the count de Rochas, Peter d'Avila and Sir Thomas Ficardo the chancellor, <as well as the chancellor of the *provedittore*,>[388] arrived and went to the citadel in order to interrogate them. And they interrogated Father John de Riviolo, whom the archbishop held very dearly <and who was the administrator in the villages of the archbishopric>, and whom the archbishop had sent as an envoy to King Ferdinand. Bringing him before them, moreover, they began to interrogate him from the time of the king's death, and said to him: 'You are a sensible man, and so tell us everything that you know. Otherwise your bones shall stay on the rack!' And he said to them: 'My lords, tell the chancellor to get some paper and I shall say whatever I know: My lords, I inform your lordships that on the king's death the count of Jaffa, John Perez, wrote a letter to me and had it sent to me in Nicosia, for me to come to Famagusta. Furthermore, I came in accordance with his command, he gave me some letters and I went to Naples'. In addition, he confessed many other things, and the chancellor wrote them down on a piece of paper. And they placed the lords in the tower.

219. Besides, on 5 February 150 men, 100 Greeks and 50 Armenians, came from Nicosia with John the Black and Stephen Koudouna, and they went and greeted the commander and introduced themselves.

220. On 8 February, moreover, as soon as day broke, the count de Rochas, the count of Jaffa, the constable and Thomas Ficardo mounted their horses and went to the galley. And the commander along with the *provedittore* came down and went to the citadel to interrogate the remainder. Furthermore, on the same day two galleasses came to Famagusta, bringing 100 warhorses.

221. In addition, on 9 February they had Peter of Armenia and Perico de Villafranca tortured, and they confessed that they had killed Sir Andrew, and that he had [sustained] two wounds before they killed him. And it was Peter of Armenia who said it, that he had killed him, and had killed him on account of Sir Rizzo and Zaplana: 'Because they told them that they were traitors, and I, not knowing about the affair and seeing that both the captain of Famagusta and Sir Rizzo were saying that they should kill the traitors, had to do that which they had ordered me [to do]. And this is all I have to tell you'. Perico de Villafranca, moreover, told them that: 'I found him [already] killed, and he had a ring, and I pulled in order to take it off and was unable to, and I cut off his finger'. Furthermore, he said other things as well, and they took them out of the citadel and placed them in custody.

222. In addition, on the same day the lords sent for and took into the citadel the children of Franceschin de Bandes, Gabriel and Hector, and they interrogated them on what letters the archbishop had given them, 'and did you take them to Kerynia?' And they replied: 'My lords, we do not know anything else to say, other than [this]: We happened to be with our mother and with our sister the countess[389] at her home, and

---

[388] This strange phrase in brackets < > which Dawkins (*Boustronios, op. cit.*, p. 49) omits from his translation exists in all three mss. and so has been included here.

[389] The 'countess' must refer to Lady Margaret, the widow of the Catalan Sir John Arognon. See above §110.

the archbishop came and summoned me, Hector, and gave me sealed papers, saying to me: "Arrange to take them to Kerynia straightaway and place them into the hands of the captain <Sir Louis Alberic>!390 These, moreover, are regarding the queen's business". Furthermore, I took them in accordance with his orders and gave them to him, and he gave me a reply, and I brought this to the archbishop in Famagusta. I know nothing else besides'. And recognizing that it was not some piece of foul play they released them.

223. In addition, on 10 February, in the third hour of the night, they hanged Perico de Villafranca and Peter of Armenia.391

224. Besides, on the 12 February a letter from the queen reached Morabit: 'he was to deprive Charles Kallergis of his horses and weapons and to order him and his brother John Kallergis to go at once to Famagusta, and he was to impound both their property and horses!'392 And so it happened. Furthermore, he sent word to them, they appeared before him, and he showed them the letter. And they said: 'Our lady's command is upon our head! As concerns her ladyship's command over our horses, we do not have any others to ride. Besides, should you so order, let us mount our horses, go there, and let them take them there!' And Morabit said to them: 'Upon your faith, do you not have any other horses?' They, moreover, took an oath that they had no others, and he said to them: 'Take them and go!' He also gave them a letter and they went to their sister,393 [the wife] of Sir Philip Podocataro.

Furthermore, a great lamentation took place there, and she was pregnant and fainted. From there they went to their mother to say goodbye to her. And who could describe her grief on seeing them, for having lost her husband, her villages and her

---

390 The words in brackets < > are found only in mss. **B** and **M**. See Kehayioglou, *Διήγησις, op. cit.*, p. 257 line 4 of both mss.

391 In a written declaration of the same day Queen Catherine announced that she had taken the county of Jaffa and the lordship of Ascalon from the heirs of the late John Perez Fabrigues, who were given land in the locality of Aglandja near Nicosia by way of exchange, and had awarded them to her cousin Sir George Contarinii. A document of 24 February 1474 records that he also received as fiefs the *casalia* or *presteries* of Vavatsinia, Dhali, Peristerona west of Nicosia, Sateni, St Sergios, Platanistassa, Tokhni, Lefkara and Kalopsida. Doge Nicholas Marcello of Venice was initially reluctant to confirm this grant, and on 20 March 1474 the Queen wrote to him imploring him to do so. George Bustron states that the award was made on 27 January 1474, but the High Court only confirmed it on 10 February. See Mas Latrie, *Histoire, op. cit.*, III, 366-369; *idem.*, 'Documents nouveaux', *op. cit.*, pp. 443-450; Hill, *op. cit.*, III, 703-704.

392 James Kallergis, father of the above, is mentioned as a fief-holder under King James II. The Kallergis family were possibly related to the prominent Greek family of this name found in Crete, and may have migrated to Cyprus. See Richard, *Remembrances, op. cit.*, no. 166 and note 19; Sally McKee, *Uncommon Dominion: Venetian Crete and the Myth of Ethnic Purity* (Pennsylvania, 2000), pp. 75-83, 101, 111, 124, 127, 130, 142, 144, 150-151, 160 and 176.

393 This was Mary Kallergis, who in 1467 was mentioned among those faithful to Queen Charlotte but who later returned to Cyprus, marrying Philip Podocataro in or shortly before 1471. See W. Rudt de Collenberg, 'Études de prosopographie généalogique des Chypriotes mentionés dans les registres du Vatican, 1378-1471', *MY* I (1984), 671.

property, was she to lose even her children on top of it all?' And even though they had never had anything good from their stepfather, were they to come to harm because of him![394] They, moreover, were comforting their mother and were saying to her: 'Stand firm with a good heart! For we reckon before God not to come to harm, because we have done no harm. Besides, the government of Venice is extremely wise, and we expect to have justice in every matter'. And the poor woman was crying and commending them to the Mother of God and prayed for them.

They, moreover, went to Famagusta, and two horsemen were with them in their company. The queen even sent word to the viscount that: 'He should impound John Guillaume's horses and weapons! And they should sent him too to Famagusta!' He, moreover, happened to be at Kolossi, and they sent people to bring him.

225. In addition, on the same day an order from the queen arrived that: 'Let no man of condition (i.e. high social station) carry weapons, on pain of being hanged!' And the viscount made a proclamation in line with her orders. Furthermore, on hearing it the people of Nicosia went to Sir John de Ras and bewailed their plight, saying to him: 'It appears to us that this is not an order from her lady the queen, but rather is your own order. And we want your lordship, who is in her place, to show us the order'.[395] Besides, the viscount turned up in the course of these words and came to Sir John de Ras' house.

And in order to see the viscount he came down to the entrance stairs and explained the reason to him, to the viscount. In addition, the viscount took out the queen's letter and showed it to them, and Sir John de Ras read it aloud, saying to them: 'This paper my boys is from her lady, the queen, and make arrangements to act according to the proclamation of his lordship the viscount!' And all said: 'Her command be on our head! Furthermore, we wish to write and to send word to her ladyship, and we wish to know what is the reason she sent word to us not to carry weapons'. They wrote a letter, moreover, and sent it to the queen. They viscount also sent one on the part of the men regarding how the matter had turned out.

226. And on 18 February the galley that took away Sir Philip Podocataro arrived at Kerynia. It was, moreover, decreed by the government that it should not make port at any place other than Famagusta, and should give the papers it was carrying to the commander of the fleet in person. And it went to Famagusta, found the commander and gave him the papers. Furthermore, it reported that it had parted company with the Venetian fleet at Modon: 'Besides, the commander of the fleet had learnt that they had

---

[394] The mother's forename is not known, but she must be the woman mentioned in *ibid.*, pp. 619-620, as James Zaplana's wife. She was the widow of James Kallergis and the mother of John, Charles and Mary, which would make James Zaplana the childrens' 'stepfather'. He must have married her after James Kallergis' death between 1468 and 1471. Dawkins, *Boustronios, op. cit.*, §222 mistranslated the Greek πατριός as father, not stepfather, which in turn caused Collenberg (Études de prosopographie', *op. cit.*, p. 671) to think that the Kallergis childrens' late father James had been the cause of their troubles. See *ibid.*, pp. 619 and 671.

[395] The words in brackets < > in this and the preceding sentence are taken from ms **M**. See Kehayioglou, Διήγησις, *op. cit.*, p. 261, **M** lines 1-2.

killed Sir Andrew and the rest and straightaway, as soon as he took possession of the papers, he sealed them without setting eyes on them and gave them to the captain of the galleys, for him to take them to Venice. And as soon as they had taken them, they sat in council and issued the order: "Let the galley turn around and go back to Cyprus!" We learnt, moreover, that: "Let Philip Podocataro not be found in Venice at this time,[396] and should he be found then let his person be at the disposal of the government, and let him not be found within three days in any territory of the government", and they said: "We gave him the order to go into exile with great leniency. Having reached a decision, however, we cannot do anything else'", and Sir Philip acted in accordance with their order. Besides, on learning of the murder of Sir Andrew and Sir Marco, the government was greatly displeased, for they (i.e. the perpetrators) had laid hands on the blood of its subjects.

227. In addition, three Venetian galleys came to Pendayia, and in passing they disembarked the men whom Marco Venier had brought over from Crete. They, moreover, forthwith mounted their horses and went to Famagusta, while the galleys went to Famagusta.

228. And on the same day they seized the count of Tripoli, Sir John Tafur, and took him to the citadel. The reason was because they had tortured Farandetto, who had been the castellan of Famagusta, and he told them: 'My lords, on the night in which they killed Sir Andrew, the count of Tripoli and Rizzo came to the citadel and summoned me. I, moreover, answered and said to them: "What are your lordship's orders?" And they said to me: 'See that we order you on the part of our ladyship the queen, upon your life and on pain of [being guilty of] treason, not to open the citadel and let anyone in without the queen herself coming in person!'

Furthermore, on hearing them I answered them and said to them: 'Should one of the governors come, should I not open for him?' And they said to me: 'Should all of us come in person, do not open for us unless you see the queen in person!' Besides, they left as soon as they had issued this order to me. In addition, after the midnight hour had passed I heard the bell sounding the alarm, and I armed myself at once, not knowing what the matter was. Furthermore, Sir Andrew arrived within a short time and called out to me to open the castle so that he could enter. And, given that those who were the governors of the realm had given me orders, I had to follow their orders, and in reply to Sir Andrew I said to him: "My lord, I inform your lordship to be aware that I am under orders not to open for anyone, unless our ladyship the queen should come in person, and for this reason I do not open for your lordship". He, moreover, was pressing me greatly, while I did not open for him in accordance with the orders I had, so as not to be considered a traitor to my queen, and I admitted him into the palisade of the citadel, because I had no prohibition regarding that place.

In addition, the count of Tripoli arrived after a short time, along with Sir Rizzo,

---

[396] Mss **B** and **M** have 'within three hours'. See Kehayioglou, Διήγησις, op. cit., p. 263, line 7 of both mss. Florio Bustron, 'Chronique', op. cit., p. 451 has six hours.

and calling me they asked me whether anyone came to enter the castle. And I said to them: "none have come other than Sir Andrew Corner < and Sir Marco Bembo >.[397] And since I have and had orders from your lordships, I did not open for them". Furthermore, they said to me: "Which way did he go?" And I said to them: "he is to be found within the palisade". And the count straightaway called out to him, while he answered him, and [the count] said to him by way of replying to him: "Come my friend, our lady the queen is summoning you!" And Sir Andrew said to him: "Leave me here until daybreak, for things to blow over!" They, moreover, did not leave and offered him a safe-conduct, taking him out of the palisade. In addition, as he was coming out the count struck his horse and went off, leaving Sir Andrew with Rizzo.

In view of this, judge whether I, wretched person that I am, did something wrong', he said to them. Besides, on account of that which Farandetto had said they brought the count of Tripoli and placed him on board the galley, and the galley sailed away and took him to Venice.[398]

229. Furthermore, on 18 February a letter came to the viscount on the part of the queen: 'Let none dare to cause discomfort in the count of Tripoli's house. And so it came to pass.

230. And on 21 February[399] the queen sent word to the viscount to make a proclamation: 'Let every person keep his weapons, and let all be law abiding!' and he was to punish whomsoever committed a crime.

231. Besides, on the same day a command reached the viscount that he was to send forthwith to Famagusta John Kallergis' black horse. And he sent for it at his house but did not find it. In addition, they told him that: 'Sir Philip de Nores has it'. Furthermore, the viscount went and showed the order to Sir Philip, and Sir Philip said to him: 'It is true and I indeed have the horse, but I purchased it from Sir John Kallergis, and I have testimonies'. The viscount, moreover, said to him: 'I shall report it in writing to her lady the queen'.

232. In addition, on the same day a letter from the queen came to the viscount that he should send people to Sir Philip Podocataro's house and should seize his pack animals and the caravan leader: 'And you shall send them to Famagusta!'

---

[397] The words in brackets < > are taken from mss. **B** and **M**. See Kehayioglou, Διήγησις, op. cit., p. 267, **B** lines 7-8 and **M** lines 5-6.

[398] The count of Tripoli never reached Venice, as a friend of his with his own ship intercepted the galley transporting him there and rescued him. He reached Naples on 28 March 1474 and at the end of this year was reported as being engaged together with Rizzo de Marino, James Zaplana, Archbishop Louis de Fabregues and Louis Alberic as plotting against Queen Catherine. See Hill, op. cit., III, 696-697.

[399] Mss. **B** and **M** both have 20 February. See Kehayioglou, Διήγησις, op. cit., p. 269 line 3 of both mss.

233. And on the same day Antonello d'Avila, who was the captain at Paphos, arrived. Furthermore, they sent John Petinal, a Venetian [in his place].[400]

234. On the same day, moreover, they incarcerated John Kallergis, Gabriel Ferrier, Master Bernard the tailor, Henry Kallergis and the abbot of [the monastery of] the Holy Cross in the tower of Famagusta.

235. And on the same day they relieved Stephen the Chiot from Chrysochou and appointed Andrew the Provençal.

236. Besides, on 24 February Morabit came to Nicosia from Famagusta. Furthermore, the queen, the commander [of the fleet] and the *provedittore* did him great honour and bestowed considerable privileges upon him.

237. In addition, on the same day four Venetian galleasses arrived at Famagusta and they brought with them 200 Italian men, along with horses, while they also had Cretans on board, all well armed.

238. And on 26 February [in the year] of Christ 1474[401] < Peter d'Avila > had a sharp exchange of words with Sir John Attar in the palace of Famagusta. He, moreover, said to him: 'Sir John Attar, know that I have learnt that you are saying many things about me, and you are saying that I am not loyal to our lady the queen! Furthermore, I consider this to be very strange, and did not wish to keep this a secret, but wished to say it to you in front of all the lords who are present amongst us. And so for this reason I ask you, should I have said something, to tell me about it here before them!'

And Sir John Attar said to him: 'Peter d'Avila, as regards your claim that I say many bad things about you, I let you know that that which I said I say it once again and I shall uphold it with a sword in my hand! That which I said I did not say it secretly, moreover, but I said it openly before all the lords who happened to be at the court of our lady the queen. Furthermore, since I can say it, you too shall admit to it by your own mouth. My lord Sir Peter d'Avila, when the traitors to our lady [the queen] had left, did you not say with your own mouth that: "They had 300 men in their company?" In addition, our lady organized a search for them and did not find other than 60.

---

[400] Antonello d'Avila was probably related to the constable Peter d'Avila, and his recall presaged Peter d'Avila's exile to Venice in May 1474. His replacement in Paphos by a Venetian, like that of Nicolas Galimberto, the castellan of Famagusta, on 6 March, of the Cypriots guarding Queen Catherine's palace at Famagusta by Italians and Cretans, and of Sir John François at the arsenal by the Venetian Nicholas Benedetti, was part of a general policy of placing Venetians and their subjects in charge of key fortresses and strong points. The Venetian Senate had resolved upon this policy as far back as 20 December 1473 and instructed Sir Peter Mocenigo, the captain-general of the sea, to implement it, stating that Famagusta, Kerynia and the other strongholds should be placed under 'our castellans and men, in the name of our dominion, either voluntarily or by force, whichever you can achieve more skilfully'. See Mas Latrie, *Histoire, op. cit.*, III, 362-364. Florio Bustron, 'Chronique', *op. cit.*, p. 449 also recounts the posting of Venetians throughout Cypriot fortresses, mentioning Chrysochou where Andrew Provençal was posted, a locality George Boustronios omits.

[401] Ms. **A** has 1473, since the New Year then began on 1 March. See Kehayioglou, Διήγησις, *op. cit.*, p. 270 line 11.

"Where are the remainder to make up the 300?" you used to say to them. You also used to say: "They are Catalans". We see now that you are seeking to make out that each and every one of them were more than they actually were. Furthermore, you say: "They are all trustworthy". It was, moreover, on account of this that I said: "It seems to me that they are not additional Franks" other than those whom you have, and I said and say this any time you like'. Besides, they exchanged many other words, and the count de Rochas came in between them. And they remained at loggerheads.

239. On 27 February, moreover, the queen knighted Sir George Corner[402] and there was a great celebration in Famagusta.

240. In addition, on 28 February [14] 73 the daughter of Sir Louis de Nores, the marshal of Cyprus, and the wife of Sir Gonsalvo Perez, who happened to be the captain of Famagusta, died. And they buried her in [the cathedral of] St Nicholas in Famagusta.

241. And on 5 March [in the year] of Christ [14] 74 four galleasses sailed from Famagusta, taking away with them many Cretans and Italians together with their horses, which they had brought with them on the assumption that they needed them. And [then] they turned them back again.[403]

242. In addition, when the lords[404] had departed, the young men of Nicosia amongst themselves organized major lootings of their houses and took what was theirs, and each one took whatever he could, while they placed the rest into the hands of Sir John de Ras, as the person acting in the queen's place until her ladyship should give orders. And in the space of a few days the queen wrote a letter to Sir William de Ras that whatever things he had in his possession 'Should all be brought together, piece by piece, in accordance with the list that Sir James Gurri[405] has in his hands!' and he was to deliver them into the hands of Sir James Gurri for him to sell them and apportion them among the people of Nicosia, because she had donated these things to them. Furthermore, in line with her decree they took them and placed them into the hands of the constable, Anthony Kalathas, until they should be sold. In addition, 15 men from

---

[402] He was the brother of Queen Catherine and subsequently persuaded her to abdicate so that Cyprus would be more secure under direct Venetian rule. See Florio Bustron, 'Chronique', *op. cit.*, p. 454; Mas Latrie, *Histoire, op. cit.*, III, 420-427, also 821-822 for a brief note on his life and descendants. He was an executor and beneficiary of Queen Catherine's will for which see Mas Latrie, 'Documents nouveaux', *op. cit.*, pp. 418-420 and 586.

[403] The words 'ταμπρός οπίσω' found in ms. **A** and meaning 'back again' are not in the other two mss. causing Dawkins (*Chronicle, op. cit.*, p. 53, no. 241) to think that the galleys were sent away from Cyprus. See Kehayioglou, Διήγησις, *op. cit.*, pp. 274-275, ms. **A** line 5, ms. **B** line 4 and ms. **M** line 4.

[404] The 'lords' were Archbishop Louis, James de Zaplana, Louis Alberic and Rizzo de Marino, as well as Count John Tafur of Tripoli, who had either fled Cyprus or had been exiled subsequently.

[405] This was a namesake of the viscount of Nicosia assassinated by King James II, and he is mentioned as the *chevetain* of Chrysochou in a document of 1 June 1468, in which King James had him replaced by John de Ronya. See Richard, *Remembrances, op. cit.*, no. 30.

among the company got up, as well as James of Epiphanios, who was himself a constable in the company, and they said to Kalathas: 'Give us the clothes that you have in your possession! Besides, we wish to sell them and for [the matter] to be between us, since we have a decree from our lady the queen'. And he took them out and gave them.

As soon as they had taken them, moreover, they grabbed hold of them and distributed them among themselves, saying: 'Just as others have taken things, so have we'. And on learning of this Stephen Koudouna and the remaining artisans reacted in a body, went and summoned the viscount and told him of the matter, saying to him: 'A great tumult is about to erupt'. And the viscount said to him: 'Master Stephen, whom are you accusing?' He, moreover, replied to him: 'My lord, [I am accusing] John Khala and George [the son] of the priest Manolis Trachonites, for they are the ones creating the disturbances'. The viscount on hearing this sent for and had them brought before him. And they said to him: 'What does your lordship decree?' And he gave orders for them to be taken into custody: 'You are the ones who are creating the disturbances in Nicosia, and it is on account of you that much evil is about to transpire in Nicosia'.

They went to the gaol, moreover, and remained there until the morning, and they made entreaties to the viscount, who had them released. Furthermore, they took it upon themselves to return the things that they had taken before the viscount and share these among themselves. In addition, on seeing that they would not bring them as they had promised, Master Peter the Savoyard ventured out and went <to Famagusta> to the queen to report [this]. < And he brought back an order to the viscount, that he should sell whatever happened to belong to the traitors and share [the proceeds] among all the comrades together >.[406]

243. On the same day,[407] moreover, they took John Kallergis out of the tower in order to torture him. As they were taking him, moreover, into the lords' presence, he said to them: 'What do you wish to find out from me?' And they said to him: 'Tell us how Zaplana's affairs turned out'. And he replied to them: 'What do I know to tell you?'

<Besides, they were found blameless in the course of their interrogation and they released them>.[408]

244. In addition, on 6 March they relieved Galimberto, the castellan of Famagusta, and appointed a Venetian.

245. And on the same day they sent out ten Italians from Famagusta, for them to go to Kerynia and replace the Cypriots.

---

[406] The words in brackets < > are taken from mss. **B** and **M**. See Kehayioglou, *Διήγησις, op. cit.*, p. 277, **B** lines 14-16 and **M** lines 14-16.

[407] Ms. **B** has 6 March. See *ibid.*, p. 277 line 17.

[408] The words in brackets < > are taken from mss. **B** and **M**. See *ibid.*, p. 279, **B** lines 3-4 and **M** lines 3-4. The narrative here inexplicably switches to the plural, possibly because the original narration referred to others also being released. Florio Bustron, 'Chronique', *op. cit.*, p. 448 states that John Kallergis was released with his brother Charles, but that both were summoned subsequently for transportation to Venice.

246. On 7 March, moreover, John Bernardin came to Nicosia, and he brought a letter from the queen: 'He should take whatever is in the possession of Bonaistre, houses and anything he has, and they should be given to Bernardin!' She also wrote him a letter [instructing him] to have a proclamation made in Nicosia: 'Anyone who has taken things belonging to Zaplana from his house, and from the remaining traitors, should return them into the viscount!' and should inform the queen. Furthermore, he was to obtain Sir John Zaplana's horse, which Philip de Nores had taken, and was to send it to Famagusta. And this is what he did.

<In addition, Peter the Savoyard the constable came from Famagusta on 9 March and brought a letter from the queen: 'They shall bring whatever things they have taken from the traitors before the viscount and sell them, and all the comrades shall share them out!'>[409]

247. Besides, on 10 March Sir Bernardin Salaha and Garcia de Navarre happened to be at the proclamation, and they exchanged high words. Since the queen had sent Bernardin Salaha to provision Kerynia and the remaining places, and had given him orders to pay for whoever's horse he might take, so that no one would be aggrieved, and among all the villages that he visited he also visited that of Garcia de Navarre, they exchanged sharp words on account of this. He (Garcia), moreover, said to him: 'The queen sent you to fetch supplies and to pay people for the transport, while you hold fast the money[410] and do not pay them'. And Bernardin Salaha said to him: 'You do not say things well, nor do you offer me proof, and you are lying through your throat!' Furthermore, [they said] many other things and people came in between them, and so they ceased.

248. In addition, John Bernardin quarrelled on the same day with Sassons de Nores, the constable of Jerusalem, inside the palace in Famagusta over Bonaistre's houses, which he wished to impound. He wished, moreover, to reserve them for Paul James Miftahah[411], saying that: 'The houses that John Bernardin is asking for do not belong to Bonaistre, but belong to James Miftahah'. And Bernardin, on hearing that Sassons de Nores was reserving the houses, exchanged many words with him. He said to him, moreover: 'Sir Sassons de Nores, know that our lady the queen, if she wishes to live well, should clear all the traitors out of her house! Otherwise, she will not be living in peace'.

249. Besides, on 12 March a Venetian galley arrived from Famagusta bringing many

---

[409] The passage in brackets < > is not found in mss. **B** or **M**. See Kehayioglou, *Διήγησις, op. cit.*, pp. 279-281.

[410] The word given for money is *cartzias*, a Cypriot coin of which 96 were worth one bezant. See Metcalf, *Gros, Sixains and Cartzias, op. cit.*, p. 133.

[411] Dawkins, *Boustronios, op. cit.*, §248 transliterates Μιφτάχας as Mustapha, but one doubts that someone with a Christian forename would have a Muslim surname. Mss. **B** and **M** omit the name Paul (Greek Πα = Pau/Paolo). See Kehayioglou, *Διήγησις, op. cit.*, p. 281, line 14 of both mss.

tidings from Venice, and a *provedittore* also arrived,[412] and he said: 'Behind us the captain is coming, while the bishop of Limassol and Sir John Mistachiel are also coming', and he also brought the news that: 'They have confiscated Doro, Sir Philip Podocataro's village', and also said that: 'a fire broke out in Crete and Sir Marco Venier's house was burnt, as well as another three mansions'.

250. And on 13 March they relieved the Cypriots who used to sleep at the palace and appointed Italians. They also changed the Cypriots guarding the doors and appointed Cretans. Furthermore, they changed the captain of the arsenal, Sir John François, and appointed Niccolo Benedetti.

251. In addition, on 15 March a letter from the queen reached the viscount, that he should make a proclamation: 'As many Franks as are recorded on the list must present themselves in Famagusta within three days!'

252. On the same day, moreover, the queen sent word to the viscount that Anthony d'Acre[413] had arrested Peter [the brother?] of James of Malta without her having ordered this. They should hand him over to his brother James, because the queen had granted them her consent that they should stay in Cyprus.

253. Besides, on 17 March the queen sent a letter to the viscount that he should straightaway conduct a search in John the Circassian's[414] house and should send a written list of his weapons and horses to his wife, while he should dispatch the weapons and horses themselves to Famagusta.

254. Furthermore, they incarcerated John the Circassian in the citadel on 18 March, since the queen had sent him on business of hers and he had said many bad things about her. In addition, he deprived him of whatever he had within the kingdom.[415]

255. And on the 19 [March], in accordance with the command she had given the Franks, they came out so as to go to Famagusta. There was, moreover, great sorrow,

---

[412] Boustronios must refer here to John Soranzo, the future *provedittore*, since the present one, Victor Soranzo, was already in Cyprus. John was elected to this office on 29 March 1474. The Venetian Senate had decided to replace Victor Soranzo on 28 March at his own request and in view of his long and distinguished service (Mas Latrie, *Histoire, op. cit.*, III, 370-371; Hill, *op. cit.*, III, 707 and note 3) but it is nonetheless strange that John Soranzo should have arrived in Cyprus prior to his election. The date given by Boustronios is perhaps too early.

[413] Dawkins, *Boustronios, op. cit.*, §252, 254 and 260 transliterates the surnames Ταρκάς and Τερκές as Tarcas, but I consider them distinct, Ταρκάς being a Greek corruption of d'Acre and Τερκές originating from Τσερκές, meaning Circassian.

[414] He is mentioned in Florio Bustron, 'Chronique', *op. cit.*, pp. 418 (Gioan Circasso) and 448 (Gioan Cenges) as receiving the *casalia* of Plessia, St Sergios, Parsada, Melini, Odhou and Kryo Nero, as well as vines at Kalliana and Marathassa from King James II sometime between 1464 and 1468. Arrested along with others in February 1474 over the murder of Andrew Corner, he was subsequently released. I believe the surnames Circasso and Cenges (var. Cerkes) given above refer to the same person.

[415] *Ibid.*, p. 448 narrates the same episode, but calls John the Circassian John Storches and places the episode after the dismissal of the Franks, whereas George Boustronios places it prior to their dismissal.

because they were all married with children. Furthermore, given that they had ordered them to go, they entered the palace and they promised all of them, on the part of God and the pope and on the part of the queen, not to separate them from their wives and children: 'For God combined us and does not separate us.[416] And so do you wish to separate us? Leave us in our homes and we do not want anything from our queen, and will live by our own labour! And if we are at fault, then have us quartered!' And for all their protestations, they made them go away.

256. Besides, on 24 March 1474 the queen deprived Sir Nicholas Zaplana, who was the Grand Commander of Cyprus, of the Cypriot commandery on account of the treason committed by Sir John Zaplana, and they declared him to be a traitor. And on account of this they deprived him of the commandery. Furthermore, the queen sequestered it and sent a letter to Rhodes, to the Grand Master, for him to appoint a Grand Commander.

And on 28 March the queen showed clemency towards John Kallergis and to his brother Charles, because they had interrogated them but they were blameless.

257. On the same day, moreover, they released Sir Camus from the citadel and ordered him to go to his home and not to leave it until the queen gave him orders.[417]

258. In addition, on 1 April they released the abbot of the Holy Cross from the citadel, Father John de Riviolo, the secretary of the archbishopric, Gabriel Ferrier and Master Bernard, the king's tailor, and they put them on board the galley.

259. Furthermore, on the 2 April they released [John] Cortese from gaol and had him placed in the palace of Famagusta, and his wife used to go there and see him.

260. And on the same day the queen showed clemency towards John the Circassian and also returned his property to him.

261. On 4 April, moreover, the silver of the Carmelite monastery[418] that had been lost was recovered, four chalices, a gold-plated tabernacle and a canapé, which Epiphanios

---

[416] This sentence recalls Mark, 10:9; Matt. 19:6 and Corinth. I, 7:10.

[417] By this time the Venetian government had further strengthened its grip on Cyprus. In a letter dated 28 March 1474, mentioned above, the Venetian Senate decreed that two councillors and a *provedittore* who would reside on Cyprus were to be appointed to assist Queen Catherine. It was also decided to send 100 crossbowmen under four captains to man the fortresses of Famagusta and Kerynia. A second letter of the same date congratulated Peter Mocenigo on pacifying the island when it was in extreme peril and especially on having Galimberto and Paolo Contarini, the castellans of Famagusta and Kerynia, replaced. It also urged him to have these fortresses as well as the city and port of Famagusta garrisoned by Venetian soldiers. John Soranzo was elected *provedittore*, Louis Gabriel and Francis Minio as councillors, and all were given detailed orders in letters of 4 June and 29 July. See Mas Latrie, *Histoire, op. cit.,* III, 370-390.

[418] The Carmelites, hermits who later became mendicant friars, initially arrived in Cyprus from Latin Syria in the mid-thirteenth century, and the first references to their house in Nicosia, dedicated to St Mary of Mt Carmel are from the beginning of the fourteenth century. See 'Amadi', *op. cit.,* p. 248; Coureas, *Latin Church, op. cit.,* pp. 217-218; Aristeidou, Έγγραφα, *op.cit.,* II, 120-123, 134-136, 274-275.

the son of the priest Stephen Flanc, who was a deacon, had stolen. And they put him in solitary confinement in [the cathedral of] the Holy Wisdom.

262. Besides, on 21 April the queen sent a letter to the viscount that the 25 Latins regarding whom she had sent word to him were to go to Famagusta upon <their lives>.[419] And as soon as they arrived they were exiled.

263. In addition, a command < from the queen >[420] reached the viscount on the same day: 'Henry Kallergis and John Kallergis must go forthwith to Famagusta, within a deadline of three days, they must be ready to depart from Cyprus!' And they acted thus, in line with the order.[421]

264. Furthermore, Charles Gonneme arrived at the viscount's house on the same day, and he said to him:[422] 'My lord, John of Emesa has arrived and has told me to say to your lordship: "Do not dare to ride forth! For the people of Nicosia wish to kill you!"' And on hearing this, he rode forth, went to Mese Street, found Stephen Koudouna and said to him: 'Master Stephen, they have come and told me just now that the people of Nicosia wish to kill me.[423] And I came to find out what is the reason for this?' Master Stephen said to him on hearing this: 'My Lord, that which your lordship has told me is something I have heard of just now'. The viscount went and found John [of Emesa], moreover, and said to him: 'Sir John, I want you to tell me, what is the reason you sent word to me that the people of Nicosia wish to kill me?' And he said to him: 'My lord viscount, as regards that which your lordship is saying, that I said to you that the people of Nicosia wish to kill you, none shall be found [to state] that I said such a thing. Furthermore, I request your lordship to tell me who is the person who told your lordship, so that I may offer the proof before you!'

And the viscount summoned Charles Gonneme straightaway and said to him: 'Didn't you come and say these words to me in my own home?' Charles, moreover, gave an answer and said to him: 'I said them to you exactly as he had said them to me'. And they had a sharp exchange of words.[424] Besides, the people witnessed this and understood that certain people who wished to cause the viscount displeasure were manipulating events. Both parties recognised this, moreover, and they subsequently requested the viscount's forgiveness, saying to him: 'My lord, we have you as our viscount and we are obliged to render every honour towards you, just as towards the

---

[419] The words in brackets are taken from ms. **M**, given that they make more sense than the rendering 'upon his (i.e. the viscount's) life found in ms. **A**. See Kehayioglou, *Διήγησις, op. cit.*, p. 288, **A** lines 10-11 and p. 289, **M** lines 10-11.

[420] The words in brackets are taken from ms. **M**. See *ibid.*, p. 289 line 12.

[421] Florio Bustron, 'Chronique', *op. cit.*, p. 448 likewise records their exile.

[422] *Ibid.*, p. 449 also narrates this episode, but prefaces it with the words 'Now the land began to quieten, but not in all respects, because there were those who wished to turn the Franks against the Greeks and the people against the nobles, and above all against the viscount of Nicosia'.

[423] *Ibid.*, p. 450 has 'I have learned that the people of the land wish to cause me displeasure'.

[424] *Ibid.*, p. 450 here has 'And John (of Emesa) replied that he could not remember any more who from among them had said such a thing'.

person of our lady (i.e. the queen). And we have understood everything'. And he said to them: 'My children, I consider you to be valued and loyal subjects of our queen and shall always hold you dearly, only be prudent and do that which is proper, just as beneficent people are accustomed to do!' Furthermore, the people exhibited camaraderie towards the viscount, while he showed them good countenance.[425]

265. In addition, on 28 April Sir Peter Bembo and Sir Lucas Corner came to Nicosia from Famagusta. And since he was the person who was related to the queen,[426] on learning of this the lords who happened to be in Nicosia and all the people went to a man to the royal court in order to greet him and to do him every honour for the love of the queen. On setting eyes on them, moreover, he took great pleasure and he thanked them.

266. And on 30 April the above mentioned Sir Peter Bembo sent for and brought all the constables, crossbowmen and Armenians, and said to them: 'Convey the order to all your companions that tomorrow all of them with their weapons must muster in the court before me!' Furthermore, in the morning they went and cut flowers for Mayday, according to custom, and they held a muster in the evening.

Besides, on 5 May [a villager with] a letter came from Paphos into the presence of Sir Peter Bembo and began shouting: 'This place has no justice, for Benedict Cartagena has taken my boy and is detaining him unjustly. And I have brought him [orders] from her lady the queen, yet he does not want to follow them but instead threatens to have me hanged'. Sir Peter, moreover, replied to the villager: 'I marvel greatly at this, if he commits such foolishness. Besides, if it is true, then his neck needs breaking'.[427]

267. Furthermore, Sir Philip de Nores exchanged high words in the queen's court with John the Black.[428] And John the Black said to Sir Philip de Nores: 'I want you to tell me, what was the reason that the queen entered the kingdom?' Sir Philip, moreover, said to him: 'Please John, don't bring these things up every so often!' In the course of the many words they exchanged, moreover, John said by way of reply: 'My lords, I inform you that amongst us there are many and numerous traitors, and they must be eliminated'. And on hearing him Sir William de Ras said to him: 'Traitors? Am I one?' And he said to him: <'No, my lord'. Sir John de Ras then responded and said to him: 'Traitors? Is Sir John a traitor, or Morphou de Grenier, the count de Rochas?' He said

---

[425] *Ibid.*, pp. 450-451 gives an account of the conversation between the viscount and the people of Nicosia in greater detail.

[426] This refers to Sir Lucas Corner, Queen Catherine's brother, who is not mentioned in the chronicle of Florio Bustron. He tried unsuccessfully in April 1475 to marry Apollonia of Pendayia, the titular countess of Jaffa and the widow of John Perez Fabrigues. See Hill, *op. cit.*, III, 704 note 3 and 722 note 2.

[427] This passage, the only one throughout the chronicle in which the sufferings of ordinary people on account of the prevalent civil strife come through clearly, is not found in mss. **B** and **M**. See Kehayioglou, Διήγησις, *op. cit.*, pp. 293-295.

[428] Florio Bustron, 'Chronique', *op. cit.*, pp. 451-452 refers to him as Gioan Sarasin, that is John the Saracen.

to him:>[429] 'No'. In addition, John said to him: 'They, whoever they are, shall be found'. And the horsemen on hearing this said to him: 'Tell us who they are, so that we too may know them!' John, moreover, said in answer: 'You shall learn of them when the time comes'. Besides, he said many other things as well, and there was a Portuguese man within the court named Joao, who was a knight and was powerfully built: 'John, you must not say that there are still many traitors in the queen's service, for I shall prove to you in person, sword in hand, that I am as good and trustworthy towards my lady as you are'. And they came in between them, and they ceased [quarrelling].

268. Furthermore, on the same day Sir Peter Bembo desired to go and worship at [the monastery of] the Holy Cross. As soon as he mounted his horse, they came and told him that: 'Benedict Cartagena has mounted his horse to go to Famagusta, maintaining that your lordship has laid plans for his assassination'. Sir Peter Bembo, moreover, was astounded on hearing this, saying: 'We had a meal together yesterday, and he said nothing of this to me. Besides, we were together today, and he said nothing, other than telling me that he was going to Famagusta. Now how did this matter transpire?' And he sent word to the viscount, the admiral and to Sir William de Ras and told them about the matter exactly as he had been informed of it.

In addition, they immediately sent four persons hard on his heels, <Nicholas the German, Nicholas Bernadin, Ferdinand d'Avila and Master John Alguazir> to bring him back.[430] And they caught up with him and told him to return: 'Besides, Sir Peter Bembo desires you, in order to talk to you'. He, moreover, said to them: 'Indeed, tell him that I am not acting for him, and that I am going there where my wife happens to be, on good testimony! Furthermore, should Sir Peter so wish, tell him to come over! And I will receive him, so that he can say what he wants, and so that I can speak to him. I, however, shall not turn back!' And they returned and reported to Sir Peter what he had said. On hearing about it, moreover, Sir Andrew[431] unloaded the clothing and wrote a letter to the queen on how things had come to pass, and sent it with Marino de Bonaventura.

269. Besides, following the passage of two hours, another item of news reached Sir Peter Bembo, that all the Franks had prepared to create a great disturbance. And as soon as he heard of this, Sir Andrew immediately sent forth John the Black with a letter, so that he would go to the queen. In addition, he gave him another six men for company. Furthermore, many men gathered on the same night within the court so as to keep company with Sir Peter Bembo.

---

[429] The words in brackets < > are taken from mss. **B** and **M**. See Kehayioglou, *Διήγησις, op. cit.*, p. 295, **B** lines 12-14 and **M**, lines 11-13.

[430] The words in brackets < > are taken from mss. **B** and **M**. See *ibid.*, p. 297, **B** lines 15-17 and **M** lines 14-15.

[431] This Sir Andrew, found in all three mss. and mentioned in §269 below as sending a letter to the queen at Famagusta, does not appear elsewhere in the chronicle nor in the corresponding passage in Florio Bustron, 'Chronique', *op. cit.*, pp. 451-452. In §270 Sir Peter Bembo states that he sent the letter to the queen, so perhaps 'Sir Andrew' is a mistake on Boustronios' part, and really refers to Sir Peter Bembo.

270. Besides, on 6 May, during the sixth hour of the night, an item of news came from Sivouri that: 'They had killed John the Black and his company'. And on hearing this news in Nicosia all the people were agitated, took up their weapons and went to the Nicosia Gate in order to cut the Franks to pieces should they arrive. Next they went to the court and began shouting: 'My lords, you who are the queen's lieutenants, we wish to have justice regarding the Franks who killed our companion whom you sent with letters to our lady the queen, in the course of his journey. And we too want to kill the Franks who happen to be in Nicosia'.

Sir Peter Bembo on hearing this came down to the courtyard, and in their company there happened to be the viscount, Sir William de Ras, Sir John de Ras and many other gentlemen. Sir Peter Bembo told them about the matter, moreover, and said to the people of Nicosia: 'My boys! Do not for the love of God wish for this evil to take place on my arrival! I did not come to Nicosia other than to see you and derive pleasure from your company, having heard of your good repute and the good service that you render for our queen. Besides, as regards the letters that I sent, the disturbance has already occurred, to my misfortune. Have a little patience, and we shall do something that redounds to the honour of all of you together!' And they were unwilling to listen in any way to any of the numerous other things that he said to them.

Furthermore, Sir John de Ras on hearing this said to them: 'Tell me my boys, what do you want? That service which you worked for, do you wish to lose it?' And they said to him: 'We wish to kill as many Franks as there are in Nicosia, because they are traitors and they killed our people who were going to the queen'. And Sir John de Ras on hearing them said to them: 'My boys, take heed! Our lady is alive, moreover, and if she learns that they have committed some treason, she shall have them punished'.

And whatever he told them, there was no way for them to calm down. And he said to them: 'Tell us what you want!' And they said to him: 'We want all the Franks, as well as their weapons, their horses and their belongings'. And seeing this, Sir Peter Bembo and the other knights and lords said to them: 'Let us now send for them and have them brought, and let us send word to the queen on everything as it has come to pass! And she shall do as seems fit to her'. The people, moreover, said to them: 'We wish to go ourselves, to take them. And let the viscount come with us, and Sir John de Ras!' And the lords went with them willy-nilly, reckoning on impounding the things with a written list and on transporting them to the palace. They (i.e. the people), however, did nothing, neither for the viscount nor for Sir John de Ras, but scattered into the Franks' houses and took their horses and their weapons, without Sir Peter Bembo discovering anything.

In addition, Sir Peter Bembo and the viscount at once wrote to her lady the queen and to the commander of the fleet on how the events had transpired.

271. On 9 May, moreover, a letter from the queen arrived [stating] that she had put forward the summons in order to discover the cause of the disturbance: 'And let whoever was the cause be punished!' Besides, she sent word to the constables to go to Famagusta, to ascertain the truth. All these things that they (i.e. ordinary people) were saying, 'and they killed John and his company' were lies.

272. And on the 14 May two galleys from the fleet arrived and brought a message to the captain,[432] that he should leave at once and go to the fleet.

273. Furthermore, on the same day Balian de Nores arrived from Famagusta bringing an order that: 'All the Franks who are salaried must go to Famagusta in accordance with the queen's command!'

274. On 16 May, moreover, they found the Franks who had hurled themselves on John during his journey, as well as another 15, and they were exiled.[433]

275. Besides, on 17 May James of Malta entered into a sharp exchange of <words>[434] with Peter d'Avila, because when Sir James had departed from Famagusta James [of Malta] had left with him, and they had taken James' possessions and had given them to Garcia Navarre, over which matter her ladyship the queen had shown compassion towards James and had written: 'Let him take back his things from Garcia Navarre!' Furthermore, in the course of the many words exchanged, d'Avila said to James: 'You traitor, you should have been dead from a long time back!' James, moreover, said to him: 'You are the traitor, and I shall prove it to you whenever you wish, in the presence of the queen and the lords, sword in hand, and let them have me beheaded should I not prove it! Know that when the archbishop took the oath, along with Sir James, the count of Tripoli, Sir Rizzo and you together with them, you swore upon the body of Christ that you would be as one! And to prove it to you, when they killed Sir Andrew and the remainder, you assigned to each one of them ten men along with their horses and weapons, from among the men whom you had, to go everywhere with them! Besides, there are many other things that I can prove to you, at any time you like! Furthermore, concerning your assertion that I departed from Famagusta with Sir James and with his company, on account of which I am a traitor, as regards this I can show to you and prove to you that when I departed, I did not depart for any reason other than because I was greatly afraid, so that they would not kill me on account of the cause that materialised. On account of that cause, moreover, in order to be in good company, I departed from Famagusta together with Sir James. And I am ready to prove it to you, on every occasion you want!' And they remained in this state until the matter was cleared up. In addition, Peter d'Avremes likewise said many offensive things to Peter d'Avila.

---

[432] This was Peter Mocenigo, the captain-general of the Venetian fleet. See *ibid.*, p. 452.

[433] *Ibid.*, pp. 451-452 also relates how the Franks were lying in wait for John the Black and his company outside Nicosia, the anger this provoked among the people of Nicosia, and how the Franks were summoned to Famagusta without their arms, but does not mention their exile. These Franks were presumably mercenaries, described by Florio Bustron (p. 451) as 'soldati forestieri'.

[434] The words in brackets < > are taken from ms. **B**. See Kehayioglou, Διήγησις, *op. cit.*, p. 305 line 8.

Furthermore, on 17 May the commander of the fleet left Famagusta, and he left behind ten armed galleys and two ships for guarding the place.[435]

276. Besides, on 19 May a great disturbance occurred [concerning] the Franks and the inhabitants of Famagusta. And they exchanged angry words with the Italians, weapons were drawn and some among them were wounded.[436] The Franks and the Cypriots, moreover, were taken into custody, and a proclamation was made: 'Let no one carry weapons!' In a short time, moreover, the *provedittore* sent people, had the Franks released and left the Cypriots in custody.

And when Gonsalvo, the captain of Famagusta, learnt of this, it did not seem right to him that the Franks had been released and the Cypriots left in custody, and he encountered John the Black, who heard about it. Furthermore, on hearing about it, John took five or six people with him and went to the *provedittore*, in order to ask him to release the Cypriots. Indeed, the captain had sent him, and he was to inform the queen if he (i.e. the *provedittore*) was unwilling to release them. Besides, numerous Cypriots accompanied John the Black, and once the *provedittore* had seen them people said to him: 'My lord, John the Black has sallied forth with his band. I believe that they are coming to kill us'. The persons saying this to the *provedittore* were the count de Rochas and Peter d'Avila. And the *provedittore* on hearing this had John seized and had him placed in the galley, in irons.

In addition, Famagusta became agitated in the course of this incident, and people took up arms. In the midst of this, moreover, a Dalmatian armed with a sword rushed in, entering the queen's chamber, and the lords on seeing him began shouting. And Sir George the count of Jaffa ran forward and said to him: 'What do you want here?' And he said to him: 'I'm seeking my fate'. And the count went to seize him, while he drew his dagger in order to stab the count. In addition, John of Emesa and James of Epiphanios happened to be there, and they grabbed hold of the Dalmatian, hurled him to the ground, and took away his weapons, his sword and his dagger. He was placed in custody, moreover, in irons.

Besides, the queen experienced considerable trepidation; word got out; all the

---

[435] Peter Mocenigo sailed for Modon, and Triadan Gritti, who replaced him, was instructed to guard Cyprus, to ensure that Famagusta had enough troops and to demand from the Hospitallers at Rhodes the surrender of Archbishop Louis Peres Fabrigues and his associates, failing which Venice would regard any venture against Cyprus as directed against herself. See Hill, *op. cit.*, III, 709 note 2. Florio Bustron, 'Chronique', *op. cit.*, p. 452 states that ten galleys and three (not two) armed ships were left behind, and that John Soranzo was elected *provedittore* of Cyprus. Hill, *op. cit.*, III, 707 note 3 dates this to 29 March 1474.

[436] Florio Bustron, 'Chronique', *op. cit.*, p. 452 states that some Italians visited the prostitutes of Famagusta and after concluding their business did not wish to pay them and swore at them. The inhabitants of Famagusta then summoned the Franks. It seems that both they and the (Greek) inhabitants of Famagusta attacked the Italians, but that after imprisoning Franks and Greeks the *provedittore* released only the former. Hill (*op. cit.*, III, 754 note 4) thinks that 'Italians' must refer to Genoese in Famagusta, but this is unlikely, for the Genoese had surrendered the city back in 1464. The Italians in question were probably Venetians, which would explain why the Venetian authorities did not imprison them.

men of the fleet and of Famagusta armed themselves and a great upheaval was about to ensue. Furthermore, John remained on the galley in irons, and the *provedittore* was reluctant to release him and said: 'I wish to castigate him, because he stirs people up and many disturbances arise'.

277. In addition, on 26 May [14] 74 ships arrived from Venice along with a captain, as well as top secret letters and 200 men, who had come to stay in Cyprus. As soon as he landed, moreover, he sent for and had Peter d'Avila brought before him and showed him a letter that he had brought from the Council of Ten, that: 'He must go to Venice forthwith!' as he had been ordered to: 'and likewise the mother of King James!' as well as the king's illegitimate children,[437] the count de Rochas and numerous other knights. And they were exiled from Cyprus.

Furthermore, with all the disturbances having passed, the queen came to Nicosia. She spent three years in Famagusta from the time of her arrival, moreover, and 13 in Nicosia. She spent 16 years in Cyprus until she departed.[438]

278. And in [the year] of Christ [14] 85 a great disturbance took place in [the cathedral of] the Holy Wisdom. While the lords were in conversation among themselves, Guyet was talking to Tristan de Gibelet, they exchanged high words, and Guyet dealt a blow to Tristan. After some time, moreover, the knights came between them and reconciled them and Tristan swore on the body of Christ that the reconciliation that had been effected: 'should be trustworthy and just for evermore!' Furthermore, in a short time Guyet went to Venice, and a little later Tristan went as well. Besides, the insult that Guyet had inflicted on him always rankled in Tristan's heart. And Tristan went to the hairdresser's and encountered Guyet having his hair done, and he straightaway drew his short sword, cut Guyet's head off and immediately boarded a ship and went away from Venice, to the lands of King Ferdinand.

The government of Venice, moreover, issued a great proclamation: 'Whoever brings him forward shall have 1,000 ducats!' and he was exiled from Venice and from all the territories subject to the government. In addition, he was planning on doing the deed that he put into effect, and prior to going he divested himself of his villages and gave them to his wife, in accordance with the power he had to do so. Furthermore, the government of Venice pronounced him a traitor: 'Because he had taken an oath upon

---

[437] George Boustronios and Florio Bustron, 'Chronique', *op. cit.*, p. 453 wrongly include the late King James' mother, Marietta of Patras, and his illegitimate children Eugene and John among the exiles and do not mention Stephen Koudouna and Sir John de Ras, or even Sir John Attar, the Cypriot knight who had been captain of Paphos under King James II and Catherine and had declared for Venice following the flight of Archbishop Louis, Rizzo de Marino and their associates. Attar remained in Venetian service even after he had been granted permission to return to Cyprus. See Hill, *op. cit.*, III, 699 and notes 4–5. King James' mother and his natural children were despatched to Venice in 1476, and the mother died at Padua in April 1503, on which see Mas Latrie, 'Documents nouveaux', *op. cit.*, pp. 489-492; Hill, *op. cit.*, III, 726-727; Richard, *Remembrances*, *op. cit.*, no. 73 note 1.

[438] One notes in passing that George Boustronios, apart from saying nothing about Queen Catherine's reign, does not even mention the death of her only son, the infant King James III, on 26 August 1474, for which see Florio Bustron, 'Chronique', *op. cit.*, p. 454; Hill, *op. cit.*, III, 710 and note 5.

the body of Christ, and Guyet put his trust in him!' The Venetian government, moreover, acted as I stated: 'Whoever should seize him shall have 1,000 ducats! And let them cut his head off!'

279. He in addition, having seen that he would <no longer>[439] have [interests in] Cyprus, came to an agreement with King Ferdinand, that Queen Catherine should be married to his son.[440] And he dressed himself in the habit of a Franciscan monk. Rizzo, moreover, happened to be in Syria, and they were planning to marry her to King Ferdinand's son after the king's death.[441] Furthermore, Tristan came to Syria <on a ship belonging to King Ferdinand>[442] and found Rizzo, <a Cypriot knight who was there in exile>[443] and told him of the matter. He, moreover, longing to return to Cyprus and in a state of distress, gave Tristan his consent. Besides, he got on board the ship and they both came to Cyprus, and Tristan left Rizzo becalmed on the high seas, came ashore and landed, in order to speak to the queen.

In addition, Lady Vera his sister was one of the queen's ladies in waiting and was at the court. Tristan, moreover, arrived and went to the court, and he remained there in hiding, in order for the papers that he wished to take with him to be readied. Besides, he spent a week at the court, did that which he wished to do and ventured forth in order to board the ship and reach his desired destination. <Furthermore, the ship that arrived remained moored by Kolliokremmos>.[444] Venetian ships spotted this ship before his

---

[439] The words in brackets < > have been taken from ms. **B**. See Kehayioglou, Διήγησις, op. cit., p. 315, **B** line 1.

[440] This was Don Alonzo. The reports of the Venetian Council of Ten state that she was favourably inclined to this union, a decisive factor in impelling the Venetian Senate to have her removed from Cyprus. See Mas Latrie, *Histoire, op. cit.*, III, 421. The involvement of both Tristan and Rizzo de Marino in King Ferdinand's schemes and the favour shown to Rizzo by the Mamluk sultan Qaitbay, whom he tried to win over to his plans against Venice, were other decisive factors, as was the interest of the Ottomans in using Cyprus, and in particular Famagusta, as a base for their fleet during the Ottoman-Mamluk war of 1485-1491, during which Sultan Bayezid unsuccessfully requested permission from the Venetians to use Famagusta as an anchorage for his fleet. See Hill, *op. cit.*, III, 738-742; Shai Har-El, *The Struggle for Domination in the Near East: The Ottoman-Mamluk War, 1485-1491* (Leiden, 1995), pp. 159-162,171-172 and 199-200.

[441] The king in question here may well be James III, who died in August 1474. Although plans to marry Queen Catherine to King Ferdinand of Naples or his son Alonzo had begun after the death of King James II, the death of King James III, Queen Catherine's only son, would have provided her with an even stronger incentive to marry and beget a new heir to her throne.

[442] The words in brackets < > are taken from ms. **B**. See Kehayioglou, Διήγησις, op. cit., p. 315, **B** lines 2-3. Ms. **A** (p. 314 lines 5-6) states implausibly that Rizzo was in Syria with one of King Ferdinand's ships.

[443] The words in brackets < > are taken from ms. **B**. See *ibid.*, p. 315, **B** lines 3-4.

[444] The words in brackets < > are taken from ms. **B**. See *ibid.*, p. 315, **B** line 10. Hill, *op. cit.*, III, 740 and note 4 thinks that the ship waited off Fontana Amorosa near Cape Arnaouti at the northwestern extremity of Cyprus. There is a cliff named Kolliokremmos near there at the village of Argaka, but it is improbable that a ship sailing from Alexandria and awaiting the return of someone coming from Nicosia would drop anchor there. A likelier candidate is the cliff of this name near the village of Psematismenos in the Larnaca district, a locality more accessible from both Nicosia and Alexandria, Egypt. For the 23 cliffs in Cyprus with this name, found in all districts of the island except Kerynia, see *A Complete Gazetteer of Cyprus*, Vol. 1, compiled by M.N. Christodoulou and K. Konstantinidis (Nicosia, 1987), p. 581.

arrival, closed in on it, <perceived that it was a foreign vessel>[445] seized it, examined it (i.e. those on board) and found out everything.

They also seized Rizzo and interrogated him, and he told them that Tristan had arrived in Nicosia and that he was waiting for him to [return and] board the ship. < In addition, he told them the sign that Tristan was going to give on his arrival so as to reach the ship. And they, taking the ship, put Rizzo in irons, and placed people of their own on board the ship. Furthermore, Tristan's sign was to fire a shot on the shore, so that the boat would go and bring him to the ship. As soon as he entered the boat, moreover, they took him to the ship. And on realising that it was not his own company, he forthwith threw the papers he was holding into the sea.[446] He too was put in irons. In addition, Tristan was holding a diamond ring and he broke it, swallowing the stone, and died. And Rizzo too was taken away>.[447] And regarding Rizzo we have not learnt what manner of death he met.[448]

280. Furthermore, the government of Venice immediately sent out the queen's mother, and she came to Cyprus to induce her to go to Venice, in 1487.[449] <In the course of the many journeys that she had to make, moreover, she told her>[450] that the Venetian government was imploring her to go, to spend a year or so there and then to come back again, the queen promised her that she would go. And she said to her: 'My daughter, I am going and I shall send your brother to keep you company'. Besides, as soon as she had departed, in [the year] of Christ 1488, the queen's brother Sir George came to Cyprus.[451]

---

[445] The words in brackets < > are taken from ms. **B**. See Kehayioglou, Διήγησις, op. cit., p. 315, **B** lines 11-12.

[446] A letter of the Venetian Council of Ten dated 22 October 1488 to Francisco Priuli, the captain-general of the Venetian fleet, states that Tristan and Rizzo de Marino had been seized with papers upon them, from the contents of which it was abundantly clear that they were scheming to have Queen Catherine married, (to Don Alonzo, King Ferdinand's son). See Mas Latrie, Histoire, op. cit., III, 419-420.

[447] The words in brackets < > are taken from ms. **B**. See Kehayioglou, Διήγησις, op. cit., p. 315, **B** lines 14-18 and p. 316, **B** lines 1-4.

[448] The fact that both George Boustronios and Florio Bustron ('Chronique', op. cit., p. 458) were unaware of Rizzo's ultimate fate vividly illustrates Venetian secrecy over the elimination of this dangerous enemy, who was tried, sentenced to death and eventually strangled after spending three years in prison. For the details see Mas Latrie, Histoire, op. cit., III, 431-435 and 441-442; Hill, op. cit., III, 741 and note 4.

[449] Ms. **B** states that she arrived in Cyprus in 1486 (see Kehayioglou, Διήγησις, op. cit., p. 397 line 7), which is probably wrong given that 1487, the date it gives for George Corner's arrival, is certainly wrong, for reasons explained below. Florio Bustron, 'Chronique', op. cit., p. 454 states that when Queen Catherine's mother Donna Fiorenza visited her she was shocked by her extravagance, and declared on her return to Venice that such profligacy was unbecoming to a Venetian lady.

[450] The words in brackets < > are taken from ms. **B**. See Kehayioglou, Διήγησις, op. cit., p. 317 lines 7-8.

[451] George Corner arrived in Nicosia on 24 January 1489 (Hill, III, 746 note 2), although his galley would have reached the island earlier, but ms. **A** (Kehayioglou, Διήγησις, op. cit., p. 316 line 10) has 1488 because the year began on 1 March. Florio Bustron, 'Chronique', op. cit., p. 454 states that he came 'to persuade her to relinquish the governance of the realm to the Venetian Republic, and to return to her homeland and live in peace among her relations there'.

In addition, on 8 February her ladyship the queen went to Apsithia on horseback to worship there, as did her brother and the *provedittore* Nicolo Michel, as well as all the ladies and knights, <and four knights on foot flanked her horse>.[452]

281. Furthermore, on 15 February 1489[453] the queen exited from Nicosia in order to go to Famagusta, to leave [Cyprus]. And she went on horseback wearing a black silken cloak, with all the ladies and the knights in her company <and six knights by her bridle and flanking her horse>.[454] Her eyes, moreover, did not cease to shed tears throughout the procession. The people likewise shed many tears. Besides, there were men drawn up, and all the soldiers had come to Nicosia. And as soon as she came out of the court, they let up the cry: 'Marco! Marco!'<In addition, on their arrival in Famagusta jousts were organised>.[455]

282. And on 1 March [in the year] of Christ 1489 she entered the galley and went to Venice.[456]

283. Furthermore, on 9 June [in the year] of Christ 1489 six Turkish pirate vessels and a brigantine went to the Karpass peninsula, and they landed at Chelones in the Karpass, carrying off men, women and children. And they destroyed the villages as well as killing 34 people, without taking into account those mentioned above whom they made off with.[457]

There were, moreover, two galleys in the island, and they were armed to deal with the above mentioned pirate vessels. Furthermore, Sir James Morabit and Sir Peter Gurri were appointed as captains. Besides, they sallied forth in search of the pirate ships, circumnavigating the island for six months without being able to find any. And so they disarmed them.

284. In addition, on 14 June [in the year] of Christ 1501 Morphou de Grenier the count de Rochas died, and they gave him a splendid funeral, bringing out ten horses with body armour and 40 with long black funereal vestments. He was, moreover, buried on top of his father, Jacques de Grenier, in [the cathedral of] the Holy Wisdom. He died at the age of 64.

---

[452] The words in brackets < > are taken from ms. **B**. See Kehayioglou, Διήγησις, *op. cit.*, p. 317 line 15.

[453] Ms. **A** has 1488 since the year at the time began on 1 March, as stated above.

[454] The words in brackets < > are taken from ms. **B**. See Kehayioglou, Διήγησις, *op. cit.*, p. 317 lines 19-20.

[455] The words in brackets < > are taken from ms. **M**. See *ibid.*, p. 319 lines 3-4. Florio Bustron, 'Chronique', *op. cit.*, p. 458 states that on Queen Catherine's arrival in Famagusta a solemn mass was held, and that the standard of Venice was hoisted in the central square in her presence.

[456] *Ibid.*, p. 458 states that she left for Venice with her brother George after 14 March, the date on which 'in this manner the kingdom of Cyprus was reduced to a province'.

[457] For other raids by Turkish pirates against Cyprus see J. Darrouzès, 'Notes pour servir à l'histoire de Chypre', ΚΣ, XX (1956), 52 and XXIII (1959), 43-44. Chapters 283-284 are not found in mss. **B** and **M** and were clearly added to the true end of the Chronicle, for which see Dawkins, *Boustronios*, *op. cit.*, p. 60 note.

BIBLIOGRAPHY

Primary Sources

'Abrégé du livre des assises de la cour des bourgeois', ed. M. le Comte Beugnot, *RHC Lois*, II, Paris, 1843

Acta Eugenii IV, ed. G. Fedalto, PCRCICO, xv, Rome, 1965

Ανέκδοτα έγγραφα της κυπριακής ιστορίας από το αρχείο της Βενετίας, ed. A. Aristeidou, 4 vols. Nicosia, 1990-2003, I (1990), III (1999), IV (2003)

The Assizes of the Lusignan Kingdom of Cyprus, transl. N. Coureas, Nicosia, 2002

'Banns et ordonnances des rois de Chypre', ed. M. le Comte Beugnot, *RHC Lois*, II, Paris, 1843

Die Byzantinische Kleinchroniken, 3 vols. ed. P. Schreiner, Vienna, 1975-1979, I

The Cartulary of the Cathedral of Holy Wisdom of Nicosia, ed. N. Coureas and C. Schabel, Nicosia, 1997

Chypre sous les Lusignans: Documents chypriotes des archives du Vatican (XIVe et XVe siècles), ed. J. Richard, Paris, 1962

A Complete Gazetteer of Cyprus, compiled by M.N. Christodoulou and K. Konstantinidis, Vol. I, Nicosia, 1987

Consulat de France à Larnaca – Documents inédits pour servir à l'histoire de Chypre, ed. Anna Pouratier Duteil-Loizidou, 4 vols. Nicosia, 1991-2002

Dated Greek Manuscripts from Cyprus to the Year 1570, ed. C. Constantinides and R. Browning, Nicosia, 1993'

'Documents nouveaux servant de preuves à l'histoire de l'île de Chypre sous le règne des princes de la maison de Lusignan', ed. L. de Mas Latrie in *Collection des documents inédits: Mélanges historiques*, IV, Paris, 1882

Une enquête à Chypre au XVe siècle: Le sindicamentum de Napoleone Lomellini, capitaine Génois de Famagouste (1459), ed. C. Otten-Froux, Nicosia, 2000

Ισπανικά έγγραφα της κυπριακής ιστορίας (ις-ιζ αι), ed. I.K. Hasiotes, Nicosia, 1972, 2003²

Lacrimae Nicossienses. Recueil des inscriptions funéraires la plupart françaises existant encore dans l'île de Chypre, ed. T.J. Chamberlayne, Paris, 1894

Lignages d'Outremer, Introduction, notes et édition critique, ed. M.A. Nielen in *Documents relatifs à l'histoire des Croisades* XVIII, Académie des Inscriptions et Belles-Lettres, Paris, 2003

Le Livre des remembrances de la secrète du royaume de Chypre (1468-1469), ed. J. Richard with the collaboration of Th. Papadopoullos, Nicosia, 1983

'Nouvelles preuves de l'histoire de Chypre sous le règne des princes de la maison de Lusignan', ed. L. de Mas Latrie, *BEC*, xxxv, Paris, 1873

Πηγές της κυπριακής ιστορίας από το ισπανικό αρχείο Simancas, ed. I.K. Hasiotes, Nicosia, 2000

The Synodicum Nicosiense and other Documents of the Latin Church of Cyprus, 1196-1373, transl. C. Schabel, Nicosia, 2001

The Trial of the Templars on Cyprus: A Complete English Edition, ed. A. Gilmour Bryson, Leiden, 1998

Chronicles and Narrative Accounts

The Chronicle of George Boustronios, 1456-1489, transl. R.M. Dawkins, Melbourne, 1964

'Chronique d'Amadi', in *Chroniques d'Amadi et de Strambaldi*, ed. R. de Mas Latrie, 2 vols. Paris, 1891-1893, I

'Chronique de Strambaldi', in *Chroniques d'Amadi et de Strambaldi*, ed. R. de Mas Latrie, 2 vols. Paris, 1891-1893, II

Felix Faber, 'Evagatorium in Terrae Sanctae, Arabiae et Egypti Peregrinationem', (extracts) in *Excerpta Cypria: Materials for a History of Cyprus*, transl. C.D. Cobham, Cambridge, 1908, repr. Nicosia, 1969

Filippo da Novara, *Guerra di Federico II in Oriente*, ed. S. Melani, Naples, 1994

Florio Bustron, 'Chronique de l'île de Chypre', ed. R. de Mas Latrie in *Collection des documents inédits sur l'histoire de France: Mélanges historiques*, V Paris, 1886

'Γεωργίου Βουστρωνίου Χρονικόν Κύπρου', in *Μεσαιωνική Βιβλιοθήκη* (= *Bibliotheca Graeca Medii Aevi*) , ed. C. Sathas, 7 vols. Venice, 1872-1894, II

'Kipriska Khronika na Georgi Bustron', ed. and trans. by P. Tivčev, *Godishnik na Sofiiskiya Universit-Istoričeski Fakultet*, Sofia, 1978

Leontios Makhairas, *Recital Concerning the Sweet Land of Cyprus, entitled 'Chronicle'*, transl. R.M. Dawkins, 2 vols. Oxford, 1932

Λεοντίου Μαχαιρά Χρονικό της Κύπρου: Παράλληλη διπλωματική έκδοση των χειρογράφων, ed. M. Pieris and Angel Nicolaou-Konnari, Nicosia, 2003

Neophytos the Recluse, 'Περί των κατά την χώραν Κύπρου σκαίων', *Μεσαιωνική Βιβλιοθήκη* (= *Bibliotheca Graeca Medii Aevi*), ed. C. Sathas, 7 vols. Venice, 1872-1894, II

Niccolo de Martoni, 'Liber peregrinationis ad loca sancta', (extracts) in *Excerpta Cypria: Materials for a History of Cyprus*, transl. C.D. Cobham, Cambridge, 1908, repr. Nicosia, 1969

'Pero Tafur and Cyprus', transl. C.I. Nepaulsingh, *Sources for the History of Cyprus*, ed. P.W. Wallace and A.G. Orphanides, IV, New York, 1997

Stephen de Lusignan, *Description de toute l'isle de Chypre*, Paris, 1580, repr. Nicosia, 2004

—-*Chorograffia et breve historia universale dell'isola de Cipro principiando al tempo di Noè per il fino al 1572*, Bologna, 1573, repr. and transl. by Olympia Pelosi 'Lusignan's Chorography and Brief General History of the island of Cyprus (A.D. 1573)', *Sources for the History of Cyprus*, ed. P.W. Wallace and A.G. Orphanides, X, New York, 2001

Τζώρτζης (Μ)πουστρούς (Γεώργιος Βο(σ)τρ(υ)νός ή Βουστρώνιος), *Διήγησις Κρονίκας Κύπρου*, ed. G. Kehayioglou, Nicosia, 1997

Secondary Works

Abulafia, D., *The Western Mediterranean Kingdoms 1200-1500:The Struggle for Dominion*, London 1997

Arbel, B., 'Cypriot Population under Venetian Rule (1473-1571): A Demographic Study', *MY*, I, Nicosia, 1984

—-'Urban Assemblies and Town Councils in Frankish and Venetian Cyprus', in *ΠΔΚΣ*, 3 vols. Nicosia, 1985-1987, II

—-'A Royal Family in Republican Venice: The Cypriot Legacy of the *Corner della Regina*', *Studi Veneziani*, new series XV, 1988

—-'The Cypriot Nobility from the Fourteenth to the Sixteenth Centuries: A New Interpretation', in *Latin and Greeks in the Eastern Mediterranean after 1204*, ed. B. Arbel, B. Hamilton and D. Jacoby, London, 1989

—-'The Reign of Caterina Corner as a Family Affair', *Studi Veneziani*, new series XXVI, 1993

—-'Greek Magnates in Venetian Cyprus: The Case of the Synglitiko Family', *DOP*, no. 49, 1995

—-'Venetian Cyprus and the Muslim Levant, 1473-1570', in *Η Κύπρος και οι Σταυροφορίες/Cyprus and the Crusades*, ed. N. Coureas and J. Riley-Smith, Nicosia, 1995

Aristeidou, A., 'Το κυνήγι με τα γεράκια στην Κύπρο από την αρχαιότητα μέχρι την τουρκοκρατία', *EKEE* XX, Nicosia, 1994

—- 'Άγνωστα στοιχεία σχετικά με τους κτίτορες της εκκλησίας της Παναγίας Ελεούσας (Ποδύθου)', *EKEE* XXX, Nicosia, 2004

Ashtor, E., *A Social and Economic History of the Near East throughout the Middle Ages*, London, 1976

—-*Levant Trade in the Later Middle Ages*, Princeton, 1983

Bekker, E., 'Die ungedruckten Byzantinischen Historiker der St Markus Bibliothek', *Philologische und historische Abhandlungen der königlichen Akademie der Wissenschaften*, 1841, Berlin, 1843

Betto, B., 'Nuove recherché sulle studenti Ciprioti all' Università di Padova (1393-1489)', *Θησαυρίσματα*, 23, Venice, 1993

Bouchard, C., 'Consanguinity and Noble Marriages in the Tenth and Eleventh Centuries', *Speculum*, LVI, Cambridge, Massachusetts 1981

Braudel, F., *The Mediterranean and the Mediterranean World in the Age of Philip II*, trans.

S. Reynolds, 2 vols. London, 1972-1973

Brayer, E., Lemerle, P., and Laurent, V., 'Le Vaticanus Latinus 4789', *REB* 9 (1951)

Cameron, A., *Procopius*, London, 1985

Chaudhuri, K.N., *Asia before Europe: Economy and Civilisation of the Indian Ocean from the Rise of Islam to 1750*, Cambridge, 1990

Constable, O.R., *Housing the Stranger in the Mediterranean World: Lodging, Trade and Travel in Late Antiquity and the Middle Ages*, Cambridge, 2003

Coureas, N., 'Η Μονή Αγίου Γεωργίου των Μαγγάνων επί Φραγκοκρατίας', *Επιστημονική Επετηρίδα της Κυπριακής Εταιρείας Ιστορικών Σπουδών*, II, Nicosia, 1994

——'Lusignan Cyprus and Lesser Armenia, 1195-1375', *EKEE* XXI, Nicosia, 1995

——*The Latin Church in Cyprus*, Aldershot, 1997

——'Non-Chalcedonian Christinas in Latin Cyprus', in *Dei gesta per Francos: Crusade Studies in Honour of Jean Richard*, ed. M. Balard, B.Z. Kedar and J. Riley-Smith, Aldershot, 2001

——'The Role of the Templars and the Hospitallers in the Movement of Commodities involving Cyprus, 1291-1312', in *The Experience of Crusading*, ed. M. Bull, P. Edbury, N. Housley and J. Phillips, 2 vols. Cambridge, 2003

——'The Place to be: Migrations to Lusignan and Venetian Cyprus', *ΚΣ* 66 2002, Nicosia, 2004

Coureas, N., Grivaud, G., and Schabel, C., 'The Capital of the Sweet Land of Cyprus: Frankish and Venetian Nicosia', in *A History of Nicosia* (forthcoming)

Darrouzès, J., 'Notes pour servir à l'histoire de Chypre', *ΚΣ* XX, 1956

——'Notes pour servir à l'histoire de Chypre', *ΚΣ* XXIII, 1959

Earle, P., *Corsairs of Malta and of Barbary*, London, 1970

Edbury, P.W., *The Kingdom of Cyprus and the Crusades*, Cambridge, 1991, 1994[2]

——'Οι τελευταίοι Λουζινιανοί', in *Ιστορία της Κύπρου*, IV, *Μεσαιωνικόν Βασίλειον, Ενετοκρατία*, ed. Th. Papadopoullos, Nicosia, 1995

——'Famagusta in 1300', in *Η Κύπρος και οι Σταυροφορίες/Cyprus and the Crusades*, ed. N. Coureas and J. Riley-Smith, Nicosia, 1995

——'John of Jaffa and the Kingdom of Cyprus', *EKEE* XXIII, Nicosia, 1997

—'The Franco-Cypriot Landowning Class and its Exploitation of the Agrarian Resources of the island of Cyprus', in *idem.*, *Kingdoms of the Crusades from Jerusalem to Cyprus*, XIX, Aldershot, 1999

Enlart, C., *Gothic Art and the Renaissance in Cyprus*, transl. D. Hunt, London, 1987

Frigerio-Zeniou, S., *L'Art "Italo-Byzantin" à Chypre au XVIe siècle*, Venice, 1998

Galatariotou, Catia., *The Making of a Saint: The Life, Times and Sanctification of Neophytos the Recluse* Cambridge, 1991

Goodwin, J.C., *An Historical Toponymy of Cyprus*, 2 vols. Nicosia, 1976, 1984[4]

Grandclaude, M., *Etude critique sur les livres des assises de Jérusalem*, Paris, 1923

Grivaud, G., 'Ο πνευματικός βίος και η γραμματολογία κατά την περίοδο της Φραγκοκρατίας', in *Ιστορία της Κύπρου, IV, Μεσαιωνικόν Βασίλειον, Γραμματολογία*, ed. Th. Papadopoullos, Nicosia, 1996

—*Villages désertés à Chypre (fin XIIe-fin XIXe siècle)*, *MY* III, Nicosia, 1998

— 'Florio Bustron, storico del rinascimento cipriota', in Florio Bustron, 'Chronique de l'ile de Chypre', in *Collection des documents inédits sur l'histoire de France: Mélanges historiques*, V, Paris, 1886, repr. Nicosia, 1998, pp. vii-viii in the Nicosia reprint

—'Une petite chronique chypriote du XVe siècle', in *Dei gesta per Francos: Crusade Studies in Honour of Jean Richard*, ed. M. Balard, B.Z. Kedar and J. Riley-Smith, Aldershot, 2001

Grivaud, G., and Papadaki, A., 'L'institution de la *mostra generale* de la chevalerie féodale en Crète et en Chypre vénitienne durant la XVIe siècle', *Studi veneziani*, n.s. XII, 1986

Hackett, J., *A History of the Orthodox Church of Cyprus*, Greek transl. Kh. Papaioannou, 3 vols. Athens, 1923, Piraeus, 1927 and 1932

Har-El, Shai, *The Struggle for Domination in the Near East: The Ottoman-Mamluk War, 1485-1491*, Leiden, 1995

Hill, G., *A History of Cyprus*, 4 vols. Cambridge, 1940-1952

Hindley, A., Langley, F.W., and Levy, B. J., *Old French-English Dictionary*, Cambridge, 2000

Holt, P.M., *The Age of the Crusades: The Islamic Near East from the Eleventh Century to 1517*, London, 1986

Holton, D., 'Cyprus and the Cretan Renaissance: A preliminary study of some cultural connections', *EKEE* XIX, Nicosia, 1992

—'A history of neglect: Cypriot history writing during the period of Venetian rule', *Modern Greek Studies Yearbook*, vol. 14/15, Minneapolis, 1998-1999

Imhaus, B., 'La mort dans la societé franque à Chypre', *EKEE* XXIV, Nicosia, 1998

Ioannou, Th., *Εμπορικές σχέσεις Κύπρου-Γαλλίας κατά τον 18ο αιώνα*, Nicosia,

2002

Irwin, R., 'Οι εισβολές των Μαμελούκων στην Κύπρο', in Ιστορία της Κύπρου, IV, Μεσαιωνικόν Βασίλειον, Ενετοκρατία, ed.Th. Papadopoullos, Nicosia, 1995

Kitromilides, P. M., Κυπριακή Λογιοσύνη 1571-1878, Nicosia, 2002.

Jacoby, D., 'The Rise of a New Emporium in the Eastern Mediterranean: Famagusta in the Late Thirteenth Century', MY II, Nicosia, 1984

——'Το εμπόριο και η οικονομία της Κύπρου', in Ιστορία της Κύπρου, IV, Μεσαιωνικόν Βασίλειον, Ενετοκρατία, ed. Th. Papadopoullos, Nicosia, 1995

Jeffery, G., A Description of the Historic Monuments of Cyprus, Nicosia, 1918

Kelly, J.N.D., The Oxford Dictionary of Popes Oxford, 1986, 1996[2]

Leventis, P., Twelve Times in Nicosia, Architecture, Topography and Urban Experience in a diversified Capital City, Unpubl. Ph.D. Thesis, Montreal, 2003

Luttrell. A., 'The Hospitallers in Cyprus after 1291', in The Hospitallers in Cyprus, Rhodes, Greece and the West, 1291-1440, Aldershot, 1979, repr. 1992, 1997, I

——'The Hospitallers at Rhodes: 1306-1421', in The Hospitallers in Cyprus, Rhodes, Greece and the West, 1291-1440, Aldershot, 1979, repr. 1992, 1997, II

——'The Hospitallers on Rhodes confront the Turks, 1306-1421', in The Hospitallers of Rhodes and their Mediterranean World, II, Aldershot, 1992

——'Τα στρατιωτικά τάγματα', in Ιστορία της Κύπρου, IV, Μεσαιωνικόν Βασίλειον, Ενετοκρατία, ed. Th. Papadopoullos, Nicosia, 1995

Maltezou, C., 'Η περιπέτεια ενός ελληνόφωνου Βενετού της Κύπρου (1571)', in ΠΔΚΣ, 3 vols. Nicosia, 1985-1987, II

Mas Latrie, Louis de., 'Histoire des archevêques Latins de l'île de Chypre', AOL, II, Paris, 1884

——Histoire de l'île de Chypre sous le règne des princes de la maison de Lusignan, 3 vols. Paris, 1852-1861

McKee, S., Uncommon Dominion: Venetian Crete and the Myth of Ethnic Purity, Pennsylvania, 2000

Megaw, P., 'A Castle in Cyprus attributable to the Hospital?', in The Military Orders: Fighting for the Faith and Caring for the Sick, ed. M. Barber, Aldershot, 1994

Metcalf, D.M., The Gros, Sixains and Cartzias of Cyprus 1382-1489, Nicosia, 2000

Moschopoulos, G.N., 'Η κυπριακή οικογένεια Στράμπαλι στην Κεφαλονία (16ος-17ος αι)', in ΠΔΚΣ, 3 vols. Nicosia, 1985-1987, II

Papadopoulou, E., 'Οι πρώτες εγκαταστάσεις Βενετών στην Κύπρο', Σύμμεικτα, V, Athens, 1983

Petrie, C.F., (ed.), The Cambridge History of Egypt, Volume One, Islamic Egypt, 640-1517, Cambridge, 1998

Pinson, M., 'Observations sur la transcription des mots français et italiens dans la chronique de George Boustron', in *ΠΠΚΣ*, 3 vols. Nicosia, 1971-1973, II

Pryor, J.H., *Geography, Technology and War: Studies in the Maritime History of the Mediterranean 649-1571*, Cambridge, 1988, 1992[2]

Richard, J., 'Le droit et institutions franques dans le royaume de Chypre', in *XVe Congrès International d'études Byzantines*, Athens, 1976

——'Le peuplement latin et syrien en Chypre au XIIIe siècle', in *idem.*, *Croises, missionnaires et voyageurs*, VII, London, 1983

——'Agriculture in the Crusader States', in *A History of the Crusades*, ed. K.M. Setton, 6 vols. Philadelphia/Madison, 1955-1989, V (1985)

——'Les Turcoples au service des royaumes de Jérusalem et de Chypre: Mussulmans convertis ou Chrétiens orientaux?', in *idem.*, *Croisades et états latins de l'Orient*, X, Aldershot, 1992

——'Culture franque et culture grecque: le royaume de Chypre au XVème siècle', in *idem.*, *Croisades et états latins d'Orient*, XVIII, Aldershot, 1992

——'The Cistercians in Cyprus', in *The Second Crusade and the Cistercians*, ed. M. Gervers, New York, 1992

——'Le casal de Psimolofo et la vie rurale en Chypre au XIVe siècle', in *idem.*, *Les Relations entre l'Orient et l'Occident au Moyen Age*, IV, Aldershot, 1992, 1996[2], 1999[3]

——'Οι πολιτικοί και κοινωνικοί θεσμοί του μεσαιωνικού βασιλείου', and

——'Το δίκαιο του μεσαιωνικού βασιλείου', in *Ιστορία της Κύπρου*, IV, in *Μεσαιωνικόν Βασίλειον, Ενετοκρατία*, ed. Th. Papadopoullos, Nicosia, 1995

Rosser, J., 'Archaeological and Literary Evidence for the Destruction of "Saranda Kolones" in 1222, *EKEE* XXX, 2004

Rudt de Collenberg, W., 'Les Lusignans de Chypre', *EKEE* X, Nicosia, 1980

——'Les dispensations matrimoniales accordées à l'Orient latin selon les registres du Vatican d'Honorius III à Clément VIII Aldobrandini (1592-1605): Flatro, Davila, Sozomenoi, Lusignan, Bustron et Nores', *EKEE* XII, Nicosia, 1983

——'Etudes de prosopographie généalogique des Chypriotes mentionnés dans les registres du Vatican, 1378-1471', *MY* II, Nicosia, 1984

——'Le royaume et l'église latine de Chypre et la papauté de 1417 à 1471', *EKEE* XIII-XVI, Nicosia, 1988

——'Les premiers Podocataro: Recherches basées sur le testament de Hugues (1452)', *Θησαυρίσματα*, XXIII, Venice, 1993

Santa, G. della, 'Alcuni documenti per la storia della chiesa di Limisso durante la seconda metà del sec. XV', *Nuovo archivio Veneto*, XVI, Venice, 1898

Setton, K.M., The Papacy and the Levant (1204-1571), 4 vols. Philadelphia, 1976-1984. II

Stewart, A.D., *The Armenian Kingdom and the Mamluks: War and Diplomacy during the Reigns of Hetoum II (1289-1317)*, Leiden, 2001

Stewart, J.R., *Lusignan Cyprus and its Coinage*, 2 vols. Nicosia, 2002

Thiriet, F., *La Romanie vénitienne au moyen âge*, Paris, 1975

Tivčev, P., 'George Bustron comme historien de l'île de Chypre au moyen age', *Etudes Balkaniques*, 4, Sofia, 1982

Tselikas, A., 'Η διαθήκη του Petro de Caffrano και οι πράξεις εκλογής Κυπρίων φοιτητών για το Πανεπιστήμιο της Παδόβας (1393, 1436-1569)', *EKEE* XVII, Nicosia, 1987-1988

Vaivre, J-B de., 'Sur les sites de châteaux disparus de Sigouri et de Gastria en Chypre', *Academie des Inscriptions et Belles-Lettres*, Paris, 1998

Ziada, M., 'The Mamluk Conquest of Cyprus in the Fifteenth Century', Pt. II, *Bulletin of the Faculty of Arts*, Vol. 2, Pt. 1, Cairo, 1934

INDEX

Numbers in bold are page numbers and footnote numbers found in the introduction. Numbers not in bold are chapter numbers and footnote numbers in the main text. The letters 'n' or 'nn' precede footnote numbers.

Abbreviations: abb.- abbot; abp.- archbishop; aml.- admiral; and. - archdeacon; Aug.- Augustinian; Ben.- Benedictine; bp.- bishop; bro.- brother; can.- canon; capt.- captain; Carm.- Carmelite; cd.- cardinal; chn.- chancellor; chr.- chronicle; cmdr.- commander; csn.- cousin; cst.- constable; ct.- count; d.- daughter; dn.- deacon; Dom.- Dominican; emp.- emperor; Fr.- French; Fran.- Franciscan; Gen.- Genoese; Gk.- Greek; hb.- husband; Hosp.- Hospitaller; hse.- house; k.- king; mgr.- monsignor; mon.- monastery; np.-nephew; patr.- patriarch; pr.- prince; prof.- professor; q.- queen; s.- sister; sen.- seneschal; Sp.- Spanish; vct.- viscount; Ven.- Venetian.

An anthology of Greek texts of the fourteenth and fifteenth centuries relating to Cyprus

Based on the Collection of

B. NERANTZE-BARMAZE

Translated and Edited by

HANS A. POHLSANDER
University at Albany, State University of New York

Preface

The Greek texts of the fourth to thirteenth centuries have been presented in vol. VII of the series *Sources for the History of Cyprus*. This section of the present volume extends the chronological parameters by another two centuries. The quotations here given are basically those found in the last two chapters of B. Nerantze-Barmaze, ΣΥΝΤΑΓΜΑ ΒΥΖΑΝΤΙΝΩΝ ΠΗΓΩΝ ΚΥΠΡΙΑΚΗΣ ΙΣΤΟΡΙΑΣ (*Collection of Byzantine Sources for the History of Cyprus,* Nicosia 1996, herafter abbreviated ΣΠΒΚΙ), nos. 91–118. We have, however, made a few additions and deletions, and all quotations are based not on the text provided by Nerantze-Barmaze, but on the best available editions and translations. In each case the appropriate reference to Nerantze-Barmaze has been given in brackets.

We have left the authors or texts quoted in the order found in ΣΠΒΚΙ. We have given their dates in parentheses, relying for the chronological information on the *Oxford Dictionary of Byzantium*, on Johannes Karayannopoulos and Günter Weiß, *Quellenkunde zur Geschichte von Byzantium* (Wiesbaden 1982), and on the *Prosopographisches Lexikon der Palaiologenzeit* (Vienna 1976–1996). We have let the *Oxford Dictionary of Byzantium* be our guide also to the spelling of Byzantine, but not classical Greek names. Thus we have written "Kantakouzenos" rather than "Cantacuzenus," but "Cleisthenes" rather than "Kleisthenes."

In two cases we have used, with kind permission of the publishers, translations already published elsewhere (see Acknowledgments). All other translations are ours. Where French, German, or Italian translations are available we have cited these as well. The Latin translations which accompany the Greek text in Migne, *PG*, are at times so free as to be mere paraphrases. For a few documents of unusual length I have given summaries rather than translations.

Interpolations in the text, providing useful information, such as dates and references, are set off by brackets.

Acknowledgments

The University of Massachusetts Press, Amherst, Mass., and Dumbarton Oaks Research Library and Collection, Washington, D.C., have kindly given permission to use copyrighted materials.

Professor Jean-Louis van Dieten, Nettetal, Germany, has kindly provided an advance copy of parts of his translation of Nikephoros Gregoras.

Bibliographical Abbreviations

BBKL	Traugott Bautz, ed., *Biographisch-Bibliographisches Kirchenlexikon*, Herz-berg, Germany, in progress; on-line www.bautz.de/bbkl.
Bréhier	Louis Bréhier, *Les institutions de l'empire byzantin*, Paris 1949.
Budé	Association Guillaume Budé.
Cammelli	Giuseppe Cammelli, ed. and Fr. tr., *Démétrius Cydonès: Correspondance*, Budé, Paris 1930.
CFHB	*Corpus Fontium Historiae Byzantinae.*
CPG	E. L. Deutsch and F. G. Schneidewin, eds., *Corpus Paroemiographorum Graecorum*, 2 vols., Göttingen 1839, repr. Hildesheim 1965.
CSHB	*Corpus Scriptorum Historiae Byzantinae*, Bonn.
Darkó	Eugenius Darkó, ed., *Laonici Chalcocandylae Historiarum Demonstrationes*, 2 vols., Budapest 1922–1927.
Darrouzès	Jean Darrouzès, *Les Regestes des Actes du Patriarcat de Constantinople*, Vol. I , fasc. 5, Paris 1977.
van Dieten	Jan-Louis van Dieten, Ger. tr., *Nikephoras Gregoras: Rhomäische Geschichte*, 4 vols. to date, Stuttgart 1973ff.
Failler	Albert Failler and Vitalien Laurent, ed. and Fr. tr., *Georges Pachymérès: Relations historiques*, 5 vols., *CFHB*, Paris: Les Belles Lettres, 1984–2000.
Grecu	Vasile Grecu, ed. and Romanian tr., *Georgios Sphrantzes: Memorii, SB* 5, Bucarest 1966.
Guilland	R. Guilland, ed. and Fr. tr., *Correspondance de Nicéphore Grégoras*, Budé, Paris 1927.
Hackett	John Hackett, *A History of the Orthodox Church of Cyprus*, London 1901.
Hill	George Hill, *A History of Cyprus*, 4 vols., Cambridge 1948–1952.
Hunger 1969	Herbert Hunger, ed., *Johannes Chortasmenos: Briefe, Gedichte und kleine Schriften*, Vienna 1969.
Hunger 1978	Herbert Hunger, *Die hochsprachliche profane Literatur der Byzantiner*, 2 vols., Munich 1978.
Hussey	Joan Mervyn Hussey, *The Orthodox Church in the Byzantine Empire*, Oxford 1986.

Krumbacher

Karl Krumbacher, *Geschichte der byzantinischen Litteratur von Justinian bis zum Ende des oströmischen Reiches (527–1453)*, 2nd ed., 2 vols., Munich 1897, repr. New York 1958.

Kyrris

Κ. Ρ. Kyrris, ʻΗ Κύπρος και το ησυχαστικόν ζήτημα κατά τον XIV αιώνα, *Κυπριακαί Σπουδαί* 26 (1962) 19–31.

Leone

Petrus Aloisius M. (Pietro Luigi) Leone, ed., *Nicephori Gregorae Epistulae*, 2 vols., Matino, Italy, 1982–1983.

Loenertz 1950

Raymond-J. Loenertz, ed., *Correspondance de Manuel Calecas*, *Studi e Testi* 152, Vatican City 1950.

Loenertz 1956

Raymond-J. Loenertz, ed., *Démétrius Cydonès: Correspondance, 2 vols.*, *Studi e Testi* 186 and 208, Vatican City 1956–1960.

Meyendorff

John Meyendorff, *Byzantine Hesychasm: Historical, Theological and Social Problems: Collected Studies.* London: Variorum Reprints, 1974.

Migne, *PG*

J. P. Migne, *Patrologia, Series Graeca*, Paris.

Misch

Georg Misch, "Die Schriftsteller-Autobiographie und Bildungsgeschichte eines Patriarchen von Konstantinopel aus dem XIII. Jahrhundert," *Zeitschrift für Geschichte der Erziehung und des Unterrichts* 21 (1931) 1–16.

MM

Franz von Miklosich and Joseph Miller, eds., *Acta et diplomata Graeca medii aevi sacra et profana*, 6 vols., Vienna 1890, repr. Aalen 1968.

Papadopoulos-Kerameus

Athanasios Papadopoulos-Kerameus, *Φιλολογικός Σύλλογος Κωνσταντινουπόλεως* 17 (1886) 49–51.

Percival

Henry R. Percival, ed., *The Seven Ecumenical Councils of the Undivided Church, A Select Library of Nicene and post-Nicene Fathers of the Christian Church*, 2nd ser., vol. 14, Grand Rapids 1956; repr. 1983.

Philippides

Marios Philippides, tr., *The Fall of the Byzantine Empire: A Chronicle by George Sphrantzes, 1407–1477*, Amherst, Mass., 1980.

PLP

Prosopographisches Lexikon der Palaiologenzeit, 12 fasc., plus addenda, ed. Erich Trapp, Vienna 1976–1996.

REB

Revue des Études Byzantines.

SB

Scriptores Byzantini.

Schopen 1828

Ludwig Schopen, ed. and Latin tr., *Iohannes Cantacuzenus: Historia*, 3 vols., *CSHB*, 1828–1832 .

Schopen 1829
Ludwig Schopen, ed. and Latin tr., Nikephoros Gregoras, *Historia*, 2 vols., *CSHB*, 1829–1830. Vol. III, ed. Immanuel Bekker, *CSHB*, 1855.

Schreiner
Peter Schreiner, ed., *Die byzantinischen Kleinchroniken*, 3 vols., Vienna 1975–1979.

TGF
Tragicorum Graecorum Fragmenta, ed. August Nauck, Leipzig 1889; 2nd. ed. with a supplement by Bruno Snell, Hildesheim 1964.

Tinnefeld
Franz Tinnefeld, Ger. tr., *Demetrios Kydones: Briefe*, 3 vols. in 4, Stuttgart 1981–1999.

Tomadakes
Nikolaos B. Tomadakes, *Ο Ιωσήφ Βρυέννιος και η Κρήτη κατά το 1400*, Athens 1947.

Tsames
Demetrios G. Tsames, ed., *Φιλοθέου Κωνσταντινουπόλεως του Κόκκινου Αγιολογικά Έργα*, vol. I, Thessalonike 1985.

Verpeaux
Jean Verpeaux, ed. and Fr. tr., Pseudo-Kodinos, *Traité des Offices*, Paris 1976.

Weiss
Günter Weiss, *Joannes Kantacuzenos, Aristokrat, Staatsmann, Kaiser und Mönch, in der Gesellschaftsentwicklung von Byzanz im 14. Jahrhundert*, Wiesbaden 1969.

TEXTS

1. Pachymeres, George (1242–ca. 1310)
[*PLP*, fasc. 9, pp. 177–78, no. 22186; *BBKL*, vol. VI, cols. 1421–23]
Historia or Συγγραφικαί Ιστορίαι (ed. and Fr. tr. Failler)

1. 7.14; vol. III, pp. 52–53 [ΣΒΠΚΙ 91.1] [1283]

He [the emperor Andronikos II, 1282–1328] decided to take the middle road, so as not to offend one party [the Arsenites, supporters of Arsenios, patriarch 1261–1265] and still to accommodate the other party [the Josephites, supporters of Joseph I, patriarch 1266–1275 and 1282–1283] by yielding to their demands (they were demanding, so to speak, the complete reform of the church). Thus he chose for patriarch George of Cyprus [Gregory II, 1283–1289], a man who was trained in letters, bore the seal of the patriarch Joseph [i.e. had been ordained by him], and held the rank of πρωτοαποστολάριος [the chief of the clerics who expound the writings of the Apostles] in the palace.
Note: See Hussey, pp. 243–46; Misch; Migne, *PG* 142, cols. 19–30 .

2. 7.22; vol. III, pp. 74–75 [not in ΣΒΠΚΙ]

Finally they admitted that he was the patriarch Gregoras; for this was his monastic name, from George [his earlier name].

3. 9.5; vol. III, pp. 226–29 [ΣΒΠΚΙ 91.2] [1294]

The emperor [Andronikos II, 1282–1328] was preparing a suitable marriage for his son [Michael IX] and sent the hieromonk Sophonias [*PLP*, fasc. 11, p. 49, no. 26424], a wise and intelligent man, to Apulia to negotiate the marriage contract. But the latter was delayed . . . and there were many who approached the emperor from elsewhere, such as from the king of Cyprus and from Armenia. He then thought that opportunities at hand were better than any that were merely expected, and besides he resented the arrogance of the pope of Rome. Therefore, ridding himself of that worry, he decided to come to an agreement with one or the other of the applicants.

4. 9.5; vol. III, pp. 230–31 [ΣΒΠΚΙ 91.3] [1294]

When the emperor learned about these developments he was saddened, as one might expect, and sent out other ambassadors, having well prepared them. These were the secretary of petitions [*magister libellorum*], John Glykys [*PLP*, fasc. 2, p. 218, no. 4271], and the *logothetes ton agelon,* Theodore Metochites [see Bréhier, pp. 266 and 276; *PLP*, fasc. 7, pp. 215–16, no. 17982]. They went first to Cyprus, approached the king [Henry II, 1285–1324], and found him readily agreeable to the things which they were seeking. There was one point which the king recognized as a source of difficulty, but on which he was willing to compromise in practice. This was that the wedding was to take place with the consent and approval of the Roman church. Such were the demands of the times and of prevailing practice. But the ambassadors were instructed to visit also the rulers of Armenia. These first made them an offer of two sisters, on condition that they should deal with it as they wanted. (For they did not know which sister to recommend more to the emperor as suitable for marriage, since if one were chosen the other one would follow.) So the ambassadors went there and escorted both ladies back, one [Rita-Maria of Armenia, also known as Xene] to marry the [co-]emperor [Michael IX], the other to find a worthy bridegroom.

2. *Chronica Byzantina Breviora* or Βϱαχέα Χϱονικά (10th c. onward,). These lesser or minor chronicles, which go down as far as the mid-sixteenth century, that is the early Ottoman period, fall into various classifications, state chronicles, imperial chronicles, chronicles from after the Ottoman conquest, regional, fragmentary and isolated chronicles. Chronicle 26 is among the group of city or regional chronicles (nos. 23-52) originating from Thessalonika, the Peloponnese, Mesembria in Thrace, Cyprus and other areas. These regional chronicles bear no relation to one another, and those originating from Cyprus (nos. 26-28) date from the late 11th to the early 16th centuries, when the island was under Lusignan or Venetian rule.
The ms. of Chronicle 26 is located in Rome (Bibl. Vat. Palat. Gr. 367, ff. 171^v. 172-172^v. 177.) and it was first published in Sp. Lampros, 'Κυπριακά και άλλα έγγϱαφα', *Νέος Ελληνομνήμων*, 15 (1921) 159, 160, 161-162, 339-340.
Ed., hist. comm., and Ger. tr. Schreiner, vol. I, pp. 23-25 and 200–204, vol. II, pp. 189–223, and vol. III, pp. 53–54
Notes: See also the genealogical tables in Hill, vol. III, pp. 1156–58. The Byzantine era begins in 5508 B.C., the presumed year of the Creation.

1. Sept. 1209–Aug. 1210 [ΣΒΠΚΙ 92.1]
   In the year [67]18 King Hugh I took possession of the country.
Note: Hugh had succeeded to the throne in 1205 at the age of 10.

2. 19 Febr. 1218 [ΣΒΠΚΙ 92.2]
   On the 19th of February in the year [67]26 he [Hugh I] died.

3. 18 Jan. 1253 [ΣΒΠΚΙ 92.3]
   On the 18th of October in the year [67]62 King Henry "the Fat" [Henry I, 1218–1253] died; he was the son of the above-named King Hugh [I, 1205–1218].
Note: The date of 18 October is erroneous; the correct date is 18 January (for a contrary view on 18 October being the correct date see C. Schabel, 'The Greek Bishops of Cyprus, 1260-1340, and the Synodikon Kyprion', ΚΣ, 64-65 [2003], 220 and note 10).

4. 25 Dec. 1267 [ΣΒΠΚΙ 92.4]
   On the 25th of December, Christmas Day, in the year [67]76, in the 11th indiction, the most noble Messire Hugh de Lusignan, son of the Messire Henry the Prince [of Antioch], was crowned as King of Cyprus [Hugh III, 1267–1284] by the Patriarch of Jerusalem, the Lord William [d'Agen], who was acting as the representative of the Apostolic See and who was in Cyprus.

5. 24 Sept. 1269 [ΣΒΠΚΙ 92.5]

On the 24th of September in the year [67]78 the above-named king of Cyprus [Hugh III] was crowned King of Jerusalem in the country of Tyre.

6. March 1284 [ΣΒΠΚΙ 92.6]

In the month of March of the year [67]92 the above-named king of Jerusalem and Cyprus [Hugh III] died in the country of Tyre. And they buried his body in Cyprus in the Church of St. Sophia in Leukosia [Nicosia].

7. 4 May 1284 [ΣΒΠΚΙ 92.7]

On the 4th of May of the year [67]92 the most noble Messire John [I, 1284–1285] was crowned king of Cyprus; he was the son of the above-named King Hugh [III] of Jerusalem and Cyprus.

8. 10 May 1285 [ΣΒΠΚΙ 92.8]

[This entry is not readable, but given that King John I of Cyprus died on this date it presumably records the king's death. See Leontios Makhairas, *Recital*, §41].

9. 24 June 1285 [ΣΒΠΚΙ 92.9]

On the 24th of June of the mentioned year [67]93 his [John's] brother, the most noble Messire Henry [II, 1285–1324], was crowned King of Cyprus.

10. Jan. 1286 [ΣΒΠΚΙ 92.10]

In the month of January of the year [67]94 the Lady of Beirut [Isabella d'Ibelin] died; she was the daughter of the Messire John d'Ibelin, the Lord of Beirut, and the wife of Sir William Barlais.

11. 26 April 1289 [ΣΒΠΚΙ 92.11]

On the 26th of April in the year [67]97 the great city of Tripolis [Syria] was seized by the Saracens [the Mameluks under the Sultan Qalawun].

12. 18 May 1291 [ΣΒΠΚΙ 92.12]

On the 18th of May in the year [67]99 the great city of Ptolemais [Acco *or* Acre in Palestine] was seized by the Saracens [the Mameluks under the Sultan al-Ashraf].

13. 13 Febr. 1302 [ΣΒΠΚΙ 92.13]

On the 13th of February, a Tuesday, in the year [6]810, the pious Sir Bertrand died in the district of Paphos and was buried in the Church of the most holy Theotokos of the Syrians in the tomb of his father.

14. 8 Aug. 1303 [ΣΒΠΚΙ 92.14]

On the 8th of August, a Thursday, in the year [6]811, in the first hour of the day, there was a great earthquake in the city of Leukosia [Nicosia].

15. 26 April 1306 [ΣΒΠΚΙ 92.15]

On the 26th of April, a Tuesday, in the year [6]814 the noble Messire Amaury, son of King Hugh [III, 1267–1284], seized control of the kingdom from the most high king, namely King Henry [II, 1285–1324], who was his own brother. And he became the governor and administrator of Cyprus and he took the oaths of the people of the kingdom, the knights, the other Lusignans, and the common people, that they would guard his person and defend him against anyone except the king.

16. 18 Aug. 1309 [ΣΒΠΚΙ 92.16]

On the 18th of August, a Monday, in the year [6]817, the noble Messire John [II] d'Ibelin, Lord of Arsuf [on the coast of Palestine], died.

17. 5–6 June 1310 [ΣΒΠΚΙ 92.17]

On the 5th of June, a Friday, of the year [6]818, at the 6th hour, the noble Messire Amaury de Lusignan, the Lord of Tyre and governor of the kingdom of Cyprus, was murdered by the knight Simon de Montolif in the chamber of his own residence in Leukosia [Nicosia]. And on the 6th, a Saturday, on the morrow, they buried his body in the Catholic church of St. Sophia.

3. Ephraim of Ainos (in Thrace; floruit end 13th c. or early 14th c.)
[*PLP*, fasc. 3, p. 137, no. 6408]
Chronographia, ed. Odysseus Lampsides, 2 vols., Athens 1984–1985

1. Vol. I, p. 123, lines 3540–46 [ΣΒΠΚΙ 93.1]

Then even Cyprus seceded, as it was held by Rhapsommates. And at the same time a man named Karykes, a dangerous rebel, seized the fertile island of Crete by force and held it for himself. But both of these islands were restored to the Roman state by a Roman fleet. [1092]

2. Vol. I, pp. 179–80, lines 5402–18 [ΣΒΠΚΙ 93.2]

Andronikos [I, 1183–1185] heard the words of the oracle and asked to learn the time when these things would happen. A second inquiry was made, and the spirit gave this response in enchanting words: "These things will begin before the day when the thrice-blessed wood is elevated" [14 September]. It was 11 September when the unspeakable deed was done. When the emperor heard of these things he thought little of them. "How," he said, "would Isaac sail from Cyprus and in a short time strip me of my power?" But he [Andronikos] did think that the tyrant of Cyprus intended to take away his power. He [Isaac] was descended from the Komnenoi, but had shown himself a rebel against the state and had established a hostile regime which led to anarchy and tyranny.
Note: Andronikos was deposed and murdered on 12 September 1185.

3. Vol. II, pp. 197–98, lines 6000–20 [ΣΒΠΚΙ 93.3]

The king of France [Philip Augustus] and the ruler of Britain [Richard the Lionheart] came again upon the sons of Hagar [the Saracens] with their ships and their soldiers. But they were unable to drive them from holy Zion and to turn it over to the Christians and returned by sea to their country. But the king of the English landed on Cyprus [1191] and seized it by force of arms and bound the tyrant of Cyprus, Isaac Komnenos, in chains, like Echetus [Hom. *Od.* 18.84–87]. And the king of the British, that is of the English, as he sailed to the places of Palestine, left his army on Cyprus, ruled it as if it were subject to him, and took from it the necessities of life. As he was about to return to his country he gave Cyprus to the king of Palestine [Guy de Lusignan] to live there when he was not engaged in battle and to rule and govern it, since it was assigned to him by his devotion to the life-giving tomb of the Lord and bordered on Palestine.

Note: Actually Richard sold the island to the Templars, who in turn sold it to Guy de Lusignan.

4. Vol. II, pp. 209–10, lines 6387–92 [not in ΣΒΠΚΙ]

Then another great and unexpected evil befell the Roman state: Isaac [Komnenos], the shameful tyrant of Cyprus, suddenly escaped to the sultan [of Iconium] and from there, having raised an army of followers, plundered [a number of] Roman villages and cities.

4. *On Transfers* or Περί Μεταθέσεων 62
Ed. Jean Darrouzès, *REB* 42 (1984)147–214 at 185 and 211 [ΣΒΠΚΙ 94]

During the reign of Isaac [II] Angelos [1185–1195 and 1203–1204], by the unanimous vote of the synod of Cyprus, Esaias, bishop of Tiberias [on the sea of Galilee], was transferred to the archbishopric of Cyprus.

5. Pseudo-Kodinos
Treatise on the Dignities and Offices or Περί οφφικιάλιων του παλατίου Κωνσταντινουπόλεως (1347–1368)
Ed. and Fr. tr. Verpeaux, p. 282 [ΣΒΠΚΙ 95]

The appointment of the other patriarchs is done in the same and unchanged manner, that is the appointment of the patriarchs of Alexandria, Antioch, and Jerusalem; and also of the archbishop of the First Justiniana, Achrida, and all of Bulgaria, since Cyprus is the Second Justiniana, and Carthage the Third.

6. Blastares, Matthew (died after 1346) [*PLP*, fasc. 2. p. 80, no. 2808; *BBKL*, vol. I, cols. 616–17]
Alphabetical Treatise, Syntagma alphabeticum, or Σύνταγμα κατά στοιχείων Ed. G. A. Rhalles-Potles, Athens 1852–1859, vol. VI, pp. 258–59; ed. Migne, *PG,* vol. 144, cols. 1281–84
[ΣΒΠΚΙ 96]

Concerning Bulgaria, Cyprus, and Iberia [Georgia]

The churches which are not subject to any patriarch are: the church of Bulgaria, which the emperor Justinian thus honored, as will be seen from his Novel which will be cited; the church of Cyprus, which the Third and Sixth [Ecumenical] Councils [Council of Ephesus, 431, canon 8; Council in Trullo, 691–692, canon 39] thus honored, as will shortly be explained; and the church of Iberia [Georgia], which was thus honored by a decision of the synod of Antioch [ca. 1057], to which it was previously subject. The archbishops of these churches are normally ordained by their own bishops.

Note: See Hackett, pp. 18–19 and 37–38.

Canon 8 of the Third [Ecumenical] Council; Percival, pp. 234–35

The eighth canon of the Third [Ecumenical] Council enjoins the bishop of
Antioch not to arrogate to himself the ordination of the Cypriot bishops on the
grounds that long ago it was the practice for a governor to be sent to Cyprus by the
duke of Antioch. Rather the ancient practice [is to be followed] whereby the ordination
of bishops is done on the island. And none other of the god-loving bishops is to assume
authority which has not been given to him from above and has not belonged to him
from the beginning. And if anyone has taken authority by force he is to return it, lest
the canons of the Fathers be ignored. Do not let the delusion of worldly power slip in
under the pretext of divine service, and let us not, without knowing it, little by little
lose the freedom which Christ has given to us by his own blood. And if anyone
procures a document contrary to the things here outlined, even an imperial decree, the
present document declares it to be utterly invalid.

Canon 39 of the Sixth [Ecumenical] Council; Percival, pp. 383–84 [1335]

The 39th canon of the Sixth [Ecumenical] Council designates the Church of
Cyprus as the New Justinianopolis, grants to it the rights of Constantinople, and
[orders] that the bishop of the Hellespont and of Kyzikos is to be ordained by him [the
archbishop of Cyprus]. But whether this canon has ever been applied is rather difficult
to discover.

7. Akindynos, Gregory (ca. 1300–ca. 1348)[*PLP*, fasc. 1, pp. 45–47, no. 495]
Letters, ed. and tr. Angela Constantinides Hero, *CFHB*, Washington, D.C., 1983; by
permission of Dumbarton Oaks Research Library and Collection.

1. From Letter 10 (pp. 38–39), to the philosopher Barlaam [*PLP*, fasc. 2, pp. 26–28,
no. 2284; ΣΒΠΚΙ 97.1] [1341]

Then again, after this, when the Cypriote Lapithes [*PLP*, fasc. 6, p. 141, no.
14479], a man well versed in philosophy, as even you have attested many times,
respectfully put forward in his letters some questions about Aristotelian philosophy
and asked for their solution as if from a teacher, instead of answering him with
consideration and kindness, you filled your letters to him with sneering and you
openly called him quite foolish. Even then I did not commend you, but you did not
heed me at all. And so, other letters came to you from Lapithes, no longer in the same
manner but full of the same kind of things as the letters you would have sent to him.
So evidently what happened to you was that, in the words of the proverb, "The sort of
thing you say [will be said back to you]" [Hom. *Il.* 20.250], just like an echo which
returns the voice it received. For, as it seems, you are not the only one disinclined by
nature to listen in humility to the words of others; they [are also disinclined] to listen
to your words, and so, in fact, am I, the man for whom you have no respect.

2. From Letter 42 (pp. 174–77 and 184–87), to the sage Lapithes [ΣΒΠΚΙ 97.2] [1345]

If we had here such pious swords, our single Divinity would not be cut into a
multitude of divinities, but the men who do this would with justice be cut to pieces by
these swords. If we made use of such rays, we would not be disturbed by the darkness

of impiety, but our light of piety would be undisturbed, detecting every impious mist or not allowing it even to start at all. And I believe that I would not fail to speak the truth if I called you a most skillful captain, one who, if here with us, would not have let this very ship—I mean the Church of Christ—run the risk of being sunk by the tempest of the impious doctrines. For you are a wise man and not one of those who appear to be wise, but [one of those] who are truly so. For your "resolve is not to seem the best, but to be," as someone said, and "you reap the harvest of your mind's deep furrowing, whence your sage counsels spring" [Aesch. *Sept.* 592–94]. And I believe that piety is the goal of a wise man's contemplative pursuits, and the conclusion of all premises, or rather, the conclusion of conclusions themselves and above that. For the sake of this, indeed, he pursues all philosophy, and for this purpose he zealously studies everything. For the first and principal attainment of philosophy, or rather of wisdom, for which you take all sorts of trouble and work systematically, is the correct knowledge of theology, so that without it nobody would be wise, even though he should seem to be most wise.

It seems, my most wise friend, that you realized this from the beginning, and you pursued philosophy in a manner so worthy of philosophy that you are no longer just a philosopher but a wise man, on account of your theological learning and strength as well as your resistance against those who offend theology. A resistance by which you not only roused yourself against the impious, but like a good and admirable general you are rousing to this war both our wise and prominent men here, [men] who are of this nature, indeed, and have sensed the evil—for how could they not?—and especially your hero and mine, the man who is named after victory. But—and they must allow me to say this at least—they have taken a softer stand towards this evil man than they should have done, because they overlooked what they ought least to overlook, since they have learnt to "avoid the profane newfangled talk," because Paul, who wrote and enjoined this, says that "those who indulge in it will stray further and further into godless courses and the infection of their teaching will spread like gangrene" [2 Tim. 2.16–17].

As for me, on the other hand, my most excellent friend, you say that I speak up against this doctrine more feebly than I ought to, and I am wonderfully delighted at your saying so, for I see that I have here an overpowering alliance against the impious. As for me, then, I happened to be an insignificant person, having nothing great or worthy as far as either wisdom or virtue is concerned, and for this reason I am disregarded by people here and deemed unworthy of consideration. This, of course, was actually to my advantage, at least before the appearance of these impious doctrines, for nothing is so suitable or so profitable for a monk as to live in oblivion or so damaging as to be honored by many and acquainted with those in power . . .

I have, therefore, sent to your Wisdom [one] of the discourses against this impiety, which, as I said, I wrote hurriedly and in commentary style. For I have written some others which are more important, but I have had no opportunity to bring them into the open for the reasons that I have already mentioned. But when you receive even this, my most wise friend, you will comprehend from them the whole impiety, for even without them, from some brief examples, you detected it very acutely and exactly as you ought to; and you will fight against this in a manner worthy of your piety and wisdom, and will send me your writings to the disgrace and downfall of this impiety and of its author, but to the glory of God and the victory of piety and to the provocation and envy of your peers who are determined, at least for the moment, to close their eyes to these things, though they hold the same pious beliefs as I do and are able to do more against the impiety due to their superior learning. For, if a few syllables from you produced here such a great change and such a turn in the state of affairs, on the one hand, amongst the pious, just as if they had been filled with Bacchic enthusiasm, and, on the other hand, amongst their opponents, just as if they had been struck by a bolt, what would happen if [you should send] here polemical tracts? What then? Be assured that I have such confidence in you and such regard for you, as the only person able to be justly the protector and defender of piety, that not only do I ask you to prepare for me over there a place of refuge, but I thought of it long ago, in case something adverse or violent should happen to me here as a result of this impiety. You have a right, on account of your own wisdom, to write to me also about my discourses, whether they seem to you to be entirely correct or, in fact, to fall somewhat short of perfection, because I already expect to have you as a law in these matters also, and especially in these, both on account of your wisdom and your good judgment regarding piety.

     As for the letter - for you must know this, too - Palamas [*PLP*, fasc. 9, pp. 108–16, no. 21546] wrote to me fom Thessalonica, because Barlaam [*PLP*, fasc. 2, pp. 26–28, no. 2284] had arrived here first and was accusing him, before the Synod, of Messalianism and of teaching false doctrines; whereas I opposed Barlaam in such away that they would not condemn the man by default, but would wait for him to arrive and to answer the charges. By saying this, then, as well as by criticizing the fact that Barlaam brought the charge of Messalianism against all our monks in general and did not blame Palamas alone, while he himself did not seem to me either to pursue these matters in an altogether correct and irreproachable manner, I restrained the Holy Synod's acute annoyance with Palamas. Wherefore he wrote to me what I have now sent you after refuting them moderately, so that you may judge both of my views, and [decide] whether they diverge from the truth anywhere, and from those of the letter, if they diverge anywhere from error. For not only did you find out correctly that beforehand also declared this first. When you have so judged these doctrines, according to the excellent learning that you possess, you will show everybody what they are by your own arguments, in a manner worthy of your learning and yourself, and you will stop the further progress of the Palamnaian deceit; rather, you will drive it out of the Church once and for all. Though in fact I do not think that you will deem them worthy of vehement arguments, because they are easily exposed to ridicule, just like the ravings of the senile; and they become so of their own accord, just as their authors do. This is how terribly they contradict and fight themselves. But the multitude, of course, is won over even by such [arguments], in the absence of vigorous refutations of the deceit. This is exactly what you have well perceived and declared. If these doctrines are to stop causing damage to most people, there is need of more serious writings against them, as you said, and of famous men who would be their authors. You are such a man, and your writings are such, and among men of this caliber you are the first and foremost.

Note: Messalianism is a doctrine which arose in Mesopotamia in the 4th century and was condemned at the Council of Ephesus in 431; it stressed concentrated and ceaseless prayer as a means of attaining spiritual perfection.

3. From Letter 43 (pp. 186–87), to the philosoper [Nikephoros] Gregoras [*PLP*, fasc 2, pp. 234–37, no. 4443; ΣΒΠΚΙ 97.3] [1345]

I am goading you on to the deeds to which the Cypriote Lapithes urges me to goad you, our common Heracles! It does not befit your wisdom that he should be first and not second to you in command of the fight for piety; for he comes from beyond the frontiers, while you live in the city where insolent acts against piety are being perpetrated, and you have the fame of being the city's foremost scholar. Besides, it is awful for the great City to appear in this respect second to Cyprus on account of you.

4. From Letter 44 (pp. 188–89), to the philosopher [Nikephoros] Gregoras [*PLP*, fasc 2, pp. 234–37, no. 4443; ΣΒΠΚΙ 97.4] [1345]

Since some pious men are here and others elsewhere and all over the inhabited world, while others are in different parts and kingdoms, all of these he [Palamas; *PLP*, fasc. 9, pp. 108–16, no. 21546] denounces as impious, because they have all detected his impiety, and he cannot escape being found out, even at the end of the world; but Antioch has had enough, and so has Cyprus (for I shall not mention us here), and Alexandria and even Rome have had enough of this man's extravagance in impiety

5. Letter 47 (pp. 200–203), to the wise Lapithes [*PLP*, fasc. 6, p. 141, no. 14479; ΣΒΠΚΙ 97.5] [1345]

Thinking that my letter would have been brought to you by an earlier ship, I wrote what was appropriate at the time. But, since it missed that [ship], I am now able to send you what I wrote then that I could not send. I am, in fact, sending you a continuous dialogue of Palamas [*PLP*, fasc. 9, pp. 108–16, no. 21546] containing all his wicked doctrines and all their proofs (of which he believes that he has an abundance) and furnishing adequate proof of his ignorance. This, though he does not make the Barlaamite give to his questions in the dialogue the answers which I would have given, but those indeed that he wants, and what he wants is full of slander and most insolent calumny. Therefore, not only does he falsely accuse me personally in many places, but also the holy Fathers, now introducing as their sayings things that they do not say and then cutting off what they say; by this he is shown to be manifestly impious and is most truly "caught by his own wings," as the proverb goes [Aesch. *Frag.* 139.4 *TGF*]. And what is most foolish, he hoped to escape the detection of wise and good men; or rather, he did not even think, as it seems, that there was any such man in the whole multitude of Church members, and for this reason he treated the matter thus. There are also my comments on these [doctrines], refuting them in an offhand manner, for it was not easy to send discourses, but even in these offhand comments my purpose is accomplished to a degree.

But now to delight me, as well as God and his whole Church, and completely confound the impious faction and their leader, the Devil, with your fire-breathing discourses which they cannot stop from their divinely-directed drive (I know it well), those tried it foolishly. For I am informed that certain members of this faction would not tolerate the great number of rebukes which have already appeared, and especially those which are expected; and they fabricated a multitude of letters, as if indeed by learned men, in defense of Palamas' wicked doctrines, and addressed them to your eminent Wisdom for the purpose of confounding you and checking your drive against them. When I heard this I was delighted, because they are "stirring up trouble" [Gregory of Cyprus 1.22; *CPG*, vol. II, p. 95] for themselves, or rather they are stirring up more the trouble which has already started for them. And they will certainly find out immediately that this is how the matter stands. For obviously my hero cannot be deceived by lies, nor can he fear the threats of pitiable men at all, not even of the most sophisticated; he [cannot] thus betray any part of truth, for, in my opinion, he is the only worthy defender of truth, even if my saying so vexes certain people; for I cannot bear to be a traitor to truth either, whether it be in matters concerning God or else in regard to a man most dear to God, who is such a champion and protector of His piety as He Himself Whom He reveres wishes. And the following fact certainly did not escape this man—for how could it escape a man who is indeed most wise and astute?— namely, that it is impossible for the heretic and impious species not to burst with passion against the rebukes of the wise men, once they are determined to persist hopelessly in the profanities into which they fell foolishly and not accept a cure from anywhere. For this race was always shown to be like this, incurable and in need of wise rebukes in order to return amiably to the state from which they fell. And they rave against those who attempt to bring them back and cure them, and thus they are pitiably confounded.

And this it was necessary to send you also the patriarchal tomes which oppose this foolishness of Palamas and cut both him and his followers off from the Church of Christ on account of his multiform heresy, and I sent to you, at the command of my most divine lord the Ecumenical Patriarch, both the tome of the Ecumenical Patriarch, in which the doctrines of Barlaam are also moderately defined, and the tome of the Patriarch of Antioch. But you, O most excellent and most wise of all men and unshakable pillar of piety, do write to me continuously, teaching me also what in your opinion is right about these matters, but not without the noble offspring for which I am forever hungrily waiting, just as young birds [wait] for their mother, as I wonder when they will come and not only feed those who are thus eagerly waiting hungrily, but will also devour that insidious snake.

6. From Letter 52 (pp. 220–21), to the Metropolitan of Monemvasia [Iakobos Koukounares, *PLP*, fasc. 6, p. 36, no. 13408; ΣΒΠΚΙ 97.6] [1345]

Or, rather, by these letters you made even those discourses shine brighter, for they too are reputed to be the work of the Metropolitan of Monemvasia. By them was the Palamnaian deceit struck at that time, collapsing to its knees. Now, as those same discourses together with these letters—the ones you write to us here and to the pastor of the Corinthians there, somewhere, and to Lapithes in Cyprus—[as these] proceed against it, it is collapsing completely, as is right, because of the assistance of the [episcopal] anointment.

7. Letter 60 (pp. 242–47), to Lapithes [*PLP*, fasc. 6, p. 141, no. 14479; ΣΒΠΚΙ 97.7] [1346]

With difficulty I grasped the sacred anchor of your letter. Why did you neglect me while I was being tossed by the tempest for such a long time, without even encouraging me with a signal light? And this, when you know full well that with you rests and yours is the sum total of my assistance against the enemies of truth, and that with your abundance of wisdom you are to others a fellow-general against heresy! And then, when I received the letter about your discourses, without having in fact yet received the discourses themselves, but being led from expectations back to expectations, you can imagine how despondent I was. When I had hoped to revive, I was further put off with different hopes, and constrained to the utmost, as if by a long and continuous famine or, to put it more moderately, by a long delay of an ardent love.

And the cause of my misfortunes is a host of troubles, which ought rather to be a reason for your discourses to be here with me, fighting bravely like champions. For helmsmen are for storms and generalship has to do with battles. And when a man is far away from both storm and danger and can be of some assistance to those who are in danger without running the same risks as they do, why should he not help them so long as he is able to do so? Just as now your Wisdom can, most safely of all, have the most decisive influence for the Church of God and cause no ordinary harm to its enemies. And if your discourses ought not to fall into the hands of the enemy, they will not. And if they ought to be read by the men who are next in the line of friendship after the most holy Metropolitan Hyakinthos, [of Thessalonike; *PLP*, fasc. 12, p. 55, no. 29453] they will be read by the same. For who is fonder of your discourses and to whom is their success more important? So, according to the circumstances, I shall display your discourses more than anyone else, and then again, if this is not the more advantageous course, I shall not display them. But if my feelings for you and your virtue and wisdom were clear to you, you would not have written these instructions. But, perhaps, you are most wise ***that no one is closer to you than I*** who do not even value my own self above friendship and close association with your Wisdom, nor do I admire Plato more with respect to wisdom, nor the most pious men with respect to piety, nor the most perfect men with respect to perfect character.

But if you have no confidence in me, remember the Cypriots. Is not the divine Bartholomew [*PLP*, fasc. 2, p.21, no. 2225] here, or the admirable Kosmas [*PLP*, fasc. 6, p. 22, no. 13253], or the divine Blasios [*PLP*, fasc. 2, p. 78, no. 2792]? And where is the most learned Leo [*PLP*, fasc. 6, p. 172, no. 14772]? To all of them you are no less than the air they breathe, and they are no less proud of your Wisdom than Gyges [a 7th c. B.C. king of Lydia] was of his ring and no less opposed to the Palamites than anybody else. And so, entrust your discourses to the hands and souls and care of such men with confidence and do not hide the sacred treasure, but give the very "talent to the exchangers" [Matt. 25.27] and—I do not mention what is sad—do not put "the lamp" of the Church "under the meal-tub" of what is merely caution, but place it "on the lamp stand" [Matt. 5.15] which is the Church itself, that it may illuminate it and show up the thieves and show forth the man who kindled the light and praise God for Whom and by Whom it was originally kindled. For the Church prevails, even if jackdaws raise a clamor. "Afraid of the huge falcon" [Soph. *Aj.* 169] they will crouch for fear when you appear with your discourses, for they are crushed even when your appearance is only through your letters, just as the Trojans were by any of Achilles' weapons, if they could not escape detection.

The confidence that I already have in you and the cause of piety persuade me to write this to you, my most wise friend, or rather they compel me. And if I carry it too far, your Excellence would rightly deem me worthy of forgiveness, for the compelling force is clear: love and need for piety, which is in terrible distress.

I wish to write to you also about the most holy Hyakinthos, the Metropolitan of Thessalonica, but I hesitate, because I did not wish to be the messenger bringing such news to you. For that man was a bishop most worthy of the ecclesiastical dignity and standard and a most able helmsman in the storm presently afflicting the Churches of God, as is shown by his short episcopate in Thessalonica. Now he is suddenly snatched away and gone, having left a great sorrow to me and the Thessalonians (for no other bishop of that city is said to have uplifted it so) and a greater joy to the Palamites, whom he cleared out of Thessalonica, exceeding all expectations. But in order not to prolong this letter beyond measure, I cease saying anything more about him and have sent you what he has written and done and what has been written about him, from which you will learn about him more exactly. And Josephos, my good friend and brother and fellow monk, will obviously add the rest.

The very same man will tell you also about the common and immense disaster that befell the Romans, or rather Christians the world over, as regards the famous and inimitable Church of the all-creating Wisdom of God, about which others also will probably write to you. And, though on account of this [disaster] you will have fallen, I believe, into extraordinary mourning—for how can you avoid it?—they will again console you, adducing the fire-breathing zeal and unity of all Christians here and everywhere for the restoration of the fallen church, unless God brings it to naught because of our sins.

I have also sent you 370 of my *Iambics*, an exposition of the pious and ecclesiastical and long-defined confession of the doctrines about God and also of the new and impious and Palamite confession. In addition to these, he is also bringing you other *Iambics* of mine, concerning which I ought not to instruct you; but you will know when you see them, and, being an expert on everything, you will judge whether anything follows closely the poetic rules as far as metrical precision is concerned, and also whether or not I deviate therein from the theological canons or from the other correct notions about other things. You will both judge and instruct me and correct what is wrong.

I gave your greetings to the friends you indicated, and they, in turn, send proper greetings to their marvelous friend. Together with others, and before others, the Princess [Irene-Eulogia Choumnaina Palaiologina] most beloved of God (the daughter of the Keeper of the Inkstand and daughter-in-law of the second emperor of the Palaiologan dynasty, a woman by nature but not in her manner, she who can compete with the most noble men in all that is best and most important and beloved of God) also exceedingly admires you for your wisdom, love of God, magnanimity and exact understanding of all matters. Know that she thinks of you no less than Croesus thought of money or Semiramis of Babylon, or she herself of the purple at one time! For no one surpasses her in her passion for piety, which is being torn asunder, and her sagacity with regard to piety and the divine doctrines of the Church. For this reason, any advocate of piety is in fact as important to her as anyone, even friend and brother and father; and if he should also be wise and excel others in sagacity, he is to her even above the afore-mentioned in rank and dignity. I have made this known to you, because I did not think that you should be ignorant of it.

8. From Letter 74 (pp. 296–97), without addressee [ΣΒΠΚΙ 97.8] [1347/48]

For it is very valuable; especially the letter of the Cypriote philosopher [Lapithes, *PLP*, fasc. 6, p. 141, no. 14479] in which he is shown to be truly a philosopher and a most accomplished champion of piety. More than anyone else he attacks from abroad the Palamnaian disease and expresses his indignation and exclaims in his letter "O what impiety" at the man who introduces a multitude of unequal divinities and at the fact that none of the men here cares to refute these doctrines with serious writings; those who appear to be our most capable men of letters keep quiet, while this doctrine feeds upon Christ's flock like poison; and one man alone—namely myself—took up the divine zeal to resist this doctrine well and correctly, but in a manner that is milder, as he says, than is required for resistance to such writings. I rejoiced indeed at this remark, more so than if he had said that I carried the war to the extreme. And yet this is the remark of a man who does not know everything about me, for he would not have thought that I oppose this doctrine mildly; I who risked even my blood for the sake of the correct and pious [doctrines]. But I am most grateful for this remark to Lapithes (for this is the philosopher's name), because he put to shame by this remark those who accuse me of contentiousness because of this [resistance]. These men, he says, should not take the attitude with regard to piety nor should they neglect the Church when it is being destroyed. For with Christians all other matters are secondary to this one, and especially when the perpetrator of impiety is extremely ignorant and unacquainted with even the first principles of philosophy, not knowing what knowledge is and how it is naturally formed, as the philosopher himself testifies that he learned from Palamas' very writings.

It is obviously necessary that learned and pious men over there see this letter also and admire the man' learning and piety and his soundness and vigor in each of these [qualities], as well as his struggle for piety in which he not only breathes fire against the impious, but also encourages and admirably organizes for the war against them those men here who are distinguished for their literary prowess. Such indeed is a soul deeply penetrated by learning and piety! For this reason it is surely necessary that your learned men both see and admire this [letter].
Note: On Hesychasm on Cyprus, specifically on Agathangelos, Nikephoros Gregoras, and Akindynos, see Kyrres.

8. Gregoras, Nikephoros (ca. 1290/91 or 1293/94–1358/61)
[*PLP*, fasc. 2, pp. 234–37, no. 4443; *BBKL*, vol. VI, cols. 812–15]
Historia Rhomaike

1. Ed. Schopen 1829, vol. I, p. 194; ed. Migne, *PG* 148, cols. 349–50; Ger. tr. van Dieten, vol. I, p. 164 [ΣΒΠΚΙ 98.1] [1294]

They [Theodore Metochites and John Glykys] boarded swift ships and sailed first to Cyprus. For word had recently reached the emperor from there about such a marriage [between Michael IX and a Lusignan princess]. But when they had spent considerable time there the proposals of the Cypriot side did not meet their expectations. So they left and sailed to Aigai; this is a city situated on the sea, in the plain of Cilicia on the Gulf of Issos.

2. Ed. Schopen 1829, vol. II, p. 689; ed. Migne, *PG* 148, cols. 917–20; Ger. tr. van Dieten, vol. III, p. 110 [ΣΒΠΚΙ 98.2] [1343]

The various Latin states had recently formed an alliance and moved against the Persian [Arab] ships, which were practicing piracy and robbery and plundering the Latins' freight ships and triremes; these carry merchant goods as they sail up and down over the whole sea for trade. The number of the ships mentioned came to 27; they were from Cyprus, Rhodes, Salamis, and Venice, as well as from the Pope and Genoa.

3. Ed. Schopen 1829, vol. II, pp. 786–87; ed. Migne, *PG* 148, cols. 1033–34; Ger. tr. van Dieten, vol. III, p. 169 [ΣΒΠΚΙ 98.3] [1347]

What happened after this can be learned more fully from others who have recorded it: how they were all dispersed, hither and thither, and how they were cast out with their free speech and their accusations; and how from everywhere by sea and by land many letters came to Byzantium from the Orthodox; these letters were full of holy zeal and passed a clear anathema on Palamas and on Isidore with him and on all of the same persuasion; these letters came from bishops and elders in Antioch, Alexandria, and Trebizond, and from the Cypriots and the Rhodians and their Orthodox neighbors; and from the Mysians [in NW Asia Minor] and the Triballians [in the Balkans] and all those who by long tradition have taken it upon themselves to abide by the rules of the holy fathers and not to accept any innovation, not even if an angel should bring it from heaven.

4. Ed. Schopen 1829, vol. II, p. 796; ed. Migne, *PG* 148, cols. 1043–46; Ger. tr. van Dieten, vol. III, p. 174 [ΣΒΠΚΙ 98.4]

[In Thessalonike] a group of so-called Zealots occupied the first rank before all others; and the city did not imitate any of the [known] forms of government. For neither was it an aristocratic form of government, such as Lycurgus made the Spartans of old follow; nor was it a democratic one, such as the first constitution of the Athenians, which Cleisthenes created by changing from a system of four tribes to one of ten. And it was not like the government which Zaleucus gave to the people of Locri Epizephyrii [7th c. B.C.], nor like the one which Charondas of Catana set up in Sicily [6th c. B.C.]. Nor was it of the newer kind, an amalgam of two or more forms, such as the government of the Cypriots or the one which the people in ancient Rome are said to have set up when they rose up against the consuls [2nd c. B.C].

5. Ed. Schopen 1829, vol. II, pp. 797–98; ed. Migne, *PG* 148, cols. 1045–48; Ger. tr. van Dieten, vol. III, p. 175 [ΣΒΠΚΙ 98.5] [1347–1348]

At this time a ruinous plague befell the people. It began with the Scythians at the Maeotis [the sea of Azov] and the mouth of the Tanais [the Don] . . . Returning the following year, it hit also the islands of the Aegean. Then it hit also the Rhodians, likewise the Cypriots, and the inhabitants of the other islands.

6. Ed. Schopen 1829, vol. III, pp. 27–39; ed. Migne, *PG* 149, cols. 17–28; Ger.tr. van Dieten, vol. V, forthcoming 2002 [ΣΒΠΚΙ 98.6]

When we had spent six years [1342–1347] in these places we departed from Cilicia with full sails and in two days reached Cyprus, where I had decided to spend considerable [reading πολύν, not πόλιν] time. The island offers many advantages, among them a well-ordered and hospitable political system and above all the company of that wise man, I mean George Lapithes [*PLP*, fasc. 6, p. 141, no. 14479]. I did not meet him immediately after debarking from the ship on that same day; that was because he did not have his home nearby but two days away from the harbor at which we had then landed. Cyprus is an island larger than Rhodes, and at the same time it is not comparable in form but oblong. In its center rises a mountain the top of which attains a great height [6404 ft.] and which is called Olympus. From it flow the headwaters of three rivers, the greatest of which, called Lapithos [now the Pedieos], on its way flows through and around the city of Leukosia [Nikosia] before emptying into the sea towards the north [actually turning east and emptying into the sea between Salamis and Famagusta]. Along the banks of this river Lapithes had his home, and his cognomen is actually derived from the name of the river. Anyone might know at once, before seeing the man himself, just from the conspicuousness and size of his buildings and stables, that he is not one of the low-born and common people, but one of the most renowned and prominent men on the island. And one would know this even more from his manner and general distinction of his life. For festivals and sacred assemblies and generous support of the needy are the ornaments of this house. He paid the greatest attention to Christian captives, who were frequently led about here, and selflessly gave the greatest share towards their freedom, while at the same time encouraging others in the study of the Holy Scriptures. He put the greatest effort of all into teaching Christians gathered in their holy churches the laws of piety in general and especially to give much thought to the care of the needy. And thus, because of his efforts the entire island became a place where compassion and faith are practiced and especially a place of freedom for prisoners.

There are in these parts also the estate and the residence of the king [Hugh IV, 1324–1359] and the most splendid buildings, while the climate in this part of the island is most pleasant and the location very convenient. For this reason and because he was nearby, George Lapithes frequently called upon the king and he very much enjoyed the king's respect and honor because of his distinction in general and especially because he possessed more wisdom than others. The king himself possessed considerable knowledge of the philosophy of the Latins and therefore always had many wise men of the Latins about him, but he loved even more the humanity and the company of George [Lapithes]. "Rulers become wise," he said, "in the company of the wise." Having Lapithes about him, he had decided to have the wisdom of both the Greeks and the Latins at the same time, and Lapithes was equally well versed in the wisdom and the language of both nations. Therefore the king often took pleasure in hearing Lapithes disputing with the wise men of the Latins, assailing them with his irrefutable arguments, and defeating them, especially when the contest was about the religious teachings of the Fathers. For then a great stream of proofs from the Holy Scriptures flowed against them and made them appear like fish, utterly speechless. And at times, when the king was roused to anger by these disputations, Lapithes calmed him with the eloquence of his words and the irrefutable demonstrations of the truth. By such means he eloquently restrained the king's anger and fittingly returned him to good cheer. To put the case briefly: among all who had at least some understanding of Greek learning or some familiarity with Latin philosophy there was no one who did not declare him easily the winner in any contest of wits. I had known this man's reputation even before leaving here. I had not only on so many occasions read the letters which he sent to you from there in response to yours and your friendship; I had also heard words of high praise from the mouths of all those who frequently came from there. And yet my admiration was kept within certain bounds. But now, that I have visited Cyprus and have lodged with this man, who has, because of you, shown me hospitality with exceedingly great care, I have come to know him and have experienced him more closely. With my very ears [I have heard] and my very eyes I have seen, so to speak, his fame living and breathing and have secured it for myself; I have received manifest pledges of the truth, and the truth has almost disproved his fame and has clearly shown it to be far from what is due.

But I have especially admired Lapithes' feeling and [sincere] friendship for you [i.e. Agathangelos, Gregoras' student and friend; *PLP*, fasc. 1, pp. 5–6, no. 67]. For he handled your writings and books with such great love that I am unable adequately to describe it. He always perused as many of them as time would permit, and he was always possessed of great pleasure, and his outer bearing was an indication of the great inner excitement of his soul. He was as if possessed by joy, applauded individual points, and, so to speak, forgot where in the world he was. At times he seemed to be conversing with you, to be in your very presence, and to hear you expounding, whatever it might be, with your own tongue; this was especially so when he went to hold in his hands that dialog which you held because of Barlaam of Calabria [*PLP*, fasc. 2, pp. 26–28, no. 2284]. He is seeking especially not only to admire your writings by himself, but also, as he converses with the Latins, to praise and admire you verbally; both in the presence of the king and wherever and whenever he might happen to be engaged in conversation and dialog. So it is that he has attached nearly all of Cyprus to your praise and has turned [the people] into your heralds before they have seen anything of you. So much did he desire to see you and to be with you and so much was he occupied with such thoughts night and day that he prayed that neither he nor you should die before he had come to Constantinople. For a long time he has wanted and cared for this, only for the sake of seeing you and being with you. His sentiments towards you are entirely natural and sincere and nothing of an artificial nature has ever been hidden in the letters which he continues to send to you and which are full of your praises.

He also brought me the astronomy books which you yourself had sent to him at various and sundry times. I was amazed to see how, to support his efforts, *you* had condensed [van Dieten: συνέκλειες] so many and such difficult theories on this subject in a few summaries. He had not neglected the *Apotelesmatica* or *Tetrabiblos* of Ptolemy [of Alexandria, 2nd c. A.D.], but had read it most carefully as well as whatever other writings on the subject there are by those who preceded or followed Ptolemy, and all that has been written by the Chaldeans and Persians of old. And all things which leap across the limits set by the laws of piety and step across the borders, those he shook off and spat out as being useless to those who wish to be pious. But all things which in a reasonable way pertain to the origins of things, these he most happily made his own. And this he did so that he might not be refuted by the Latins there, who boast about such things, or by the king himself; for the Latins devote considerable effort to this part of learning. This they do because the Arabs of Egypt are nearby and often travel across the sea to the king for the sake of stimulating conversation and, at the same time, because of their ambition. Among these Arabs ambition goes hand-in-hand with their great desire to show off, and they spend an entire lifetime [in seeing] if by chance any sign of the ancient knowledge of the Chaldaeans has been preserved. They say this: it has been ordained by the Creator that all things which are subject to a beginning and an end are governed and shaped by the nature and the movement of the heavenly bodies; and the stream of physical substance is ruled and regulated, so to speak, by the constellations of these bodies and their relationship to things on earth. Therefore it is necessary to stress that one cannot be content with knowing only one but not the other. Indeed anyone not willing to join the practical to the theoretical or vice versa would step into a blind alley. Since philosophy is seen from these two perspectives, any man to whom it does not occur that he must pursue the mysteries of philosophy in both forms would hardly understand the reasons for things and would fall far short from being called wise.

But enough of this. Either because he mostly had the time, or else because for your sake he deemed it better than leisure to be of service to me, he [Lapithes] went with me as a guide and showed me all the things on the island which are worth seeing. This included all that went on in the theaters, market places, and law courts. [He pointed out] that in the minting of coinage there had been stability at all times and no change whatsoever and how in weights and measures and scales all manner of wares are sold and bought not as each seller might want but as the ancient ordinances of the state provide; not as the greed of the more affluent people wants it for more gain, but as the salvific laws of the old order ordain it for all time. Neither a man of greater wealth nor one who happens to be of advanced age would be able there, under such conditions, to take advantage of those who might be disadvantaged in either regard. For anyone who would dare in any way whatsoever to cheat them would quickly lose, if not his head, those limbs of his body which the laws of the state prescribe as a recompense for the offense. This, if it is preserved, he assured me, is what unifies and binds states, cities, continents, and islands, both in private and in public affairs. But if it is overthrown, it in turn, in its sharp decline, takes along, in both public and private affairs, whatever goes on in violation of the laws in cities and states. A firm and lasting foundation can, by its very nature, not co-exist with the lawless, but in a very short time the whole fabric of society is shaken and dissolved, like the harmony [of an instrument] when the strings are broken. When the body politic as a whole is sound, then by obvious necessity the parts do well also, since they model themselves after the whole. Conversely, when the whole is ill, the parts are ill with it; for they imitate the prototype and use the governance and condition of the state as a sure guaranty of their own wickedness.

The Lord, since he is righteous and, naturally, loves righteousness, raises those nations which do not have a law, but by nature do the things of the law; so the holy apostle says [Rom. 2.14]. But he hates those who have chosen and promised to live according to the commandments and laws of righteousness but then by their deeds show their promises to be but lies and shake off every standard and norm of righteousness. But a man who turns away from righteousness, chooses instead the lot of unrighteousness, has no respect for God's laws, and sets himself above every human fate, such a man has willingly and clearly separated himself from God, who sits on the throne of righteousness, and has cast his lot with the devil. Therefore, in this area, where such evils are fostered, the worse elements gain the advantage, and the better elements are at a disadvantage. In such a place there is a veritable desert, devoid of any good things, and the devil really triumphs over piety itself, all the time encouraging his followers to deny it. This is what has happened in the state of the Byzantines. Hating the truth and a just political order but welcoming injustice and falsehood, it has with both hands opened its own gates to impiety. And since the devil needs a body and a suitable tool for his purposes he has found Palamas [*PLP*, fasc. 9, pp. 108–16, no. 21546], a little man, who, as I have heard and learned more fully from his own writings, is quite insignificant except that he is vain and for this reason espouses false doctrines, knowing nothing further that is sound. And the devil persuaded those in power to make an alliance with this man. To tell the story briefly, whatever impure and spurious teachings have by stealth at various times crept into the churches of God, all these he gathered at this one time, and among the churches of Christ he scattered his evil seed, which was to bear rich fruit. For this wretched man not only taught polytheism, but even added atheism, and at the same time Arianism, iconoclasm, and, simply speaking, the denial of the incarnation of the Son and the Word of God. What need is there to give a detailed account when it is possible to examine and to disprove it all from the books of the holy Fathers? Such thoughts the wise and God-loving man presented to me, and at times he brought out books which he himself in a labor of love has gathered from all of Holy Scripture and has given as weapons to those people there who choose to observe piety; and also books which other learned and orthodox men who live nearby have produced, clearly speaking out against the false teachings of Palamas.

In the meantime word came to the Cypriots that the emperor Kantakouzenos had secretly at night entered Byzantium and had seized sole rule, and this through the active cooperation and preparations of Palamas [February 1347]. First Kantakouzenos had sworn awful oaths and had assured Palamas that he would confirm and ratify the latter's polytheism and all the impure and newfangled notions which had entered the churches of God; and, which is to say the same thing, he had sworn by [the very] God, whom he promised to deny. All this very much upset my wise friend George Lapithes, not so much that Kantakouzenos had seized the emperorship, but that he had committed himself by such oaths and had become bound to the impieties of Palamas. Thus he was disappointed in those noble hopes which had given pleasure to his soul for so long; he was distressed, he was troubled, and all manner of disturbance and perplexity possessed his soul. He had hoped to travel with me on my return from Cyprus as far as Byzantium, for the sake of seeing you and being with you, as we have previously mentioned, because of his desire for more wisdom; additionally, perhaps, because he wanted to see the extraordinary things which the city of Byzantium possesses more than other cities. But now, when he saw that in a moment just the opposite had prevailed, he was very sad; and he wept because piety had so obviously fallen into acute danger in the inscrutable ways of God, who had allowed it to happen. He also wept because he suspected that you were dead, knowing of your fiery zeal in the service of God and what resistance on behalf of the teachings of the fathers you will show until your death.

What need is there to describe in detail all the things which I have seen on this island in more than two years and all the commodities which can be found in its cities, harbors, and other places? There are other, more important things which drive me on. Therefore I shall let these things go and mention my departure. Right after the summer solstice, when I was about to depart, the good George [Lapithes] accompanied me to the harbor, weeping and his heart bursting, so to speak, over my departure. And thus, when the ship was taking us on, set its sails, and with a favorable wind sailed out onto the open sea, he stood for a long time watching me and shedding many tears. He did so until slowly we lost sight of land as the distance increased. After a good voyage we reached Crete on the ninth day; this is an island well populated and much larger than Cyprus, but like Cyprus oblong in shape.

7. Ed. Schopen 1829, vol. III, pp. 182–83; ed. Migne, *PG* 149, cols. 157–58; Ger. tr. van Dieten, vol. V, forthcoming [ΣΒΠΚΙ 98.7] [1341–1347]

Now he [Gregory, Patriarch of Alexandria, *PLP*, fasc. 2, p. 249, no. 4588] was sent by the governor of Egypt and all of Arabia on an embassy to the Roman emperor. But when he had departed and had learned that Roman affairs were in a state of confusion and sedition because of the imperial succession, he decided to put off his journey until he should find out more clearly which of the contending emperors [John V Palaiologos and John VI Kantakouzenos] had secured power, lest the embassy might appear foolish and laughable to him. Therefore, having departed from Egypt, he landed in Cyprus and from there sailed to Crete; he spent a lot of time on both islands because the Romans' dispute about the emperorship had not been concluded.

9. Gregoras, Nikephoros (ca. 1290/91 or 1293/94–1358/61)
[*PLP*, fasc. 2, pp. 234–37, no. 4443]
Letter to King Hugh IV [1324–1359]; ed. P. A. M. Leone, *Byzantion* 51 (1981) 220–24; ed. Migne, *PG* 145, cols. 397–404 (attribution to Theodoulos Monachos alias Thomas Magister) [ΣΒΠΚΙ 99]

Nikephoros Gregoras to the king of Cyprus [Hugh IV, 1324–1359]

1. Most high, renowned, noble, and illustrious great king of Cyprus: Most people who come to this great city [Constantinople], if they have traveled through many countries, cities, islands, and continents, are anxious to talk about their travels to anyone whom they might meet by day or by night. This is especially true of those who by nature have sufficient language skills to reveal the innermost thoughts of their mind; such people become even better speakers than they would otherwise be when they sing your praises and release all restraints on their tongues. Often they are asked by their listeners why it is that those who by nature are fond of sightseeing and have passed through many places and have visited the cities and learned the minds of many men [Hom. *Od.* 1.3] prefer to praise the state of Cyprus, your justice, and your many fine qualities. Then they answer by citing a well-known wise saying of Aristotle; he, when he was asked why we spend more time in the company of those who are attractive, answered that this was the question of a blind man [D. L. 5.20]. Just so these travelers, when they are asked by someone why they dwell so much on your praises and consider

stories of you the sweetest delight, answer that this is the question of a deaf person. These people, as already mentioned, often and emphatically hold forth about your good qualities, and all listen and are amazed. If there be anyone who has not heard he would be, people say, completely deaf from birth and deprived of the best of his senses. There are many seas and many oceans and in them there are many islands, some large, some small, and some of medium size; but neither from the Indian Ocean, nor from that which is beyond the Atlas Mountains, nor from that which is bounded by the Pillars of Heracles has any report come to us bringing fame comparable in greatness or kind to that which your Cyprus brings. Neither [from] the so-called Golden Chersonesos, nor [from] Thule, foremost in the northern regions of the world, nor [from] any of the British Isles. And not [from] those who live in the southern parts, Indians and Aethiopians, or on Taprobane [Salike, Sri Lanka, or Ceylon], astonishing by its size. Nor [from] the Caspian Sea, which is next to the Hyrcanian tribes. And not [from] that region which begins at Cadiz and the Pillars of Heracles and stretches all the way to the Hyperboreans in the North, but ends at your Cyprus, or rather begins at Cyprus and ends at the Pillars of Heracles: for that would be the better way of putting it. There are two end points to this sea which is civilized and which we claim as ours; in front of one lies renowned and wonderful Cyprus, while the other is marked by the Pillars of Heracles. In my judgment the sea which flows around Cyprus takes precedence and the whole body of water flows from there as far as the pillars of Heracles and ends there, rather than the other way around. And I declare that this rule and law consequently applies to both end points and that the beginning of this sea of ours is established at Cyprus, not at the Pillars of Heracles. And through the ages all men have seen that the heat of the sun, which nourishes all things and provides daylight to the whole world, begins there. From that area in which Cyprus was planted by God and from these parts we see the light of the condescension of our spiritual sun and of God, our Savior, and the mystery of gladness to the whole world. Thus, to the extent that the regions around the Pillars of Heracles are dark, without light, and wild, to that same extent the regions around Cyprus are civilized, gentle, and filled with light. And they delight not only our bodies but also our very souls, which spiritually see God the Word, who for us was incarnated, suffered, and rose again. To summarize: just as truth is better than falsehood, so the East and Cyprus excel the West. If all the myths, which are redolent with falsehood, provoke laughter, then certainly all the exploits of Heracles, which are based on myth and fiction, provoke much laughter and invite every kind of joke. Therefore, how fitting would it be for falsehood to rule over truth and for laughable things to govern those which are praised and deemed blessed? Thus, in every way and quite clearly, your Cyprus deserves to be given the first prize.

2. And these advantages seem to have been granted to the island of Cyprus directly by God long ago. Who would be able to describe adequately the things which have been added afterwards through you and because of you, the best possible servant God could have? And who, having given an inadequate account, would not be ashamed, when the proof is right before his eyes? You have torn out the foundations of all injustice from the island, casting it out everywhere, and allotting it to utter disappearance. In its stead you have brought in justice, and established it firmly. For justice is the foremost of all virtues and the root and foundation of good order; it is an ornament of states and gives harmony to all human affairs . . . Not only have you graced with words of virtue that

which is august, the scales of justice and the accuracy of such rules, but you have strengthened the good order of your words with deeds. And you have appointed judges, choosing the very best men, to be guardians and champions of economic justice and of equality before the law, lest that which is proper might secretly slip away. Market supervisors, price watchers, and judges are continually patrolling the markets and the entire island, supervisors of all transactions and tireless guardians of justice. [These are] officers and governors, maintaining good order, not only in public affairs, but also in the people's manners, speech, and behavior, so that the bad may disappear and vanish, all that partakes of the temerity of falsehood or of perjury, and so that the good may prosper and flourish. Dignified conduct, propriety of speech, and a becoming adherence to truth are found everywhere on the island, just as flowers in the fields and warm winds in the summer, clearly delighting mind, speech, and senses. I believe that Plato, if he were alive, would imitate you and would love your political system more than the one which he established in antiquity; and, giving up his frequent trips to Sicily, he would prefer to come to Cyprus for your sake and for the sake of your political and legal system.

3. Such are the virtues of this island, and you are the reason; and so is your righteousness, which has become the unshakeable base, groundwork, and foundation of a beautiful house with excellent harmony and rule. For this has been built with and upon such good principles, and the greatest of these is love, which pervades the entire structure; just as the color of gold improves upon and gives joy to body and soul, or rather, just as a certain bond embraces and ties together the whole assembly of good qualities which I have mentioned. For without love no good thing is good. This is clearly the reason for your openness to strangers and, above all, for your liberating prisoners. How many are wandering about and are led about everywhere in the world and are experiencing the evils of being prisoners! But when they come to your Cyprus—and those who do come here are those upon whom God casts a kinder eye— at once they see a change in their lives and a release from their misfortune; just as Christ, working miracles, cleansed the lepers, so that, in a way which defies reason, hopelessness becomes the mother of confidence and ill fortune the source of good fortune. Many are the evils which attend the condition of being a prisoner, and all men curse them and pray to escape them. All these evils have been brought to an end for those who have experienced your island and have turned their mind to your good deeds. For one cannot say that a chance circumstance has brought them there or that time, bringing forth what was hidden [Soph. *Aj.* 647]. has shown something new to them in their wretched condition. But divine providence above, being favorably and kindly disposed toward them, has brought them under your jurisdiction. And so the awful condition of being a prisoner has turned into the beginning of good cheer for them and into a thing that easily persuades them not at all to curse, but even to thank those who took them into captivity in the first place. Thus you have amazed all with your good report and easily lead them to love you, even from afar, men who love goodness and virtue and who are learned and wise. This happens when they listen to those who constantly come here from there and talk about such things and even more; especially that just from seeing you and from the kindness of your countenance there comes, as if by magic, a certain unspeakable joy to the souls of those who see you, similar to what we feel when we see the heavenly brightness of the rays of the sun.

Note: This panegyric is attributed to Theodoulos Monachos, alias Thomas Magister, by Krumbacher, vol. I, p. 550, and by Hill, vol. II, p. 306. The latter rightly describes it as "merely a rhetorical exercise, extolling in vague generalities the natural excellences of Cyprus and the virtues of its ruler, and inspired, not improbably, by hopes of a reward for the flatterer." For the attribution to Nikephoros Gregoras see Hunger 1978, vol. I, p. 130.

10. Gregoras, Nikephoros (ca. 1290/91 or 1293/94–1358/61)
[*PLP*, fasc. 2, pp. 234–37, no. 4443] [1354]

1. From Letter 87, ed. Leone, vol. II, p. 236 [ΣΒΠΚΙ 100.1]

I would like to describe heroic deeds and send any such accounts, and, to speak frankly, whatever occurs to me to write, to various people about various people; and especially [I like to write] about the king of Cyprus and the kind and number of good things which he has brought to the island during his reign: among other things he has established a well-ordered political system and a standard of justice, constantly frees prisoners and releases captives, forgives debts, and cares for those who have been wronged. And he has done all the things which make for true excellence and have made the island more renowned, and many other things besides. These I have assembled and included in my books on Byzantine History, setting them up as the best model of goodness for those in authority.

2. From Letter 44, to Athanasios Lepentrenos [*PLP*, fasc. 6, p. 169, no. 14743] on Cyprus, ed. Leone, vol. II, pp. 152–56; ed. and Fr. tr. Guilland, pp. 252–59, no. 156 [ΣΒΠΚΙ 100.2] [1350–1355]

You know the Illyrian [Agathangelos, *PLP*, fasc.1, pp. 5–6, no. 67], who during his visit to Cyprus stayed with you and enjoyed your hospitality as proper as possible. He is the one who conceived a strong desire to see the holy places of Palestine and proceeded in haste, being a lover, so to speak, of beautiful things across the seas. He visited Egypt and Babylon [in Egypt, not Mesopotamia], bypassing Canopus, Pelusium, and the other mouths by which the Nile empties into the sea there, and then came to Palestine. Leaving there, having satisfied his desire as much as possible, he skirted Syria Coele and Phoenicia and came to Cyprus, already thinking of his return. And when, by good fortune, he had met you and, as we mentioned, had enjoyed your kind attention, he at last returned to us; and he was full of stories about you and all the other numerous and various things which he had explored with his own eyes. And he has kindled in us a desire for a close friendship with you, has persuaded us to write, and promises that we will receive a response . . .

Here is the point: Are there still any traces of the former splendor of the Hellenes in Athens, in Thebes, or on the Peloponnesus? Why are Sparta, Crete, and Carthage held in such esteem by scholars of former times while Cyprus is not? Furthermore, is Lycurgus still giving laws to the Spartans, Zaleucus to the people of Locri Epizephyrii, Charondas of Catana to the people of Sicily, or Numa Pompilius to the residents of Rome? [cf. **8**.6]

11. Lepentrenos, Athanasios (ca. 1350) [*PLP*, fasc 6, p. 169, no. 14743]
From Letter 18, to Nikephoros Gregoras, ed. Leone, vol. II, pp. 414–16; ed. and Fr. tr.
Guilland, pp. 284–89, no. XXI [ΣΒΠΚΙ 101] [1350–1355]

Athanasios Lepentrenos from Cyprus to Gregoras:

We are indebted to your kindness on two accounts: First, because you have initiated our friendship when we had given you no reason to do so; and then because you cheer us with the bright hope that you will always maintain it in sincerity . . .

And now our beautiful capital, Phoenicia, Coele Syria, and any district inhabited by Greeks will clearly be amazed - and I will not be silent - at your wonderful letter. Anyone judging it would rightly pronounce it a collection of all manner of wisdom, like a standard that has been set up and proclaims its father, more than a thousand mouths. Neither will most of the barbarians, at least those who have had some schooling, be without a part in this beautiful feast; for there are Cypriots who are competent in three languages and can translate Greek into the language of the Syrians and of the Italians. So be it.

You are by nature fond of learning, and this is a natural attribute of one who excels in wisdom. It prompts you to examine not only the things here but all other things of which we have been eyewitnesses. Let me tell you then, my friend, that it is possible, if one believes the prescriptions of the medical profession, to charge Cyprus with having a climate which is disagreeable and detrimental to the health of most visitors, if they live carelessly. I fear that I might seem to offend Fate, which looks upon this island so kindly. And I think that even the zodiac, which completes its own movement in the regular cycles of the years, is strangely inclined toward the south, exposed to the north, one might say.

And now, my good friend, Aphrodite is far removed from the Cypriot people, who were once devoted to her, as the myths of the Greeks might tell you. But Hermes goes about everywhere, as does Athena, and any other god who takes an interest in reason and wit. Therefore you might see people coming here from every land and every sea, like pieces of iron to a magnet. These, in short, are the qualities of this island. And it would be right if she were found worthy of the greatest fame not only by the wise men of old, but by our contemporaries.

The Athenians, the Thebans, and those who live on the island of Pelops, once celebrated by many poets and historians, have sunk from their former blessed condition into barbarism. And you might see those who once refused to yield even a little of their land or their sea to the Great Kings of the Persians reduced to the worst of servitude. The Carians you might call fortunate by comparison. As for Lycurgus, Charondas [of Catana], and Zaleucus [of Locri Epizephyrii], and other ancient lawgivers, those to whom they gave their laws do not even know of their existence.

It remains to discuss the third point, the arrogance of the Latins. But I must refrain from [excessive] length and have [already] gone beyond the limits of a letter; I shall do what is necessary. Take care of yourself, my wonderful friend. You are the [only] treasure of learning that is left in Byzantium. Do not tire of being our friend and of sending us your noble letters as tokens of your friendship, giving us at the same time pleasure and an incentive to do likewise, even if we should seem to run on foot next to a Lydian messenger [proverb].

12. John VI Kantakouzenos (ca. 1295–1383, emperor 1347–1354)
[*PLP*, fasc. 5, pp. 94–96, no. 10973]

1. *Historia* 3.31; ed. and Latin tr. Schopen 1828, vol. II, pp. 190–91; ed. Migne, *PG* 153, cols. 881–82 [ΣΒΠΚΙ 102.1] [1341]

Also the emperor sent an embassy to the eparch Monomachos [*PLP*, fasc. 8, p. 30, no. 19306], who was the governor of Thessaly, to the protostrator Synadenos [*PLP*, fasc. 11, pp. 136–37, no. 27120], who was the governor of Thessalonike, and to Sir Guy de Lusignan, who was the cousin of the emperor Andronikos [III, 1328–1341], the son of the king of Cyprus, [the usurper Amaury de Lusignan, 1306–1310], and governor of Pherae [more correctly, Serres in Macedonia] himself. The latter had a daughter [Isabella, also known as Margaret or Mary], whom the grand domestic of that time [John Kantakouzenos] had betrothed to his son Manuel while the emperor Andronikos was still alive.

2. *Historia* 4.24; ed. and Latin tr. Schopen 1828, vol. III, p. 171; ed. Migne, *PG* 154, cols. 185–86 [ΣΒΠΚΙ 102.2] [1351]

But Nikephoros Gregoras did not desist [from speaking out], neither earlier nor later, but he wrote to his associates in Trebizond and accused the Byzantine church of having abandoned the correct doctrines and boldly taught the need of secession from it as it had become diseased. And then he wrote also to his friends on Cyprus, especially to a certain George Lapithes. Writing to the latter he not only accused the church in general but also its leaders individually.

13. John VI Kantakouzenos (ca. 1295–1383, emperor 1347–1354)
Letter to Bishop John of Karpasia [*PLP*, fasc. 4, p. 145, no. 8448]; ed. Jean Darrouzès, Κυπριακαί Σπουδαί 20 (1956) 60 [ΣΒΠΚΙ 103] [post 1355]

To the Lord John, god-loving Bishop (ἐπίσκοπος) of Karpasia and Bishop (πρόεδρος) of Constantia and Ammochostos [Famagusta]. Even if My Highness ordinarily had nothing to write . . .

And these things My Highness has written to Your Holiness so that you yourself and all the Christians there might know the slanders of these men of ill fame. I was going to write about these matters in greater detail. But because I have been deposed [?] and in exile from Constantinople, as you will learn from the man who brings you this message, I have written nothing further about this. Write to me then, so that I may know that the present message has safely reached you, and then My Highness will write to Your Holiness more fully and more clearly, and from that you will understand the evil fame and impiety of these men.

John Kantakouzenos, faithful king [βασιλεύς] in Christ the God and emperor [αυτοκράτωρ] of the Romans, whose name has been changed by God and the designs of the monks to Joasaph the monk.

Note: The evil men referred to are the opponents of Hesychasm, of which John Kantakouzenos was a supporter. On Kantakouzenos see Weiss.

14. *Acta Patriarchatus Constantinopolitani*

1. Ed. MM, vol. I, p. 400, no. 175.I; ed. Darrouzès, pp. 342–43 [ΣΒΠΚΙ 104.1]
Cyril, metropolitan of Side [*PLP*, fasc. 6, p. 96 no. 14044], writes from Cyprus, where he had stopped on his way to Constantinople. [ca. 1360]

A letter has come to us from our divinely guarded and holy emperor [John V Palaiologos], ordering us to come finally and at once to the royal city, I mean Constantinople. This is our plan: if the Lord God will grant us health, peace on the way, and calm seas, we anxiously plan to leave the island of Cyprus during the month of February. Pray to God on our behalf and ask that we might be granted to accomplish such a long journey. But I, having been blessed by God, certainly owe it to you to speak to you words to the benefit and salvation of your soul. Strive mightily, above all, for the good and the salvation of your soul, so that you might inherit the blessings of Jerusalem above, which no eye has seen, which no ear has heard, and which have not entered upon the hearts of men [1 Cor. 2.9], but which God has prepared for those who love him. But because of the love of our Lord Jesus Christ see to it as much as you can that you keep the purity of your piety and of your faith, which you have received, handed down to you from your fathers. For the present time has become utterly corrupt, not the time itself, but the people of this time: wicked, devilish, murderous, haters of mankind, or rather, to speak the truth, haters of Christ, atheists, faithless, and partakers of all manner of evil. Consider the wolves in sheep's clothing, of whom the present time nourishes and harbors many. You should also know that letters against the godless and polytheistic Palamites have been sent from Constantinople to the patriarchs of Antioch, Alexandria, and Jerusalem, and also here to Cyprus; these letters were carried by the Christians who are here.

2. Ed. MM, vol. I, pp. 405–407, no. 176.II; ed. Darrouzès, pp. 341–43, no. 2413 [ΣΒΠΚΙ 104.2]
To [Cyril,] the most holy and honorable metropolitan of Side: [post 1360]

The letter which you wrote by your own hand and sent from Cyprus to the chartophylax of the holy metropolis of Side has been forwarded to us [Kallistos I, patriarch of Constantinople 1350–1353 and 1355–1363; *PLP*, fasc. 5, pp. 44–46, no. 10478] by the grace of God, who brings hidden things out into the open, and has been read by us and the holy synod. We have noted the unholy thoughts which are contained in that letter, the corruption of the sound dogmas of the church, furthermore the calumnies against the orthodox, and finally the propositions which you advance as if they were dogmas. In these, without reason or knowledge, you represent the orthodox as believers in two or more gods, thus slandering the church of God as believing these things. Understand that we have been especially saddened and distressed by your error and by your corruption of orthodox doctrines. And we have been astonished at how you are thoughtlessly assailing the church of God, of which you consider yourself a member and a high priest, without recognizing the impious dogmas which have been secretly introduced into the church of God by that man fom Calabria and friend of the Latins, Barlaam [*PLP*, fasc. 2, pp. 26–28, no. 2284], and by Akindynos [*PLP*, fasc. 1, pp. 45–47, no. 495], who teaches his [Barlaam's] doctrines with him.

Note: Cyril was ordered, under pain of deposition, to appear before the synod and to defend himself. He was posthumously rehabilitated by the patriarch Philotheos Kokkinos in 1364/65. On Hesychasm see Meyendorff, especially Study I, pp. 90–102, for brief biographies of Barlaam, Akindynos, and Palamas.

15. *Acta Varia*
Ed. MM, vol. V, p. 273 [ΣΒΠΚΙ 105] [1363]

The master Lord Petro de Pestagali [*PLP*, fasc. 9, p. 213, no. 22513], who had previously been physician to Pope Innocent VI [1352–1362] and then to the king of Cyprus, Lord Hugh [IV, 1324–1359], came here to the divinely protected, divinely glorified, and divinely made-great Constantinople to purchase holy relics of some saints.

16. **Philotheos Kokkinos** (patriarch of Constantinople 1353–1354 and 1364–1376, died 1377/78) [*PLP*, fasc. 5, pp. 204–206, no. 11917]
Life of St. Sabas the Younger, ed. Tsames, pp. 159–325 [ΣΒΠΚΙ 106]

1. 17, ll. 1–2, p. 189
After this, having visited Patmos and some of the islands in between, he [Sabas] reached the great island of Cyprus.

2. 19, ll. 1–2, p. 195
Thus, when he had shed even his last cloak, as I mentioned, the noble man passed through all the cities and districts of the Cypriots.

3. 28, ll. 1–6, p. 214
As a result of these deeds and others like them there was so much devotion to him at that time among the Cypriots and so much light shone forth from him, that they not only experienced the things mentioned with great joy, but also engraved his likeness on painted panels and venerated him in their homes with candles, fragrances, incense and other such things.

4. 30, ll. 1–11, p. 216
The Cypriots searched every place on the island, I mean cliffs, mountains, deserts, and caves, but the man whom they sought was nowhere. Then heavy grief came upon them and they took their lot very hard (for everyone believed his lot to be an unbearable punishment). And they suspected the whole thing to be the beginning of God's wrath and prophesied renewed calamities for themselves, now that such a counselor, a sleepless guardian of their souls and bodies, had been taken from them. But he headed for the city that he had long desired, not without toil and not without

the trials and dangers of a voyage, but he reached Jerusalem, wonderful anciently and now, and his desire made the hardships of the voyage easier to bear.

5. 57, ll. 23–27, p. 269

On the island of Cyprus he suffered many trials for the sake of Christ, but then, on account of these, he was deemed worthy by God of many gifts, was called a dwelling place of the Holy Spirit, and performed many wonderful miracles.

17. Kydones, Demetrios (ca. 1324–1397/98)[*PLP*, fasc 6, pp.78–79, no. 13876; *BBKL*, vol. IV, cols. 859–62]
Letters, ed. Loenertz 1956

1. From letter 31; Ger. tr. Tinnefeld, letter 49, vol. I.2, p. 306 [ΣΒΠΚΙ 107.1]
To the Lord George the Philosopher [*PLP*, fas. 2, pp. 201–202, no. 4117] [1361]

It is madness to write to someone in Cyprus who is traveling in Palestine . . . For all are saying that you have had your fill of Cyprus and are thinking of the Alps . . . But I would like for you to beware of Cyprus in the future even if you should enjoy the advantages its ruler does.

2. From letter 97; Ger. tr. Tinnefeld, letter 63, vol. I.2, pp. 374–75 [ΣΒΠΚΙ 107.2]
To George the Philosopher [1365]

Someone brought a letter from us to you in Cyprus . . . I have sent many letters to Syria and Cyprus, more to Rhodes, and no fewer to Crete.

3. From letter 35; Ger. tr. Tinnefeld, letter 87, vol. I.2, p. 484 [ΣΒΠΚΙ 107.3]
To [John] Kyparissiotes [*PLP*, fasc 6. p. 82, no. 13900] [1371]

I know that Cyprus is not a pleasant place for strangers. But is better to live there in poverty but security than to be exposed to the dangers in this city [Constantinople]. Note: John Kyparissiotes was a leading opponent of Hesychasm and Palamism.

4. From letter 46; Ger. tr. Tinnefeld, letter 44, vol. I.1, p. 270 [ΣΒΠΚΙ 107.4]
To Astras, governor of Lemnos [*PLP*, fasc 1. p. 150, no. 1598] [1358–1359]

But you are busy about the harbors, fortifying the hilltops, dealing with shipbuilders, enlisting an army, and contending with Cyprus, Sicily, and, I might add, even Britain.

5. From letter 108; Ger. tr. Tinnefeld, letter 55, vol. I.2, p. 339 [ΣΒΠΚΙ 107.5] [1363]
To Astras

And then, how is not disgraceful to state that Lemnos produces such things, an island of which you yourself say that it is in no way second to Cyprus or Sicily!

6. From letter 93; Ger. tr. Tinnefeld, letter 59, vol. I.2, p. 355 [ΣΒΠΚΙ 107.6]
To Bishop Simon Atoumanos [*PLP*, fasc. 1. p. 155–56, no. 1648] [1364]

They called for a consideration of the case of the king of Cyprus; he, they pointed out, had asked for an alliance not through ambassadors but in his own person and had believed that, given their common faith, his high birth, and his considerable expense, he would not fail in anything. Now, they said, he was in danger of returning home blaming himself for his hopes and having gained nothing other from his journey than to seem a big spender and magnanimous.

Note: "They" refers to the ambassadors whom the emperor John V Palaiologos (1341–1376) intended to send to Pope Urban V (1362–1370). The king of Cyprus is Peter I (1358–1369), who in 1362–1365 was on an extended journey through Western Europe seeking support for a proposed crusade. John V visited Urban V in 1369 and in the course of his visit converted to Roman Catholicism.

7. From letter 400; Ger. tr. Tinnefeld, letter 93, vol. I.2, p. 501 [ΣΒΠΚΙ 107.7]
To the monk Joasaph, the former emperor John VI Kantakouzenos [*PLP*, fasc. 5, pp. 94–96, no. 10973] [1371–1372]

You have sent many [messengers] to Ionia and many to Cyprus, Crete, Palestine, Egypt, Trebizond [modern Trabzon in Turkey], and Cherson [on the Crimea], spreading this new theology [Hesychasm].

8. From letter 269; Ger. tr. Tinnefeld, letter 246, vol. III, p. 59 [ΣΒΠΚΙ 107.8]
To John Laskaris Kalopheros [*PLP*, fasc. 5. p. 68–69, no. 10732] [1382–1383]

Rhodes and Cyprus receive you.

9. From letter 325; Ger. tr. Tinnefeld, letter 67, vol. I.2, p. 391 [ΣΒΠΚΙ 107.9]
To John Laskaris Kalopheros [1365–1366; ΣΒΠΚΙ erroneously 1385–1386]

How you have saddened us by being silent on events after [your arrival on] Cyprus!

10. From letter 331; Ger. tr. Tinnefeld, letter 327, vol. III, pp. 278–79 [ΣΒΠΚΙ 107.10]
To John Laskaris Kalopheros [1386–1387]

The news of the disease which has befallen your eyes has put on the eye of my mind, too, a dense cloud of discouragement, and I think that I have been equally affected by the ingratitude of the Cypriots.

11. From letter 359; Ger. tr. Tinnefeld, letter 323, vol. III, p. 267 [ΣΒΠΚΙ 107.11]
To John Laskaris Kalopheros [1386]

Therefore I have sent [word] to Cyprus, assuming that you were with the king there [James I. 1382–1398], and I have given letters to pilgrims on their way to Jerusalem and the life-giving tomb.

12. From letter 436; ed. and Fr. tr. Cammelli, letter 49, p. 127; not yet in Tinnefeld [ΣΒΠΚΙ 107.12]
To John Laskaris Kalopheros [1391 or 1395?]

You have lived a pleasant life sitting in Cyprus, but my friends have persuaded me that, if I have any sense, I must abandon my hopes like a toy, since it is not possible that I will ever be with you in the future. For Cyprus and its pleasures are full of many drugs which are able to beguile and hold in their power anyone who has once tasted them.

18. Kalekas, Manuel (died ca. 1410) [*PLP*, fasc. 5, p. 27, no. 10289]
Letters, ed. Loenertz 1950

1. From letter 60, pp. 135 and 253–54, lines 23–46 [ΣΒΠΚΙ 108.1]
From Crete to Manuel Raoul [*PLP*, fasc. 10, p. 106, no. 24128] in Cyprus [1400]

To us, it seems, it has been allotted to suffer misfortune not only together but also as an individual Greek, wherever in the world one might be. Therefore, in addition to both shared troubles and that part which pertains to me, there is the lack of a letter from you. If a letter were to come it would to no small degree take away from my concern over both shared and individual problems, but I would at the same time think that I had received what I asked for, and I would know more clearly about coming to you. I say this not because other options have already been closed to me and it remains only to look towards Cyprus; for there are those who advise me to go to Italy, and, to speak with God, I am not entirely useless. But it is first of all, to speak the truth, for the sake of your company and because the inhabitants speak Greek. I will add also that I will receive more help from you, if this is my decision. Perhaps when we are together we will be of importance to each other, as far as the books of the ancients are concerned, looking at some collections. For we will enhance their voice to us whenever circumstances might permit you.

And we will think that we are enjoying our homeland in turn. And if there were any devoted to philosophy it would, perhaps, not prevent my presence from becoming the cause of the culture of the ancients not entirely disappearing. For Cyprus, too, is the ancient homeland of the Greeks, and its achievement in learning is appreciable. Do then, my noble friend, whatever can readily be done, whether you think that I will have some place at the court of the king [John II, 1398–1432] or whether there are any students of philosophy worth the effort. I think I would be unfortunate if I were not to find both of these and if I were to come to you without a letter. I would like for me to be assured that I am on firm ground and not to care about other matters, and for you to receive no small thanks for it from me.

2. From letter 70, pp. 140–41 and 267, lines 20–32 [ΣΒΠΚΙ 108.2]
From Crete to a Byzantine emigrant in Cyprus [1400]

But I am not yet released from my bonds, even if God himself were willing! And I shall not be sorry to set my sights on Cyprus, but it will be one or the other of two things: either, since I have received that man's letter - and that has given me much hope - and have learned where in the world you live and what the state of your affairs is, to rush to your side; or, if the state of my homeland has improved, to return to it. But may it be the latter and may we soon see that day when both you and I will regain our homeland, share one another's company and good fortune, and forget the misfortunes which we suffered on foreign soil. But as long as the present circumstances prevail I must unfurl my sails and try to gain, instead of my homeland, your harbor, which alone offers me safety. Having gained that, even if it involves some unpleasant things, I would ignore them, valuing one thing only, your company.

3. From letter 77, pp. 144–45 and 275, lines 3–11 [ΣΒΠΚΙ 108.3]
From Italy, to Manuel Raul on Cyprus

I am amazed myself at the things which happen to us every day, in which we sometimes do one thing and sometimes another, and at how we often choose the opposite of what we had intended, either because our own free will takes us in another direction or because circumstances force us. Indeed I say that I had planned the opposite of this. For, when many factors from many directions were weighing upon my mind, one was to set my sights on Cyprus; and there was no necessity driving me, but rather it was for the sake of your company and because the inhabitants of Cyprus speak Greek.

19. Chortasmenos, John (ca. 1370–ca. 1436/37) [*PLP*, fasc. 12, p. 224, no. 30897]
Letters

From no. 11, ed. Hunger 1969, pp. 79–82 and 161–62 [ΣΒΠΚΙ 113]
To the most honorable monk and philosopher, the Lord Joseph [Bryennios]:

When I learned from your letter the things which recently happened to you on Cyprus I praised your tongue, which so ably champions the truth, and I pitied the condition of the Cypriots, [seeing] into what lawlessness they have fallen. Yet, when I first perused your letter, I was driven to much laughter, whenever I thought I could hear these arguments, and, unable to control myself, I took to barbaric and discordant shouting, as Euripides says, assaulting my own ears. Then, a little later, when I gave more thought to the matter and reflected on the loss of so.many souls, I changed my attitude concerning them. I perceived that the Cypriots are more wretched than others who have given in to the Latins, in as much as the evils of irrationality are added to their error; indeed, this is a double affliction, which can take those who are affected by it down to the very bottom of Hell, as the saying goes.

There are many who, without thinking, suffer nothing out of the ordinary and instead of good things do those things that give them pleasure; but those who are set before them in positions of holiness are becoming models of every kind of wickedness to the people, and sometimes worse. What could be worse than this? And yet, in preliminary discussions, they gave us a bright hope, and all believed that they regretted their communion with the Latins. There were some who deemed you fortunate to have come there, as if you had come to the garden of Alcinous [king of the Phaeacians]; but, it seems, it has been allotted to this island to fully endure the arguments of the Latins, which is more able to destroy cities, I believe, than the emanations of Aphrodite Urania which strike the country of the Cypriots, if we must believe the myth on this point, too.

Therefore the well-deserving ambassadors—ours, I mean—and mediators of peace, as one might say, were forced to sit in a foreign country and to be treated like prisoners; what is worse, they were suspected, like some evildoers, of having come for the purpose of spying on the affairs of the Cypriots. Thus the embassy turned out contrary to their every hope and expectation, and, to quote the proverb, having come for a treasure they found only coals [*CPG*, vol. I, p. 9, and vol. II, p. 32]. But neither the lack of necessities nor the unexpected turn of events tempted these noble men to undertake anything unworthy of those who had sent them or to stoop to anything low. And, being truly ambassadors of truth, when it would have been possible for them to receive much money, they rejected it; and they did not cease to admonish these wretches to look up from the depths of deception and to cast their eyes upon the sun of truth. To put it briefly, they demonstrated to all by their actions that there is no false pretense and no evil intent on our side, but just the opposite, and that we value nothing more than the correctness of our doctrines, even if the Latins unceasingly tell lies about us. In all things, as I said, our ambassadors showed admirable fortitude; for this is what I call their disdain of money, which they could have obtained there for their private use rather than to use it for its proper purpose. Even more admirable was their unanimity, by which, as if they were an unbreakable wall, they left no opening against them to flattery and deceit, which might have broken down the strength of their mind.

Therefore the reason for all these things is clearly the virtue of the three ambassadors, according to my reasoning. But someone else might name, aiming at accuracy, that great marvel among monks, Joseph, unless he more than others contributed to the task and they gladly yielded to him the first place; and this they did because of his character, his speech, and his zeal for the truth, because of which he risked, yesterday and the day before, so to speak, to become a victim of malice, but was saved by the foresight of God, as even his worst enemies feared the man's righteousness.

And this is no miracle: everywhere you claim for yourself the lesser place, my good friend, and demonstrate this in words and deeds alike; therefore you obtain from us who know your virtue and even more so from the truth itself the greater place. And, if nothing else, I think, this alone suffices for those who wish to praise your qualities, that, when you deserve much praise, you do not think that you are different from the others.

Note: on Bryennios' unsuccessful mission to Cyprus see Hackett, pp. 141–42.

20. Chalkokondyles, Laonikos (ca. 1423 or 1430–ca. 1490) [*PLP*, fasc. 12. p. 187, no. 30512]

Historiarum Demonstrationes, ed. Darkó, vol. I, pp. 133–134 [ΣΒΠΚΙ 114]

This king [Richard the Lionheart] possessed considerable naval power in the area of Samos, both transports and triremes. Having sent the transports and an army with them to Rhodes and Cyprus, he subjected Cyprus. Then he sailed across, laid siege to the city, plundered the island, and attacked the walls for a fair number of days. But when the capture of the city made no progress he left for his homeland. Nevertheless he subjected Cyprus and led its king [Isaac Komnenos] away in captivity. Since that time Cyprus pays a tribute to this king, and it seems that the island has been under this king for a long time. The Franks arrived at the tomb of the divine Jesus. They enslaved this island and subjected it to themselves, bringing in an army and considerable force.

[1192] And the Venetians seized the blessed city of Amathous and held it for a considerable time, using it as a base for their trade with Egypt. From this time on successive Frankish kings have reigned on this island; nevertheless the Arabs inhabit a part of this island, specifically the city called Ammochostos.

21. Sphrantzes, George (1401–1477/78) [*PLP*, fasc. 11. pp. 153–54, no. 27278]; translations by permission of University of Massachusetts Press

1. *Chronikon* (*Chronicon Minus*) 33.2; ed. Grecu, p. 86; tr. Philippides, p. 64 [ΣΒΠΚΙ 115.1] [1451]

Once this had been decided, the emperor [Constantine XI Palaiologos, 1449–1453] one day issued the following orders to me: "First lord of the imperial wardrobe [protovestiarios; see Bréhier, pp. 130–31], as I have decided, I command you to travel to the Morea and, however you manage it, see whichever of my two brothers is willing to come here. Then you are to sail to Cyprus and visit my niece, the queen [Helena Palaiologina, died 1458, wife of King John II, 1432–1458]. I will prepare the necessary provisions so that, when you return from Cyprus, you will proceed to Georgia [Iberia] and bring your future empress."

2. *Chronikon* (*Chronicon Minus*) 33.8; ed. Grecu, p. 88; tr. Philippides, pp. 65–66 [ΣΒΠΚΙ 115.2] [Constantine XI to Sphrantzes, 1451]

"Concerning Cyprus, do you know the monk I met a few days ago? He brought me a message from my niece that she is in need of something; she would have told me in her own voice what she wanted; had it been possible, she would have sent her message through a loyal, trusted courtier, but she has none. As she does not have one and cannot make the trip, I must send a man whom I consider appropriate to hear her message."

3. *Chronikon* (*Chronicon Minus*) 34.7; ed. Grecu, p. 92; tr. Philippides, p. 67 [ΣΒΠΚΙ 115.3]

I discussed these matters with my relatives, friends, and members of my household. It seemed best to accept whichever post I would be given and to travel to the Morea and Cyprus. I would take with me my good son, who was one of the most prominent of the young nobility, and the greatest part of my portable wealth. We would travel by a land route so that my son could visit the places and learn all of those things which would be of use in his life.

22. Pseudo-Sphrantzes or Makarios Melissenos (16th c.)

Chronikon (*Chronicon Maius*) 3.2.16; ed. Grecu, p. 370 [ΣΒΠΚΙ 116] [Constantine XI to Sphrantzes, 1451. Cf. 25.2]

You know yourself also the monk who was sent by the queen of Cyprus [Helena Palaiologina], my niece, and said to me that I should send her an approved and reliable man from my court; for the queen did not have a reliable and suitable person through whom she might communicate with me whatever might be necessary, nor was it possible for her to speak to me in person, as she desired. Therefore there is no other man apart from yourself qualified to know our secrets; and no one is more qualified than you, and indeed you are the only one, because you have dealt with her, supported her, talked with her, and informed her of all things also on a previous occasion; therefore this project cannot be accomplished by anyone else.

Note: On Sphrantzes and Pseudo-Sphrantzes see the excellent introduction to Philippides' translation.

23. *Chronica Byzantina Breviora* or Βραχέα Χρονικά (10th c. onward), Chronicle 28 the ms. of which is located in Paris (Bibl. Nat. gr. 624, ff. 1 –2ᵛ and was first published by J. Darrouzès, 'Notes pour servir à l'histoire de Chypre (troisième article), *ΚΣ* 22 (1958), 240-246.
Ed., hist. comm., and Ger. tr. Schreiner, vol. I, pp. 207–212, vol. II, pp. 430–45, and vol. III, pp. 56–58

1. 3 Aug. 1425 [ΣΒΠΚΙ 117.1]

On the 3rd day of August, a Friday, in the year 1425 of Christ the fleet of the Saracens came upon Cyprus and landed in the district of Ammochostos [Famagusta], at Constantia, and there were 40 ships, both large and small.

2. 6 Aug. 1425 [ΣΒΠΚΙ 117.2]

On the 6th day of August, a Monday, in the year 1425 [of Christ] the Lord, Prince [Prince Henry of Galilee, brother of King Janus] came to fight the Saracens and to ambush them, and they killed 15 Saracens. In this ambush Tzanot Mephtach, the son of Nicolas Mephtach, died, and many others. And they died from the excessive heat at that time at the village of Styli [modern Styllos, near Famagusta], and may God grant them rest.

3. 1 July 1426 [ΣΒΠΚΙ 117.3]

On the last day of June, a Monday, in the year [1]426 of Christ the fleet of the Saracens came upon Cyprus, to Lemesos [Limassol], and a day later they took the castle of Lemesos and burned it at once.

Note: The date of 30 June is erroneous; the correct date is 1 July.

4. 7 July 1426 [ΣΒΠΚΙ 117.4]

On the 7th day of July, a Monday, of the year [1]426 of Christ, the lords of Cyprus fled and came to Kerynia [Kyrenia]. And the remaining people of that place [Nicosia], young and old, abandoned it and fled into the mountains and villages, and the country was blessed [?] with the old and the useless.

5. 4 Aug. 1425 [ΣΒΠΚΙ 117.5]

On the 4th of August, a Saturday . . . the prince [Prince Henry of Galilee] the brother of the king of Cyprus [King Janus], went out with the army and went to face the Saracens . . .

6. 19 Sept. 1425 [in French, not in ΣΒΠΚΙ]

On Wednesday on the 19 day of September in the year of Christ 1425 the viscount *** of Nicosia took possession of the houses that had belonged to Janot the *bailli* which were on the road of St. Nicholas *** that *** (translated by Nicholas Coureas).

7. 3–6 July 1426 [ΣΒΠΚΙ 117.7]

On the 3rd of July, a Thursday, of the year [1]42[6] of Christ, our lord the king came with his army to Potamia because of the Saracens, and he stayed until Sunday, that is the 6th of July. And on that same Sunday the Saracens came to face the king's army at the village of Cherokoitia [Khirokitia], and in this same place they defeated our army and seized the king [Janus] and took him to Cairo . . . upon the Christians. And it was punishment for many people, young and old.

8. 10–16 July 1426 [ΣΒΠΚΙ 117.8]

On the 10th of July, a Thursday, at noon, of the year [1]426 of Christ, the army of the Saracens came and entered the town [Nicosia] and stayed until Saturday. And on Saturday they plundered the whole town, destroyed the houses of the people, and took their belongings. And they took all the men, women, children of all ages, and priests. And they burned the court of the king . . . of Petra [in the district of Morphou]. Similarly they destroyed the churches, plundered, and seized monks, women and men, and took many captives . . . The chief of the Saracens was named Taghribardi . . . to sell them . . .

On the 16th day, until . . . the Lord Peter of Lusignan . . . and Sir Henry de Giblet came to this place, seized it, hung many robbers and pirates, and made a great effort to put an end to the piracy and the robberies. And the people began [to return], and they went into their houses and found them ruined and utterly destroyed by the piracy of the Saracens and especially by the Cypriots and by every sort of people.

9. 12 May 1427 [ΣΒΠΚΙ 117.9]

On the 12th of May of the year 1427 of Christ, on the feast day of St. Epiphanios, the king [King Janus, having been ransomed] came to Cyprus, and there was great joy and the people rejoiced. He came heavily in debt and placed a great burden on the people.

10. 7 January 1427 [ΣΒΠΚΙ 117.10]

On the 7th of January in the year [1]427 of Christ . . . Viscount of Leukosia [Nicosia] Sir Pierre Lezes [*PLP*, fasc. 6, p. `158, no. 14638] . . .

11. 17 June 1429 [in French, not in ΣΒΠΚΙ]

On Friday on the seventeenth day [of June] in the year of Christ 1429 it came to pass (?) at the court of the viscount of Nicosia that at the request of the monk Guy Mermat, the viscount summoned the court and *** they were at the residences which were d*** for the revocation of the banns *** of the residences which had belonged to

the monk Philip Granze the *** 100 bezants (?) regarding which the court *** did not
(?) *** if the said Guy should do *** to the said Philip Granze by charging *** on the
said wall whereby that the said Philip would have to construct in *** the said wall at
his own cost and also construct the other walls which are *** the residences of the said
Guy for among *** the said residences at the expense of the said Philip, without the
said Guy spending anything, and for as many times as the said [Guy] might wish to
alter the walls he would have (?) power (?) to do his pleasure in building on the said
walls and the structures of the said walls belonging to the said Philip (translated by
Nicholas Coureas).

12. 28 June 1432 [in French, not in ΣΒΠΚΙ]

On Saturday on the 27 (28?) day of June in the year of Christ 1432, at the hour of
vespers, King Janus of Lusignan the son of King James died, and on the next day he
was buried in the abbey of the Dominicans *** (at the side?) of his father (translated
by Nicholas Coureas).

13. 24 Aug. 1432 [in French, not in ΣΒΠΚΙ]

On Sunday, on the 23 day of August in the year of Christ 1432, King John [II] the
son of the late Janus of Lusignan was crowned king of Jerusalem, and he was crowned
by the bishop of Fa[magusta] Brother Salomon Car[dus], at the church of St. Sophia,
and there were great celebrations and expenses (translated by Nicholas Coureas).

14. 15 Nov. 1425 [in French, not in ΣΒΠΚΙ]

On 15 day of November in the year of Christ 1425, it came to pass (?) at the court
of the viscount of Nicosia that that James, a clerk of *** of the *** house gave himself
up at the street *** having given back (?) *** some payments *** to express his
gratitude (translated by Nicholas Coureas).

15. 9 June 1429 [in French, not in ΣΒΠΚΙ]

On the 9 day of June in the year of Christ 1429 it came to pass (?) at the court of
the viscount of Nicosia that the monk Guy Mermat granted a pardon to Philip Granze
*** 40 bezants (?) *** karoubles *** which were *** (translated by Nicholas Coureas).

16. 20 June 1508 [in Greek, not in ΣΒΠΚΙ]

On 20 June in the year of Christ 1508 on a Monday, at night, in the second hour
of the night, an earthquake took place, first a small one and immediately afterwards
another major one. And nothing was destroyed, neither in Nicosia nor the villages,
except that in places further off, in Crete, it destroyed many villages. And I, the priest
Athanasios Pharis from [the village of] Kophinou, wrote this by way of remembrance,
in the above day and year (translated by Nicholas Coureas).

17. 24 April 1491 [in Greek, not in ΣΒΠΚΙ]

In the year of Christ 1491 a great earthquake occurred on Sunday the 24 day of
April, which Sunday happened to be that of the Paralysed Man. Furthermore, St.

Sophia and many churches in Nicosia were damaged, the great cross of Our Lord was damaged and the dome of the cathedral church of Limassol dedicated to the life giving cross was damaged. The [monastery of] the Holy Cross near Lympia, which was upon the mountain, also suffered damage, and the church at Pentaschinos of our holy father Athanasios of Pentaschinos was damaged down to its foundations. By way of remembrance I, the priest Athanasios Pharis from the village of Kophinou, wrote this on 24 April in the abovementioned year (translated by Nicholas Coureas).

18. 7 November 1510 [in Greek, not in ΣΒΠΚΙ]

On Thursday, 7 November in the year of Christ 1510, it rained a great torrent descending from the road of Mersiniki like a river. And it destroyed people and some horses and none could cross (ράξου = ρέξουν?) and it flooded all the orchards of Alaminos and demolished them (translated by Nicholas Coureas).

24. *Chronica Byzantina Breviora* or Βραχέα Χρονικά (10th c. onward), Chronicle 27, the ms. of which is in Paris (Bibl. Nat. gr. 546, f. 324ᵃ [recto – verso] was first published by B. de Montfaucon, *Paleographia graeca*, Paris 1708, 55.
Ed., hist. comm., and Ger. tr. Schreiner, vol. I, pp. 205–206, vol. II, pp. 238, 272, and 521, and vol. III, p. 55

1. 9 November 1330 [ΣΒΠΚΙ 118.1]

On the 9th of November, a Friday, there was a great downpour from heaven, and a great river descended on the inhabited area and destroyed two-thirds of Leukosia [Nicosia], that is to say many houses, at the hour of midnight and in the early hours of Saturday. And many people were killed, numbering six or seven thousand. And [the flood] killed many beasts and destroyed the bridges and many churches, in the year 6839.

2. 10 December 1347 [ΣΒΠΚΙ 118.2]

On the tenth of December, a Monday, of the year 6857 there was an attack on Cyprus, on the castle of Kerynia [Kyrenia], at the noon hour. That is to say, the Turks, without warning, first entered the castle where the castellan was located, and forthwith cut off his head and cast it into the castle, and they killed many others, all the residents of the castle, as well.

3. 5 November 1479 [ΣΒΠΚΙ 118.3]

On the fifth of November, a Tuesday, in the early hours of Wednesday, there was a great storm in Leukosia [Nicosia] and on the whole island, and many herds . . . And much damage was done on the whole island of Cyprus. And many birds fell to the ground, many beasts drowned, and in Ammochostos [Famagusta] many houses collapsed . . . many people, in the year 1479 . . . and a mighty river.